Cape Horn and Antarctic Waters

including Chile, the Beagle Channel, the Falkland Islands and the Antarctic Peninsula

RCC PILOTAGE FOUNDATION

Paul Heiney

Imray Laurie Norie & Wilson

Published by
Imray Laurie Norie & Wilson Ltd
Wych House The Broadway St Ives Cambridgeshire
PE27 5BT England
✆ +44 (0)1480 462114 *Fax* +44 (0)1480 496109
Email ilnw@imray.com
www.imray.com
2017

First edition 2017

ISBN 978 184623 836 9

British Library Cataloguing in Publication Data.
A catalogue record for this title is available from the British Library.

Printed in Croatia by Zrinski

Updates and Supplements

Corrections, updates and annual supplements for this title are published as free downloads at www.imray.com. Printed copies are also available on request from the publishers.

Find out more

For a wealth of further information, including passage planning guides and cruising logs for this area visit the RCC Pilotage Foundation website at www.rccpf.org.uk

Feedback

The RCC Pilotage Foundation is a voluntary, charitable organisation. We welcome all feedback for updates and new information. If you notice any errors or omissions, please let us know at www.rccpf.org.uk

CAUTION

Whilst the RCC Pilotage Foundation, the author and the publishers have used reasonable endeavours to ensure the accuracy of the content of this book, it contains selected information and thus is not definitive. It does not contain all known information on the subject in hand and should not be relied on alone for navigational use: it should only be used in conjunction with official hydrographical data. This is particularly relevant to the plans, which should not be used for navigation. The RCC Pilotage Foundation, the authors and the publishers believe that the information which they have included is a useful aid to prudent navigation, but the safety of a vessel depends ultimately on the judgment of the skipper, who should assess all information, published or unpublished. The information provided in this pilot book may be out of date and may be changed or updated without notice. The RCC Pilotage Foundation cannot accept any liability for any error, omission or failure to update such information. To the extent permitted by law, the RCC Pilotage Foundation, the author and the publishers do not accept liability for any loss and/or damage howsoever caused that may arise from reliance on information contained in these pages.

Positions and Waypoints

All positions and waypoints are to datum WGS 84. They are included to help in locating places, features and transits. Do not rely on them alone for safe navigation.

Bearings and Lights

Any bearings are given as °T and from seaward. The characteristics of lights may be changed during the lifetime of this book. They should be checked against the latest edition of the UK Admiralty *List of Lights*.

CONTENTS

RCC PILOTAGE FOUNDATION

The RCC Pilotage Foundation was formed as an independent charity in 1976 supported by a gift and permanent endowment made to the Royal Cruising Club by Dr Fred Ellis. The Foundation's charitable objective is to advance the education of the public in the science and practice of navigation.

The Foundation is privileged to have been given the copyrights to books written by a number of distinguished authors and yachtsmen. These are kept as up to date as possible. New publications are also produced by the Foundation to cover a range of cruising areas. This is only made possible through the dedicated work of our authors and editors, all of whom are experienced sailors, who depend on a valuable supply of information from around the world by generous-minded yachtsmen and women.

Most of the management of the Foundation is done on a voluntary basis. In line with its charitable status, the Foundation distributes no profits. Any surpluses are used to finance new publications and to subsidise publications which cover some of the more remote areas of the world.

The Foundation works in close collaboration with three publishers – Imray Laurie Norie & Wilson, Bloomsbury (Adlard Coles Nautical) and On Board Publications. The Foundation also itself publishes guides and pilots, including web downloads, for areas where limited demand does not justify large print runs. Several books have been translated into French, Spanish, Italian and German and some books are now available as electronic versions.

For further details about the RCC Pilotage Foundation and its publications visit **www.rccpf.org.uk**

PUBLICATIONS OF THE RCC PILOTAGE FOUNDATION

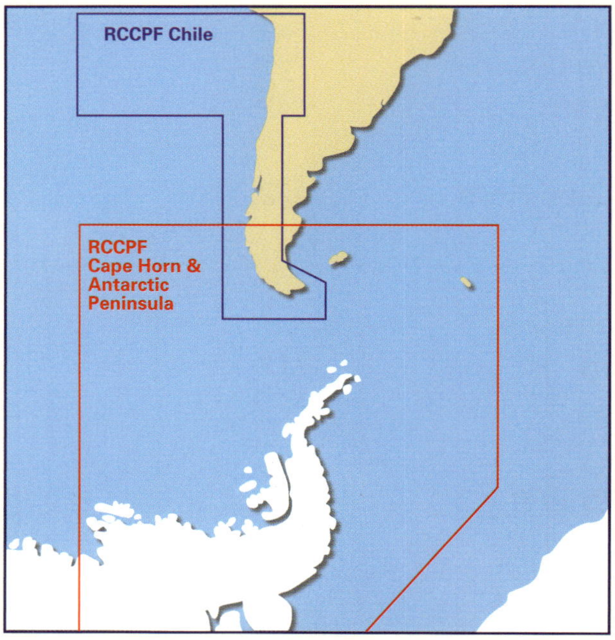

Adlard Coles Nautical
Atlantic Crossing Guide
Pacific Crossing Guide

Imray
Chile
Arctic and Northern Waters
Norway
The Baltic Sea
Channel Islands, Cherbourg Peninsula and North Brittany
Isles of Scilly
Atlantic France
South Biscay
Atlantic Islands
Atlantic Spain & Portugal
Mediterranean Spain
Islas Baleares
Corsica and North Sardinia
North Africa
Black Sea

On Board Publications
South Atlantic Circuit
Havens and Anchorages for the South American Coast

The RCC Pilotage Foundation
Supplement to Falkland Island Shores
Guide to West Africa
Argentina

RCCPF website www.rccpf.org.uk
Supplements
Support files for books
Passage Planning Guides
ePilots - from the Arctic to the Antarctic Peninsula

FOREWORD

Over more than twenty years the RCC Pilotage Foundation has published information about southern Chile, Argentina and the islands in the far south of the Atlantic, from the Falkland Islands to the Antarctic Peninsula. However, all of these were published in isolation, many as downloads from the website. Following the success of Arctic and Northern Waters, and in recognition of the increasing numbers of yachtsmen and women who choose to cruise the far south, the Pilotage Foundation had, for some time, been contemplating pulling together a single publication to provide an overview of the region as a planning resource, but we needed an author with first-hand experience. We were delighted when Paul Heiney, fresh from his voyage around Cape Horn, agreed to bring together all the necessary material to create this book. Nevertheless, the decision to publish was not straightforward. The most experienced sailors based in the region are, quite rightly, reticent about encouraging the unprepared and the unwary. Paul would be the first to emphasise that sailing these waters requires serious consideration and thorough preparation. The hope is that this book will encourage appropriate levels of planning and risk assessment, whilst at the same time serving as an inspiration for wider dreams.

Sailing in the far south remains a pioneering activity and, in the most remote areas, this book is really only sharing seeds of knowledge in the hope that they will grow and develop over time. To this end, the Pilotage Foundation is dependent on the yachtsmen and women who cruise the waters of Cape Horn and the Antarctic to help to build on the foundation of this book by contributing more information based on their own experience of the region. If you have some information for us we would love to hear from you at info@rccpf.org.uk. Any feedback will be published on our website at www.rccpf.org.uk and annual correctional supplements to the book will be available via the Imray website at www.imray.com.

The RCC Pilotage Foundation is very grateful to Paul Heiney for all of his efforts in the researching and writing of this book, and to the many experienced contributors who have supported him with information, photographs and pearls of wisdom. We are also grateful to the whole team at Imray who bring all of their expertise to the production of such a high quality publication.

Jane Russell
Editor in Chief
RCC Pilotage Foundation
February 2017

Nereid *Peter Smith*

Beaulieu, Seno Pia *Vicky Jackson*

INTRODUCTION

I don't think there has ever been a cruising guide where the author can honestly say that danger lurks on almost every page. Yet there is hardly an anchorage or harbour described here where the cruising sailor does not have to look over his or her shoulder for one reason or another. It is true that in these nervous times such books as this must issue warnings at every stage, shout our disclaimers, ring the alarm bells, pour a hefty dose of caveats over everything we write. The difference with this book is that we mean it.

This book covers some of the most dangerous waters in the world; from the infamous storms of Cape Horn, to the standing waves of the Le Maire Strait, and onward to the icebound anchorages of Antarctica. These are places for hardy sailors, not those for whom the romantic idea of high latitude sailing has eclipsed the tough reality of it. Be in no doubt that if you choose to venture into the areas described in this book, there will be times when you will wish you were anywhere else. It will be tough, relentless, frightening, and humbling, and all within the space of a few hours tough sailing. That's all I can promise you for certain.

So don't read this book and imagine that somehow you have been given the secret of how to overcome all these things, for you haven't. You are given, here, enough information to plan for what most people would consider the voyage of a lifetime. There is nothing in these pages that tells you it is going to be easy.

That's the bad news. The good news is that the reward will be beyond your wildest dreams. It is easy to sit at home and imagine what it will be like to round the Horn or make an Antarctic landfall, but nothing you can imagine will live up to the eventual experience. Within this book is information that can help you to achieve that dream. If used wisely, you will make a voyage you will never forget. To successfully sail these waters can be considered the achievement of a sailing lifetime. This book is intended to help you make the first, small step towards it.

How to use this book

If this book were a pilot guide in the true sense, you might find it heavier than you would care to carry - it covers a vast and intricate area. It is instead a cruising guide; an aid to planning, a primer intended to give you an overview of the waters in which you hope to sail.

You will not find here every harbour or anchorage in the regions described. The havens I have chosen are included for their strategic value to someone in the early stages of planning their cruise. For example, in the Chilean channels I have chosen places which offer reliable shelter in all weathers, or where you can get provisions, or fuel, or somewhere to effect a crew change. The places described are harbours or anchorages around which you can draw a ring on the chart and know that there will be some comfort to be had. There are also the 'must see' places (and there are many of them in this spectacular cruising ground) which might be easy to miss if no one points them out in advance. I have included these as well.

To say that this book should not be used for navigation might appear to defeat the whole object, but that is the case. The charts given here are not a substitute for properly drawn and printed navigation charts, and this book is no substitute for a pilot guide.

As far as waypoints go, you will find none given here. Any coordinates given are to help with identification, which is not always easy in these tangled waters. Many of the anchorages are no more than tiny bays invisible on a large scale chart and impossible to spot without some kind of aid. By all means punch the coordinates into your plotter, but don't think you can then simply steer for the mark. The best our locators can do is indicate the area you are aiming for. I have assumed that anyone sailing in these complex waters is an experienced navigator more than capable of getting from where they are to where they wish to be.

ACKNOWLEDGMENTS

Those who first took small boats into these waters back in the days before GPS, to places where few had gone before them, when yacht systems were less reliable and radio communications did not exist on small craft, were true pioneers. A lot of the information in this book can be traced back to their early surveys, and it is on the basis of these that recent adventurers have been able to compile the more modern cruising and pilotage notes to which I have had access.

I am grateful to the following people who have given permission for their work to be used in this book: Annie Hill, Pete Hill, Andy O'Grady, Ewen Southby-Tailyour, Tim Barker, Tony and Coryn Gooch, Jerome and Sally Poncét, Pete Smith, Andrew and Máire Wilkes, Brian and Sandy Duker, James Boyce and *Adventure 2013*, Vicky Jackson, Mike Jaques, Nick Coleman, Chris Cromey and Suzanne Hills.

My thanks also the Royal Cruising Club's Pilotage Foundation for commissioning this book, and to its Editor-in-Chief, Jane Russell, for her support and the wide experience which she has brought to the project.

I hope that you, in turn, will support this book by offering corrections, clarifications, and updates as they arise. Corrections should be sent to info@rccpf.org.uk

Glaciers in every direction - Seno Pia from the Beaulieu anchorage *Vicky Jackson*

1 BEFORE YOU GO

PREPARING FOR THE EXTREMES

Fitting out for a trip to the regions described in this book is a complex business, not only for the boat but for the skipper and crew as well. Most yachts heading for South America and onwards will need to prepare for two distinct climates. Some, if not most, will be sailing from tropical islands to a land of icebergs, and there can be no bigger contrast anywhere on earth.

Keeping your boat warm, or keeping it cool, is the first problem you will have to solve. Providing fresh air in the tropics when sailing hard is not always easy. It is not long before a closed-up boat becomes untenable with an equatorial sun blazing down upon it, and hatches cannot be opened because there is green water across the decks. Then, when it is icy water falling on the deck, you'll be avoiding every draught of cold air that you can.

When considering these steamy/chilly scenarios from the comfort of your boatyard back home, you will be trying to decide which heater will keep you warm as toast in the harsh winds of Patagonia. How are you going to rig that temporary double-glazing you might need if heading even further south? But at the same time your mind will be on how to rig a cockpit shade to stop you frying under the tropical sun. Is your wardrobe of thermal gear as complete as that you have packed for lazy, hot days under clear, blue skies? Have you enough power to keep the fridge cool in the tropics, and will the watermaker work when the sea temperature is only just above freezing? These contrasting demands on your imagination may give you sleepless nights.

You will also be sailing at both ends of the maritime weather spectrum. You may spend many days, if not weeks, in the very light airs of the doldrums; only if you have given such conditions some thought beforehand and equipped yourself suitably will you make decent progress. One of the common mistakes of ocean sailing, at whatever latitude, is lack of preparation for light airs.

On the other hand, you are certain to meet storms which will test you and your boat to the limits, and not to have prepared for those would clearly be equally foolish. There might be weeks on end when you never see the bottom half of your mainsail. Then, for the ambitious who venture to the deep south, sailing in ice will bring its own challenges for which you will need to be properly equipped. It is a lot to get your head round.

These are just some of the confusing questions that will present themselves. Never forget that you are preparing for one of sailing's greatest and most dangerous challenges.

But before you start considering your boat, perhaps you might be well advised to look at yourself and see if you think you are up to the job. Unless you have sailed in remote regions of the world before, this is sailing unlike any other you will have experienced.

It is difficult to over stress how important it is that you understand you are completely on your own in almost all the waters described in this book.

You will have to be self-sufficient in all respects; carrying out your own repairs and servicing, having plentiful supplies and spares. There will be none within easy reach. Assume that no harbours will have any means of helping you. You need to be meteorologist and navigator, with enough skills to get safely to shelter if your electronic support lets you down. You must not be just a sailor, but also a bosun and mechanic. And probably an inventor too: there will doubtless come a

'Self-sufficiency will lead to success'
Adventure 2013

moment when something breaks, no spare is in the locker, and only invention will see you through.

You might also need to play doctor, in charge of a comprehensive chest of medicines and with the skills to deploy it. You may also be called upon to be a counsellor and a mediator, and know how to deal with crew who might be losing their confidence in testing times, or deal with the inevitable frictions that can arise when a group of people in a confined space are put through the mill. In other words, you may have to make an outward show of being a tower of strength, even if deep down you are not feeling it. The crew will be depending on you. All these things fall well outside what might be learnt at a sailing school, but they can be just as vital as a knowledge of how to set the sails and steer a course.

But most important of all is the confidence that you are a true seaman/woman; ever vigilant, ever knowing what to do next, always ready with plan B. You need to develop a nose that smells danger. You need to be able to look both forwards and over your shoulder at the same time. There will not be many days when you can give only half your mind to the job and expect to get away with it. These waters test not only boats and gear but also the people who sail them. They will find every weakness. Sailing down here really is hard work. Your boat must become an extension of yourself and not a machine you are operating. The connection between your brain and your boat must be as instinctive as that between brain and fingers. You must know all her ways, her virtues and her faults, and how to turn each of them to your advantage.

So, have a long hard look at yourself in the mirror and if you can't put a tick against all of the things above, then you might decide you need a little more experience before embarking on a trip like this. *It is no place for beginners*. Many of the qualities I have outlined - and doubtless there are many more - can be learned or acquired but it takes time, and if you haven't put in the hours then you are not ready to sail in these high latitude waters.

None of the above means that you have to be superman/woman. There will be countless coastal sailors who are capable of making voyages into waters like these. Nor do you have to be an athlete or a hero. But you have to know what you are letting yourself in for, and be certain that you and your boat can face it when the time comes. Only you can answer that question for certain.

When it comes to considering a boat, a different set of questions present themselves. Harsh climates demand tough ships, but that does not mean that battleships are the only suitable craft for hereabouts. In my time in the Beagle Channel I watched many boats preparing for Patagonian adventures. Some fell into that 'warship' category; built in aluminium or steel, with heavy gear, towering masts, sails as big as playing fields, massive anchors, and large crews that were up to the job of handling them. But they were not the only ones which had taken on the challenge. There were standard GRP production boats (mine included) which were proving themselves more than up to the task because size alone offers no guarantees. There are no rules about what will or won't work in these waters. The secret of any boat's success is a skipper that understands not only their virtues, but their shortcomings as well. Seamanship is more than the sum total of your knowledge. It is partly an instinct, and it will tell you if a boat is right for the job or not. Those who have to go round asking others, should perhaps venture no further.

What will get you through, in the end, is preparation. The number of nights when you sleep soundly will be directly related to the effort you have put into preparing your boat. You will get not a wink of sleep when the *rachas* are sweeping down the Chilean mountains unless you are certain that you have moused the anchor shackle tightly. You will spend days biting your nails as you motor through the calms if you're not sure that there are enough spare fuel filters on board. Have you thought about connectors which might enable you to refill your gas tanks in every country you visit? Is there twine and a needle on board if a sail has to be repaired? These are problems to solve before you leave home, not when the crisis is upon you.

This is not a book which tells you how to fit out for ocean sailing and remote cruising, but let the above act as a reminder that the success of a voyage in these waters rests fair and square on your shoulders in ways that might not be immediately obvious.

It takes a great deal of effort, application, and strength to cruise successfully here. But those who have done it will tell you that the sense of achievement in successfully cruising these waters is enormous.

For a taste of sailing in these waters, sit at the feet of a master and watch Skip Novak's Storm Sailing Techniques at **www.yachtingworld.com/storm-sailing-techniques**

SPECIAL EQUIPMENT AND TECHNIQUES FOR THE FAR SOUTH

Living with kelp

Kelp is a stringy, tough and rubbery seaweed, well known to sailors, and its wafting leaves can reach 80m long and grow at a rate of half a metre per day. The stems can be very thick, up to 20cm in diameter, and the leaves are full of air sacs which is why the kelp rises to the surface despite the weight of the thick stems.

It makes itself a real pest by preventing anchors from digging in, tangling round anchor chains, disabling outboards, and potentially making rowing impossible. It is common in all the areas covered in this book and you must learn to live with it.

It is certain that on most mornings your anchor will bring a large bundle of kelp to the surface. It needs to be cut away as the chain rises and for this you need some kind of kelp knife. It need not be a sophisticated device. A machete can be used and a good model can sometimes be bought at the small ironmonger in Puerto Williams. Some have used a pruning saw. A sharpened garden hoe on the end of a long pole works, as will a lashed bread knife. Apart from cutting kelp, long poles will be useful for deflecting any ice growlers as a conventional boat hook will tend to slip before it becomes effective.

In certain situations kelp can be your friend, sometimes showing you the position of isolated, shallow rocks, giving you a clue to the way the current flows, and, if sufficiently dense, providing some shelter by breaking any fetch.

It takes time to master the identification of kelp by sight but it can prove a useful aid to navigation. Even at night, in calm water, with a slight moon or starlight, it is unmistakeable as it shines on the surface of the water. Kelp can also break swell and ships have been known to shelter behind it. While it can clog engine cooling water inlets, it is easily seen and thus avoided.

Kinds of kelp

Frond kelp is the most common and lies on the surface of the water, drifting with the tide in long streamers. It suggests the presence of rocks and should be avoided. As a general rule, the thicker the kelp bank, the shallower the water, but no kelp bank should be passed

A typical morning's harvest of kelp
Vicky Jackson

A bread knife lashed to a pole will make a kelp knife
Paul Heiney

through without undertaking a survey first. The shallow water is always on the upstream side of a kelp patch, or in a kelp-free area surrounded by kelp. In areas with a strong tidal flow the absence of kelp may not necessarily indicate the absence of dangers as the kelp 'runs under' in these conditions.

Tree kelp is very thick with dense fronds and it lies close to the surface, its leaves often jutting out of the water. Some call them 'dead man's hands'. It always indicates a danger close to the surface and should be avoided at all times.

Drift kelp is a frond kelp that has broken free from from the bottom and is found drifting in dense masses on the surface; it resembles a tangled jumble of growth. It can be safe to pass through, if correctly identified as being adrift.

Pete Smith is the designer of the Rocna anchor and his website is a good starting point for gaining an understanding of modern anchors, how they work, and how they can be best be deployed.

www.petersmith.net.nz

www.manson-marine.co.nz

www.spade-anchor.com

and

www.fortressanchors.com

An internet search will reveal many anchor comparisons conducted over the years, mostly by yachting magazines.

Anchoring

Cruisers heading for this part of the world should already have a wealth of anchoring experience under their belts. However, there are one or two unusual anchoring techniques which are frequently used in these waters and time spent planning how to quickly and effectively deploy your anchor and lines will be time well spent.

Equipment

The range of anchors now available to cruisers is broad to say the least, and there seems to be hardly one of them which does not claim to outperform all the others. The author took a straw poll of anchors found amongst the charter fleets in Ushuaia, many of whom were bound for Antarctica. The results were inconclusive with every anchor under the sun to be seen, from the old fashioned Fisherman's (rare) through the venerable CQR (a couple) to several of the so-called modern anchors such as Rocna, Manson etc. As all of these anchors, and more, were to be found on substantial charter yachts taking many passengers to some of the most remote anchorages on the planet, we must assume their skippers had complete faith

A simple rig for storing lines (and sausages)
Paul Heiney

in them. In other words, the choice of anchor is yours and there isn't one which doesn't have a fan somewhere.

What is certain is that your anchor should be substantial, matched to the boat, and be one in which you have the greatest confidence. If given the choice between two sizes of the same anchor, go for the heavier - it's doubtful that anyone was kept awake in a gale with the nagging thought that their anchor was too heavy. On the other hand...

You will also need more than one, and the more variety you have the better for some will set better in mud, others in shingle or rock. At least three are recommended. Two should be of a size to act as the boat's main anchor if required, the third might be light - some yachts choose a lightweight Fortress for this.

If you are increasing the weight of your anchors and the size of your chain, then you must ensure that your windlass is going to be up to the job of lifting them, and that you have gypsies to fit all the grades of chain you carry. Your windlass is really going to earn its keep in these waters and you need to have confidence in it.

100m of chain would seem to be a basic requirement, but the author had no trouble in the Beagle Channel anchorages with 60m of chain and 40m of multiplait.

You will also need 100m coils of polypropylene rope. Some people advocate four lengths so you can deploy a line from each quarter. If you have stowage room on deck and the stuff is cheap, why not? However, for most situations three lengths will do, and some boats have got by with just two.

How to store these lines needs a bit of thought. The best method is, without doubt, on permanently mounted drums. You'll see these on each quarter of most high latitude charter boats, or sometimes near the foot of the mast. There are times when you will need to deploy the lines quickly, and this provides the speediest method. Likewise when retrieving.

If you don't have space for drums, then large baskets can be used. These might be laundry baskets, or even plastic containers designed for collecting garden rubbish - you need to be inventive. Line handling will not be as speedy as with drums, and the line has to be carefully flaked when retrieving. There is also a greater risk of snagging when deploying, but polypropylene rope seems to behave well in this respect and, providing it is stowed with care, it should pay out smoothly. It is much easier to load the dinghy with line first and let the line pay out as you row to the shore, rather than dragging the line off the deck.

Why polypropylene? Simply because it floats. You can see where it is and where it might be snagged. It is also easier to retrieve than a line which sinks, and there is less danger of fouling your prop. Buy yellow for a better chance of spotting it in the dark. It can be bought quite cheaply on the south America coast if bought from a fishing boat chandler where it will usually be sold by the kilo. If buying in Argentina, then Mar del Plata (see p. 36) is a good place to purchase. For a 12m boat 14mm lines tend to be sufficient. It is tempting to buy larger than you really need only to be faced with stowage problems.

In addition to the lines, you need a way of making them secure ashore and preventing chafe. If tying off to a strong tree, then chafe is less likely to be a problem. If using sharp rocks, some cruisers have used heavy canvas, galvanised wire strops or short lengths (2–3m) of anchor chain.

Anchoring and mooring techniques

The use of lines ashore together with a bow anchor is common practice in many of the anchorages found in the regions covered by this book, most commonly in Patagonia and the Chilean channels. The reason is that many of the anchorages are narrow, steep-to, the holding is indifferent and the swinging room is very limited. Add to this the unpredictability of the *rachas* or *williwaws*

Secure lines ashore make for a good night's sleep
Vicky Jackson

Lines ashore can be the hardest work of the day *Vicky Jackson*

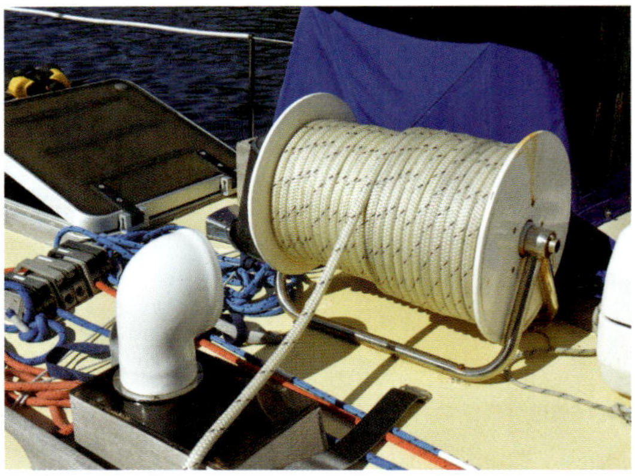

An ideal set for warp drums *Vicky Jackson*

A turning block will give a better lead and reduce chafe *Vicky Jackson*

and you begin to see why lines to the shore will became part of a daily routine.

The *rachas* can be deadly. They are caused by accelerating down-draughts and can exceed 100 knots, although only for short periods of time. But during that time, the winds might strike from any point of the compass. Only if you are held in place by more than a single anchor can you expect to survive in many Patagonian anchorages.

The usual formation is to lie with the stern to the shore, an anchor to hold the bow in position, and lines ashore to prevent her swinging. The advantage of having an anchor to seaward is that you can pull yourself backwards, tight up to the shore, so there is no fetch to worry about; by carefully choosing your spot you can get shelter from the wind under trees or a rocky outcrop. Whilst it might feel counter-intuitive to anchor stern to the wind, remember that your anchor will be pulling 'uphill' making for a much more secure attachment. Many cruisers report peaceful nights in such anchorages while a storm rages overhead. There will be bays where it is perfectly safe to swing to a single anchor, but generally these will be more open and provide less shelter than the snug caletas.

How to set your lines

You will soon arrive at a method which works for you and, after a little practice, have it down to a fine art. However, the first couple of attempts will be interesting, and the first occasion on which you have to do it in a rising gale will be testing. It is worth remembering that it will be the lines rather than the anchor doing all the work of holding your boat, they must therefore be given your full attention. Allow for the rise and fall of the tide to ensure you can easily retrieve the lines if you have too.

Remember that any boulders you attach to may have to take the full weight of a yacht subjected to 70 knot squalls. Making fast to trees does away with the need for chafe protection, and is common practice. Choose strong, living trees and not rotten ones!

Sometimes, the tying-in process can take an exhausting hour or two. Rowing through kelp, then climbing over rocks, and fighting the thorny bushes, can make this a testing experience and you should plan for this when considering an ideal arrival time. Consider also that another yacht might have beaten you to it, leaving no room in your chosen spot.

The process of tying up is made easier by good communication between yacht and dinghy, usually with a hand-held VHF. There will be times when a dinghy might have to be sent into an anchorage ahead of the yacht, in which case a hand-held depth sounder is also useful. Although expensive, some have used a laser finder to judge distances from the shore which can be deceptive, especially in heavy conditions.

There is no single method of taking lines ashore that guarantees success. Speed is often

Getting lines ashore can be a scramble, particularly at low tide
Paul Heiney

***Mina*[2] well secured by four lines** *Tim Barker*

of the essence, for even in the short time it can take to row the first line ashore the yacht can be blown far from its intended spot.

Lines before anchor

If the yacht can be held in position under engine alone, take the line, in its bag, to the shore, and then bring it back to the yacht ready for the crew to grab and make secure. Once that line is on board, the anchor can be dropped as the shore line is hauled in with the engine in reverse. Now held in position by one line and the anchor, the rest of the shore lines can be quickly deployed. .

Anchor before lines

If you choose to anchor first, you should get a line ashore as quickly as possible: tie the polypropylene line round your waist and the dinghy painter round your leg. That way you won't waste time tying up the dinghy as it is attached to you and won't go anywhere. Once secure, it's quickly back to the boat to do the same again until all lines are ashore. This is the method advocated by Andy O'Grady, author of *Chile* (3rd edition, RCC Pilotage Foundation) (Imray).

Stern anchor

Another option is to motor straight into the anchorage, drop a stern anchor in the desired spot and hold the yacht in position with minimum power once the anchor has bitten. The lines are then quickly taken ashore. The advantage of this method is that the bow is facing into the direction of the strongest wind and the boat is held by the lines with the anchor doing little work. Also, if you should ground while approaching the shore, it is the forefoot and not the rudder or propellor which takes the hit.

There are many ways to deploy your lines, and there have been countless arguments over which is the best. Most people will end up using a blend of all of them. But only by practice will you discover the method that best suits you, your crew, and your boat.

Tandem anchoring

With a little practice, tandem anchors are easy to deploy and recover. Two bow rollers, port and starboard bow cleats and a good chain and rope windlass are required. The 'first-down' anchor lies in the port side roller. Its shaft is connected by 6–10m of chain, running around the outside of the pulpit and back to the crown of the main anchor lying in the starboard roller. Attach a retrieval line of floating rope with a bight in its end and 3m longer than the chain connecting the two anchors to the crown of the first down anchor.

Prior to anchoring, the 'first-down' anchor is held in place on its roller by the retrieval line. The main anchor is held in place by the chain from the windlass. With the boat slowly in reverse, let go the 'first-down anchor by hand using the retrieval line. Then, dropping the floating retrieval line into the water, release the windlass and pay out the main anchor. Set it hard with the engine. Place a nylon snubber (5–7m) on the main anchor chain and leave the chain slack between windlass and snubber. Make sure that the snubber is protected from chafe over the roller.

To retrieve the anchors, haul up the main anchor on the windlass until the shaft reaches the roller. Lock the windlass and pick up the bight of the floating line with a boat hook and haul in the second anchor over the other bow roller.

Andy O'Grady

Although this seems a convenient way of getting extra holding from your anchoring set-up, there are those who will argue that it is a poor substitute for your primary anchor being big enough in the first place.

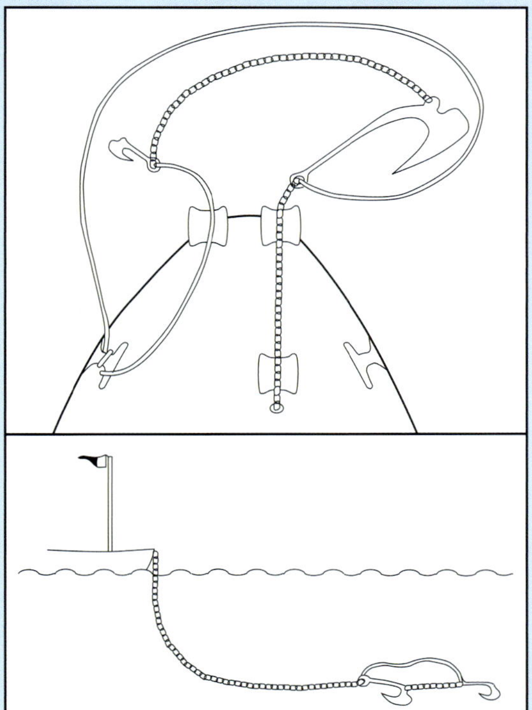

TANDEM ANCHORING

Keeping warm

Clothing

The range of protective clothing available to sailors is now so advanced that it is a wonder that anyone should ever feel cold or wet. However, there are still lessons to be learnt from those who spend their working lives at sea in harsh conditions, and work boots used by Canadian and Alaskan fishermen are worth considering. Many Antarctic sailors report that conventional sailing footwear is simply not up to the job of keeping their feet warm.

Add to this a little merino wool underwear (highly recommended, if expensive) and you will have gone far when it comes to keeping the cold out. The old advice of wearing cotton next to the skin has now passed into history with some even going so far as to say 'cotton kills' as it retains moisture and you will never feel dry. If this layer were to be accidentally exposed to freezing temperatures, the result could be life-threatening.

Fancy yachting gloves will hardly be up to the task of keeping your fingers protected when handling cold, wet ropes or anchors. Thick rubber gloves can be best when worn with liners, of which you should have several pairs so that there is always a dry pair to reach for.

Ski goggles are often recommended even when sailing outside snowy areas. When cold spray is flying, there is no better eye protection.

www.myhuntingshop.co.uk (Baffin Endurance boot)
www.dunlopboots.com (Purofort thermo full safety)
www.muckbootcompany.com
uk.icebreaker.com

A good cabin heater can be your best friend in these waters – a drip feed diesel heater
Vicky Jackson

A simple oil lamp can raise the cabin temperature a few useful degrees
Paul Heiney

Blower heaters
www.eberspacher.com
www.webasto.com

Drip-fed heaters
www.refleks-olieovne.dk
www.dickinsonmarine.com
(also solid fuel heaters)

Bottled gas systems
www.socal.co.uk
www.whayward.com

Heating systems

I once lay alongside a small French yacht which had overwintered in the Chilean channels with a baby on board. They had built their own boat stove out of tin cans riveted together, and had bought some chimney pipe from a scrap yard in Ushuaia. For fuel, they foraged the shoreline and plundered dead trees. They voted it a huge success both in terms of warmth and economy, although cleaning the deck of drops of tar was a daily task.

At the other end of the spectrum is the sophisticated diesel blower heater, commonly found in modern yachts and providing ducted warm air to all parts of the boat. Somewhere in between lies the old-fashioned drip-fed diesel heater, a favourite with fishermen. Each has its plusses and minuses.

The blower heater consumes electricity, particularly at start up, and without it will not work. Also, they come with electronic systems to set temperature and prevent overheating and if these were to fail then there is little chance of a DIY repair. The advantage is that there is no conventional lighting process to go through - you just press the button. The blower heater is also immune to the effects of the wind and requires only an exhaust and no conventional chimney.

The drip-fed heater, on the other hand, behaves more like a conventional fire and requires an efficient flue if it is to burn properly and safely. A problem can occur when strong down-draughts, often found in these anchorages, come whistling down the chimney and blow out the flames. The result is a boat full of suffocating fumes. You can guard against this by choosing a chimney in the shape of a letter H, and by experimenting you will find a configuration that works for you. In almost every town in southern Chile you will find someone who stocks chimney parts and can advise. Some yachts, however, have found a conventional chimney to be perfectly fine if extended by a metre or so. No two boats will be the same in this respect.

This would seem to make the drip-fed heater the less desirable of the two but it has no electronics, needs no electricity, and as long as there is a supply of diesel you will get some heat from it.

Whichever stove you choose, your boat should have a working carbon monoxide alarm. Carbon monoxide kills.

Quick thoughts from those who have been before

Equipment

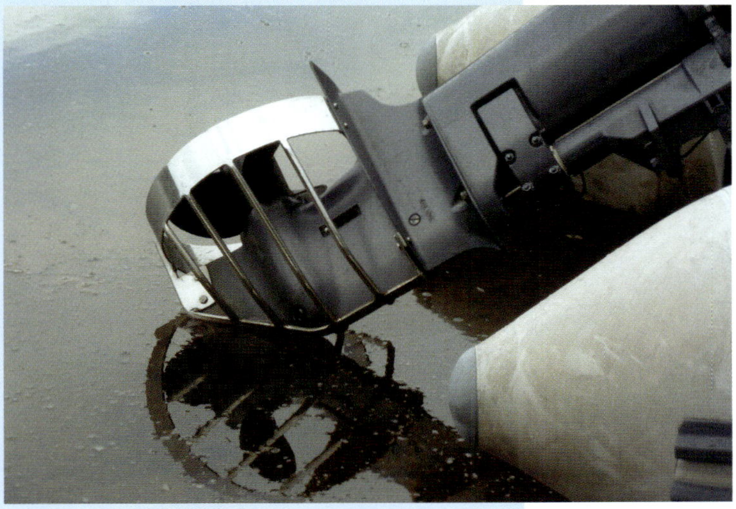

An ice-guard protects the prop from damage
Tim Barker

Have a pair of fishermen's waders - then you can jump ashore before the dinghy grounds.

Wind-driven self steering always seem to work, electric autopilots can let you down.

Protect dinghy propellors from ice.

You will use more diesel than you think.

Unless you have large tanks, you will be carrying spare fuel on deck. Think about how you are going to decant it in rough weather.

If sailing south, use up all your diesel bought in warmer climes as it will 'wax' when it hits the colder waters.

A barometer is useful, but a barograph is better.

Learn how to get the best out of the radar before you need it - especially in ice.

Take every opportunity to get fresh air through the boat to dry things out.

Gas

Propane works in low temperatures, butane doesn't.

Pressure cookers use less gas.

Have a set of universal adaptors and then you can buy gas anywhere in the world.

Safety

Do not expect to be rescued and plan accordingly.

Wherever you are moored, have an escape plan and know where to head for next.

Carry two dinghies. It is easy to lose one or have one punctured by inquisitive animals.

There will be times when it is not safe for all the crew to go ashore together.

Know where hospitals and doctors are, and then you'll never need them.

Don't leave a snug anchorage unless you are certain conditions are manageable outside.

Plan for the electricity to fail - have a small solar panel to charge the satellite phone.

Make sure *everyone* on board knows where *everything* is.

The GPS can lead you astray in the Chilean canals and your plotter will often show you sailing over a mountain. However, electronic charts are useful for identification of islands etc in channels where it is easy to lose track. Electronic charts become much more reliable in the commercial waterways.

Always remember....

... there will be no sailmaker/rigger/engineer/electrician or anyone who can help you, so carry spare sailcloth and needles and a full set of engine spares. If you are lucky enough to find a diesel engineer he certainly won't be able to get any parts.

A good canvas cockpit sprayhood/dodger is good to have, but a solid one is a blessing.

If cruising the Chilean canals in the winter, an anchor dangling from the bow will crack thin ice to allow you into an anchorage.

If you expect to be sailing in ice, don't bother to antifoul - it will get rubbed off.

Even a little Spanish will help you greatly (in Chile and Argentina).

Wine boxes are good and cheap in Ushuaia, and along with cigarettes can be traded with fishermen for crabs etc.

Don't expect any parcels to arrive, ever.

An extra layer of glazing on the back of the sprayhood keeps out the cold and rain and can make a considerable difference to comfort
Sandy Duker

Double glazing

In Antarctica, a considerable difference can be made to the warmth of a boat by employing a little ad-hoc double glazing, especially if the boat has large saloon windows. This need not be sophisticated. Some have reported good results with polythene stretched across the hatches, or thin acrylic attached with velcro.

MEDICAL

In many of the areas covered by this book, particularly in Antarctica, you will be far from any medical resources and evacuation in the event of illness should not be expected. You must carry a full medical kit and know how to use it. An up to date medical formulary can be very helpful. You should also carry appropriate medical texts books such as the '*Ship Captain's Medical Guide*' available as a free download here:

www.nauticalmind.com/81810/ship-captains-medical-guide-ebook-free/

This book is written to be understood by those without professional medical training, but it would be wise to have someone on board who has attended more than a routine first aid course. Medical kits are worthless if you don't know how to use them.

In the UK medical training courses are available at:

Warsash Academy
www.warsashacademy.co.uk

Glasgow Maritime Academy
www.glasgowmaritimeacademy.com

North Kent College
www.northkent.ac.uk

Similar courses are available worldwide.

For medical kits consult:
www.oceanmedix.com/?action=sku&sku=cOM-marine3000
www.msos.org.uk
www.oceansafety.com/product-range/medical-equipment/category/medical-kits

Those with existing medical conditions should make the skipper aware of them. If taking regular medication then details should be written down, placed in a sealed envelope, and kept where everyone can find it. The information might have to be given over the radio if the patient is not able to do so.

SHIP'S PAPERS

Throughout South America, bureaucracy is practiced as if it were an art form. There is no way of avoiding it, no way to speed it up, and certainly no way to pull the wool over its eyes.

Officials are rarely empowered to make exceptions to the rules, so you must ensure that your paperwork presents them with no opportunity for doubt.

Each chapter gives detailed information on visa/administrative issues, but there are some general points which apply to all countries and territories in this region:

- It goes without saying that your passports and any necessary visas must be up to date
- Your ship's papers must include your registration certificate
- It is useful to have a copy of your insurance policy in Spanish, and also in Portuguese if calling at Brazil. Most insurance companies will supply this
- If you have any sailing qualifications, of whatever kind, have the documents with you. In fact, the more official documents you have, the happier they will be, even if they don't understand a word of them. Also ensure you keep any paperwork you are given at every port you have been to. You never know when someone down the line will want to see it
- Everyone on board should go ashore for clearance in every harbour, and be dressed in what might be considered a respectful manner
- It can help to present a ready-prepared crew list, and official-looking blanks can be downloaded from the IMO website.
  www.imo.org

Have carbon paper, and take it with you when you check in. Take your own pens.

Customs may ask you for details of electronic equipment on board. It can be useful to prepare this in advance together with any serial numbers.

WEATHER INFORMATION

Be aware that the sources of weather information may be far fewer than you are used to, and are reported to be less reliable and often out of date by the time they are broadcast. Each chapter gives further information on weather forecasts available for that particular area.

Off the Argentine coast, the *prefectura* make regular broadcasts but the forecasts are reckoned to be poor. If you have sufficient Spanish they will give forecasts on request but these will be no more reliable and, unless your Spanish is good, confusion can result. The Chilean forecasts are reported to be more accurate and up to date see Chile p. 47.

You should be self sufficient when it comes to forecasting the weather, and not rely on shore stations. Certainly you will find none in Antarctica.

Remember, as a first-line forecasting tool, a simple barometer or barograph will more than repay their cost in these waters.

If you are equipped to get a satellite broadband internet connection, there are any number of online forecast services and charts are easily downloaded. The cost, however, and the size of the hardware, can put satellite broadband beyond most cruisers. Fleet Broadband, which delivers speeds up to 432Kbps, can cost as much as $14,000 plus data. The more modest Iridium Pilot will deliver 128kbps at a cost of $5,000 plus data.

Before deciding which satellite provider to go for, check the coverage maps. Inmarsat coverage shows the Antarctic peninsula to be on the fringes. Iridium claims its coverage extends to the poles. Satellites are constantly being replaced and upgraded and you should check latest coverage maps.

A modest satellite phone, although too slow for web browsing, is adequate for obtaining GRIB files.

www.inmarsat.com

iridium.com/products/details/iridiumpilot

GRIB files

These are your best bet for high latitude sailing, but be aware that they contain raw data from the major computer forecasting models, usually the American GFS, and they come with no guarantee of accuracy for specific locations. They are merely the computer's output, no more than that. Neither is there any human intervention which is so vital in successful forecasting for a small sea area. Consequently, they must be treated with great caution and are best used when viewed with an experienced and sceptical eye. Their inclination to underestimate wind speeds by 10 or 15% is well known. Nor can they factor in local influences, as a human forecaster would. An excellent outline of GRIB files is available here:

weather.mailasail.com/Franks-Weather/Grib-Files-Getting-And-Using

These small data files, about 10Kb, are economically downloaded on a slow-speed connection and can contain wind, temperature and sea-state information which can then be displayed on a PC or tablet using a GRIB viewer. A list of current viewers can be found here:

weather.mailasail.com/Franks-Weather/Grib-Files-Apps

but note that some can only be used when a broadband connection is available.

GRIBs by HF/ SSB radio

HF radio may seem an antique communication system by modern standards, but it still has its uses and GRIBs can be downloaded using it. The advantage is that the GRIBs are free unlike those downloaded from a satellite phone, which come with considerable data charges.

You will need an efficient SSB installation with Pactor modem, experience of how to use it, and a licence to operate. The SSB GRIB service operates through Sailmail

www.sailmail.com

who provide GRIBs not only for SSB but also for satellite connections.

For SSB, an email retrieval service such as that operated by Saildocs allows you to tailor your request for information to suit your precise needs. Your starting point if you are considering this route is:

weather.mailasail.com/Franks-Weather/Saildocs-Free-Grib-Files

It cannot be stressed enough that even modern satellite phones and computers, or SSB radio and Pactor modem, rarely work straight out of the box. You should allow many hours of operating and practising

before you can consider yourself proficient. It would be unwise to set off expecting to 'pick it up along the way'.

Weather routers

Detailed weather information, together with suggested passage plans can be purchased from professional forecasters, known as weather routers. The amount of advice you get will depend on how much you pay. There are also software packages which can offer you advice - temperature, sea state, grib forecast data etc - based on as much data as you can feed in but these require considerable data input, beyond the scope of most yachts.

When choosing a professional forecaster, you must ensure their experience covers high latitudes. It is a good idea to make contact with those who have gone before you for recommendations.

A much cheaper option than a weather router is to use a friend back home (preferably a sailor) with a decent grasp of how to read a weather chart. With the wealth of information that is available online, it is not difficult to come up with a reliable forecast, certainly for a couple of days ahead. Forecasting fog, or swell, might be problematical for an amateur, but windspeed and direction, which is what most sailors want to know, is not to difficult to predict given a bit of experience of reading data. An amateur will not give you the fine detail, or the minute by minute changes in the wind, but few sail to those fine tolerances.

A good routine would be to send a text message via satellite every morning giving location, speed and direction. Your friend back home then consults his many charts and sends back a message giving his wind forecast for the next couple of days, with any possible warnings of looming events. Text messages sent to Iridium phones via the Iridium website are free.

NAVIGATION

Charts and pilot books

If sailing in waters used by commercial shipping, then charts can be relied upon to be up to date and the surveys recent. But you don't have to stray far from the commercial routes before you are into waters which might have last been surveyed a century or more ago. There may even be places that have remained unsurveyed since the *Beagle* went through, or perhaps have never been surveyed at all. Charts should always be treated with suspicion, and since many of the electronic charts are derived from the same original data, they should likewise be considered suspect if you are sailing well off the beaten track.

However, the Chileans, in particular, have made great efforts to update their charts and correct inaccuracies between the charted and the GPS positions, which can be up to two miles in places. Avoid navigating with charts of differing vintages and use ones all of the same age, the more modern the better.

Charts of the Falkland Islands are an exception as their waters have been recently surveyed and the charts redrawn to WGS84, a standard coordinate system most recently

UK Admiralty **www.ukho.gov.uk**
or available from **www.imray.com**

Argentina **www.hidro.gov.ar**
(Spanish only)

Chile **www.shoa.cl** (English and Spanish)

Uruguay **www.sohma.armada.mil.uy**
(Spanish only, but with useful weather info easily translated)

revised in 2004. You should always check the source and date of the data on the chart and be aware of the datum. Older charts will not be drawn to WGS84.

Depths shown on UK Admiralty charts will accord with those shown on Argentine and Chilean charts.

Chilean charts are of the highest quality and they are produced jointly with the UK and USA. There are chart agents in Puerto Montt and Punta Arenas, but the *Armada* office in Puerto Williams will order charts for you, and most likely have local ones in stock. Prices are similar to UKHO charts.

A very useful publication is *Atlas Hidrográfico de Chile*; a substantial catalogue in which every chart is shown in reduced size, but carefully printed. See p. 45.

Electronic charts

Electronic charts cover all the regions described in this book with varying degrees of accuracy and detail. Expect to find your position shown on a plotter as halfway up a hillside in more remote places due to uncertainties in the original cartography. Although charts of Antarctica are offered, some regions show no more detail than a school atlas. All navigators, using whichever data source they choose, should remember that less than 10% of the world's seas have been charted to the same resolution as maps of the moon and Mars (International Council for Science).

Note Google Earth is a useful tool for armchair planning, and is accurate, but sometimes the pictures are taken in heavy shadow and detail is lost. Also, the last time the author looked in detail at Antarctica, he found that the pictures were taken in the winter and it was impossible to see any division between land and sea - everything was white.

Electronic charts do not display their source, which adds to the caution needed when using them. For close, rock hopping navigation in out-of-the-way places they cannot be fully trusted but they remain invaluable for orientation and 'having a rough idea what you are looking at'. They are best considered an aid to eyeball navigation, which will be your primary means of working out where you are.

A recent development by Navionics allows its users to provide 'live' sonar data as they cruise. This is then fed back into the charts increasing their accuracy over time. However, given the few yachts found in these waters, it might be a while before high latitude charts benefit greatly from this.

www.navionics.com/en/sonarchart

Pilot books

You should have the latest editions of the following:

Chile

RCCPF Chile: Arica Desert to Tierra del Fuego Revised 3rd edition, Andy O'Grady (Imray)

Admiralty Sailing Directions: South America Pilot Vol 2 NP6 (UKHO) (The northern reaches of the Chilean channels, including Puerto Montt and Valdivia, are not included in NP6, so you will have to purchase NP7 Vol 3 expecting only to use a small part of it).

Patagonia and Tierra del Fuego 2nd edition Mariolina Rolfo, Giorgio Ardrizzi (Editrice Incontri Nautici). This is widely known as 'the Italian book'.

Argentina

Argentina Pete Hill and Andy O'Grady download from **www.rccpf.org.uk** or a printed version from Imray.

Patagonia and Tierra del Fuego (the 'Italian Book') includes harbour information from Mar del Plata southwards.

Falkland Islands

Falkland Island Shores (FIS) Ewen Southby-Tailyour (RCCPF). This book is now quite elderly but an essential supplement by Pete and Annie Hill is available from Imray.

Antarctica and South Georgia

Admiralty Sailing Directions: Antarctic Pilot NP9 (UKHO)

South Shetland Islands Pete Hill. Download from **www.rccpf.org.uk**

South Orkney Islands Pete and Annie Hill (1994/5). Download from **www.rccpf.org.uk**

South Georgia Pete and Annie Hill (2005). Download from **www.rccpf.org.uk**

Antarctic Peninsula Noel Marshall (2008). Download from **www.rccpf.org.uk**

Southern Ocean Cruising Sally and Jerome Poncet (2007), Environmental Research and Assessment). Geographical and environmental information.

Pilot charts

Pilot charts for both the South Atlantic and Pacific Oceans for all times of year can be found as a free download here:

www.offshoreblue.com/navigation/pilot-charts.php

Tides and lights

Each country publishes its own list of lights and tide tables, but the UKHO's are perfectly accurate and easier to use if you are already familiar with them.

In 2016, the UKHO made some changes to its tide tables in order to include more standard ports and to make them easier to use. The E coast of South America is now found in NP207 Volume 7, and the W coast NP207 Volume 4.

There is a free tide programme, WXtide 32, which has proved accurate in Chilean waters. Other programmes, including the Imray Tides Planner app, are available.

Chart agents in Puerto Montt and Punta Arenas will supply the Chilean *Armada* tide tables, called Tables De Marea.

Be careful to check time differences and be aware of daylight saving. In 2015, the Chilean government decided to abolish daylight saving, DST, and so their time is now 3 hours behind UTC year round.

Argentina no longer has DST (2017) but reviews it on a year by year basis, so check. Like Chile it is in the UTC-3 zone.

In Uruguay, DST begins on the first Sunday in October and ends on the second Sunday in March every year. The time zone changes from UTC-3 to UTC-2.

Magnetic compasses

Problems arise with the use of magnetic compasses at high latitudes, and although hardly significant southwards towards the Horn, yachts intending to cruise on to Antarctica ought to be aware that the functioning of a magnetic compass can be compromised.

A 'northern hemisphere' compass carries a small counterweight at the S end of the needle to compensate for the downward attraction of the N end to the magnetic north pole, by a factor known as the angle of dip.

If the same compass is then taken into the southern hemisphere, where it will be the S end which experiences a downward attraction, the effect of the counterweight is to make matters worse. It is commonly reported that although compasses might eventually point in the right direction, they can be sluggish and very slow to respond to changes in course. This has not been widely reported as being a problem since the advent of GPS, although a conventional GPS receiver requires you to be on the move in order to confirm which way you are heading. GPS will be of no help if you are standing still.

A way round this is to use a satellite compass, although these are very expensive. You may prefer to have your magnetic compass adjusted before leaving the northern hemisphere. Some modern compass manufacturers claim to have developed a 'global needle' which they say will work at an angle of dip up to 20°, which more than covers the areas described in this book. Some yachts have reported carrying two compasses - each balanced for different hemispheres.

As a rule of thumb, a magnetic compass can be reckoned to perform safely provided you are no closer to the magnetic pole than 1,000M. The latest position of the magnetic S pole (2017) is 64°13S 136°15E.

Be aware that magnetic anomalies are frequently found, particularly in areas of volcanic activity, and within the Chilean channels.

Dusky dolphin
WDC U Ludewig

WILDLIFE OF THE SOUTHERN OCEAN

The wildlife in these rich waters can provide spectacles which easily match the majesty of the land and seascape. Whales might be your companion off the Argentine coast as they migrate towards their favoured breeding grounds off the Valdez Peninsula, and dolphins will chase and cavort and generally add to the gaiety of life on passage. When you meet your first penguins, your heart will be gladdened and the first time the albatross flies in your wake you will feel humbled, and honoured.

It would be a shame not to have a full appreciation of all the wildlife that is around you - it is a large part of what ocean sailing is all about. You should, therefore, stock your bookshelf accordingly; some suggested books are listed at the end of this chapter.

The Global Penguin Society has a comprehensive website in both Spanish and English.

www.globalpenguinsociety.org

The WDC, Whale & Dolphin Conservation, is a valuable resource on marine mammals.

uk.whales.org

In the meantime, here is a quick guide to the most common species you are likely to encounter.

Dolphins

There are several species of dolphin only to be found in southern Atlantic and Antarctic waters.

Peale's dolphin

Medium sized with no beak. Dark grey or black face which ends abruptly near the chin. They swim slowly and in small groups. Only found south of 40°S and as far as the Drake passage.

These are found around the Falklands and, while similar to the Commerson's dolphin (below) at first glance, they are longer at about six feet, and sleeker. They are often found in Stanley harbour and famously enjoy shallow water close to the shore. Falkland explorer, Ewen Southby-Tailyour writes,

> *On a number of occasions I have watched them from a beach patrolling back and forth about two hundred yards offshore... and watched them surfing in on breakers of some size and just before the water becomes too shallow they will suddenly turn (even so in about three feet of water) - almost always to the right - and burst out of the water to about half their length well clear and fall back in, facing out to sea, on their right side. They will do this all afternoon....When in a dinghy, they will slowly rise out of the water alongside so that it is possible to stroke them as they dive past.*

Hourglass dolphin

Named for the striking black and white patterning on its body, it has a small, hooked, dark dorsal fin and is the only dolphin seen in these waters with this characteristic. The beak is short and stubby. The 'hourglass' is white and divides the upper from the lower body. It is a fast swimmer with low leaps and enjoys bow riding.

Dusky dolphin

This has a distinctive dark eye patch, white below, and a pale-faced appearance. It can be found in groups of up to 500 and is a fast swimmer, is highly acrobatic displaying twists and turns in the air. Enjoys the company of boats and is quite nosey.

Commerson's dolphin

The pure white body makes it impossible to confuse this species with any other. They have a black face which runs down to the flippers. They can swim upside down and spin underwater, and enjoy surfing on inshore waves. In the Falkland Islands they are known as 'puffing pigs'.

Ewen Southby-Tailyour described them perfectly in a note submitted to researchers at Cambridge University:

> *No longer than four foot. Very playful - like a kitten. Can be seen in numbers of 20 or so. Usually seen in the narrow passages and seldom further offshore than a mile. Play for hours on end around the bows and obviously fascinated by the propellor. They are known throughout the islands as the 'puffing pig' due to the noise they make when coming to the surface. They can swim considerably faster than a ship can sail and I have estimated on one occasion that they could probably swim at something approaching 20 knots, but that is my guess. By far my most favourite animal in the Falklands!*

Chilean dolphin

Found in Chilean coastal waters although a few may appear on the eastern side of the Horn. They are small, stocky, and beak-less and generally grey but with a large white patch on the belly. They swim somewhat like a sea lion and may come and have a look at boats. They are only found in small groups. They prefer areas with a strong tidal flow, or the waters found at the entrances to fjords. Numbers are thought to be quite low.

Commerson's dolphin
WDC M Iniguez

The albatross

It is worth getting to understand the ways of the albatross for no sooner are you below 45°S than these magnificent birds will become your companions, often for long periods of your voyage. They will hover and swoop around you, never letting you out of their gaze. It is for you to decide if they feel like friend or foe - seafarers down the years have often been unable to make up their minds. If you are lucky enough to be followed by the Great albatross, you may find its wingspan of up to 12 feet intimidating, although undoubtedly spectacular.

To watch the flight of the albatross is to witness one of nature's great creations. An albatross can travel 1,000km without ever flapping its wings due to a technique which allows it to gather energy in a long, slow descent which is then expended in turning and upward soaring. This does have disadvantages for, if there is no wind, the albatross must ride the surface of the sea until the breeze returns. The take-off process can be long and lumbering. It is almost comic and in complete contrast to the balletic gliding displayed once airborne. In fact, you sometimes wonder if the bird is going to get into the air at all.

Although a south Atlantic bird, found anywhere between Antarctica, Australia, South America and South Africa, they may also be seen in the north Pacific. There is geological evidence to suggest that they were once a north Atlantic bird too, and they may have been victims of rising sea levels in the period of glacial melting. It is also possible that they gave up on the north Atlantic because getting across the windless doldrums was simply too much of an effort.

Their endurance at sea is remarkable. Once a bird is nine months old it will leave the nesting site and not return for up to ten years, spending all its time at sea. One is recorded as having circumnavigated Antarctica in just 46 days.

Albatrosses are being lost at an increasing rate, often when diving for hooked bait set by tuna fishermen, and populations on South Georgia are in measurable decline, which is worrying because the albatross takes many years to produce enough offspring to replace the annual losses. Longline and trawl fishing are thought to be the greatest threats.

Samuel Taylor Coleridge's poem *The Rime of the Ancient Mariner* (1798) warns of the dangers of not treating this bird with due respect. Although generally reckoned by seafarers to be a sign of good luck, this can change. To have an albatross around your neck is no good thing; an expression which derives from this poem.

The Royal albatross in flight
Vicky Jackson

At length did cross an Albatross,
Through the fog it came;
As if it had been a Christian soul,
We hailed it in God's name.

It ate the food it ne'er had eat,
And round and round it flew.
The ice did split with a thunder-fit
The helmsman steered us through!

And a good south wind sprung up behind;
The Albatross did follow,
And every day, for food or play,
Came to the mariner's hollo!

In mist or cloud, on mast or shroud,
It perched for vespers nine;
Whiles all the night, through fog-smoke white,
Glimmered the white Moon-shine.'

'God save thee, ancient Mariner!
From the fiends, that plague thee thus!—
Why look'st thou so?'—With my cross-bow
I shot the ALBATROSS.

And from then onwards the voyage went decidedly downhill. So be kind to the albatross if you are lucky enough to have one as a companion.

King penguins off for a swim, Falkland Islands *Vicky Jackson*

King penguin *Vicky Jackson*

Penguins

Without doubt, these creatures are one of the highlights of southern ocean cruising.

Emperor penguin

The largest of all the penguins, they are generally 1.15m high, weigh 30kg and breed in the depths of the Antarctic winter. They are only found on sea ice near the coast of Antarctica and very rarely on land. They eat fish, krill and squid and can dive to 500m holding their breath for up to 20 minutes thus enabling them to catch food inaccessible to other species.

Although their breeding programme, which happens at the coldest, darkest, most inhospitable time of year, appears bizarre, in fact it allows the growing chicks to be fully ready to lead an independent life at a time of year when the oceans are coming alive with food.

As their name suggests, they are upright, dignified creatures. They do not mix with King penguins and are never found with them. Identifiable by their yellow ear patches which fade into the white of their breasts.

Their enemy is the Leopard seal which might eat 15 penguins a day.

King penguin

The King penguin has remarkable colours and is the most vibrant of all the penguin species. They can grow to 1m tall and tend to make

King penguins with chicks, Falkland Islands
Vicky Jackson

their homes on the sub-Antarctic islands where they form huge colonies, usually with access to the sea via a beach. Throughout their lives (which can be up to 30 years) at breeding time they will always return to the same spot where they were born. You can recognise the King by an orange patch round the ear enclosed in a band of black feathers. There are over two million in the world.

Gentoo penguin

Notable for their loud trumpeting for which they throw their heads backwards, and easily recognised by a white stripe extending across the top of its head. They have the longest tail of all penguins and are the third largest species.

They prefer shallow, coastal waters and are not found on ice. The main colonies are on the Falkland Islands and South Georgia, with smaller numbers on South Shetland.

Their diet is fish, squid and lobster krill, and overfishing in the 1980s led to a decline in the Gentoo population, which has since recovered and is currently stable.

Adelie penguin

With its rather fat tummy, this is the penguin which looks as though it ought to go on a diet. In fact, their appearance is due to the fact that they are short but rather wide. Rarely taller than 80cm, they are the smallest of the Antarctic penguins. They have white rings around their eyes and a red beak with a black tip. There may be five million of them in the Ross Sea area.

Gentoo penguin
Tim Barker

Adelie penguin
Nick Coleman

They are extremely social animals and give the impression of getting a lot of fun out of life. These are the penguins who slide into the water on their bellies and slither down snow slopes. They have powerful feet with a strong grip on the ice, and can propel themselves into the sea without sliding.

Chinstrap penguin

There is no mistaking the chinstrap. The narrow band of black under its head has the look of something that is keeping its helmet on its head, and the bill is notably black. They prefer to breed on hillsides or rocky slopes. They are found in the greatest numbers on South Georgia, South Orkney and Shetland, and the Sandwich Islands where there might be as many as 10 million. They migrate north of the pack ice in the winter, spending the time at sea until they return the following spring. They are fast swimmers and are often seen 'tobogganing' down slopes on their bellies. They are said to be the most aggressive of all the penguins.

Chinstrap penguin
Nick Coleman

Rockhopper penguin

You can't mistake this penguin due to the colourful feathers on its head - it is a punk of a penguin. They get their name from their habit of hopping, rather than walking, from place to place, and tend to argue a lot with other penguins. Although small - they are amongst the smallest penguins in the world (0.50m) - their flippers are powerful.

They are skilful climbers and will sometimes get themselves up cliffs to 300m above the sea. They are easily distinguished by their blood red eyes and pink webbed feet. They breed in tussock grass near the shore.

They were once the most numerous penguin on the planet but their numbers are now in steep decline.

Magellanic penguin
Paul Heiney

Magellanic penguin

The Magellanic penguin, a small bird at 70cm tall, is found in the greatest numbers on the east coast of South America, south of 40°S, and in the Falkland Islands; in total there may be over two million breeding pairs. It differs from other penguins in that it nests in burrows, or amongst scrub. They are easily recognisable by the thick black band running under their chin. A male and female will pair for life and return to the same burrow every breeding season, the male arriving first. They recognise each other by their calls.

They are shy and nervous birds and unlike others will run for cover at the slightest sense of threat.

Blue whale *WDC L Molleson*

Whales of the Southern Ocean

The whales you will come across as you sail the length of the South Atlantic will also be on a journey. This is a place of migration where whales travel in order to breed in the warmer waters of the north, where the climate is less harsh and the newly-born more likely to survive. They return south during the summer to the rich feeding grounds found closer to Antarctica, moving ever closer inshore as the ice recedes.

Every contact with a whale is a moment of great excitement and, at times, some anxiety. But to be in the company of these giant creatures is one of the most inspiring and humbling experiences to be had in these waters. They are the most remarkable of creatures, intelligent, sociable, and able to communicate over long distances.

A well equipped yacht should carry a comprehensive book to enable positive identification of the many species to be found. However, as a sighting of a whale can be a fleeting thing with little time to make a certain identification, what follows are one or two clues to the above-water shapes you are likely to see.

Blue whale

This is the largest creature living on earth. Their tongues can weigh as much as an elephant and their hearts weigh the same as a car. They are usually found alone or in pairs. Some will live to 100 years. They are balleen whales which means they have a kind of mesh attached to their upper jaws. They take a huge quantity of seawater into their mouths which they then expel through this mesh leaving behind the krill which is their basic feedstuff. Their stomach can hold a ton of krill and they need four tons a day to survive. They are also the loudest creatures on earth with a sound output equivalent to a jet engine, but at much lower frequencies.

They are about 20-25m long and have a very small dorsal fin in relation to their body size. Blue/grey mottled in colour, they often expose their tail flukes when diving.

Fin whale
WDC B Smith

Fin whale

Second in size to the Blue whale, but much thinner, the Fin whale is very streamlined and has a clear ridge along its back behind the dorsal fin which gives it the name 'razorback'. They are now less common in the south Atlantic following intensive hunting.

They are generally 18–22m long, the dorsal fin curves well back, like a sickle, and it is not visible when the whale blows. It will rarely show its tail when diving.

Unusually, the right lower lip is white, the left is black. Dark grey body to brownish black with pale or white undersides.

Humpback whale

This gets its name from the way it raises and bends its back when preparing for a dive, which makes the dorsal fin more prominent. They are considerable show-offs and collect in groups near land to display their diving and breaching skills. They are slow swimmers and tourist boats are more than able to keep up with them. 11–15m long with a small, stubby dorsal fin, a black body with bumps and knobs on the head, and long fins with a white underside. The humpback often raises its tail flukes in preparation for a prolonged dive.

Humpback

The distinctive outline of a Humpback whale *Nick Coleman*

Sperm whale *WDC C Millard-Dawe*

Sperm whale

Toothed rather than baleen whales, they feed on squid and are the deepest diving of the whales. Their name comes from a bulbous organ found in their heads which contains a waxy fluid once used to make medicines and soap. They have the largest brain of any animal on earth, and the largest intestine. Only males are found in Antarctic waters.

16m long with a dorsal fin that is little more than a triangular, rounded hump.They have wrinkled, dark skin with a huge, square head and a blowhole very close to the front.

Lifts its tail high in the air before diving.

Southern Right whale

This is perhaps the most easily distinguished of the whales as it has no dorsal fin. The callosites, or areas of thickened skin on its head, also aid identification. They are known to be curious creatures, and for fun raise their tails in the air to catch the wind and propel themselves forward, pretty much as yachts do. They are called the Right whale because the early hunters recognised them as being the right, or correct, whale to kill.

15m long with a dark, rotund body, no dorsal fin. Blows in a V shape and may raise tail flukes when diving.

See Bibliography page 206 for further reading on the history, geography, nature and culture of the areas covered in this book.

2 HEADING FOR THE FAR SOUTH

SOUTHWARDS FROM EUROPE

An ideal passage plan

Distances
UK to Canary Islands 1,400M
Canaries to Cape Verdes 850M
Cape Verdes to Rio 2,600M

It is roughly 9,000M from Europe to the Beagle Channel, which could make for a non-stop three/four month passage, allowing for hold-ups in calms and heaving-to in gales. Such a passage is quite hard on crew, yacht, and provisions. But unless you are in a hurry to get south, the great circle route from Ushant to Rio provides interesting stopping places and makes for a proper cruise.

If you are free to carefully choose the time of your European departure, a passage as far south as Rio (roughly 5,000M) should present few difficulties. If there is a concern it is likely to be lack of wind at certain latitudes rather than excess of it.

An ideal passage plan would involve departure from northwest Europe in time to be across Biscay by mid August, allowing you to take advantage of the dying breaths of the NE Portuguese Trades which will take you south to the Canaries, aided by the south-flowing Azores current. Early October would be a good time to leave the Canaries for Cape Verde as there is then a much reduced chance of meeting any of the nasty little depressions that form off the African coast east of Cape Verde and develop by mid Atlantic into hurricanes. By mid November they have given up completely.

On departure from the Canaries, the NE trades take over and you will enjoy day after day of warm following winds. Most yachts choose to make a stop in the Cape Verde Islands. Mindelo is a well developed little town with a marina now managed to European standards, fully equipped with a surprisingly well-stocked chandlery. Mindelo used to be famous for petty crime, but no longer. The streets are safe to walk and the people helpful and welcoming.

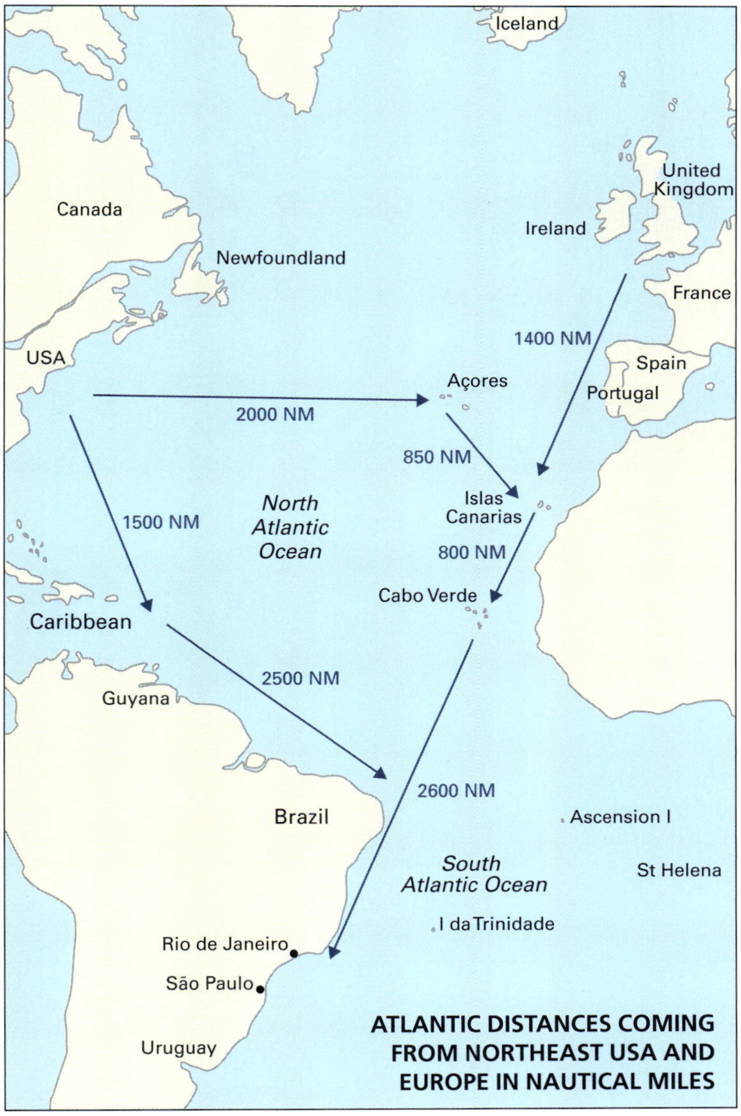

ATLANTIC DISTANCES COMING FROM NORTHEAST USA AND EUROPE IN NAUTICAL MILES

The anchorage, Mindelo *James Boyce*

The marina, Mindelo *James Boyce*

The foreshore off Mindelo, Cape Verde *Máire Wilkes*

Plenty of fresh food but expensive and not long-lasting *James Boyce*

You will want to take on fresh stores for the next leg, but be aware that fruit and vegetables may be of poor quality here. The islands have no fresh water and what they have is desalinated, which is why water in the marina is metered. This water, therefore, comes at a cost, which is often too much for it to be used for watering crops. You will find plenty of fresh produce, but it does not seem to last long, so choose green tomatoes, and hard, white cabbages which seem immune to the passing of time.

Further information on the Canary Islands and Cape Verdes can be found in *RCCPF Atlantic Islands* 6th edition by Anne Hammick and Hilary Keatinge (Imray).

South of Cape Verde you are heading for the Equator, and you will feel you are truly on your way. It will be hot and the visibility poor due to the Saharan dust in the air, but the sea is deep blue and inviting.

You can expect a few pleasant days of downwind sailing before coming to a grinding halt as you hit the doldrums – an area of light and unpredictable weather which marks the boundary between two great atmospheric circulations. This area of calm winds, properly known as the Inter Tropical Convergence Zone, can extend up to 300M and although not wide can make for a very slow passage. It always lies north of the equator, but shifts north or south according to season and its movements cannot be easily predicted. Sometimes it behaves with a mind of its own and yachts have reported less than 12 hours of calm in transiting from the NE to the SE trades; others have been less lucky and slopped along for a week or more. Yachts with ample fuel tanks (diesel available in Mindelo) can disregard the doldrums, but to motor through them is to miss a unique mid-ocean mix of eery calm, dramatic skies, terrifying electrical storms and vivid sunsets.

Beware wrecks, Mindelo, Cape Verde *Paul Heiney*

The weather in the doldrums belt tends to be at its least predictable when the trade winds are strongest so if you have had a fast passage down the African coast, expect the doldrums to be more troublesome.

Squalls can be a nuisance in the doldrums, although in daylight their tall black clouds are well defined and, if you have steerage way, they can be avoided. Radar is also effective at picking them up and if you are under way you can take avoiding action. However, if struck, be prepared for hasty reefing and torrential rain, although this may not last long. It is worth taking advantage of any following wind they offer, but there is no point chasing the wind all the way round the clock for you will find that after enormous effort in tropical heat you will be pretty much back where you started. It might be best to heave-to when a squall heads you and wait for it to pass. It won't take long. It is considered a rite of passage to shower under a passing rain squall, and by tradition the rain will give out before you have washed off all the soap.

> Sailing in squalls
>
> **www.yachtingworld.com**
> Search for 'bluewater sailing techniques part 3'

Doldrum sky *Paul Heiney*

If you have access to weather GRIB files then you might be able to see in advance where the narrowest band of calms is to be found; but this can change wildly on a daily basis and trying to chase the GRIBs would be a futile business. The doldrums tend to become narrower the further west you sail until they almost cease to exist close to the Brazilian coast.

Of greater importance is getting yourself into an ideal position for crossing the equator which you should do between 25° and 28° W, and certainly no further west than that. The currents in the equatorial region can be strong, especially the west flowing North Equatorial current which runs between 10°N and 20°N, and will be trying to take you to the Caribbean. This is joined at about 5°N by the South Equatorial current which extends to 20°S but splits either side of Cape San Roque to form the helpful south-going Brazil current (see p. 30). These currents are partly generated by the wind and are difficult to predict with precision.

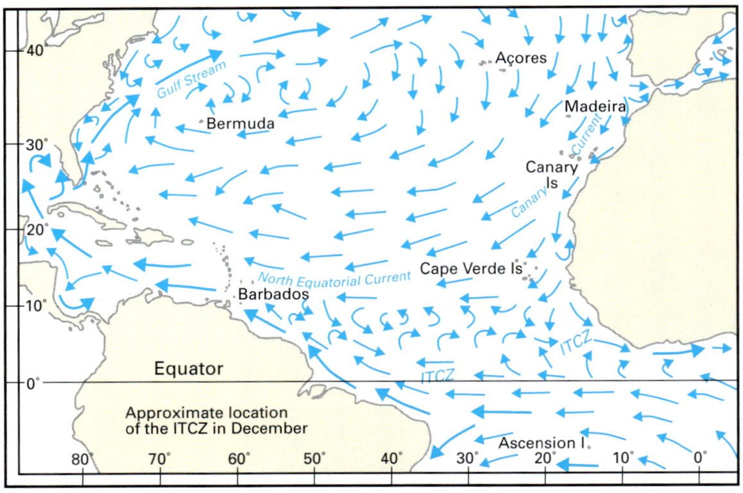

ATLANTIC OCEAN CURRENTS

If you meet strong southerly winds when you leave the doldrums, take care that you are not taken so far west by wind and current that you have hard work on your hands to weather Cape San Roque at the eastern tip of Brazil. This was the great fear of the old sailing ship masters who knew that if they failed to weather that headland, the next attempt would require them to have made a full circuit of the north Atlantic first. It is unlikely that a modern, weatherly yacht would have the same problem, certainly not to that extent, but windward work is always best avoided so don't cross the equator too far to the west.

SOUTHWARDS FROM NORTHEAST USA

This route is problematical. Even if a passage is made as far as the Caribbean there remains the difficulty of fighting both the E/NE trade winds and the North Equatorial current until it is possible to round the bulge of Brazil and bear away for the south. Some yachts have done it but at the expense of a hard slog and much diesel. The North Equatorial current is weaker close inshore, but there is the added risk of shallows making for short, steep seas which result in an even more uncomfortable passage against wind, current and substantial swell.

A passage directly from the NE USA towards a mark off Brazil might seem attractive, and it would certainly move the NE trade wind further aft making for slightly easier ride, but to arrive in Brazil at the most favourable time (October onwards) would mean sailing through the hurricane belt at the height of the season.

An easier, if more lengthy passage, would take a yacht from the US eastern seaboard towards the Azores, and then onwards to the Canary Islands where it would join the route from NW Europe. This can be safely done by leaving the US no later than May, expecting to cover the 2,000M within three weeks. A later start runs the risk of meeting an early season hurricane.

A departure from the Azores for the Canary Islands in mid/late July (800M) would have you there by August. By the time you had rested, re-fitted and re-stocked, it would be an ideal time to commence moving south towards the Cape Verdes as outlined above.

For other times of year see *World Cruising Routes*, Jimmy Cornell (Adlard Coles).

South Atlantic weather systems

The SE trade winds will be found several degrees south of the equator in the South Atlantic summer and extend as far as the latitude of the Cape of Good Hope, although on the western side of the Atlantic easterly winds are more likely to be found.

If sailing southwards through this trade wind belt, you are moving towards the centre of the permanent South Atlantic high pressure area and light and variable winds will develop, although be aware of coastal effects such as those found off the Plate estuary (p. 32). The centre of this high pressure area is found between 25°S and 32°S, moving northwards in the southern winter and south in the southern summer.

At 40°S the infamous 'roaring forties' are to be expected, gaining in strength the further south you go until you meet the 'furious fifties'. The weather at these latitudes, from the Plate down to the Horn, is volatile. Low pressure areas travel at speed and the passage of cold and warm fronts can be violent.

Tropical storms

Hurricanes were thought not to occur in the south Atlantic. However, in March 2004, Catarina became the first known hurricane to form in this region. Five have occurred since, all making landfall on the Brazilian coast. Typically, tropical storms will not form when the sea temperature is less than 26°C.

South Atlantic currents

The patterns of both weather and current are of the greatest importance in planning any passage in the South Atlantic and advantage can be gained by making the best use of them. The south-flowing Brazil Current is a great aid to yachts making south from Europe as, together with an E or NE wind in October/November, it can make for a fast passage. However, the Brazil Current is unpredictable, particularly inshore, and can change from a

The distinctive outline of Fernando de Noronha *Paul Heiney*

fair to a foul flow within a short distance, often driven by the weather. South of the River Plate, the adverse north-flowing Falklands current may hold you back, but this is less powerful further offshore. This is an offshoot of the Southern Ocean Current which circles the globe south of Cape Horn, but an arm of which is deflected northwestwards towards the Falklands. The good news is that it varies considerably in strength and width depending on surface winds, and at times can be hardly felt at all. You cannot plan to avoid it completely.

BRAZIL

If you are able to follow the ideal plan, it will be November by the time you reach Brazil and NE winds can be found off the Brazilian coast from October to February making for an easy coastal passage down the length of Brazil. A popular stopping place is the island group of Fernando de Noronha, (3°51'S 32°25'W) which lies 200M E by N from the shoulder of South America.

This small group of 20 volcanic islands is a World Heritage Site and the Brazilians are fiercely protective of them. Two problems present themselves: you may find it expensive to anchor, and even more expensive to land, with a charge being made for each crew member. In 2016, the anchoring cost per day for a 12m boat was around $75, and about $65 per person to land.

If there is any swell from the NE, which is likely given the proximity to the NE trade wind belt, it may be impossible to land by dinghy. Even on a quiet day, there is a fierce undertow. Within the arm of the recently extended jetty is a floating pontoon used by local dive boats, and you may moor to this if you use the inside and keep out of the way of the working boats. But if you manage to get ashore, you will feel you have at last reached a real tropical island. Climb the hill to find a supermarket, which is not badly stocked but at island prices which are, as always, higher than shore prices.

It is possible to complete the immigration process here at a hut on the beach, but there is no customs officer as the island's airport only deals with local flights. You will have to deal with immigration, customs and *capitania* at your next Brazilian port of call.

Credit cards are not accepted for anchoring or landing charges, but sometimes the officer in charge will drive you to the airport's ATM. To avoid this, bring local currency with you. Other currencies might not be accepted.

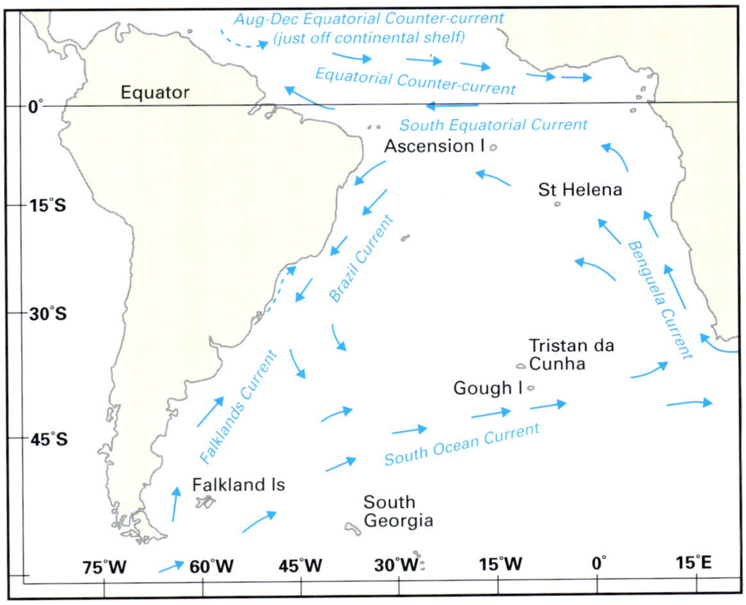

SOUTH ATLANTIC CURRENTS

You are now, of course, in the southern hemisphere and it is approaching midsummer in Patagonia and the Beagle Channel. If you wish to arrive there in the summer months then you are already late, and most of the summer is going to be over by the time you get there. You may, therefore, decide to linger as you make your way down the South American coast. Some cruisers have spent pleasant winters in Uruguay waiting for spring to return in the deep south.

Under certain circumstances, usually in winter when ground temperatures are low, an area of high pressure can form over Patagonia, deflecting the depressions either to the north or south. This can be of great advantage to cruisers (unless you are in northern Chile when you may get gales) who can then enjoy light airs in the Beagle Channel under clear skies and sail in crisp air. For this reason, winter cruising in the Beagle and Chilean channels should not be ruled out. Many have found it to be hugely enjoyable, but see p. 10 - cabin heaters!

Harbours on the coast of Brazil

For details of Brazilian harbours and anchorages see:

Brazil Cruising Guide Michel Balette (Imray)
Brazil, Pete Hill (Kindle/ **www.rccpf.org.uk**)

A word about Brazil

The country presents few navigational difficulties but its social problems, arising from a sharp divide between the rich and the poor, can often result in crime and violence. Cruising yachts can be seen as easy targets so all warnings about personal security should be taken seriously and acted upon and local advice should be heeded.

Pampero **felt in Piriápolis**
Paul Heiney

URUGUAY AND THE RIVER PLATE

On arriving in Uruguay, many sailors give a sigh of relief that Brazil is behind them. The Uruguayans are pleasant and helpful people, the crime rate is low, and you will spend far less time looking over your shoulder ever alert to street danger. Also, the bureaucracy is less burdensome than in Brazil although, as you will find everywhere in south America, paperwork has been raised to the level of an art form. Nevertheless, the Uruguayan *Prefectura* are generally helpful and will not deliberately make life difficult for you.

The weather of the Plate Estuary

There is some debate amongst geographers as to whether the River Plate is an estuary or a gulf, but its 14,000 square miles provides a perfect breeding ground for volatile weather systems and, for this reason, a close eye should be kept on the forecasts when sailing hereabouts.

For the first time since leaving the Bay of Biscay, you are now entering a region where stronger weather becomes an issue. Sudden and violent storms can appear, fuelled by fast-moving depressions which breed in central south America and intensify as they meet the Atlantic Ocean. There are three in particular.

Pampero

A *pampero* is born in the Andes and reaches maturity as it passes over the vast grasslands of Patagonia, known as the pampas, hence the name. It is experienced as a line squall which occurs during the passage of a cold front, and is notable for a swift backing of the wind from a northerly quarter to south or southwest with rain, thunder and lightning. They are more frequent between June and September. A typical *pampero* would be heralded with a slow fall in pressure, and a hot northerly wind. A rise in water levels in the Plate estuary will be seen and dense clouds of insects in the air are said to be a portent. The wind may then die for a short time before a squall appears from the SW and severe winds of 70 knots or more at first, but moderating.

Zonda

Preceding a *pampero*, a *zonda* may be experienced. This is a hot, humid north wind which blows in advance of the depression as it tracks eastwards.

Sudestada

Between March and October, of greater danger is the *sudestada* which blows with great vigour from between E and SE and can last several days giving rise to steep and breaking seas. The outer reaches of the Plate provide little shelter from that direction. A sudestada can occur anywhere between 30° and 45° south and again it is a product of the movement of a depression across the Plate estuary, but unlike the pampero the strong winds occur when the depression collides with the South Atlantic High. The winds can be of gale force or greater and last for several days producing steep and damaging seas. If forced to heave to, a yacht might soon find itself on a lee shore.

One thing you must remember – and until you have been here some time it is easy to forget – if your home waters are north of the equator you have learned over many years the direction in which weather systems revolve. Once south of the equator, everything is reversed. This means that if someone says 'there's a depression on the way' you must remember that in southern latitudes a low pressure area has clockwise rotation, and an anticyclone anti-clockwise. Until you are used to it, it is easy to make a hasty mistake.

Uruguayan Prefectura

The concept of *Prefectura* is not easily understood by Europeans and North Americans who have no such organisations in charge of their navigation.

It is best to think of them as a cross between the Police and the Coastguard and their directions must be heeded, especially in Argentina.

Although uniformed, and despite the fact that they operate small launches (sometimes), they are essentially an organisation dedicated to paperwork which must be complied with in every detail. This can appear onerous and pointless at times, but there is little to be gained by showing impatience or frustration - it will only slow things down even further.

They have full authority, but little responsibility, which can make them a formidable foe should you cross them.

The author experienced no problems with the *Prefectura* in either Uruguay or Argentina, but took the precaution of always dealing with them with a smile on his face, and with honesty.

Useful harbours of the outer River Plate

Piriápolis, Uruguay

34° 52'·4S 55° 16'·9W
Charts UK 2004, 3064 H113

Piriápolis provides a useful port of call if heading south, offering good shelter and a 60-ton travel-hoist. Its neighbour to the east, Punta del Este, is more famous, glamorous and expensive, but for shelter and facilities Piriápolis is the better of the two. If you need to haul-out the next lift will be in Puerto Montt on the Pacific coast of Chile, over 2,000M away. (Haul-out facilities can be found further up the Plate at the Yacht Club Argentino's branch in San Fernando, but this calls for a considerable detour and an extra stop in Argentina).

Piriápolis has a large and well maintained area of hard-standing providing good lay-up facilities and yachts can be left here in perfect safety. It is an ideal place to break your journey south and a popular laying-up spot for charter yachts at the end of their Antarctic season. Charter yachts come here not only to haul out, but to avoid prolonged exposure to the attentions of the Argentine customs and *Prefectura*, both of which can be unpredictable, and expensive, in their interpretation of the law. In Piriápolis, the bureaucracy is more relaxed.

The only drawback to this popular place is that it is not possible to book ahead either for a berth afloat or ashore, and so you must trust to chance. December to the middle of February is the high season here and during

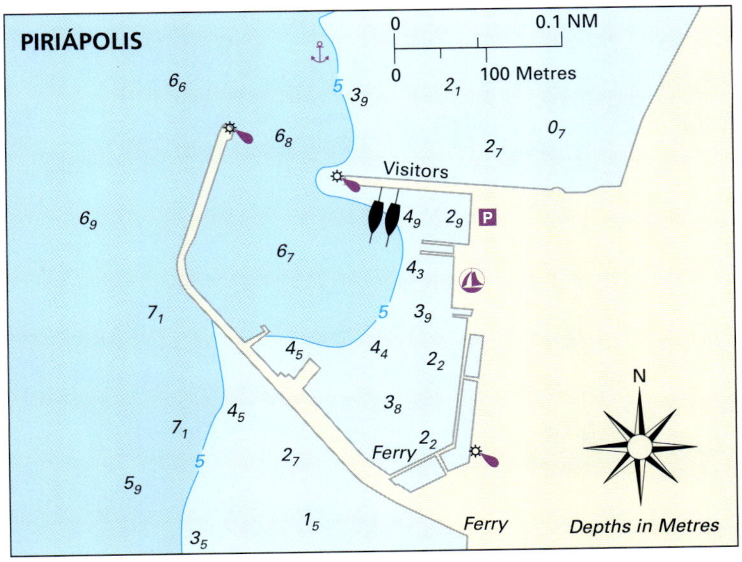

Approaching Piriápolis *Paul Heiney*

that period berthing afloat might be scarce. If looking to lay up ashore, the best option might be to get there just after the season ends, and before the big boys arrive from the south, towards the middle of March. If you then plan to re-launch in September you will be sailing south as the days lengthen and the air turns warmer.

Entry

Coming from the direction of Brazil, a Q(6)+LFl cardinal buoy to the south of Punta Del Este (34°58'·6S 54°57'·7W) should be left well to starboard and a course made to the WNW to give a good clearance to Pta Colorado to avoid the sunken rocks 1 cable off. This headland is marked by the light on Pta Negra (Fl.W.5s7·5M).

Strong adverse currents can flow round this headland driven by wind and tidal flow. Note, also, the submerged rocks 2 cables to the southwest of Punta Iman (unlit). From here a roughly northerly course can be made to the western pier marked Fl.R5s8·5M.

It is advisable to make a radio call (VHF 16) to *Control Piriápolis* so the *Prefectura* can log your arrival. It may smooth things for when you visit them face to face.

Local boats on the right of this picture, visitors on the left *Paul Heiney*

Berthing

On entering the harbour between the piers, the yacht berths will be seen running the length of the northern pier. You should tie up bow or stern-to with a line from each quarter to a buoy. Look out for directions given by marina staff from the shore. Beyond the travel hoist, the moorings are reserved for locals and the western pier is home to the fishing fleet.

If the place appears full, or you arrive at night and want to wait until morning to make an entry, there is a good anchorage in 3m north of the north pier taking care not to impede access to the harbour. From here you will have a good view of the berths and can pounce as soon as one becomes free. This anchorage can become choppy quite quickly in westerly winds.

Formalities

You will first deal with the *Hydrografia*, a state-run body which administers the marina and the yard. They will ask to see your insurance and warn you that they carry no insurance whatsoever. If you are going to be hauled out, check if this is OK with your insurer. The marina office can be found in the row of low buildings which form the back of the boatyard, and where you will also find the showers. The berthing rates in-season can be high but quite modest out of season. The low season usually begins around 1 March.

To find the *Prefectura* you should leave the marina, turn left, and follow the waterfront promenade, Rambla de los Ingleses, for 400m or so. Note a useful, English-speaking chandler 200m on the right after you leave the marina. You will come to a roundabout and on the right, flying the Uruguay flag, is a low, white building which houses the *Prefectura*. They may operate 24 hours during the high season but normal hours at other times. You will be lucky to find an English speaker here.

Note: you cannot carry out the immigration procedure here. For that you will have to go to the local airport in the direction of Punta Del Este. Take a bus. Ask at the airport information desk for immigration - they are helpful and English is widely spoken. There will be a small charge for stamping your passport, both on entry and departure. There is a bus to the airport from the Piriápolis bus station some 15 minutes' walk from the marina, or a 20 minute taxi ride. You will have to visit the airport again if you leave Uruguay for Argentina or Chile.

The inner harbour, Piriápolis
Paul Heiney

Services

The chandlery is surprisingly well-stocked, especially during the season, and the chandler is a helpful man. For example, there is only one sailmaker in Uruguay, in Montevideo, and the chandler will put you in touch.

Propane gas is quite common hereabouts and there are two bottle-filling stations in town. The chandler will advise. Butane is not obtainable.

Diesel appears to be available from pumps near the travel hoist, but it is not that simple and requires a phone call and a visit from a tanker which may not deal in small quantities. There are several filling stations but none close enough to the marina to be useful. A taxi is the only option.

Water (drinkable) and electricity is available on the pier.

There are many small shops in town, a decent supermarket close to the *Prefectura*, and a larger one further up the hill.

Piriápolis is a pleasant little seaside town with a first class beach where you will be made to feel safe, secure and welcome. Alongside affordable family hotels are ones offering considerable luxury, some with casinos. During the season, the air will be full of the scents of woodsmoke and barbecuing meat from the *parillas* (grills) of the many steak houses. You will enjoy Uruguay.

ARGENTINA

The 200M crossing of the Plate estuary provides a good shake-down if you have been ashore for any length of time in Piriápolis. Providing you have been cautious and checked the forecasts, the crossing presents few problems although the Plate is shallow in places, particularly in the region of the English Bank, where depths can fall to 6m. If any sea is running, it would be prudent to steer a southerly course on leaving Piriápolis and give this area a wide berth. For the first time in many miles you will be sailing in murky, shallow waters.

The River Plate is a major maritime highway serving the capitals of Argentina and Uruguay and you can expect it to be busy when crossing the well-defined shipping lanes. AIS is very useful.

If taking a more or less straight line south from Piriápolis, the last 70M will find you sailing parallel to the Argentine coast and soon an endless vista of high-rise apartments will appear. This is where the richer residents of Buenos Aires flee in the hot summers, making for a smart and wealthy resort with the longest beach in the entire country. Mar del Plata attracts seven million tourists a year but despite this it is known as the 'Happy City,' and also the 'Pearl of the Atlantic'. In high season, December to February, the beaches have been described as 'shoulder to shoulder'. The intensity of the high-rise building has led to portions of the beach being in the shade for long parts of the day.

Mar del Plata

38°2'·0S 57° 31'·2W

Charts H -114, UK 3065

Callsign *Prefectura L2U*

(When calling the Argentine *Prefectura* on VHF or SSB, they will not respond to a simple 'Prefectura Mar del Plata'. You must use the callsign allocated to each station)

Entry

The entrance is made between two piers. The eastern breakwater (Fl.G.3s) should be avoided as there is considerable and unpredictable shoaling here despite repeated dredging. In fact, even in settled weather white water may be seen across much of the harbour entrance. The deepest water is found closest to the northern pier (Fl.R.3s) and from here a roughly SW course will bring you to a swing bridge to starboard, to be found after passing a red pile (F.R.5s4·7m) marked NAUTICO, Be careful to avoid 'poles' and a jetty clearly marked on the chart.

Soon after entering the outer harbour you may be called on VHF (in English) by the *Prefectura* who will ask you to identify yourself. They will want to know your last port, number of crew and nationality. In strong weather, they may close the port.

The small swing bridge marks the entrance to the yacht moorings. Access is limited by tide and there can be less than 2m at LW. In high season you can assume that if the bridge is open there is sufficient water for most boats

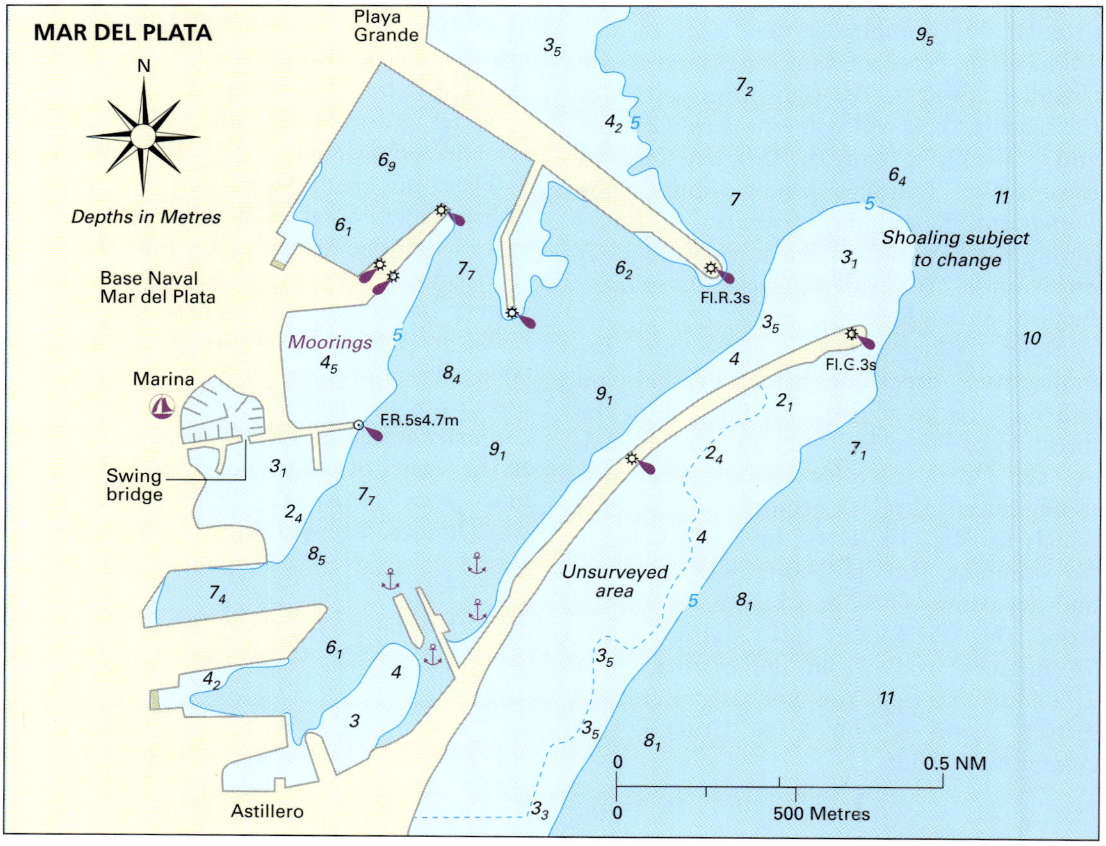

Mar del Plata in full holiday mode
Vicky Jackson

to access. Alternatively, it is possible to anchor and wait (holding may be poor) or use one of the buoys provided. Out of season, a fog horn will summon the bridge keeper, or try VHF 71.

After passing through the swing bridge, turn left to find the pile moorings of the hospitable Yacht Club Argentino.

In fact, there are two clubs here, both of which welcome visitors. The YCA offers free berthing for no less than 7 days. Possibly for this reason it seems more popular with foreign yachts than the Club Nautico Mar del Plata, which is mainly a motor yacht club, but welcomes all.

Formalities

The YCA's berthing master will advise on where the authorities are to be found including *Prefectura*, Immigration and Customs and can provide forms for you to fill in before you leave the boat - this saves much time. It is a good idea to travel with a supply of carbon paper. All offices are within 20 minutes walking distance of the marina but take his advice on the order in which they should be visited.

You may be asked for a Port Health Clearance. This is conducted in the marina and merely requires you to state if you have any diseases or animals on board. There is no examination. A sum of money is then required in exchange for the certificate. If you are lucky, the official will accept cash there and then. Otherwise you will have to travel some distance into town to a government office to make payment. Reports say this can be time-consuming.

Customs

It is beyond the scope of this book to detail Argentine customs regulations. Suffice it to say that they are complex, ever-changing, and inconsistent from harbour to harbour. The penalties for contravention can be severe and disrupting. The only thing you can do is to give your full attention to the form-filling and answer all the questions honestly. If you are planning to leave your boat in Argentine waters you must take advice, possibly from a lawyer or customs agent, before doing so. Current advice would be to avoid leaving your boat in Argentina if possible.

The swing bridge (open) at the entrance to the yacht basin, Mar del Plata
Vicky Jackson

The yacht basin, Mar del Plata
Vicky Jackson

If you want to leave from Argentina for the Falkland Islands, special rules apply; these can be found on p. 119. There are severe penalties if you break these rules.

Diesel

Diesel is available in large quantities from the fish docks but is said to be of poor quality and best avoided. There is a large filling station 10 mins walk from the marina and the YCA will loan you a wheel barrow to help with this.

Services

There are several chandleries to be found in the direction of the *Prefectura*, but these are geared to the needs of the large fishing fleet and not yachts. However, for the anchorages further south you will need several coils of polypropylene rope (see page 5 on mooring) which can be found in abundance here, usually sold by the kilo at a good price. This will be your last chance to purchase before heading south.

Repairs

There are no repair facilities for yachts, but fishing fleet support engineers may be able to help with engine repairs if you have the spares on board. It should be stressed that ordering spares from Europe can lead to lengthy delays in customs.

Crew change

If planning a crew change, the local airport is Astor Piazzolla International which is 7km north of the city and from here it would be a short flight to Buenos Aires. Note that Buenos Aires has two airports and you should allow at least an hour to transfer from the local, downtown airport (Jorge Newbery, code AEP) to the international one (Ministro Pistarini, code EZE).

The train journey from Mar Del Plata to Buenos Aires takes roughly six hours and three services operate. The price depends on the level of comfort and catering. This can be the cheapest way to travel between the two cities. In high season reservations are needed well in advance. Tickets can be purchased at the Ferrobaires office (✆ 451-2501; Alberti 1602; 0800–2100) at the bus terminal. The fares decline considerably out of season.

Mar del Plata to the Beagle Channel

On leaving Mar del Plata, you are 1,000M from the entrance to the Beagle Channel. 54°18'S 64°49'W provides a suitable mark to aim for as it gives you the option of making either directly for the Le Maire Strait, seeking shelter to the west, or visiting Staten Island. Which you choose will largely be determined by the weather.

Although the straight line option seems the simplest, it might not always be the most comfortable given that you will be sailing into the Roaring Forties and towards the Furious Fifties and will be, at times, 200M offshore. A passage closer inshore is longer but means smoother water in less fetch. Balancing distance sailed with comfort is tricky, but a good option on leaving Mar del Plata might be to head towards Puerto Deseado to a mark at 47°5'7S 65°13'W (650M) thence towards the entrance to the Magellan Strait at 52°20'S 67°35'W (260M) and then a SE course takes you towards the Le Maire Strait, a modest 150M. You will have lengthened your passage by less than 100M and may have had a far less rough passage.

The pilot chart for October - a good time to be making a passage down the Argentine coast if you want to arrive in time for the Patagonian spring - will show that the majority of the winds south of the Plate will be from N through W to SW, and the strongest will be from the NW and the SW. These sometimes violent winds are generated by the passage of fronts.

MAR DEL PLATA TO THE BEAGLE CHANNEL

Beagle E end
Paul Heiney

Pilot charts of the south Atlantic and Pacific for every month of the year are worth close study and can be downloaded from:

http://www.offshoreblue.com/navigation/pilot-charts.php

A typical passage of a depression might go as follows: you will start with (relatively) steady and modest winds from the NW accompanied by a steadily falling barometer. This is where a barograph (mechanical or electrical) repays its cost. Just before the front arrives, the pressure may fall more rapidly before bottoming out. The wind will slowly start to shift to W. This is when you should prepare for the cold front which will not be far behind.

The front can often be seen as a clearing of the cloudy sky to the SW due to the change from a moist to a cold, dry air mass. If you see such a clearing then reduce sail without delay. The cold front will hit with amazing rapidity and winds can increase from 15 to 35/40 knots in a matter of minutes and can strengthen to as much as 50 knots. You will need a stout vessel indeed to continue sailing and the best advice is to heave to until the front is through and the wind and seas have moderated and there is a shift of wind back towards W.

It is some consolation that the weather systems are highly mobile and the weather ever-changing. With luck, you might be held up for less than 12 hours. With even better luck, it might be another couple of days before the next front goes through by which time you will have made good progress with the wind just free.

It is worth considering making a stop in the Falkland Islands. If you had sailed the east coast of South America as far as, for example, Caleta Horno 45°02'·37S 65°41'·02W, a popular anchorage, then a course to the Falklands would bring the prevailing winds further aft giving an easier ride. If heading for the Beagle Channel after that, it would be a case of waiting for a good forecast before undertaking the passage, which is only 300M.

Weather information off the Argentinian coast

GRIBs are able to give good predictions of approaching depressions. There are no weather forecasts issued routinely for this coast either on HF or VHF, although the *Prefectura* will give forecasts on request on VHF although you are unlikely to be within range.

If you have internet access, the website below provides live information of weather conditions at several coastal airports.

http://en.allmetsat.com/metar-taf/argentina.php?icao=EGYP

GMDSS Metarea 6 covers this area. Broadcast 0230 / 1730 UT via Inmarsat C.

Navtex

Navtex 518-kHz Service in NAVAREA 6

Navtex Coast Station	Transmission times UTC
La Paloma (URG)	0050, 0450, 0850, 1250, 1650, 2050
Ushuaia (ARG)	0200, 0600, 1000, 1400, 1800, 2200
Rio Gallegos (ARG)	0210, 0610, 1010, 1410, 1810, 2210
Comodoro Rivadavia (ARG)	0220, 0620, 1020, 1420, 1820, 2220
Bahia Blanca (ARG)	0230, 0630, 1030, 1430, 1830, 2230
Mar del Plata (ARG)	0240, 0640, 1040, 1440, 1840, 2240
Buenos Aires (ARG)	0250, 0650, 1050, 1450, 1850, 2250

Yachts have found the Navtex service to be unreliable at times and the forecasts often out of date due to the fast-changing nature of the weather.

Harbours on the coast of Argentina

There are intriguing harbours and anchorages to be found between Mar del Plata and the Le Maire Strait but details are beyond the scope of this book and it should be said that all have their drawbacks either in terms of shelter or ease of access. Certainly you should expect to find no completely safe harbour south of Puerto Deseado until you are in the Beagle Channel, and even Puerto Deseado can present a challenge with close navigation needed in fast tides, shallows, and often strong winds.

If you decide to cruise this coast, consult the following:

Argentina Andy O'Grady and Pete Hill (RCC Pilotage Foundation)

Patagonia and Tierra del Fuego Marionlina Rolfo and Giorgio Ardrizzi (Editrice Incontri Nautici).

APPROACHING THE BEAGLE CHANNEL FROM THE PACIFIC

The Pacific offshore route to the south

This is the traditional sailing ship route from the Pacific coast of North America to S Chile or the Horn, and the following advice is given by Andy O'Grady in RCCPF *Chile* 3rd edition (Imray).

"The theory is to sail close-hauled on a S course between 90° and 120°W until westerlies are encountered around 35° to 40°S, and then run into Valdivia (39°50'S) or Puerto Montt (41°30'S). Much depends upon the time available for the passage. If coming through Panama in January or February, some yachts visit the Galápagos, about 900M. They then go on to Tahiti and the Australs before turning towards Valdivia or the Horn. Going this way, the distance from the Galapagos to Valdivia is about 8800M. A middle route lies via Gambier, about 7000M, and an even shorter route passes by Isla de Pascua, about 4000M.

A more direct route is to sail S from Panama to Salinas, Ecuador, about 670M, and then make an off-shore loop of about 3100M to Valdivia or crawl down the coast. At first, the winds in the Gulf of Panama are light and variable and thunderstorms are common. It is advisable to stay well off the coast of Colombia, closing the coast around the border with Ecuador. If going offshore, most of the remainder is close hauled, beating across the SE trades with a reach or run in to the coast at the end. For a boat that is happy beating in rough conditions, this route may be preferable as it takes less time than the other routes. Unfortunately the high is unstable. In the centre of the high the winds will be very light.

The Pacific inshore route

The inshore route is against the prevailing S wind and the Humboldt Current. A not untypical passage following the coast from Salinas, Ecuador to Valdivia logged a total of 3360M, 1460M under motor and 1,900M under sail.

The Humboldt Current flows up the coasts of Peru and Chile at a rate of 0·5 to 1·5 knots. The prevailing wind is from the S and follows the coast. During the day it is reinforced by the thermal effect of air flowing over the cold waters of the Humboldt Current and onto the warm land and the strength of the thermal wind increases during the summer months. It is often easier to travel at night when the wind is lighter and frequently has an offshore slant.

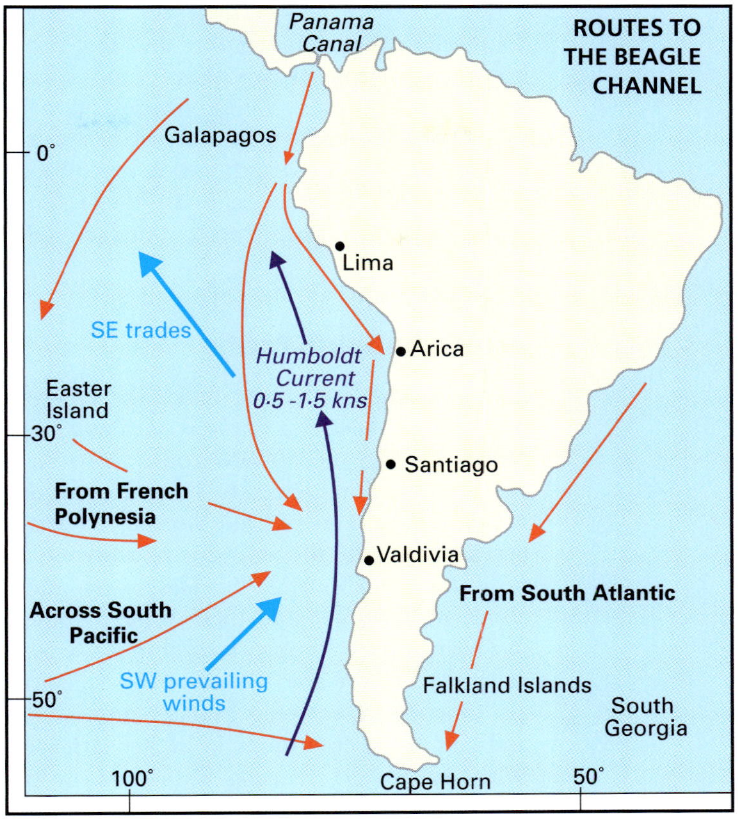

Dealing with the officials in Peru is time consuming, frustrating and expensive. Fortunately there are anchorages where there are no settlements and hence no officials. The Peruvian coast is 1150M long with few sheltered anchorages, necessitating several overnight legs. In Chile, the anchorages and towns become more frequent. The straight-line distance from Arica to Valparaíso is 870M but under sail as much as 1150M may be logged and the average distance between anchorages rises to about 60M. Although the prevailing winds are decidedly from the S, there are occasional N winds lasting 12–24 hours with calms during the night. There are fewer anchorages along the 600M from Valparaíso to Valdivia, though there is a greater likelihood of W or SW winds making for easier sailing on a close reach.

This route takes more time than the offshore route but has a number of attractions. The coastal towns in N Chile are worth visiting; so few yachts travel this coast that the welcome is generous. The anchorages in the Atacama Desert are a unique experience. Given the availability of anchorages, the inshore route is a great deal easier than the rough offshore passage, particularly for smaller yachts.

Local advice, concerning the prevailing southerlies, is that November and December are the months of strongest winds. Two yachts travelling S in these months experienced no night-time decrease in winds S of Caldera. Wind strength varied between 15 to 25 knots with occasional 30–35 knot winds off Caldera, Puerto Huasco and Valdivia.

Across the South Pacific

Several yachts each year make the crossing direct from Australia or New Zealand. The weather along the 5000M route from New Zealand is dominated by the depressions which track across the Southern Ocean between 50° and 60°S producing a strong W flow up to about 35°S. Gales are most common in winter and their number lessens in November. Tropical cyclones, which generally keep to the W end of the S Pacific, are most likely between January and March and can affect conditions in higher latitudes. With an eye to cruising Patagonia in the spring, the best choice appears to be to cross in November or December between 40° and 45°S but the decision will be affected by conditions at the time of the start. In January some vessels have experienced frustrating E winds along this route as far S as 50 degrees. Places to aim for are Puerto Williams after rounding Cape Horn, Puerto Montt via Canal de Chacao or Valdivia. To enter the Patagonian *canales* elsewhere is more difficult: the landfall is highly complex and there are no ports of entry."

For Chilean landfalls see Puerto Montt (p. 53) and Puerto Williams in the Beagle Channel (p. 87).

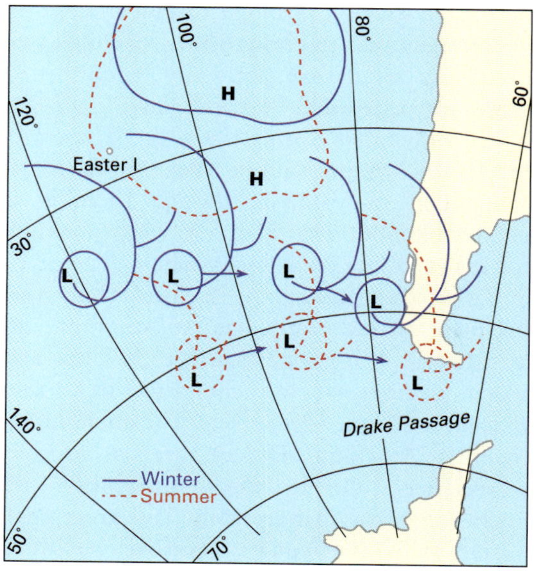

MAJOR WEATHER SYSTEMS

Pacific currents

"The Peru or Humboldt Current comes inshore near Cabo Ráper and drifts N along the coast in a band some 50–150 miles wide at about half a knot. It often slants towards the coast, which can be dangerous, as it cools the surrounding air and causes fog. Off Cabo Ráper the current may drift any way, even E, but the tendency is either N or S. Along the S coast the W wind drift moves SE and increases up to 1kn towards Cabo de Hornos. Between summer and winter, sea temperatures vary from 20°–15°C in the N and 9°–5°C in the S.

El Niño

Once or twice a decade, the system is upset by *El Niño*, a mass of warm Pacific surface water. This, when it reaches the coast around Ecuador, pushes S, blocking the lower rungs of the food ladder and causing wide disruption to dependant life as well as upsetting the climate in places as far apart as Australia and Brazil, California and Tierra del Fuego. Experience suggests that El Niño years are more settled in the far south.

South pacific weather systems

The S Pacific High sits within the area bordered roughly by the Galapagos to the N, Easter Island to the W, and the continent of S America to the E. It moves N in winter and S in summer. The N part of the Chilean coast is on the fringe of the SE trades; to the S is a wide area of moderate southerlies gradually becoming stronger westerlies. Inshore, the westerlies may be diverted by the Andes, generally to the N. Winds from an E quadrant are rare or short lived on the coast although they may blow 200M or 300M offshore.

The S Pacific High is generally powerful enough to keep the frontal systems of the roaring forties to the S of Valparaíso. Some systems slip through, especially in winter. In winter, the extreme cold of the mountains and Argentine pampas can result in the temporary development of a stable high over Patagonia. This can push depressions to the N or S. It is not unknown for the Golfo de Penas to be calm and sunny whilst a gale rages in Valdivia. It is the development of this high, that tends to be strongest and last for longer periods in the months of July–September, that makes winter the best season for winds and sun (though not for heat) S of Golfo de Penas."

3 CHILE, FROM VALDIVIA TO THE BEAGLE CHANNEL INCLUDING THE MAGELLAN STRAIT

There is no other country so long, and at the same time so slender, as Chile. It sits off the W coast of South America like a thin skin, roughly 2,300 miles long and on average less than a hundred miles wide, except at its southern limit where its Pacific coast meets the Atlantic Ocean at Cape Horn and the landmass briefly swells. It really is a thin sliver of a place, but for a cruising yachtsman it is bloated with anchorages and adventure as you sail between the temperate greenness of Puerto Montt to the bleakness of Cape Horn, passing through some of the most remote and spectacular anchorages on the continent.

For the purposes of this book, and as far as most cruising sailors are concerned, it is the bit of Chile which lies between 40°S and 60°S that is of interest, for most will have entered the country somewhere along that 1,000M route. Strangely, for a country with such a long coastline, it has few coastal harbours and yachts arriving from the west have few choices. Certainly, after what might have been a lengthy ocean crossing, a lee shore in a westerly wind and swell, as the southern half of Chilean coast is most of the time, can hardly be considered welcoming - prepare to be unnerved at the number of charted wrecks on this coast.

I have sliced Chile in two, from Valdivia (roughly 40°S) to the Beagle Channel (roughly 55°S), and then the Beagle Channel including Cape Horn which will surely be the highlight of any voyage to these waters and is therefore described in some detail.

As far as the passage from Valdivia to the Beagle (or vice-versa) is concerned, I give only details of stopping places where some kind of facility exists such as food, diesel, public transport etc - and there are not many of them. On the other hand, spectacular anchorages abound, and you will need them as overnight navigation is forbidden. For about 1,000M, a yacht will be on its own, far from human contact and support, swinging to its anchor sometimes, but often tied to the shore for security. All the warnings already given with regard to self-sufficiency must be heeded here.

Pilot books, cruising guides, charts and tidal information

The revised *RCCPF Chile* 3rd edition edited by Andrew O'Grady (Imray) contains useful pilotage photographs not included in earlier printed versions. Andy has drawn on his own experiences and those of many others to whom he gives full credit in his introduction and I, in turn, have drawn heavily on his work, which is the most up-to-date available for these waters, with grateful thanks.

Patagonia & Tierra del Feugo (Editrice Incontri Nautici) is not only a vital and detailed source of information from two intrepid Italian explorers, Mariolina Rolfo and Giogio Ardrizzi, but also a work of literature and penmanship in its own right. Ensure you have the latest, second edition (2007). Although outstandingly comprehensive, note that this edition is now 10 years old.

Admiralty NP6 & 7 are comprehensive pilot books from which yachts can glean useful information. South America Pilot Volume 2 (NP6) covers the Chileans channels from 50°S to Cape Horn.

Those parts of South America which are covered by US pilot books (and other useful information such as pilot charts) are available as free downloads
http://msi.nga.mil/NGAPortal/MSI.portal

A useful source of up to date information while cruising (if you have a rare internet connection) is the Chilean Armada's website
www.shoa.cl/pagnuevaing/index_ing.html
which has an option to be read in English. Apart from having Notices to Mariners, tide times, and other current navigational data, this is also a good source of chart information (see below).

Valdivia
40°S
Puerto Montt
G de Ancud
Chiloé
Península Valdés
Golfo Corcovado
Archipiélago de los Chonos
Aysén
Golfo San Jorge
Cabo Rapér
Golfo de Penas
CHILE
Cabo Banco
Cabo Tres Puntas
ARGENTINA
Puerto Edén
50°S
Bahía Grande
Puerto Natales
CHILE
Strait of Magellan
I Riesco
Punta Arenas
Isla Grande de Tierra del Fuego
ARGENTINA
Ushuaia
P Williams
I de los Estados
I Navarino
I Hoste
Borders are approximate
Cape Horn
75°W
65°W

Apart from the above website, most electronic chart packages include tidal information which has been found to be reliable. In addition, *UK Admiralty Tide Tables* NP207 Volume 4 gives some coverage, but for detail the Chilean information is more comprehensive.

Charts

Chilean charts are of high quality and while the UK, USA and Chilean navies share information, it is advised that Chilean charts should be your first choice. The Chilean authority is the SHOA who have their HQ in Valparaiso, but charts can be bought through their website (see above). If you want to buy charts 'over the counter', they are available in Puerto Montt, Punta Arenas, Aysén, and from the *Armada* office in Puerto Williams.

On the website there is also the option to make online purchases and buy downloadable electronic charts.

Of great use is a substantial book called *Atlas Hidrografico de Chile* which, remarkably, contains all the Chilean charts drawn and printed to a very high standard. It is intended as a catalogue but with the aid of a good magnifying glass the charts are useful and much information can be gleaned from them. This Atlas represents terrific value for money and if travelling the length of the Chilean channels you should have a copy on board. However, be aware that these charts are not intended for navigation and have not been corrected since they were first published. Important information may be missing.

Remember, the first priority of the chart makers is coverage of the main navigation channels; yacht anchorages and passages may be unsurveyed.

Warning: Although the *Armada* are updating many charts, discrepancies can occur between charted positions and those shown by GPS. This problem is more likely to occur in the south where errors of up to 2 miles have been found, although some of these may be due to errors in the original surveys.

The SHOA website (above) will give corrections to be applied to the various datums so that they agree with WGS84. These corrections, of course, do not rectify any inaccuracies in the original drawing of the charts.

Buoyage

Chile, like the rest of the American landmass, has adopted IALA B as its system of buoyage. This is best remembered as 'red, right, returning'. This is the opposite of the IALA A system with which European cruisers will be more familiar.

The direction of buoyage is as follows:

From S to N along the coast, except in the Straits of Magellan where it is N to S

From W to E in channels which lie in this orientation, expect the Canal Cockburn where it is E to W.

The buoyage always runs inwards towards ports. In channels outside the main routes, the buoyage will follow the direction of the flood tide.

Dealing with the authorities when you arrive

The most important thing is to arrive in the right frame of mind. At first you are going to find the processes tedious and often pointless, but they have to be endured and so you might as well relax and enjoy them. You can make it easier for yourself by attempting some Spanish (very few other languages will be spoken). Simple phrases can be useful and prepared in advance. Keep smiling, don't turn up looking like a tramp and always be honest with them. Remember, unlike in some other countries, the Chilean navy are on your side and have no intention of making life difficult. Chile is famously one of the most welcoming countries in the world and the authorities are merely seeking to carry out their procedures to the letter.

Visas

Always check the latest requirements before you leave your own country, but at the time of writing (2017) you do not need a visa if you are a citizen of the European Union, Canada, USA, New Zealand, Australia, South Africa, and many other countries listed here

https://en.wikipedia.org/wiki/Visa_policy_of_Chile

It must be remembered that in South America administrative advice (visas, customs etc) can change and updates on these topics might be found at

www.noonsite.com/Countries/Chile

A useful glossary of English–Spanish nautical terms can be downloaded from the US Coastguard.

http://icdept.cgaux.org/pdf_files/English-Spanish-Glossary-Nautical-Terms.pdf

Even so, before departing for Chile you should check for yourself through websites/embassies/travel agents etc to be sure of the latest position regarding visas. The Chileans are helpful people, but arriving anywhere in South America with the wrong paperwork can end in tears, fines, and loss of good cruising time.You will be given entry for 90 days, and the permit should be kept in a safe place. It can generally be renewed once for a further 90 days, and this must be done before it expires. You can 'reset' your entry from certain anchorages by leaving Chile and taking a bus across the border to Argentina. On returning, you have another 90 days. This can be done by sailing from Puerto Williams in the Beagle Channel across the 25 miles to Ushuaia in Argentina.

Quarantine

Chile has introduced new quarantine laws covering the import of food, animals and animal products A declaration must be made at every port, not just at the port of entry. Failure to do so can result in a $4,500 fine. Fresh fruit and vegetables may have to be destroyed. A declaration form can be found here:

www.sag.cl/sites/default/files/f-iit-ing-001_declaracion_jurada_conjunta_aduana_sag_02.pdf

Entry

There are three authorities you must deal with.

The *Armada* (navy), who have total control over all craft of whatever size in Chilean waters.

The *Aduana* (customs)

The *Policia International*

The customs and police may come to your boat or you may have to call at their offices. The *Armada* will advise.

Armada (navy)

Prepare for your first meeting by having all your paperwork ready, along with photocopies of passports, crew lists and ship's papers. You will be asked to supply details of your water, oil, fuel and life-saving gear, as well as serial numbers for radios and navigation equipment and licences, certificates and so on. You may also be asked to show evidence of insurance and your insurer will often supply a certificate in Spanish, which will make life easier. If you have all this information to hand, the process will be much smoother.

You should arrive at a port of entry which, within the scope of this book, will be either Valdivia, Puerto Montt, Punta Arenas or Puerto Williams.

It is the way of South America to introduce taxes at short notice and to vary the amounts. In 2015 Chile asked for a payment for light dues calculated on the size of the vessel. This was not large at about $3 for a yacht below 25 tons. It is useful to have local currency in hand to pay for this.

Aduana (Customs)

Generally found to be helpful. On arrival, you must apply for a *Declaracion de Admission Temporal* for which you will have to repeat much of the information you gave to the *Armada*. It is valid for a four month period and can be renewed, although this can be a slow process. You can make a special request for a two year permit. After that you must leave the country or be prepared to import your boat which will have VAT implications.

The Policia International

They may board your boat on arrival and ask to see your passports. This seems to be the limit of their interest.

CRUISING IN CHILE

The *Zarpe*

Leaving one Chilean port bound for another initiates another batch of paperwork, but it becomes familiar and less painful over time. To travel from one port to another requires a *zarpe* (permit). This document, usually issued by the *Armada* in your port of departure, lists your itinerary and will not be issued if the officer does not think you have fulfilled the safety requirements: if you were given clearance on arrival, this is less likely to occur.

Once your passage is completed and you have arrived at the stated destination, the arriving officer will ask to see your zarpe and passports. If he is satisfied, you will be given entry to the port. When you wish to leave, a further *zarpe* will have to be applied for. This is how the system works. You should allow at least an hour (on a good day) for the issuing of *zarpes*.

At first, the *zarpe* can seem a restrictive document since it outlines the route you must take to your destination - the kind of outside control which does not sit easily on the shoulders of cruising sailors. Certainly in the region of Cape Horn there is little room for interpretation, and the route given by the *Armada* is the route you must stick to. They claim this is in the interests of safety as well as security since they will know where you are heading at any particular time. There is some weight to this argument.

Away from the Cape Horn region things seem to be a bit more relaxed, and if you are careful about your wording then you can build a certain amount of flexibility into your *zarpe* application. For example, you can give your destination as one of the channels without specifying which particular anchorages you wish to use. Be generous with your ETAs as overdue yachts can attract often unnecessary attention, but no one is bothered if you arrive ahead of your ETA.

Yachts travelling south have successfully applied for a *zarpe* to travel 'between Isla de Chiloe and Puerto Williams', a good 1,000 miles, without specifying any stops. Sometimes the *Armada* will allow this, sometimes they will insist you renew your *zarpe* along the way.

Reporting in

This is yet another burden but must be observed.

All yachts in Chilean waters are required to be equipped with VHF and to monitor Ch 16. Your set must be tuned to US VHF channels, and not European ones.

You must report your position twice a day, at 0800 and 2000 local time. If you are close to an *Armada* station or a lighthouse, this is easily done. If not, and you are lucky enough to meet a passing ship, you can ask them to forward your details. You can also check in using HF radio on channel 4146.0 KHZ upper side band. However, the waiting lists at 0800 and 2000 can be very long and stretch over hours. You may not wish to stay glued to your radio for that length of time. For this reason, some yachts do not declare their HF/SSB radios on arrival in Chile. Keep a log of all attempts to make contact.

The information required is the name of vessel, number of persons on board, flag, present position, last harbour/anchorage, next port/anchorage and ETA.

If you do not have VHF, this same information can be sent by email to

mrccchile@directemar.cl

This may prove simplest as no conversation is involved. Do not expect a reply.

You will find that as soon as you come within sight of a lighthouse or shore station, you will be called on VHF by the officer in charge. There is little chance that they will not spot you.

You can also make contact via HF using 4146kHz USB, and a listening watch is also kept on 2182kHz. If you fail to make regular radio contact you will have to offer an explanation at your next port of call, so if you make any unanswered calls you should log them. Rescue services are generally well organised in Chile and these may be initiated if the *Armada* are unable to make contact with you after a period of time.

You should make an effort to conduct these exchanges in Spanish. They all follow the same pattern and it might be useful to have a written template of Spanish words and numbers.

Weather forecasts

Chile is divided into 10 zones. The Patagonian channels from Puerto Montt to Puerto Williams are in zones 6, 7 and 8.

The *Armada* transmit the local weather forecast twice daily at 0835LT and 2035LT on 4146 KHz. In the southern canals, Magallanes Radio gives the forecast for zones 6, 7 and 8 but also for 9 specific places. The forecast for these 9 places is very useful and more accurate than GRIB weather files because it is a locally generated forecast.

The nine specific places are:

Puerto Natales
(the town north of Magellan Straits)

Faro Evangelistas
(western extremity of Magellan Straits)

Paso del Mar
(western end of Magellan Straits)

Punta Arenas
(eastern Magellan Straits)

Punta Delgada
(eastern end of Magellan Straits – first narrows)

Canal Brecknock
(western most canal west of Beagle Channel)

Canal Ballerno
(west of Beagle Channel)

Puerto Navarino
(Beagle Channel)

Puerto Williams
(Beagle Channel)

You can pick up the forecast for the area you are in if you know the sequence order and after listening carefully a few times - it is a very poor quality pre-recording so it makes it a lot easier if you know the sequence. They always say the name before the forecast, e.g. 'Paso del Mar .....' Until you have got used to

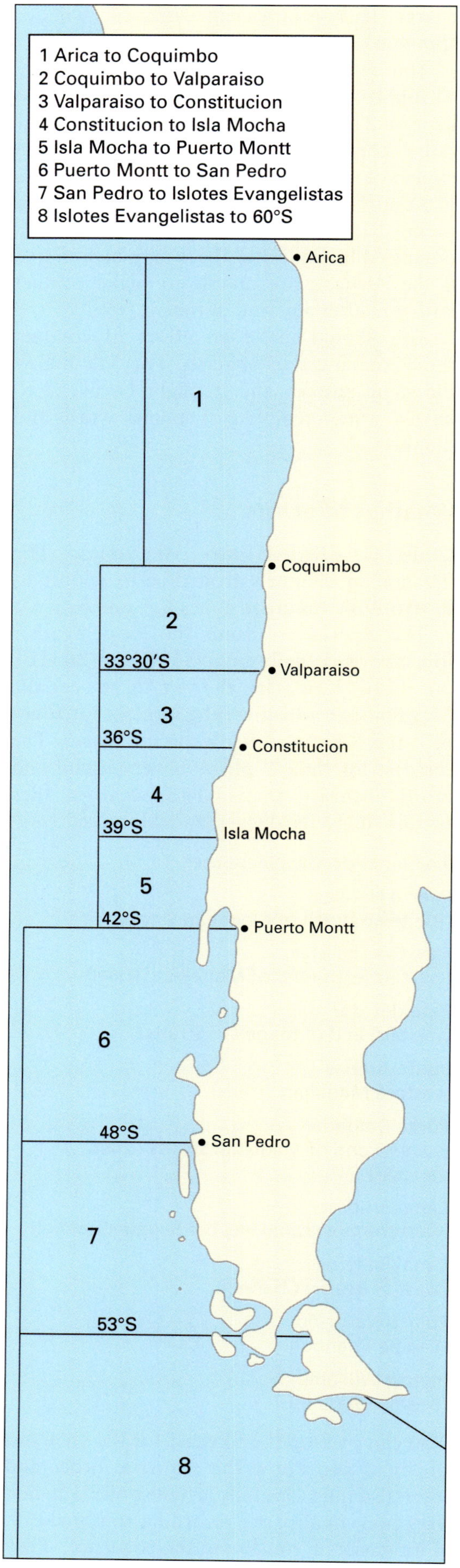

CHILE FORECAST AREAS

it, it might be worth recording the transmission for later playback. The sequence order is

1. Notices to mariners (buoys etc)
2. Weather warnings
3. Forecast for zones 6, 7 and 8
4. Forecast for the 9 places listed above every 12 hours (the evening forecast gives details for the following day, the morning forecast for the following night). They give cloud coverage, visibility, the wind speed and direction, strength of *rachas* (gusts) and sea state.

Provisions and fuel

Yachts heading south will stock up in Puerto Montt where pretty much everything can be found. From there onwards well stocked supermarkets become rare and are replaced by smaller shops where the stock levels can vary depending on deliveries. If starting from Puerto Williams heading north, the supplies are very much limited in variety, and fresh food depends on the weekly arrival of the ferry from Punta Arenas. It is worth knowing when the ferry is due to dock and heading for the shops as fast as you can before the fresh stuff goes. Given the generally cool nature of the climate, there is a good chance that fresh food taken on board will last some days even without refrigeration. Of course, there are several well-stocked supermarkets 20M to the west of Puerto Williams in Ushuaia but this involves an emigration process from Chile and an entry into Argentina, doing your shopping, then going through the reverse process before returning to Puerto Williams to commence your Chilean cruising.

Expect a good variety of stores to be found at Valdivia, Puerto Montt, Castro, Aysén, Puerto Edén, Puerto Natales, Punta Arenas and Ushuaia (Argentina). Leaving Aysén heading south, it might be 600M or more before the next provisions; the same applies if leaving northwards from Puerto Natales. Remember that some of these stopping places require a considerable detour from the most direct route north or south. You will have no problem buying good South American wines at decent prices. Underway, fishermen are often ready to trade or sell fresh fish - but beware shellfish (see below). As a general rule, the further south you go, the more fish is eaten, but the fewer fishing boats you will see. Cigarettes seem to be useful for bartering. Fishermen tend to lead poor lives and anything will be appreciated.

DO NOT HARVEST YOUR OWN SHELLFISH

Most of the Chilean waters south of 44° are infected with an algae which is highly poisonous and can cause paralysis and swift death. It is called Red Tide (*Marea Roja*) and infects mussels, clams, oysters, whelks and similar. This disease is not to be taken lightly. It is not a passing tummy upset - it can kill you and there is no antidote. All shellfish brought ashore by fishermen are tested and can be bought in safety, but a yacht would have no way of knowing if their catch was safe if buying directly.

Not all waters are infected with Red Tide and the *Armada* provide latest information on their regular VHF and SSB transmissions. You will be warned of Red Tide when your *zarpe* is issued. Crabs, lobster and finfish are generally reckoned not to be infected by Red Tide, and if you are offered one by local fisherman, a polite mention of *Marea Roja* should provoke a reassurance.

Diesel

Leaving Chiloé and heading south, it may be 1,000M before fuel next becomes available and it is not uncommon to spend far longer under engine in the channels than you would on a conventional passage. As such, most cruisers without large tanks have many cans strapped to their decks. Fuel can be obtained at Puerto Edén (with notice), Chacabuco (Aysén) or Puerto Natales, but may be up to 50% more expensive than in less remote spots.

The quality of the diesel is good and will run Primus stoves. Where diesel can be obtained, petrol and oil are also usually available. Methylated spirit (*alcohol blanco*) can be bought at a pharmacy. Burning alcohol (*Alcohol de quemia*) can be found in hardware stores but it gives off foul fumes when burning.

The *Armada* will give information on fuel availability if you are able to reach them on VHF.

Gas

Propane is widely used for domestic heating and cooking in Chile and supplies seem cheap. The problem of gas bottle fittings is an abiding issue. But in the more remote parts the gas stations are helpful and inventive, and if they can possibly get gas into your canisters they will. If you have a problem you can always buy a local canister and with an appropriate regulator, connect your supply to that.

Money

The currency is the peso and one peso is divided into 100 centavos. There is no point giving exchange rates here as it is something of a volatile currency, for which reason many people seem happy to trade in US dollars, although these will rarely be accepted in shops. In 2017, the average value of the peso was 650 pesos to the US dollar.

ATMs now appear in most places, and cash can certainly be obtained from one in Puerto Williams, and most likely in other stopping places going north or south. Travellers cheques are little known or understood. It is worth checking with your bank before you leave as to whether or not their card will work. The author's experience was that Mastercard worked everywhere in South America.

Telephone and internet

The code, if making phone calls to Chile, is +56.

If using conventional telephones then cards (*fichas*) can be bought at train and bus stations and cigarette kiosks. It is difficult to imagine a mobile phone of being much use in the more remote areas, and local SIMs will only be available and effective in major centres such as Puerto Montt, Punta Arenas, and Ushuaia. Internet cafés are now appearing everywhere, as is WiFi.

Metric

The metric system of weights and measures has been adopted.

Staying safe

Crime barely exists in southern Chile, particularly in the villages. You need not, therefore, worry about your personal safety.

PUERTO MONTT TO THE BEAGLE CHANNEL INCLUDING THE MAGELLAN STRAITS

Which way to sail the Chilean channels?

Most yachts will have little choice. If you are arriving from the Atlantic, you will have to start at Puerto Williams and head north, unless you enter by the Magellan Strait. If you have crossed the Pacific, your only real choice is Valdivia, or Puerto Montt, unless you want to round the Horn before approaching the Beagle channel from the east. The western entrance to the Magellan Strait is lit, but this is essentially a small gap in the rock-bound lee shore where gales are an everyday matter and will not be most people's first choice.

Generally speaking, heading south through the channels from Puerto Montt is easier. However, the prevailing weather must be carefully considered. Near Puerto Montt, southerlies predominate in the summer and northerlies in the winter. Further south, northerly winds become more dominant throughout the year with active fronts crossing the region and producing wind shifts from NW to SW, and vice-versa. However, the issue is further complicated by the deflection of the winds by the Andes, and the funnelling effect of the high-sided channels. Even if a W wind is forecast, it could just as easily become a northerly or a southerly, depending on your luck. Given this unpredictability, any anchorage giving shelter from N round to SW is the best one to seek.

From roughly 42°S southwards the incidence of bad weather increases, with stronger winds from W and N. The deflection created by the mountains here seems to turn winds to the N more than any other direction. The further south you go, the more frequently violent squalls, known as *rachas*, are encountered. These are caused by eddies created in and around the mountains and can appear from any direction. For short periods of time, possibly minutes, they can blow at 100 knots, shifting anchors and uprooting trees to which you might be made fast.

On balance, for an easier ride, plan to make the passage N to S, and sail on wet and windy days when the wind is in the N/NW; use the quieter SW periods, which are likely to be dryer and brighter, to anchor and explore ashore.

That said, many do make the trip S to N and enjoy it. Patience is the game, and if you are willing to enjoy an anchorage until things are in your favour, you will have a much more pleasant time.

If you are taking it slowly and getting the very best out of it, either passage could take 3 or 4 months. It is possible to do it in as little as a month, but it will be hard work and at times you will, no doubt, feel that you are banging your head against a brick wall.

Salmon farms - a warning

You are likely to come across salmon farms in the clean, sheltered waters of the fjords. They are often unmarked by lights, and uncharted. On the plus side, if they are large enough, they can acts as breakwaters and lessen the chop in an anchorage.

Harbours and anchorages

Note tide times below are given in relation to the standard port, Valparaiso

Valdivia

(Remember that in Spanish 'b' and 'v' can be similar in sound. So you may hear this place pronounced 'Baldibia')

39° 48'S 73°15'W

Charts BA 3075, 3081; US 22335; Chile 6000, 7000, 6251

Tides +0236hrs

A cultured city with a fine climate and a youthful feel, Valdivia is a major tourist centre, dubbed 'The Pearl of the South', and a university town. Cheap accommodation and budget eating places can be found and there is a strong café culture.

Frosts are very rare here and the January temperatures can top 30°C. In the summer expect average highs of 22°C, and in the winter, 10°C. 100 inches of rain falls every year, at its heaviest between March and October. Close by is the remarkable Bosque Valdiviabo, one of the world's three great temperate rain forests, which gives a strong clue to the climate you can expect. The population is 12,000 with a strong German influence - expect to find beer and sausages on many menus - and the German language can still be heard.

If you are heading south it is a good place from which to say goodbye to the delights of 21st-century living before facing the loneliness of the anchorages and fjords ahead of you. If you are arriving from months in the channels you may also welcome a little of the hedonistic lifestyle that Valdivia can provide. If you are there in mid February, you might catch the *noche Valdiviana* (Valdivian night) which marks an end of summer celebration in which people take to the water in huge numbers.

Valdivia suffered badly in the earthquake of 1960, reckoned to be the world's largest at a magnitude of 9·5. The epicentre was beneath the Pacific Ocean and the quake left two million people homeless and many dead, most of the fatalities occurring in the subsequent tsunamis experienced on both sides of the Pacific. Further north, a 38ft tidal wave lifted houses and deposited them two miles inland. Entire coastal harbours disappeared. Puerto Montt also suffered greatly. You may come across half submerged houses standing on what was once the shore.

Valdivia lies 10M up the tidal Valdivia River and is approached from Bahiá Corral. Two lights mark the entrance to the bay, which is just under a mile wide and has no obstructions, the deepest water is to the W:

Roca El Conde to the west 39°52′·1S 73°25′·2W

Morro Niebla to the east 39° 51·9S 73°24′·0W

Good anchorage can be found off Puerto Corral on the W side of the bay opposite the entrance to the river. Once inside the bay make roughly SW ensuring you have identified the Wreck of the *Haverbeck* marked by a green buoy with a horizontal red band. Pass to the W of it. The bay of Puerto Corral lies ahead.

For most shelter you need to be close in, but this may be crowded with fishing boats. Space may be found further south but in deeper water.

If sheltering from a W wind, Isla Mancera gives shelter. The northern tip of the island is marked by a red conical pillar (Fl(3)R.9s6m3M). Approach from the NW and anchor just beyond the small ferry pier in 3m with good holding in mud, mindful that the tide runs strongly. This is a popular anchorage with a good restaurant ashore.

The river up to Valdivia is well buoyed and marked (least depth 3m) and you should keep to the middle of the fairway. Beware of submerged moles along the way.

Call the *Capitán del Puerto* on VHF 88 before entering the river.

In strong northerly winds, breaking seas can be found off Isla Mancera and the river may be closed. In that case, you will have to use the anchorage off Puerto Corral (above) until the weather improves. The *capitán* will arrange to visit you to carry out the formalities. There used to be no customs (*aduana*) office here, and it was necessary to make a two hours bus ride to Osorno. This was said to be a delightful trip, well worth the effort, and a good way of seeing some of the Chilean countryside away from the water. However, customs can now be dealt with on arrival and a visit will be made to your boat. You will also be asked to pay light dues, which may involve making payment through a bank, usually open only until 1400.

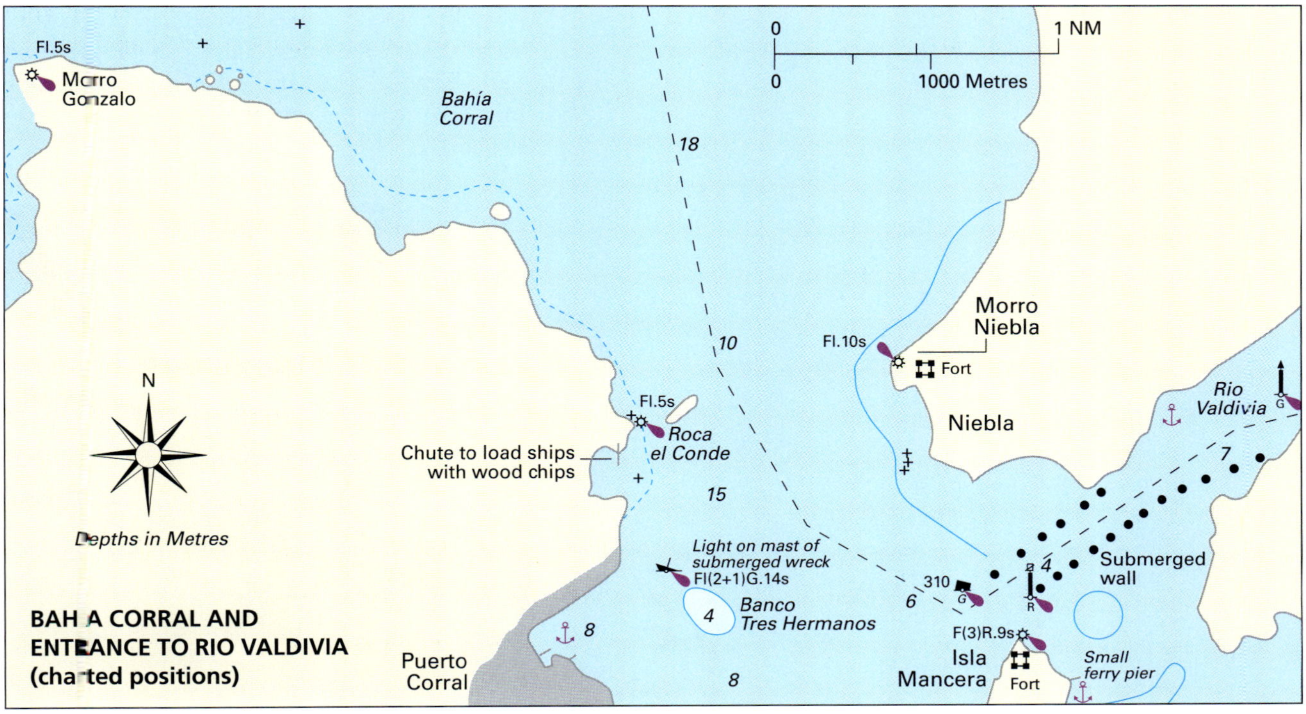

BAHIA CORRAL AND ENTRANCE TO RIO VALDIVIA (charted positions)

The docks at Alwoplast, Valdivia *Vicky Jackson*

There are three possible places to moor:

Alwoplast

39°50'S 73° 16'W
✆+56 63 2203200
rrpp@alwoplast.cl

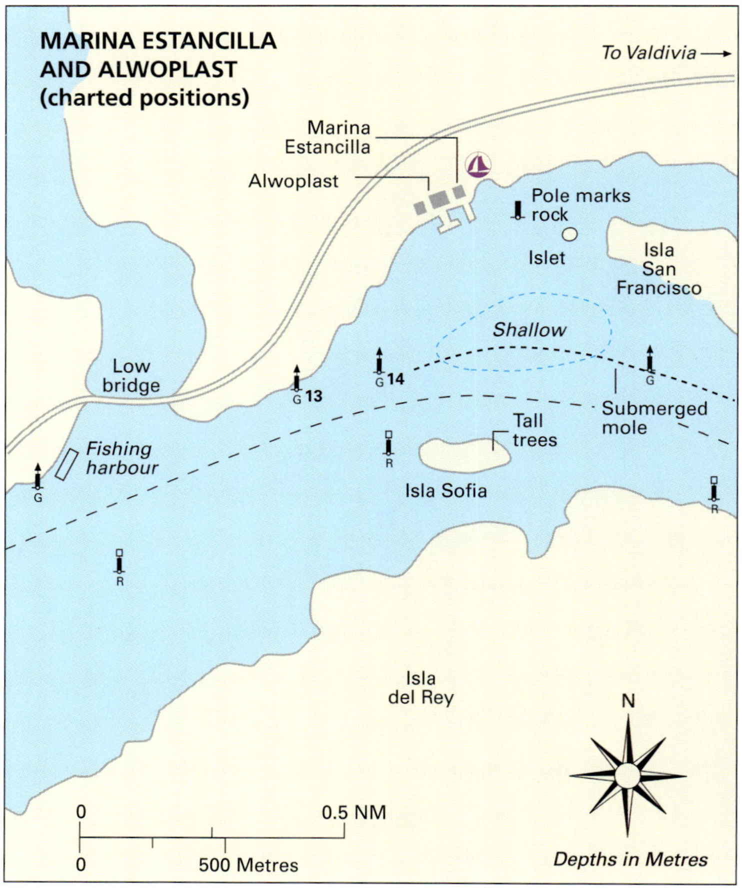

This is the base of a Chilean company (under German management) which builds high-end multihulls and other craft. It is not only a marina but a boatyard with all the services you could wish for.

Approach by passing midway between buoys 13 and 14 (this marks the end of a submerged mole). Alwoplast will now come into view and is the most westerly of the two boatyards ahead of you.

There is a 35-ton travel-lift which can handle boats up to 65ft. English and German is spoken and the marina has 220VAC as well as all usual facilities. Sails can be repaired here. Labour costs are lower than in Europe but use of the travel-lift can be very expensive.

Alwoplast boatyard, Valdivia *Máire Wilkes*

Marina Estancilla

39°50'S 73°19'W

Next to Alwoplast is Marina Estancilla. This is part of the Club de Yates Valdivia, which can be found further upstream. It is a safe, well-equipped marina just 20 minutes from town with a regular bus service. A good, secure place to leave a boat for a spell, especially over winter.

Club de Yates Valdivia

✆ +56 63 63 221-028
VHF 68
administrador@cyv.cl

The Club de Yates, founded in 1912, is 4–5M further upstream, near the town centre. This is a busy club which might be full in the high season. Space starts to free up at the end of the summer, from February onwards.

Everything a yacht needs to either prepare for an ocean leg, or recover from one, can be found in Valdivia and any of the above will direct you to chandlers, hardware stores, gas, diesel etc. There are several launderettes and well-stocked supermarkets.

If needing repairs, M & F Naval Service can cope with aluminium, fibreglass, electrical work and painting. English is spoken. ✆ +56 63 228 699.

You should take time to linger in Valdivia where you are on the fringes of the spectacular Lake District. The city has excellent bus connections to all parts of Chile and if you can endure the 7 hour bus ride, you can reach the Argentine ski resort of Bariloche; a trip that brings the joint benefits of offering a spot of sightseeing and enabling you to reset your 90 day entry by briefly leaving Chile.

The passage south

To enter the channels you will have to put to sea and undertake the 120M passage south to the Canal de Chacao which leads to, amongst other places, Puerto Montt. This can be no easy trip, especially against a prevailing SW wind and a north-going Humboldt current. If the wind is against you, leave Valdivia late in the afternoon as the winds generally slacken overnight and you will be able to motor-sail. There are bolt holes along the way, described in *RCCPF Chile*, 3rd edition, Andy O'Grady (Imray).

It might be better to wait for a northerly wind; the clue to its arrival will be a change to wet, chilly and overcast weather in Valdivia. If it's a bright, sunny day, you can bet the wind will be against you.

The Canal de Chacao separates Isla Chiloé from the mainland and the tidal streams are strong here, running at up to 10 knots in the centre, where there are tide rips. Correct timing is vital because entrance must be made with a fair tide - there is no slack water. However there are waiting places either end, as described in *RCCPF Chile* 3rd edition.

W going stream commences HW –1
E going at LW –1

On approach you should contact Corona Light (*Faro Corona*) on VHF 16 .This is a helpful station and if you are in any doubt about the sea state they can provide information and give weather and tidal forecasts.

Local conditions are broadcast on VHF 14 at 0500, 0650,1250, 1850 UT

The *Chile* pilot book offers several anchorages where you can wait in safety if conditions are against you.

Once through, you have entered what is considered to be one of the finest cruising grounds in the world. This is the northern gateway to the Chilean channels, and many cruisers will have their eyes on the splendours that are to come, but the area around Puerto Montt and the Golfo de Ancud to the south should not be overlooked as it offers splendid sailing in gentle winds, decent temperatures and flat water, likened by some to lake sailing.

Having said that, close to mountains, *rachas* can occur and good attention should be given to anchoring - good practice for later. Because of the purity of the water, salmon farms proliferate, and what might look like a good anchorage on a chart could be occupied by a salmon farm, often marked by a flashing yellow light. Mussel farms tend to be unmarked and found inshore of salmon farms. The salmon farm workers are said to be helpful when it comes to finding places for yachts to secure.

Puerto Montt

41°29'S 72°57'W
This is a standard tidal port

A major tourist centre and common first port of call for yachts arriving from the Pacific, it is also a terminus for the ferries working their way south to Aysén and Puerto Natales. Puerto Montt is an air and road transport hub serving this most visited part of Chile with its glacial lakes, snow-capped volcanoes, and mountainous hinterland. All facilities and provisions can be found. It is worth remembering that if you are heading south, this will be the last travel-lift before the River Plate on the east coast, some 2,500M away.

The waterfront, Puerto Montt
Máire Wilkes

The airport, Aeropuerto El Tepual, 16km west of town, has flights to Santiago and Punta Arenas making this an ideal place for crew changes.

The town is sheltered by Isla Tenglo to the SE, and entrance to the harbour should be made from the SW which is well marked and easily navigated by day or night starting with the Punta Anselmo light buoy Fl.G.5s.

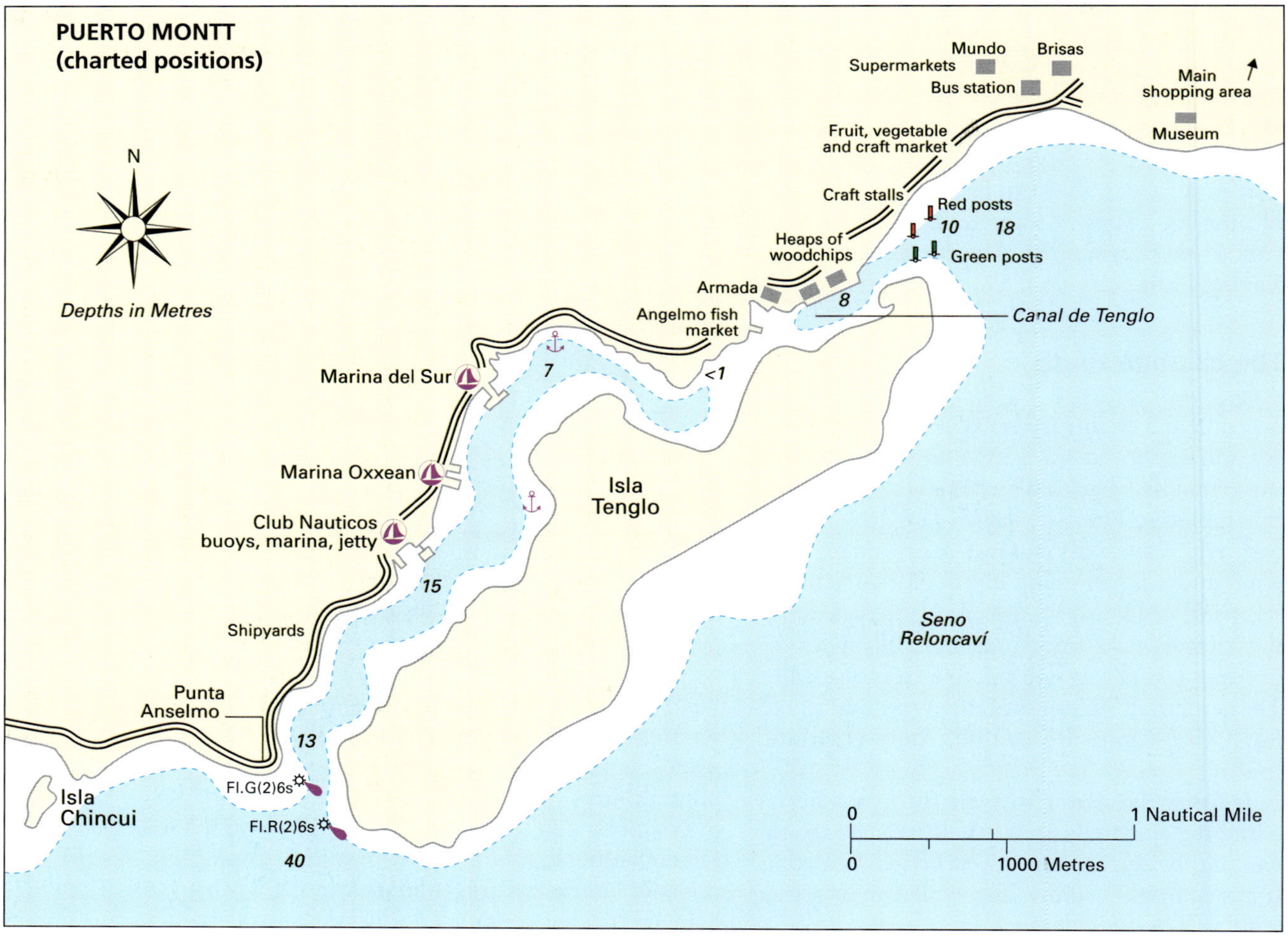

Charts

The *Armada* office in Puerto Montt has a stock of charts, possibly limited. If a chart needs to be ordered from Santiago the waiting time can be up to a month. A useful contact is Mani Suanto, an experienced sailor and engineer who lives aboard his vessel in Marina Oxxean. He runs a support service and helps in acquiring spares.

manisuanto@yahoo.com

There are three places to moor:

Marina Oxxean

41°29'S 72°59'·6W
✆ +56 65 255 544
VHF 16, 71
www.marinaoxxean.cl
marina@oxxean.cl

A very safe marina with water, electricity, fuel and a slipway. An underwater repair service is available. You can dry out against a concrete wall on sand in order to scrub.

Marina del Sur

41°29'·6S 72°59'·7W
✆ +56 65 251 958
VHF 16
www.marinadelsur.cl

Customs and immigration clearance can be done here. A good marina with all facilities and a boat service company on site for refrigeration/watermaker/electronic repairs. Boats up to 65ft and 40 tons can be handled.

Their website states that repairs to foreign-flagged vessels are free of VAT. It is also worth noting that the time a boat spends out of the water does not count as part of the two year import period.

Club Deportes Nauticos Reloncavi

41°29'S 72°59'W
✆ +56 2255022
VHF 16 (daytime only)
www.nauticoreloncavi.com
nauticos@surnet.cl

A smaller marina, 7km from Puerto Montt, with 70 berths for boats up to 18m. There are both pontoons and moorings and the marina is . There is hard standing and a 27 ton travel-lift. All boatyard facilities are available here. It is the most exposed of all the marinas with reports that it appeared unmaintained in places. You are less likely to find English spoken here.

It is possible to anchor opposite the yacht club to the NE of this marina although the canal is very busy. There is NO anchorage directly off the town.

Transport from the marinas into the city is plentiful and cheap and will take you through Angelmo where you will find the *Armada* office for clearance. There is also an excellent fish market here. Marina staff will give you the precise location of capitania, aduana and immigration.

Castro, Chiloé Island

42° 28'S 73° 46'W
Charts BA 3749, US 22352, Chile 7000, 7370, 7372

Although Castro is less than 100M from Puerto Montt, most cruisers will not want to miss the capital of Chiloé, a tidy and well preserved town famous for its traditional wooden stilt houses. The best of the island's renowned timber churches can be found here - it is a national monument.

Many cruisers in these waters will have a copy of *The Voyage of the Beagle* on board. Rest assured that modern Castro is nothing like the scene which confronted Darwin in 1834:

> *The place was so poor that, although inhabited by hundreds of people, one of our crew found it impossible to obtain a pound of sugar or a simple knife. None of the locals owned a watch or a clock and the bells were tolled by an old fellow supposed to have a decent notion of time.*

Shoreside has improved since with good supermarkets, hotels and restaurants. The next place for re-provisioning is 200M south

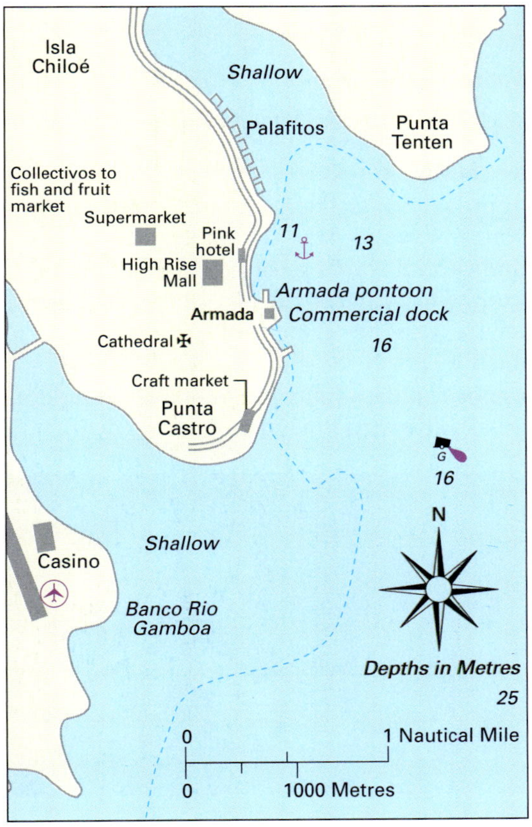

CASTRO (GPS positions)

The Castro waterfront
Vicky Jackson

so a little fresh food might usefully be taken on board here. Be warned that this is a very busy place in the high season of January and February.

Shelter would appear to be good as the harbour is almost landlocked, although it can be choppy in strong winds from N or S. The approach is straightforward, but shallow water is found over the Banco Rio Gamboa and careful watch must be kept for a large G buoy which marks the end of it. From here a course can be made towards the town to anchor north of the *Armada* station and opposite a pink hotel in 6–14m, good holding and sheltered in E winds.

A rural scene typical of these islands. Estero Pailad, Isla Chiloe
Vicky Jackson

Formalities

Call the *Armada* on VHF 16 and prepare to go ashore to check in. On request, they may allow you to land your dinghy at their pontoon (dinghies left on the shore have gone missing). Permission is not automatic. If you have to leave your dinghy on shore, remove the outboard. There are no customs at Castro. Water is alongside at the commercial harbour, but make arrangements first.

Facilities

Diesel must be carried from filling stations using small, open trucks called *fletes* which operate like taxis.

Propane is easily obtained if the connection issue can be overcome.

There are many small shops providing everything from hardware to food, the best supermarket is reported to be HiperBecker, north of the cathedral.

Credit cards are widely accepted, and all banks have ATMs.

Since 2012, LAN flights can be taken from the new airport a bus ride north of Castro.

South from Chiloé

The most direct route south would be to head 30M to Canal Moraleda (43°55′·7S, 73°23′·2W) but this route risks the often exposed nature of the Canal and ignores some marvellous cruising to be had in the Chonos Archipelago; an intricate maze of islands and fjords in sheltered waters, where many weeks could be spent safe in the knowledge that provisions and fuel are not too far away.

RCCPF Chile 3rd edition advises on various routes which can be taken heading north or south. Close attention must be given to complex tidal flows.

Note that if you need to renew your *zarpe*, you can do so at Melinka (43°54′S 73°45′W) on the SE corner of Isla Ascension. The anchorage is in front of the town between the *Armada* building and a newish ferry jetty, 14m good holding. It is protected from N, but exposed to chop from the S. Check in with the *Armada* by VHF and in person.

Water supplies may be limited, especially in summer, and the electricity supply ashore may be cut off early in the evening.

There is a butcher and freshly smoked fish from the tin house with the yellow second floor near the fishing boat quay.

Puerto Aguirre

45°09′S 73°31′W
VHF 16 callsign *CBP31*
Charts BA 1288, US 22371, Chile 8000, 8200, 8620, 8621

This is a useful and pretty little harbour on Isla Las Huichas, well sheltered from N and with some shelter from SE provided by Isla Eugenio. There is an *Armada* post here where a *zarpe* can be renewed and you must report by radio and in person. Anchor in front of the *Armada* if possible, in 12m, or seek permission to lie alongside the wall (5–6m). Ignore the fishing jetty built to the W of Punta Ancla.

If you are able to lie alongside, this is a useful place for picking up fuel.

Fresh food arrives here on the weekly ferry - you might be lucky.

Close by to the NNE are the sheltered and beautiful anchorages of Caleta Poza and Estero Copa. Secure to trees in both of these.

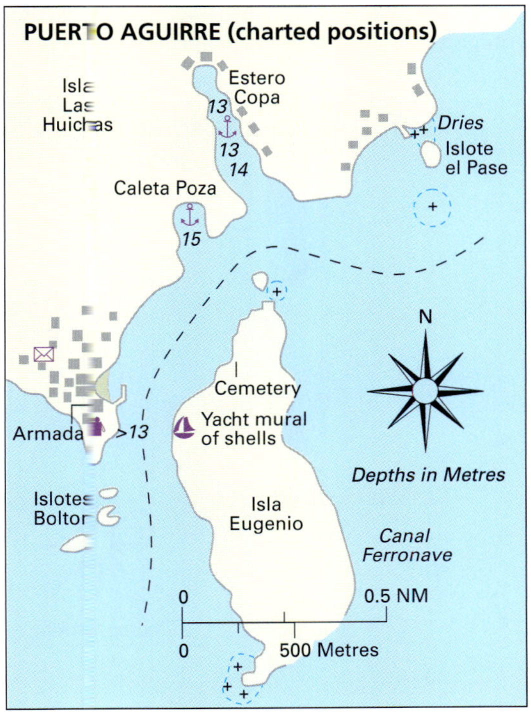

Puerto Chacabuco - Seno Aysén

45°28′S 72°49′W
Charts BA 1288; US 22371; Chile 8000, 8600, 8610, 8611

This is a working port and a diversion from the direct route north or south, but a useful one from a cruiser's point a view for there is a nearby airport for crew changes. There is also an opportunity to travel inland and cross the border into Argentina before returning with another 90 days on your permit. A ferry service runs from here to Puerto Montt, which has more reliable air connections.

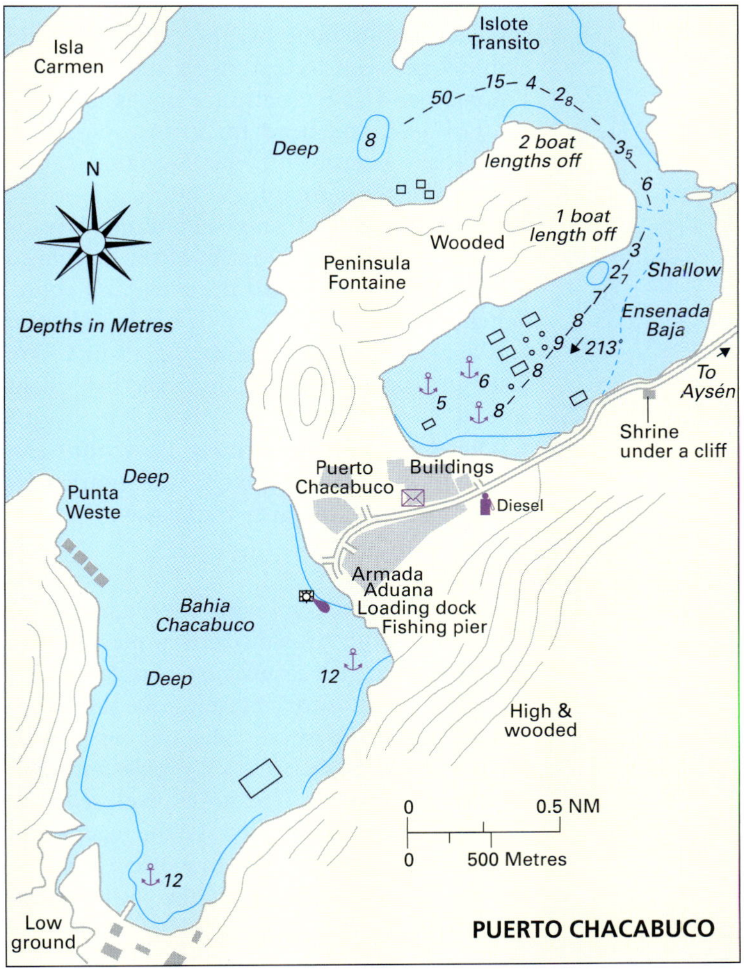

Fiordo Aysén, which leads to Chacabuco, has its own microclimate and is noted for whirlwinds (*remolinos*) and *rachas*. The main bay opposite the town is exposed and the winds here can be strong and gusty, but if you need water you will have to go alongside the busy fishing pier for a short while before making for a safer anchorage in Ensenada Baja (below).

There is a notable average rainfall of 3 m here, making it the sort of harbour where you might find yourself waiting several days for the weather to clear. By way of comfort, the town of Aysén is close by with shops and banks. You are now in the glacier and fly fishing country of northern Patagonia, surrounded by National Park and described as 'the supreme wilderness'. There has been controversy surrounding the government's plan to flood parts of this region to produce hydro-electricity, destroying much beauty in the process.

Ensenada Baja

This wide bay which lies to the east of Chacabuco is the best bet for yachts. The holding is extremely good, which is necessary as this can be a windy place. The entrance is not difficult but must be approached with caution as it can be shallow and un-surveyed. It is best taken at half tide rising, and at HW there is a minimum of 3m. Approach mid channel between Isla Transito and Península Fontaine and as the entrance opens up come to starboard and head for a position about two boats lengths off the Fontaine shore. Follow the coast round, closing to about one boat's length at the E end of Fontaine. Depths will start to drop to 2–3m but keep well in to avoid a drying patch off the mainland shore. When a course of 213° can be made, follow it and anchor beyond the salmon pens in 4–7m. The scenery is stunning but the fish plant smelly.

Diesel is available in cans. Provisions can be found in Aysén at a large supermarket by the bridge at the entrance to the town.

Formalities

You should check in with the *capitania* at Chacabuco both by radio and in person. You will be issued with a new *zarpe* on departure. To renew your visitor's permit, take the bus to Aysén, and from there take one of several buses to Coyhaique, which is a pleasant town with good shopping. You are now close to the airport. From Coyhaique take the bus or taxi to Balmaceda Airport, which is a few hundred metres from the border. If the immigration officer is not feeling helpful, you may have to travel further inland to Chile Chico or Los Antiguos before returning. You should be able to make the trip there and back in a day, renewing your permit as you go.

Crossing the Golfo de Penas

Whichever way you have come, then Caleta Suarez in Bahía San Andres is a good place to take a breath after crossing the Gulf heading north, or somewhere to wait for the ideal weather for your passage south.

Caleta Suárez

46°36.8'S 75°27.69'W (this s position of the anchorage if using WGS84 as a datum. It may show differently on the chart)
Charts 8000, 8112, 8800

This is the answer to many a passage-maker's prayers: a safe harbour with wonderful scenery and protection from all weather. This is a convenient spot for breaking a long journey north or south.

Even in bad weather the bay can be approached, although reliable radar would be needed in fog. It is well used by fishermen and in bad weather they can be hiding here in large numbers. In good weather, the most notable landmark will be the impressive cone of an old volcano, Monte Cono, which rises 488m and was climbed by Darwin. It marks a division between the northern and southern ends of the bay, and you should be passing south of it heading for Caleta Suárez.

Islote Cono gives some shelter but do not be tempted by Caleta Monomo to the south of it as fishermen advise against its use. (Note: there is a warm water spring here to which you can row in settled weather.)

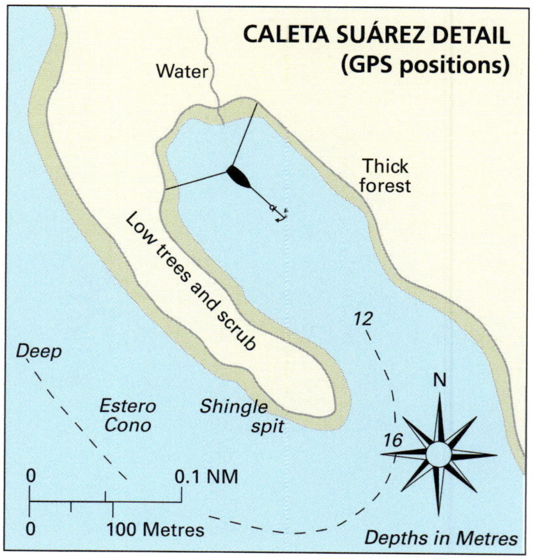

The Estero Cono is deep and the anchorage is 2½M from the entrance in a small bay behind a narrow wooded spit. There is deep water right to the edge of the spit. Anchor in 12m, mud, and take lines ashore or to lines already rigged by fishermen. There is perfect shelter from N but extra lines may be needed in S winds. There are worse places to have to kill time if stormbound. The eastern shore can be walked, and there is a large rock pool for swimming on a warm day. Bird life is abundant, and so is the flora at the edge of forest, described as being as rich as an English garden. The only downside to this place is that it might be a stiff beat out.

Golfo de Penas

Charts BA 1287; Chile 8800, 9000, 9300, 9311
(Charts 9300 and 9311 are new charts drawn to WGS84 datum)
VHF 16. Weather forecasts for the Golfo will be given.
Lights
Cabo Ráper 46°49.3'S 75°37'.3W
Fl.5s61m18M white concrete tower and building 14m 337°-vis-175°
Isla San Pedro 47°41.9'S 74° 51.9'W
Fl.W.10s38m16M white GRP tower with red band

The passage is a direct line between these two lights and should be timed so that landfall at San Pedro is in daylight. There is considerable foul ground to the NW of this island and close attention needs to be given to navigation here. The entire crossing deserves respect for, although just 67M, the bay is shallow and nasty seas can kick up.

If heading S, clearly the best time to leave Bahía San Andres is after the passage of a warm front when the wind veers to NW or N, although the visibility might be poor. If the weather is light and the wind from SW, then an easy crossing can also be had.

If forced to break the passage across the bay, then good anchorage can be found in Puerto San Salvador (47°11'·6S 74° 14·9'W – by GPS, not charted position). See *RCCPF Chile* 3rd edition for details.

On arrival off San Pedro (mindful of the shoals already mentioned) a confused sea can be found depending on the state of the tide at the mouth of the Messier Canal.

There are a number of anchorages around the entrance to the Messier Canal and you should consult *RCCPF Chile* 3rd edition for details.

Caleta Tortel

47°50·5'S 73°35'W
Charts BA 1287, Chile 9000, 9100
(Note that the ranges shown on some charts are no longer in use. Large differences have been reported between GPS and charted positions)
Light Pta. Mancilla Fl.G.5s36m5M G GRP tower

It is a diversion of over 60M to the east of the shortest N/S route, and Canal Baker is not often visited by yachts. However, Tortel can provide facilities and transport connections which may be of use. There is also an *Armada* station. The area has some magnificent scenery with good anchorages and is recommended for exploration, particularly by dinghy up the Río Baker, although you will need a powerful outboard as the river is said to discharge more water into the sea than any other Chilean river. There are commercial river trips here.

The village is found on the W side of Caleta Tortel and there has been much recent development. You will find a Post Office, telephones, a small airstrip and a few shops. Gas, and diesel are available from the EMZA store.

Of the two anchorages shown, the northern is best for anchoring with lines ashore and is close to the village. The more

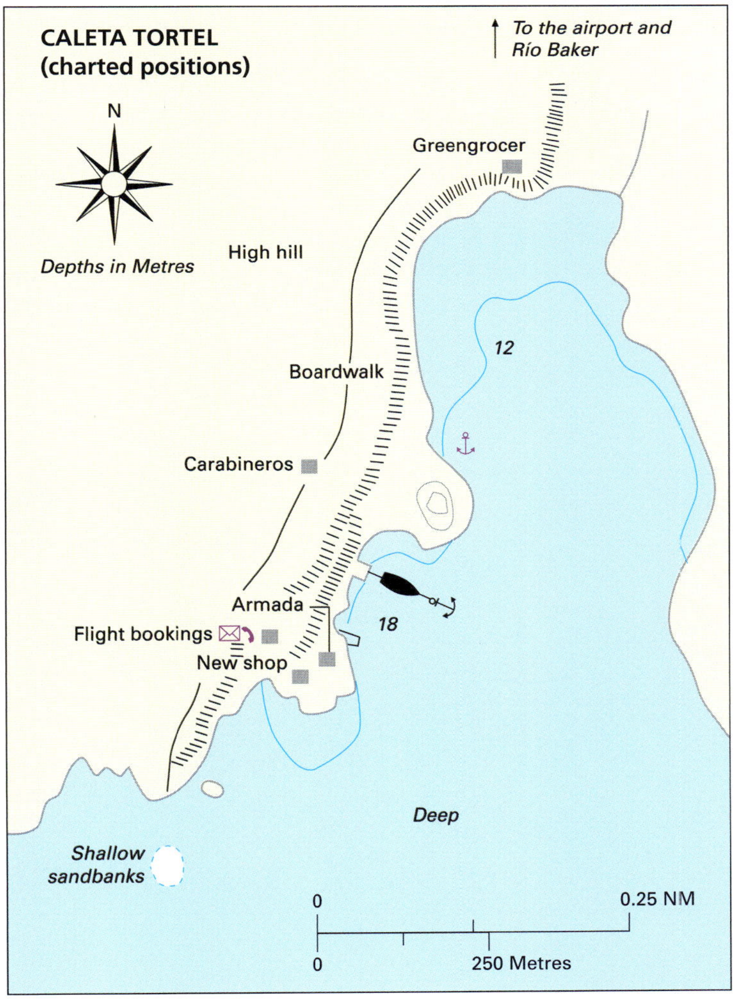

southerly, in the central bay by the N pier, is used by the police launch. If choosing this spot, anchor in deep water - the holding can be poor - and take lines to the pier. The S pier is for timber loading and not for yachts.

It is hardly a convenient place for a crew change, but it might be possible. Buses run to Cochrane (3 hours), from here it is a 6 hour journey by daily bus to Coihaique, from where there are services to Osorno (22 hours) and Puerto Montt via Argentina.

If you are lucky enough to coincide with a flight, then there is an irregular service to Coihaique and flights from there to Santiago via Puerto Montt. Your first port of call should be the Post Office, who will advise.

Angostura Inglesa (The English Narrows)

48°59'S 74° 27'W
Charts 9000, 9400, 9510

This area lies 15M N of Puerto Eden and requires close navigational attention with tides that can flow at 8 knots, shoals and narrow passages to be negotiated. This passage is used by commercial shipping and special rules apply to them, set out in *Chile* 3rd edition. There is room for yachts and ships to pass, but you should be aware of the constraints large ships are working under.

Yachts should pass through at slack water, if possible, mindful that prolonged wind, especially from N, can cause HW times to vary by more than an hour. In settled weather, the N-going stream will commence at HW+45mins, and the S-going LW+45mins. The narrows are well marked with port and starboard markers. If you are in range, then call *Capitanía de Puerto* in Puerto Edén and seek advice on tides and shipping movements.

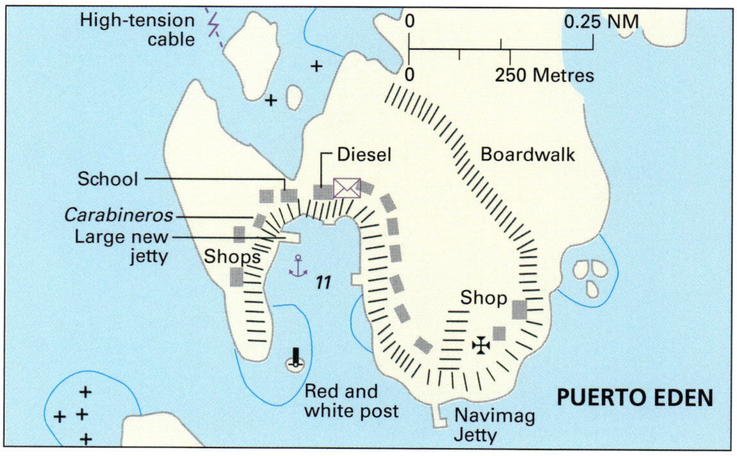

Puerto Edén

49°08'S 74°25'W
Charts BA 1286; Chile 9000, 9400, 9510, 9511

Be aware that the positioning of Puerto Edén can vary according to which chart you consult.

You will get a warm welcome here, and excellent shelter both off the village and in the many small bays around. If you are lucky, your visit will coincide with the twice weekly visit of the ferry which runs from Puerto Montt to Puerto Natales, bringing fresh food. There are small shops, fresh bread baked on request, and *centollas*, the famous Southern King crab with its sweet meat.

Diesel can be had in drums, but as in all such places be careful of the price which can be 75% higher than you might have paid in Puerto Montt. The quality of the fuel, though, is said to be good.

There is an *Armada* station here off which you can anchor. Holding is excellent in mud, rock and kelp. Or make use of their buoy, with permission. The *Armada* building is blue with a white roof.

There is a fine new jetty (GPS 49°07'·62S 74°24'·84W) which yachts may be invited to use, but they should leave the steps free for coming and going of local craft. You must make radio contact with the *Armada*, even if you are passing and not intending to stop. If stopping, your *zarpe* will be checked and re-issued if necessary. On occasions, the *Armada* officer has come to boats to complete the formalities and this is reported to be a friendly station.

Puerto Natales

51°44'S 72°31'W
Charts Chile 10600, 10610, 10611

A visit here represents a considerable diversion from the N/S route which, due to tidal constraints along the way, can add an extra couple of days to your passage. Puerto Natales also lacks a secure and sheltered anchorage.

However, to reach here you will undertake some spectacular sailing into the heart of the Andes and the Torres del Paine National Park, famed for its granite peaks, lakes and glaciers. If you leave Canal Collingwood and take the route through Seno Union, along Canal Morla Vicuna, taking either Canal White or Canal Kirke (where you must transit the narrows at slack water), you will pass through some of the finest waterways in Chile.

Puerto Edén *Vicky Jackson*

The *capitania* (VHF 16) is an easily spotted, blue-roofed building between the main shipping pier and Muelle Arturo Prat, the most northerly of the piers. Your *zarpe* will be checked and a new one issued if required.

There are also immigration authorities here and it is possible to obtain a 3-month extension to your visa. However, it is only a one hour bus ride to the (unattractive) town of Río Turbio which is across the Argentine border. You can take the bus here in the morning and return by evening with your passport 'refreshed' for another 90 days.

In strong winds, the anchorages are poor, if not dangerous. The entire waterfront is exposed to the N and W and winds can build rapidly. There is an anchorage to the N of the mooring buoys at the N end of town, but it is not recommended. It may be possible to negotiate use of one of the buoys but these too will be very exposed.

Of the piers, only the most southerly, Terminal Pesquero, might be of use to yachts and the L shaped head to the pier can offer some shelter from the strongest winds. Because of the shelving nature of the shore, it is only the outermost parts of the pier that can be used. Some yachts have tied alongside

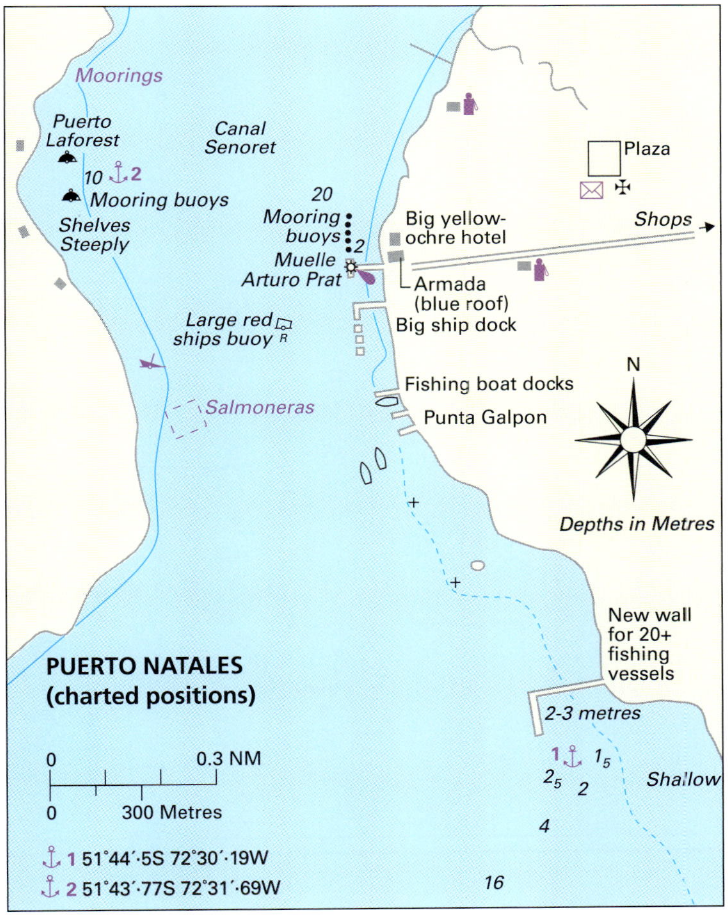

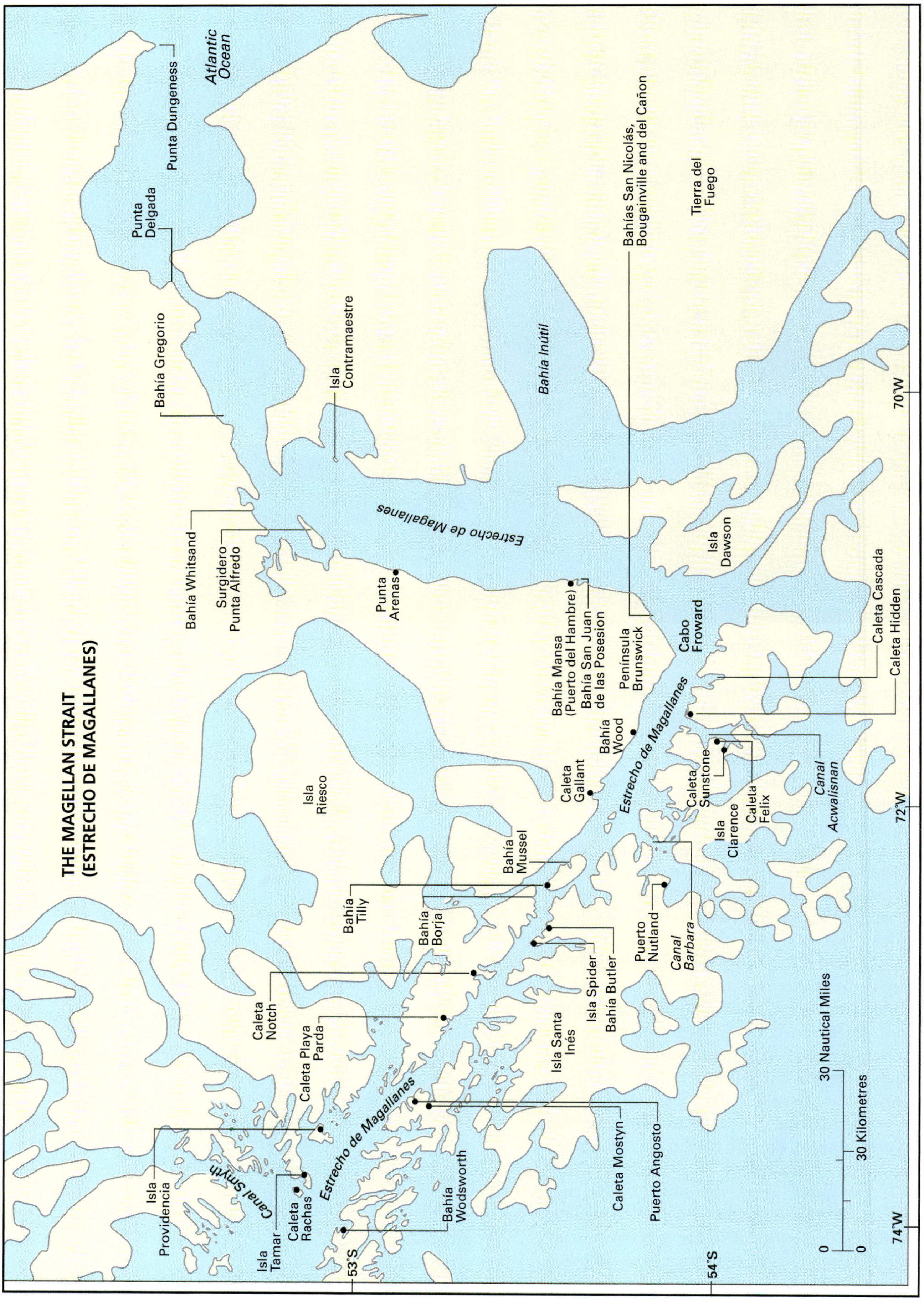
THE MAGELLAN STRAIT
(ESTRECHO DE MAGALLANES)
Atlantic Ocean
Punta Dungeness
Punta Delgada
Bahía Gregorio
Isla Contramaestre
Bahía Inútil
Bahías San Nicolás, Bougainville and del Cañon
Tierra del Fuego
Bahía Whitsand
Surgidero Punta Alfredo
Estrecho de Magallanes
Punta Arenas
Isla Dawson
Isla Riesco
Bahía Mansa (Puerto del Hambre)
Bahía San Juan de las Posesion
Península Brunswick
Cabo Froward
Caleta Cascada
Caleta Hidden
Bahía Wood
Caleta Gallant
Caleta Sunstone
Caleta Felix
Canal Acwalisnan
Isla Clarence
Bahía Mussel
Bahía Tilly
Bahía Borja
Puerto Nutland
Canal Barbara
Isla Spider
Bahía Butler
Caleta Notch
Caleta Playa Parda
Isla Santa Inés
Isla Providencia
Canal Smyth
Isla Tamar
Caleta Rachas
Bahía Wodsworth
Caleta Mostyn
Puerto Angosto
30 Nautical Miles
30 Kilometres
0
0
53°S
54°S
74°W
72°W
70°W

The anchorage off Puerto Edén *Máire Wilkes*

fishing vessels, but in the summer this is a busy harbour and you should expect much movement at all hours. It might be possible to anchor within the shelter of the pier but be aware of floating and submerged lines.

There are toilets here, clean showers, and the office can arrange deliveries of fuel. Water is available. Yachts should not be left unattended due to the unwelcome attention of local children who will not hesitate to play around them.

Opposite the town is a small bay, Puerto Laforest, which can be used as an anchorage but part of it is occupied by a salmon farm. Although less than a mile from the town on the opposite side of the canal, this stretch of water is very exposed and dangerous for a dinghy under windy conditions.

There are all the facilities you could ask for including internet, hospital, dentist and museums. Small workshops may be able to offer assistance with welding and metalwork. There are supermarkets, excellent fruit and vegetable shops, hardware and a launderette.

However, it is Puerto Natales's transport connections which might prove most useful to a yacht on passage. There are buses here connecting to Punta Arenas (3·5hrs), and to Argentina for passport renewal. There is also a small airport with flights to Punta Arenas, Puerto Montt and Concepción. There is car hire but check the spare tyre as some roads are not tarmaced.

A crew change would be easy to organise from here.

THE MAGELLAN STRAIT (ESTRECHO DE MAGALLANES)

This is the long-sought-after passage between the Atlantic and Pacific Oceans avoiding Cape Horn, and was much used before the building of the Panama Canal in 1914.

It is the jagged slash of a waterway, 300M long, that marks the southern end of the South American landmass and creates, to its south, the many islands collectively known as Tierra del Fuego. Apart from the very easternmost tip, it lies entirely in Chile.

The Straits are exceptionally challenging for yachts. If you imagine it divided in two, the boundary being Cape Froward, then to the west the weather can be unremittingly bad, both wet and with violent winds. The eastern section is drier and the land flatter, but the winds still blow and strong tides in the narrows create further navigational obstacles. There is the major centre at Punta Arenas in the eastern arm but the shelter here is poor and yachts can have a difficult time. However, there are safe anchorages to be had along the way (and no less than 40 lights and lighthouses the length of the Straits) and despite what will be a challenging trip, whether exploring or passage-making, you will be sailing in deeply historic waters.

The first passage by a European was achieved by Ferdinand Magellan between October and November 1520. From here his ship, the *Trinidad*, went on to accomplish the first circumnavigation of the world, although

Magellan himself was killed along the way in the Philippines in April 1521. It was originally called the Strait of All Saints as Magellan first entered on 1 November, All Saints Day. It was also Magellan who gave the name Mar Pacifico to what we call the Pacific Ocean when impressed by the placid waters that awaited him once he was free of the Strait.

More recently, Joshua Slocum, writing of his experience at the western end of the Straits in the 1890s, said

> *The* Spray *neared Cape Pillar rapidly, and, nothing loath, plunged into the Pacific Ocean at once, taking her first bath of it in the gathering storm. There was no turning back even if I had wished to do so.....The sea was confused and treacherous. In such a time as this the old fisherman prayed, 'Remember, Lord, my ship is small and thy sea is so wide!"... .the wind shifted to southwest, then back suddenly to north west, and blew with terrific force. The* Spray, *stripped of her sails, then bore off under bare poles. No ship in the world could have stood up against so violent a gale.*

Navigation in the Magellan Strait

From Punta Arenas to Cape Pillar, tidal ranges do not exceed 2m.

In December, daylight can last from 0230 until 2030. In July only from 0800 to 1600. The eastern section is well lit and night navigation would present no difficulties.

The Straits lie on the latitude of the breeding ground for the depressions that sweep through on a regular basis. It is rare for a depression to pass to the N of the Straits. The Andes represent a considerable barrier to the weather systems fresh off the Pacific and the resulting collision causes the often torrential rainfall experienced towards to west, and the relative dryness of the eastern side.

Irrespective of what the GRIBs might be saying, in the E part of the Strait the wind will blow from WSW or W, often exceeding 50 knots in the period from mid September to the end of March and strongest in October and November. This is a peculiarity of the wind hereabouts, particularly off Punta Arenas, and is known as a *panteonaro*. Wind comes from WNW at up to 50 knots in the early hours of the morning and reaches a crescendo by mid afternoon. It then drops and can be light by the time night comes. A *panteonaro* occurs mostly in the summer months.

There is a constant SE flow in the W arm, which is also the direction of the flood tide, and together they can reach 1.5 knots. The NW flowing ebb is much slower but if running against the wind can create rips and overfalls almost anywhere. The currents are much influenced by the strength and direction of the wind, particularly in the middle sections of the Strait.

Correctly judging the tides in the E part, especially when navigating the Narrows, is of the utmost importance.

The Magellan Strait: western section

Light Islote fairway 52° 43'.8S 73° 46'.3W
Fl.5s39m19M white tower with orange bands

Yachts which are taking the Canal Smyth, in whichever direction, should know that the keepers of this light welcome yachts. It is possible to lie alongside large rubber tyres on the N shore of the island and entry is made via a narrow passage between the rock and small island to its north. There is shelter here from the worst of the weather to be found in Straits but, clearly, this is a settled weather approach.

On leaving Canal Smyth bound for the Straits, yachts will have to pass W of Isla Tamar (52°53'S 73°52'W) and although this is a passage of less than 20M, it can involve some of the roughest waters in Patagonia. You should watch the weather carefully over a period of days, and only when you think you can get to the next anchorage avoiding a blow (the first usable anchorage is 10M beyond Isla Tamar) should you set out. Sailing north towards Canal Smyth can call for great patience as wind, swell and tidal streams will be against you. You have no option but to wait in Puerto Angosto (see below) for favourable conditions.

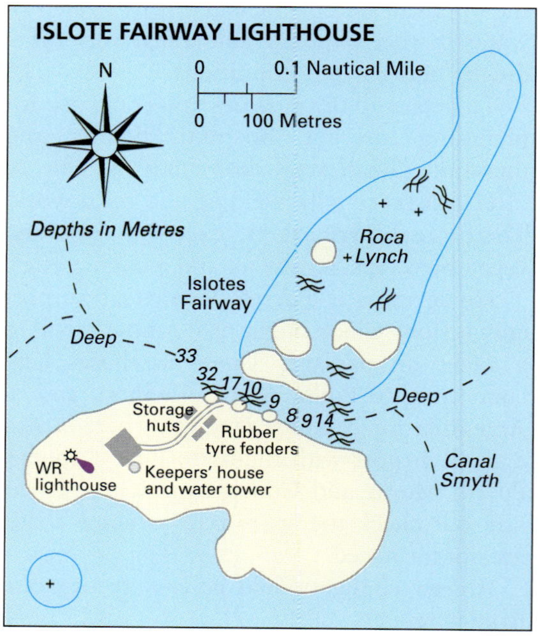

Two anchorages, Puerto Angosto and Celata Mostyn, both on the SE side of Isla Desolación, can prove useful either for entry or departure from the Straits, although see Caleta Sylvia on Isle Providencia in *Chile* 3rd edition for details of an emergency anchorage due south of Canal Smyth.

Isla Desolación, Puerto Angosto

53°13'S 73°20'W
Charts BA 1281; Chile11000, 11200, 11212

This is where you connect with Joshua Slocum again for it was here that he received his famous greeting from the locals:

> *I think it was on the second day, while I was busily employed about the decks, that I heard the swish of something through the air close by my ear, and heard a 'zip'-like sound in the water, but saw nothing, Presently, however, I suspected it was an arrow of some sort, for just then one passing not far from me struck the mainmast, where it stuck fast, vibrating from the shock - a Fuegian autograph.*

Once you are in the entrance you will straight away feel the shelter from W winds. The entrance is wide, and a mid line is best steered to avoid rocks off the N shore.

The bottom of this bay is rocky and subject to *rachas*.

There are three places to moor:

- Fishermen tie to steel drums against the wall, as seen on the plan below
- There is a small bay S of Punta Hoy (53°13'·2S 73°21'·8W) where it is possible to lie to anchor(s) ahead, with lines ashore from each quarter. This is secure, if subject to gusts
- Anchor at the head of the bay near the waterfall descending from a hanging valley lake. Use lines ashore. This is a fair weather anchorage for yachts drawing less than 2m.

Slocum used one of the last two anchorages and described it as

> *an exceedingly snug nook...no wind ever reached there.*

Isla Desolación, Caleta Mostyn

53°16'S 73°22'W

A small bay with a narrow entrance marked by two islets on the port side when entering. Caleta Mostyn is located in the north arm at the head of Estero Cormorant and provides much better shelter than Puerto Angosto (above). Follow the N shore of Estero Cormorant to find it. Inside, there is good shelter but the anchorage may be exposed to strong S winds.

Anchor in the NW corner in 10m, mud on rock but good holding and take a line ashore.

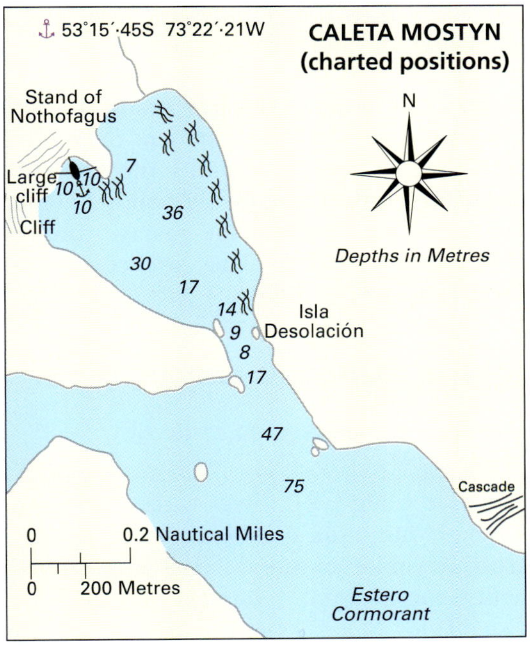

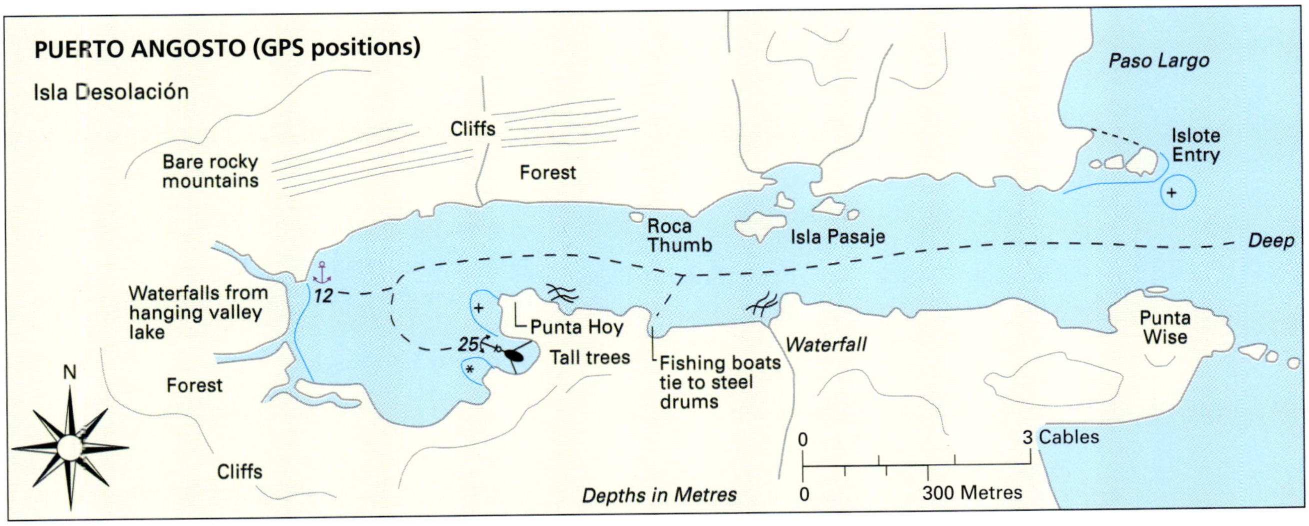

Typical Magellan weather - a full gale
Vicky Jackson

There are reports that this is a particularly good anchorage in NW gales.

Many anchorages of great grandeur, and varying degrees of shelter, present themselves between Isla Desolación and Cabo Froward, the southern tip of mainland South America and a halfway mark in the passage through the Magellan Straits. They are covered in detail in *Chile* 3rd edition.

The Magellan Strait: eastern section

Light Cabo Froward 53°53′·7S 71°18′·7W
Fl(3)9s21m6M

This is a white GRP tower with a red band, 4m high. But more striking is the huge, white cross 5 cables to the NNE (with flashing lights) consisting of a wire frame, called the *Cruz de los Mares* – the Cross of the Seas. It stands atop the cliff 360m above sea level and marks the end of the American continent. The collection of islands to its south are known as Tierra del Fuego - the Land of Fire. The cross was first erected here in 1913, but like so much hereabouts it succumbed to the weather, and the latest cross was placed here in 1987 to mark the visit of Pope John Paul II who blessed it. In clear weather, the lights of the cross are said to be visible for 20 miles.

The Cape itself has been described as looking not unlike Cape Horn. In his book, *Mischief in Patagonia*, the sailor and mountaineer, Bill Tilman, wrote

> *Whether it is done under sail or power, the rounding of a great cape, more especially a cape that divides two oceans, has about it something both solemn and elating. Although it is a normal and long-forseen step, the moment the cape looms in sight the pent-up hopes and fears of a long voyage focus themselves upon its successful rounding.*

The Admiralty Pilot is less romantic:

> *In the vicinity of Cabo Froward exceptionally heavy squalls may be experienced; the weather frequently changes to heavy rain or snow obscuring the shores. This change in the weather is often very striking, but it seldom happens that there are not occasional clearances in the weather conditions which enable a position to be ascertained visually.*

It is roughly 50 miles from Cabo Froward to Punta Arenas where most yachts will make a call if heading either north or south. Along this stretch, there is no easy shelter from E winds, but several anchorages can be found in which to break what might be a tiring, wet and cold passage.

Anchorages

Bahía San Nicolás is a useful bay between Cabo Froward and Cabo San Isidro, which lies to the NE (Fl.W.5s9M). The bay is found in 53°50′S 71°05′W and has a forest, a beach, and two anchorages, depending on the wind. Note Islote Sanchez in the middle of the bay when entering. The SW corner of the bay gives shelter from WSW winds and the northern shore, close in, gives shelter from NE winds.

Just north of Bahía San Nicolás, and north of Isla Nassau, is a narrow inlet much used by fishermen - Bahía Bougainville. Anchor near the head in 10m, tucked well in, and tied to trees. There is good shelter here.

Bahia del Canón, a further 2½M, can be located by reference to Cabo San Isidro light (Fl.W.5s9M) which lies just over a mile to the NE of it. The beach shelves so shore lines cannot be used and it is very deep unless anchored well in.

Further north, and immediately south of Cabo San Isidro, is Bahía del Águila with very good holding but subject to gusts, requiring you to be firmly attached to the shore with lines.

Bahía Mansa

53°36′·6S 70° 55′·5W
Charts BA 1281, Chile 11300, 11400
(avoid chart 11432 which is reported to be 'dangerously inaccurate')

This is a useful place for yachts under 14m as there is easy access by road and public transport to Punta Arenas (30M) where yachts can only lie with difficulty and with exposure to the worst of the weather.

The bay lies to the NW of Punta Santa Ana (Fl.10s.10M) and south of Punta Askew. Anchor in the middle of the bay or on the W side with a line to a tree ashore. There is much fishing traffic here and the boats crowd the head of the bay. Make sure your lines do not impede their passage.

Although there are no facilities, there are frequent buses and *fletes* to Punta Arenas. The *fletes* are pick up trucks for hire, useful for hauling supplies and fuel from the town.

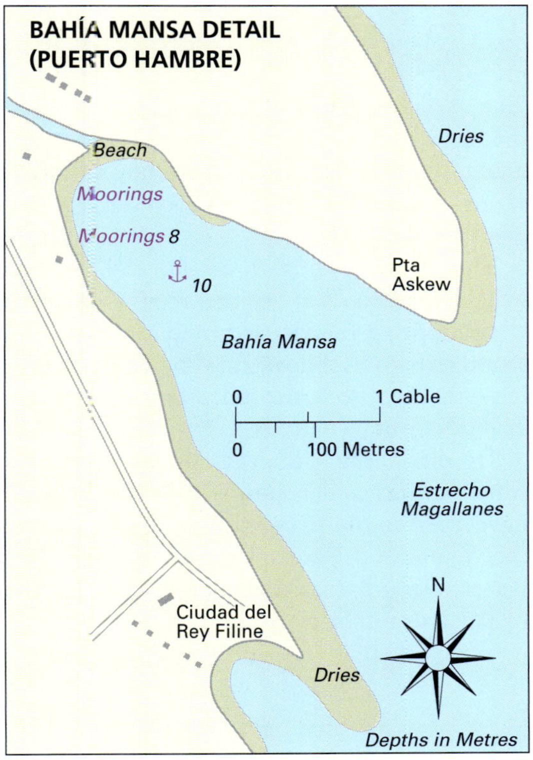

There is an *Armada* station at the head of the bay VHF 16. There is also a walk of about an hour to Fuerte Bulnes, an old military establishment and historic monument on Punta Santa Ana. This was once known as Port Famine, and Darwin and the Beagle anchored here on 7 June 1834 before heading south for the Magdalen Channel.

Punta Arenas

53°10S 70° 54′W
VHF 16, 09
Local telephone code 061
Charts Chile 11000, 11400, 11411
Light Muelle Arturo Prat (light on the end of) Fl.W.10s20m, 53°10′·23S 70°54′·36W
Tides The flood tide runs SW past Punt Arenas, the spring range is 2·4m. In the summer (January) the average high temperature will be 14·3°C, and in the winter (July) the average high is 3·7°C

Punta Arenas translates as 'Sandy Point', named by the 18th century English explorer John Byron, and a look at the chart will reveal that it is little more than that, from a cruiser's point of view. Before the opening of the Panama Canal, it was a hugely important coaling station for ships passing between the Atlantic and Pacific oceans and achieved

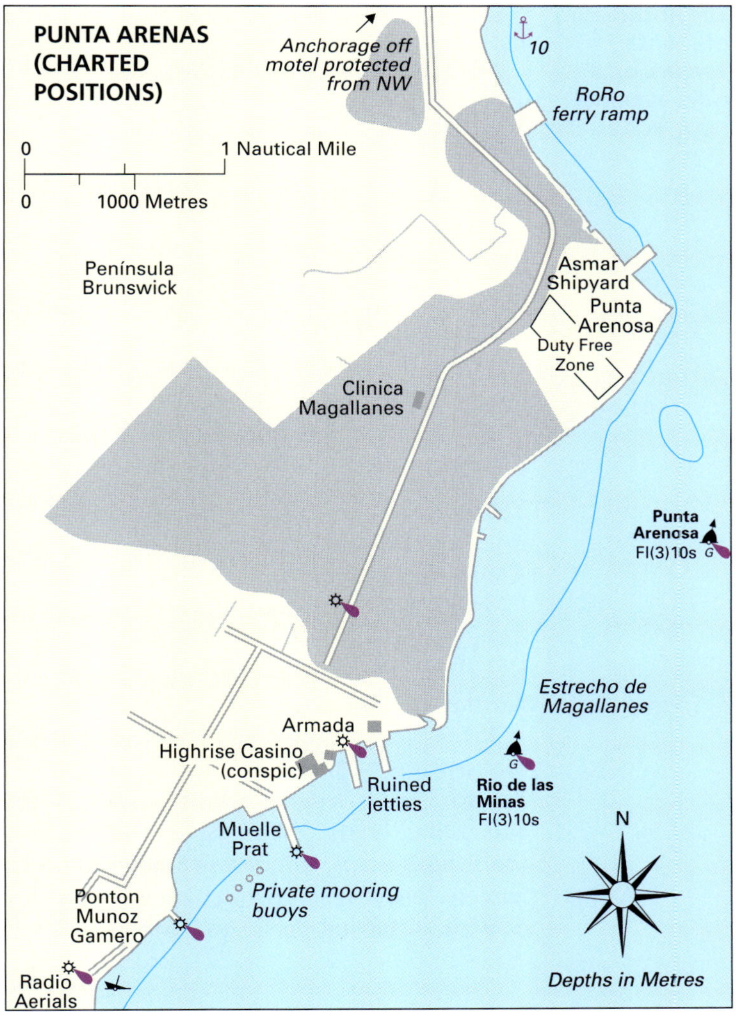

The anchorage off Punta Arenas, on a calm evening
Máire Wilkes

great prosperity during the California Gold Rush when ships carrying fortune hunters made the passage through the Straits.

This is a friendly and welcoming city which once made its fortunes in the sheep industry but now looks to a booming oil exploration and petrochemical industry in the Magellan Straits for its wealth. It is a popular tourist destination (with mega shopping malls and a duty free area) and cruise ships are regular visitors here.

It was in Punta Arenas that Slocum was advised by a Chilean Naval officer to

> *ship hands to fight Indians in the Straits further west.*

These days the fight will be against the weather and the poor nature of the Punta Arenas anchorage.

There is no real anchorage here, only an open roadstead through which the wind can whistle in the unpredictable manner of the weather hereabouts.

If the weather suits, you have two options on arrival. The first is to identify the Muelle Arturo Prat, a lengthy wharf used by ships and fishing boats. Yachts have rafted against the fishing boats, which use tractor tyres as fenders. There is frequent coming and going, as with all fishing fleets, and you should not leave the boat unattended. Keep a listening watch VHF 16.

If you are lucky and arrive in settled conditions, you will be able the visit the *capitania* and *Armada* by foot. The former is found near the head of the pier, and the latter is at the head of a ruined wooden pier a short distance to the northeast.

Remember, though, that conditions change quickly here and you are very exposed. Be prepared to drop your lines at the slightest hint of deteriorating weather, especially from the E, which is thankfully rare. There are many written accounts of yachts suffering severe damage by lingering too long on this wharf.

The alternative is to anchor SW of the Muelle Arturo Prat in the region of some large mooring buoys used by pilot boats and workboats. The buoys may be available on request, but check the price first. Otherwise anchor in 5m.

Despite the attractions of shops, supermarkets and restaurants which will all have been in short supply on the way here, this remains a poor place for a safe visit. Better to use Bahia Mansa (above) and come by truck or public transport.

Facilities

There are several options here for carrying out repairs. There are two travel-lifts near the Asmar Shipyard, 5 cables south of the pier. One is said to be 'yacht friendly'. In emergency, yachts have found ASMAR (a naval shipyard) to be helpful.

Diesel is available at Muelle Prat and arrives by truck from the local COPEC station who can be contacted VHF 83. The capitania can advise.

Water is available on request.

There are many supermarkets, and a duty free area to the north of the town where bargains may be found. It is worth remembering that goods produced in South America are often of a lower standard than those found in North America or Europe.

It may be possible to buy yacht equipment tax free; the dealers will advise. Be cautious, however, as you may incur charges for the paperwork and wipe out any saving you have made.

The fish market in the centre of town is highly recommended.

Charts and pilot books may be obtainable at the *Armada* office, otherwise the local branch of Ultramar Agencias Marítimas (which may also stock British publications) can be found at Independencia, 865. ✆ 204 723.

Medical and dental facilities can be found. There are two hospitals.

There are consulates representing many European countries, including the UK, and other south American countries.

Transport

Punta Arenas is without doubt the best connected city in this part of the world with flights from its modern airport to all parts of South America, and also direct (and spectacular) flights to Puerto Williams which can be useful if planning a crew change in the Beagle Channel (see p. 104).There are bus links to all parts of Chile and Argentina, although you will find no bus station since each operator prefers to use his own stops. There is a tourist office by the central square which will advise.

East of Punta Arenas

Punta Arenas to Punta Dungeness at the eastern entrance to the Straits is roughly 120 miles, a passage obstructed by two troublesome sections known as the First and Second Narrows – *Primera and Segunda Angostura*. Careful attention must be given to the tidal flows which may reach 8 knots, and if heading SW with the tide against a strong wind, considerable seas can form which would prevent a yacht from making progress. Sailing NE, with the tide and prevailing wind, is easier but the timing of the tides may be less convenient.

Fast currents found in the narrows also create tide rips, eddies and overfalls in the vicinity of both the entrance and exits to them.

With reference to the tides at Cabo Vírgines, the flood tide runs into the Strait and then to the SW at HW+3.The ebb tide runs at HW–3. Slack water in the narrows is very brief and cannot be relied on.

If travelling E, yachts are advised to be off the entrance to Segunda Angostura as the E-going stream is starting, which is HW Cape Horn –0230 (*Admiralty Pilot*).

If inward bound from the Atlantic, you should be off the NE approach to Primera Angostura just before the SW stream starts HW Cape Horn +0230.

The narrows are well lit and some report it easier to navigate this stretch at night.

Useful anchorages

Cabo Gregorio

(no light)

Having transited the Segunda Angostura NE bound, or if arriving from the NE and waiting for a tide, a good anchorage with shelter from SW to N can be found to the N of Cabo Gregorio in 52°38·2'S 70°12'W in 6m, good holding. This lies between the Cabo Gregorio oil jetty and an oil installation ashore at Punto Sara, with a derelict jetty which has two mooring buoys off it, which must be avoided in the dark.

Punta Delgada

Fl.W.5s

At the northern entrance to the Primera Angostura, on the N side, is an anchorage off Punta Delgada giving good shelter from SW to NW with good holding in 52°27·1S 69°32·7W.

Mount Sarmienta stands guard over the Canal Magdelana *Máire Wilkes*
The Chilean Channels *Pete Smith*

The eastern entrance to the Magellan Strait

This is marked by two lights on each of the N and S shores.

North shore

Cabo Virgenes 52°20'S 68°21.2W, Fl.W.5s69m27M. Note that this is in Argentina and the Argentine *prefectura* keep watch on VHF16. A nasty rock, the Roca Nassau lies 3·6 miles off the Cape bearing 124° from it. Inshore of this rock, and a mile off the light on the same bearing, is the Roca Virgen. Although it is possible to pass inshore of Roca Nassau, it seems more sensible to give it a wide offshore berth, given that the Roca Virgen is awash and the currents can run strongly.

Five miles to the SW is Punta Dungeness light, 52°23.7S 68°26.10W, Fl.W.10s28m22M. This is in Chile and the lighthouse staff will give weather, tide and traffic information, VHF 16.

South shore

On the S shore is the Cabo Espiritu Santo light (52°39.5S 68°36.6W), Fl.W.15s66m23m. The line joining this to Punta Dungeness is the border between Chilean and Argentine waters. There are two implications for cruisers: you may be called by either country and asked your intentions, crew numbers, destination etc. Also, if you are arriving from the Falklands and intending to enter Chile at Punta Arenas, even though you are not entering Argentina, you may still be stopped by Argentine patrol boats and charged with an unauthorised visit to the Falkland Islands. This can prove costly and time-consuming, and can occur even though you might be in international waters.

To the south of the Espiritu Santo light is the Argentine Faro Magallanes, a light beacon Fl(3)10s12·5M.

Ever vigilant, the Chilean *Armada* *Máire Wilkes*

The magic of the Beagle anchorages, Beaulieu, Seno Pia *Tim Barker*

4 THE BEAGLE CHANNEL AND CAPE HORN

On the 31st January 1833, on seeing the Beagle Channel for the first time, Charles Darwin recorded in his diary

> *The channel now ran between islands; and this part was entirely unknown; it rained continually and the weather well became its bad character.*

Welcome to the Beagle Channel where your log may record similar sentiments. Little has changed down here since Darwin set eyes on it, and certainly not the weather. It is true that it can be wet, windy and cold, but there is hardly a passage anywhere in the world which can stir emotions like the Beagle and few places have majestic scenery to match it. This is a place where you should plan for time to linger.

There are three natural passages between the Atlantic and Pacific Oceans – the Magellan Strait, the Drake Passage and the Beagle. Of the three, the Beagle is the narrowest but most sheltered; its discovery meant that for the first time ships had a relatively easy, if tight, passage between two great oceans, which avoided rounding the Horn or facing the tumultuous Drake Passage. It is perhaps less a highway and more a useful 'rat run' between oceans.

The Beagle is 150M long, and runs from Cabo San Pio in the east (55°03'.44S 66°31'.45W) to somewhere to the west of Isla Gordon in roughly 70°13'W, although the western extremity is not clearly defined and the channels carry many different names. At 69°05'W the channel divides to form the southwestern and northwestern arms which pass either side of Isla Gordon. The Beagle is well lit and isolated dangers are few and well marked. Although presenting no problem for yachts, the passage south of Gable Island (approx 67°29'W) narrows to less than a mile at the Beagle's narrowest pont.

The only inconvenience to navigation is the fact that until you reach 68°36'W (if heading westwards) the border between Chile and Argentina runs down the middle of the channel. It is jealously guarded by both sides neither of whom trust each other. If you are able to keep to one side or the other then you will have no problem, depending on the state of your paperwork – see below. But if forced to tack you may find that you have to deal with repeated radio calls as you cross from one side of the channel to the other and consequently in and out of either Argentina or Chile. As each of these radio calls is initiated from a string of observing stations which don't seem to communicate with each other, you may find a great deal of repetition and much patience is required.

If you set aside for one moment the sheer sense of adventure that comes from sailing these waters, there are good, practical reasons to cruise here. In Ushuaia (Argentina) you have a decent sized town with supermarkets, a hospital, an airport and bus connections, and some possibility, if small, of getting repairs done, although only shallow draft boats will be able to lift out here. Also, for what is probably the first time in a thousand miles you will have a novel choice of clothing and coffee shops. Whether arriving from east or west, Ushuaia will feel like stepping back into a small European town/ski resort in the winter. This, and Puerto Williams across the water, are the only bits of the Beagle that Darwin would not recognise.

Puerto Williams is a much smaller settlement built around a naval base from which the Chileans keep control of their portion of the Beagle and the channels running northwards towards Puerto Montt. You will find far less in the way of provisions and support systems. But it is a friendly and helpful place and, most importantly, it is the only place in the Beagle Channel where a boat can safely be left unattended for any period of time. There is also an airport linking to the rest of Chile, but not Argentina. This can present logistical problems if trying to organise a crew change – see p. 104.

ARRIVING IN THE BEAGLE CHANNEL

These waters can present quite a challenge for the sailor thanks to the changeable and often tempestuous winds and equally testing dealings with the authorities.

You should base your plan around which country you last sailed from.

From the east

If arriving from the east, having first checked into Argentina somewhere in the South Atlantic, you will already have been given clearance for Ushuaia which you must make your first port of call.

If arriving in Ushuaia from the Falklands having left for there from Argentina, you must already be in possession of a *permiso* from Argentina giving you permission to have sailed in Falkland waters (see p. 119) otherwise you will be subject to a fine of several thousand dollars and risk having your boat impounded. For this reason, yachts arriving from the Falklands often choose to make a first stop at Puerto Williams. If you have been to the Falklands without a *permiso*, it would be wise to ensure that you stay in the Chilean half of the Beagle Channel, but the risk remains of being stopped in international waters by the Argentine navy as you approach from the east.

From the west

Arriving from the northwest, from the direction of Puerto Montt and the channels, check the *zarpe* obtained at your last port of call. This will state the route and anchorages you are allowed to use. For extended exploration of the Chilean parts of the Beagle Channel you may have to sail to Puerto Williams, apply for a more detailed *zarpe*, and then retrace your steps. You should discuss this at the last *Armada* station before leaving the Magellan Strait.

If you have braved the south Pacific, then a landfall at the western entrance to the Beagle Channel is not recommended except in perfect conditions and with confident navigation. A better plan is to round the Horn eastwards so that you will be sailing into shelter as you make your way north to the eastern end of Navarino Island, thence to Puerto Williams to 'check in'. This is what the Armada would probably insist on.

Crossing the Chile-Argentina border

If you want to 'change sides' you must go through an emigration procedure at the first port, and immigration at the second. Despite the fact that this is a daily occurrence, particularly by the charter fleets, no attempt has been made to streamline the process, so although the two ports are only 25M away from each other, as far as the paperwork goes they might as well be a thousand.

Tides and currents

The tidal rise and fall is not extreme anywhere in the Beagle Channel. At Ushuaia, for example, the average range will be 1·6m at springs and 0·7 at neaps.

It can generally be assumed that there will be a constant set of about 1 knot running west to east the full length of the Channel, but this is largely driven by the prevailing wind and can cease or reverse depending on wind strength and direction.

For those with an oceanographic interest in these waters, then the results of extensive surveys and explanations of the coastal currents can be found here:

www.icm.csic.es/scimar/pdf/63/sm63s1023.pdf

From a cruiser's point of view, the simplest approach is to assume an eastwards set but maintain careful observation if attempting anything where the current may be a determining factor.

Weather forecasts

See Chile page 47

If you are using GRIBs to obtain weather forecasts in the Beagle Channel, the anecdotal evidence gleaned from experienced charter skippers is that they invariably under-read. One skipper told me that to get a better idea of the coming weather in the Beagle, he looked at the forecast wind speeds for Cape Horn, usually 10 or 15% higher, and assumed that's what he would get.

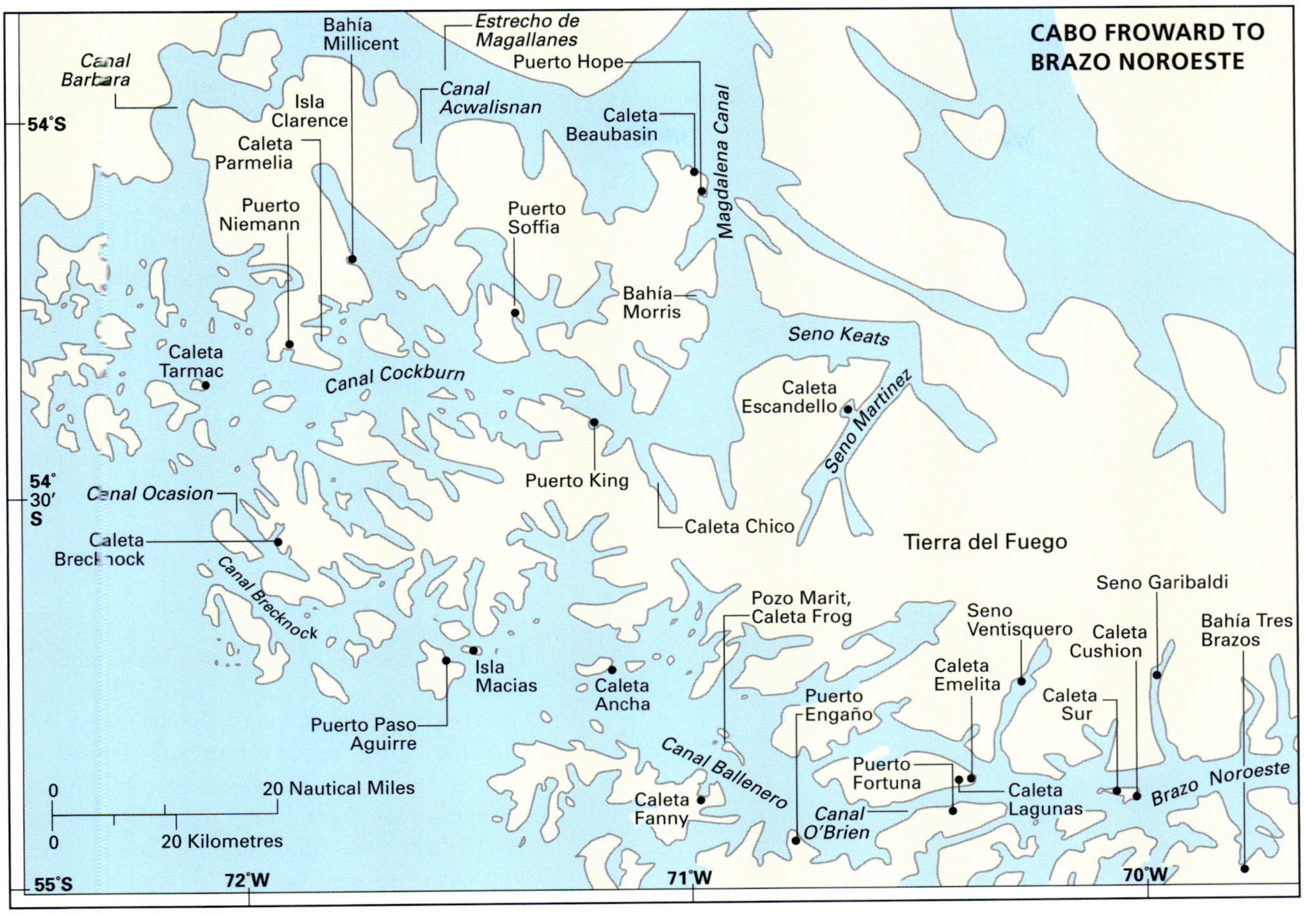

LEAVING THE STRAITS FOR THE BEAGLE CHANNEL

Heading for the Beagle Channel from the Magellan Strait, three opportunities present themselves. All lead to the Canal Cockburn from where you must leave the shelter provided by the islands and face the open ocean before making south a short way to find the western entrance to the Beagle.

The first option is to leave the Straits at the Canal Barbara, the entrance to which is found at 53°47′·5S 072°05′·8W, west of Cape Froward. It is a passage of 40 miles to the Cockburn and although this route is much used by fishermen, and is undoubtedly impressive, the pilotage can be complicated as the canal is quite open, and subject to *rachas*. Nor are the anchorages good if you are overtaken by bad weather.

The Seno Pedro/Canal Acwalisnan 53°55′S 71°37′W, also west of Cape Froward, is the easiest of all the routes and is well protected. The distance to Canal Cockburn is 60 miles. There are narrows to be negotiated at Paso O'Ryan but these are straightforward at slack water.

The problem with these two passages is that they remain (at the time of writing) forbidden to yachts. Your *zarpe* will not allow passage through either. Some yachts have chosen to take these routes, but the bureaucratic risks are great, and now that you are in the waters of Tierra del Fuego, the *Armada* enforce the rules more strictly than in other parts of Chile. If you happened to be in one of these channels and were discovered by a patrol boat, you would be told to return to the authorised track, which may prove troublesome and probably incur a fine.

The Canal Magdalena is the recognised main shipping channel and this is the one you will be told to use – the entrance is found in 54°S 71°W, southeast of Cape Froward. Do not feel in any way cheated if you are forced to use this route for it is the most spectacular of the three and for much of it you will be sailing with Mount Sarmiento, the highest peaks in Tierra del Fuego, looking down on you.

Adventurous navigators will look at the chart and see other interesting route options. However, the policing of these waters by the Chilean *Armada* moves up a notch or two and your journey south will have been handled with a much softer touch than in the waters to which you are now sailing. You will have been given a permitted route at the last *Armada* station you visited, and you must stick to this. Whereas in the channels south of Puerto Montt you would be given a little more freedom, here a passing patrol boat

SENO CHICO

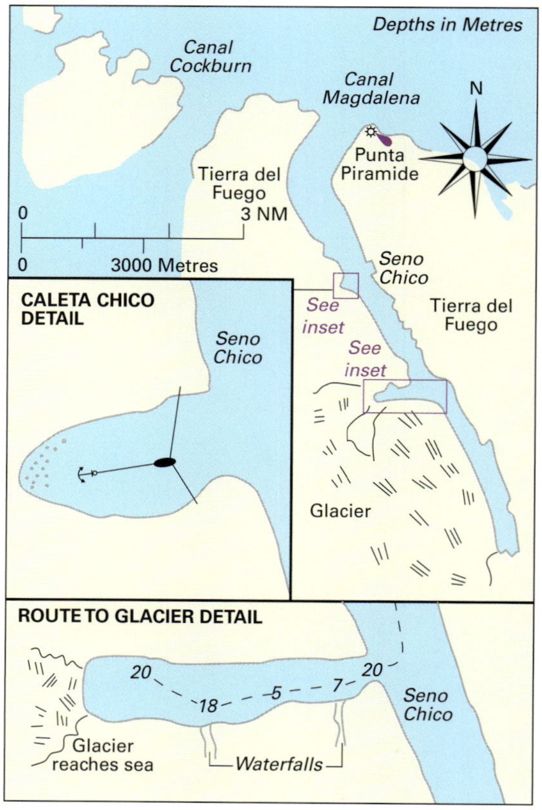

might examine your papers, insurance etc, and if you are found deviating from the intended track then penalties can follow. However, they do understand that in the interests of safe navigation you may choose to depart from your intended track in order to reach a safe anchorage. If you are in VHF range and seek permission to deviate from your *zarpe*, it will usually be given in cases of bad weather.

You must report your position at least daily by radio or email otherwise a search and rescue operation may result.

Canal Cockburn

Caleta Chico

54° 28′S 71° 08′W
Charts BA 554,1373, Chile 11000,12400

This is a useful and spectacular anchorage where the Canal Magdalena joins the Canal Cockburn. Seno Chico is a long, narrow inlet and 4M down the western side is another inlet leading to a spectacular glacier. There is no anchorage here but a little way to the north there is a small notch, Caleta Chico, where it is possible to lie with lines ashore to trees in good shelter. This can be useful if waiting for improving weather, remembering that the western end of Canal Cockburn is open to the Pacific.

Caleta Brecknock

54° 34′.3S 71° 57′ W
Charts BA 554, Chile 12400, 12600, 12711

Yachts wishing to minimise their exposure to Pacific swell when rounding the northern end of Peninsula Brecknock, can take the Canal Ocasión which leads between Canals Cockburn and Brecknock. This is the favoured route used by fishing boats and small ships seeking to avoid rough water.

Brecknock is a very popular anchorage with excellent hiking. Anchor in the NW corner in a well protected notch with four lines ashore. Fresh water can be found here in settled weather by going alongside E of the waterfall, lying against truck tyres.

From Caleta Brecknock, passage can be made to the NW arm of the Beagle which lies to the north of Isla Gordon.

Anchored with lines ashore, Caleta Brecknock *Máire Wilkes*

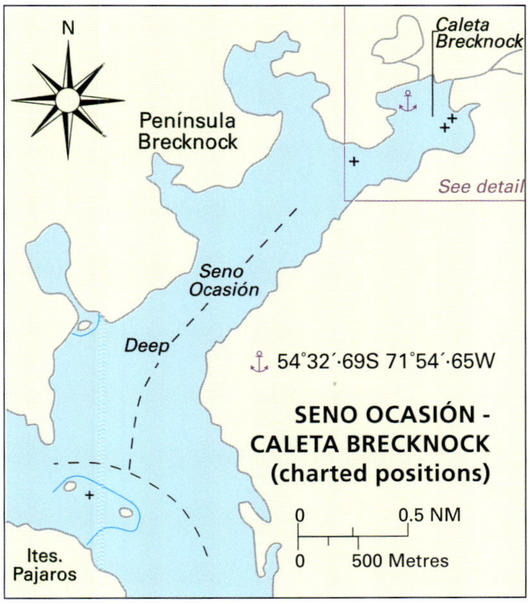

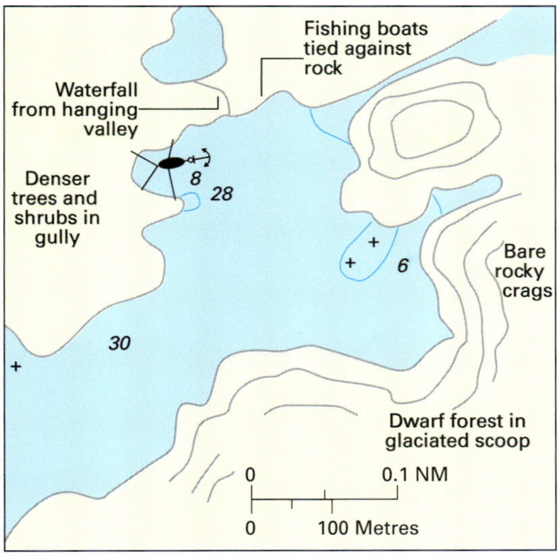

CALETA BRECKNOCK DETAIL

Good walking from the Brecknock anchorage *Vicky Jackson*

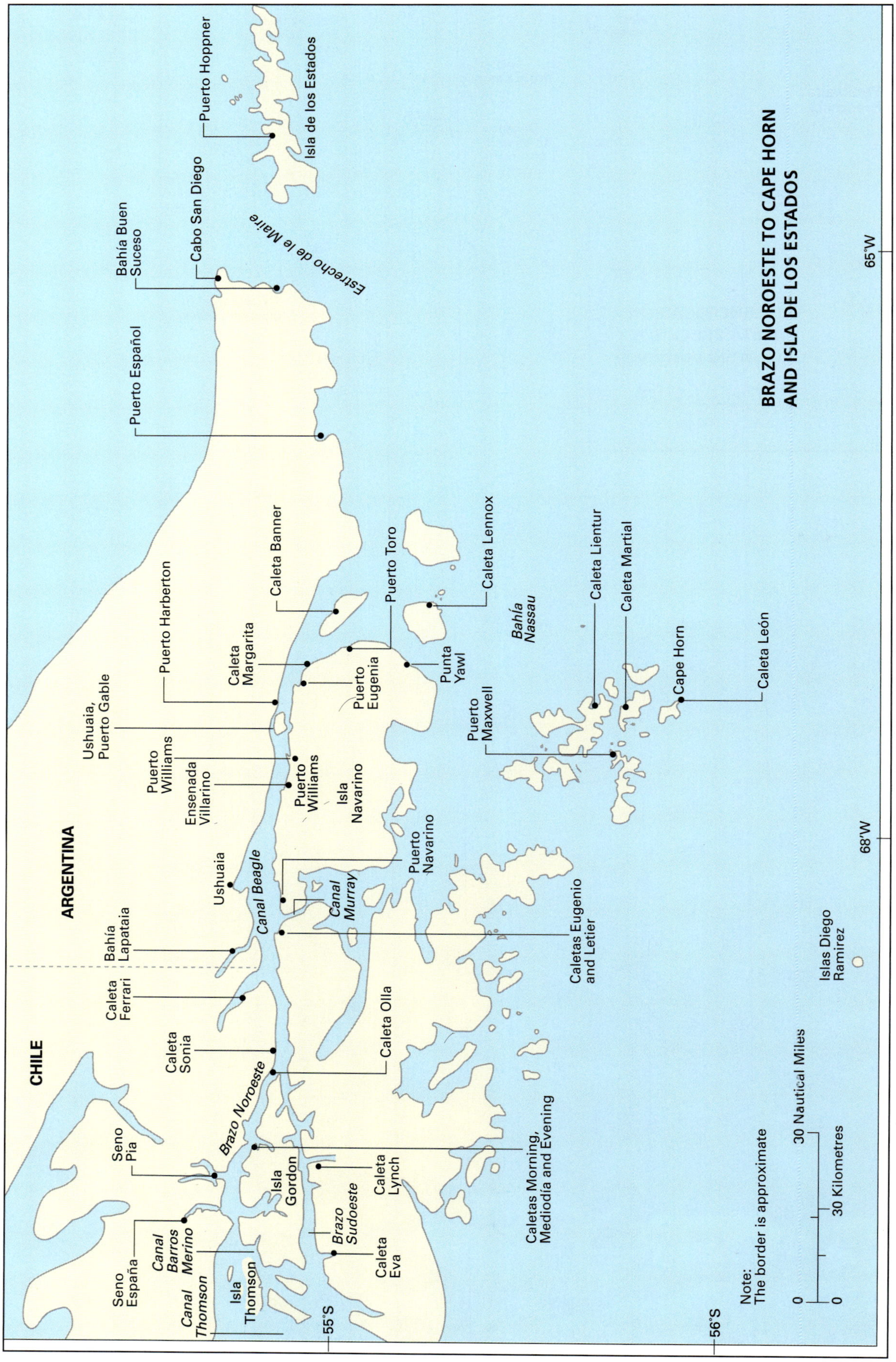
BRAZO NOROESTE TO CAPE HORN
AND ISLA DE LOS ESTADOS
CHILE
ARGENTINA
Puerto Hoppner
Isla de los Estados
Cabo San Diego
Bahía Buen Suceso
Estrecho de le Maire
Puerto Español
Caleta Banner
Puerto Harberton
Caleta Margarita
Puerto Toro
Caleta Lennox
Bahía Nassau
Caleta Lientur
Caleta Martial
Cape Horn
Caleta León
Puerto Eugenia
Punta Yawl
Puerto Maxwell
Ushuaia, Puerto Gable
Puerto Williams
Ensenada Villarino
Puerto Williams
Isla Navarino
Puerto Navarino
Ushuaia
Canal Beagle
Canal Murray
Caletas Eugenio and Letier
Bahía Lapataia
Caleta Ferrari
Caleta Sonia
Caleta Olla
Brazo Noroeste
Seno Pia
Caletas Morning, Mediodía and Evening
Isla Gordon
Caleta Lynch
Brazo Sudoeste
Caleta Eva
Seno España
Canal Barros Merino
Canal Thomson
Isla Thomson
Islas Diego Ramirez
55°S
56°S
68°W
65°W
Note:
The border is approximate
0
30 Nautical Miles
0
30 Kilometres

The Brecknock anchorage - *Sunstone* and *Taraki*
Vicky Jackson

THE BEAGLE CHANNEL EASTWARDS: NORTHWEST ARM (BRAZO NOROESTE) AND NORTHERN SHORE TO USHUAIA

As far as 68°S 36°W (12M west of Ushuaia) you will be sailing in Chilean territorial waters (eastwards from here is Argentina *but only on the northern shore*).

The northwest arm (Brazo Noroeste), which runs to the north of Isla Gordon, has some of the most spectacular anchorages to be found in the Beagle Channel and is known as 'glacier alley'. The frequency of the glaciers is breathtaking and the experience of taking your boat to within spitting distance (with due caution) will never be forgotten. This was where Darwin first set his eyes on glaciers and wrote

> *It is scarcely possible to imagine anything more beautiful than the beryl-like blue of these glaciers, and especially as contrasted with the dead white of the upper expanse of snow.*

There are many anchorages in and around Isla Gordon, and opportunities to explore. To list every little hole, and there are many, is beyond the scope of this book. The anchorages I have listed come under the 'must see' category, but don't hesitate to look further afield for this is a place laden with possibility. However, beware that many anchorages are forbidden and those you may use will be listed on your *zarpe*. Take advice from local charter skippers who are usually free with their advice about where you may and may not go.

There are no navigational hazards in the northwest arm and the waters are as deep and clear as the mountains are steep and dark. When the sun blazes on the trees tumbling to the waterline, and glistens on the snowy peaks, this is as inspiring a place as you could wish for. But when the wind howls and funnels, and the rain falls and the clouds are low, you can feel as if you are in a corridor leading to hell. It is one of the great virtues of this part of the world that the weather is ever-changing and it is possible to experience the many varied faces of the Beagle within an hour or so of each other.

Note that cartography in many of the fjords can date from more than a century ago and only in the main navigation channels can the surveys be considered up to date. It would be unwise to rely on electronic charting which on occasions will have you high and dry. This is a place for eyeball navigation.

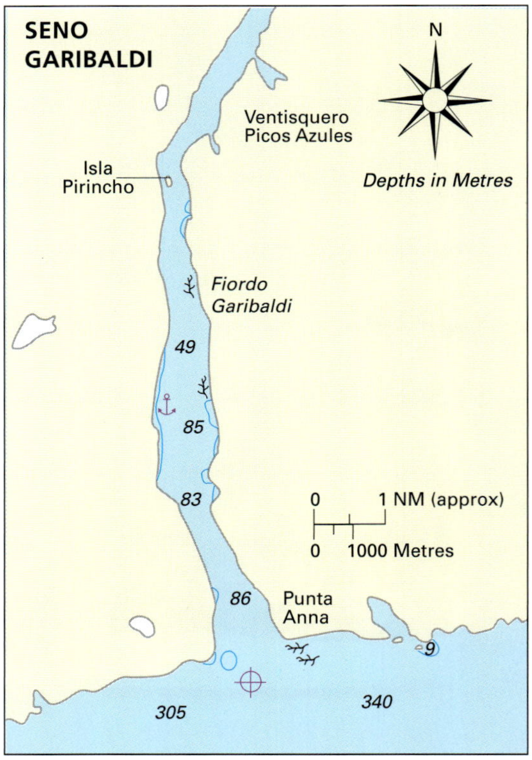

Seno Garibaldi

54° 51.3S 69° 56.4W
Charts BA 554 1373

This runs to the north for 11M from the western end of Brazo Noroeste and leads to a fine glacier at the head. It is clear of hazards although when making an entrance keep well to the west to avoid rocks off Punta Anna on the eastern side. The mountains on either side are steep so be prepared for any strong winds to funnel here.

It is possible to anchor when the fjord starts to turn towards the NE. A small island will be seen, Isla Pirincho. It is possible to lie off the SW corner of the island in 4m with a bow anchor and a line ashore providing you can be certain of no strong southerly winds. The island and the shallows on its western side will also protect you from any breakaway ice which flows from the glacier.

More adventurous, but difficult to find, is a small cleft in the rock on the western side, less than a mile south of the island. This is Caleta Scherzo. You can lie here bows out with lines astern and good shelter is reported.

Seno Pia

54° 50.5S 69° 41.3W
(use this as a safe position from which to enter)

Guarded by a reef through which there is a narrow passage, Seno Pia justifiably carries

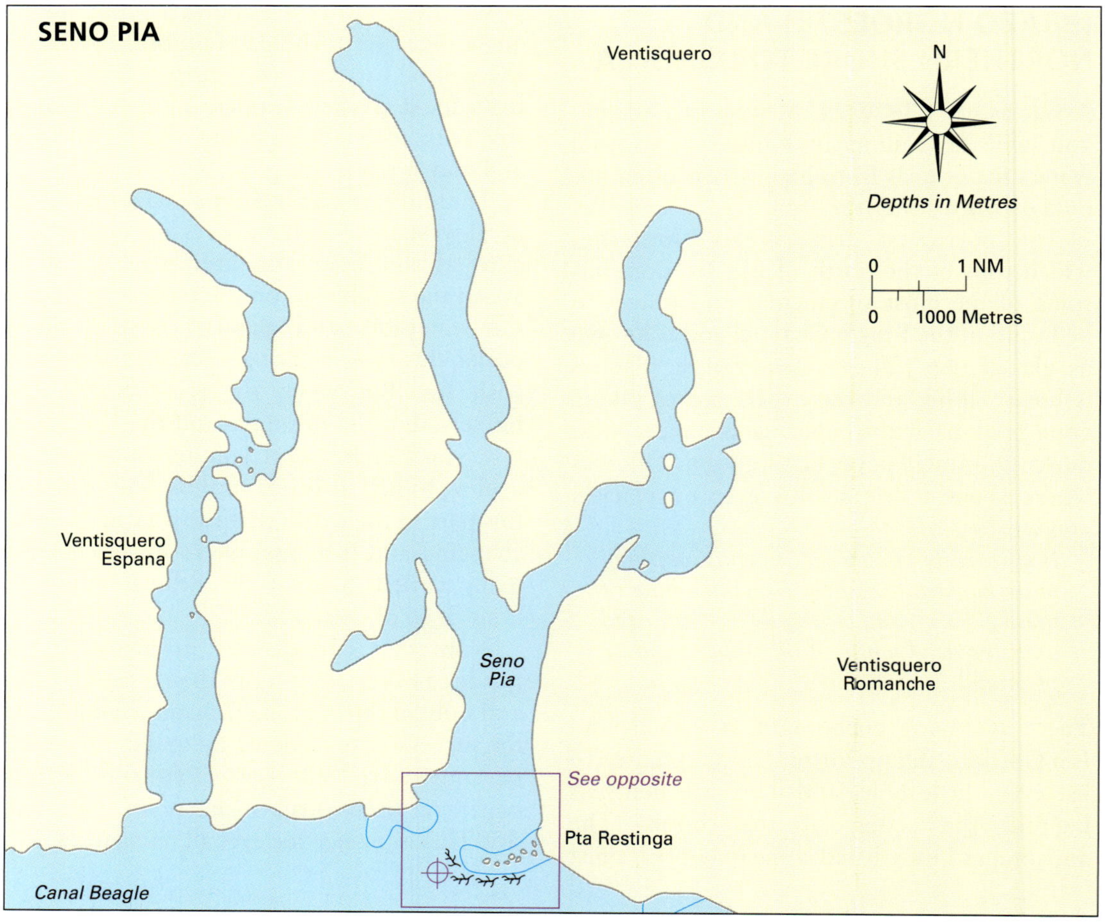

the name Seno Wow! At first you may think there is nothing special about this inlet but as you wind your way northwards you find yourself with a glacier of immense grandeur ahead of you, and a couple more to your right just for good measure. If the air is still you will find a silence here that is almost painful. If you only get to visit one fjord on this stretch of coast, make it this one.

The entrance requires care. A rocky bar runs across the mouth of the fjord. The eastern side of it is partly visible with rocks showing and you should note the position of the smallest outlying rocks and pass well to the west of them. The western side of the entrance is less troublesome although thick kelp grows on the submerged portions of the bar. From the waypoint given, you should be able to turn NE and enter with safety, after which there are no hazards.

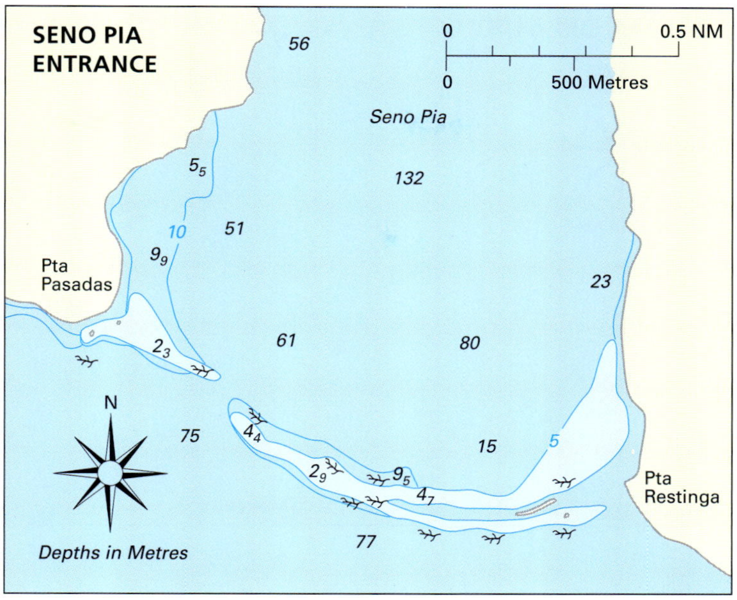

The western arm of Seno Pia

From the entrance it is 9M to the head of the western arm where you will find two massive glaciers tumbling down to the sea. This is a place of breathtaking beauty and you will want to linger. The temptation to nose up to the ice is great, especially in a dinghy, but be aware that colossal chunks of ice can calve at any moment, and even if they don't hit you, the wash could overwhelm you. In summer the water will be strewn with ice all around you but the pieces are small and unlikely to inflict damage.

Seno Pia western arm
Paul Heiney

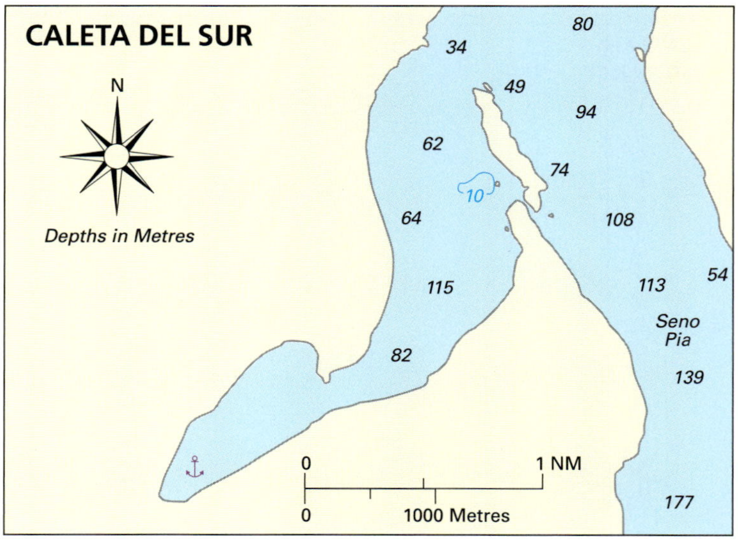

Caleta del Sur, western arm, Seno Pia

This inlet is on the western side and 4M north of the entrance. Enter by turning west then south and a fine, safe anchorage can be found at the far end of the bay, anchoring in 4m with lines to the shore.

The Beaulieu anchorage, Seno Pia, perfect shelter *Vicky Jackson*

Caleta Beaulieu, eastern arm, Seno Pia

This is another spectacular bay and if you want to anchor for the night within sight of a majestic glacier, this is the place to come to. It is famous for its good shelter.

Heading northeast towards Islote Punta Falsa, do not turn to starboard until you are sure you are clearing Punta Storaker. The water to the north of it is shallow. Once you have rounded it, make to the SW and anchor in 5m, good holding, from where you can get lines to trees ashore. The views of the glacier to the north of you will be stunning, and if you are able to make a visit ashore to climb the heights and look down at a remarkable scene, you will not be disappointed.

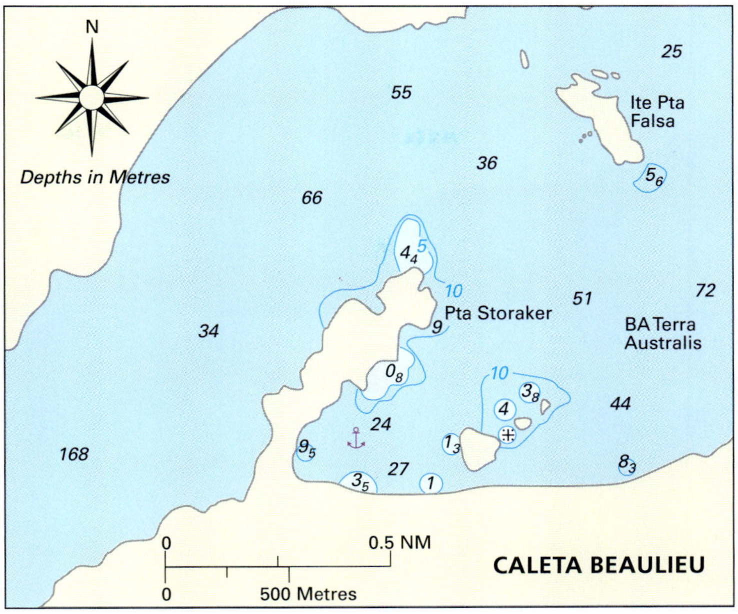

Caleta Mediodiá, Bahía Romanche
Paul Heiney

Bahía Romanche

54°54.7S 69°28.1W (at the mouth of the bay)
Charts Chile 1203, 1206, 13000

This bay lies on the north side of Isla Gordon and is worth visiting for the remarkable anchorage on its eastern side, Caleta Mediodía. The bay itself is spectacular enough with high mountains on all sides, but this little anchorage is quite unlike any other. It is like anchoring in a shoe box, and it is not easy to find. Proceed with care down the eastern side of the bay to find a small headland sticking out to the west. Follow this round and you will see a narrow indentation in the rock. The entrance can be found by reference to a flat rock to the north of it.

Drop your anchor and reverse in, then tie with four lines to the shore. Amazingly, there is a rock wall to which you can tie and there may even be some tyres left by fishermen to act as fenders but this option is for settled weather only.

A magical place.

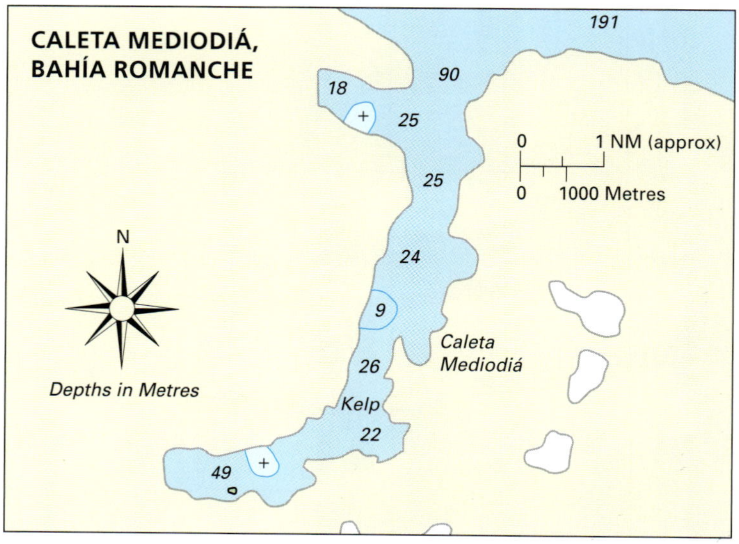

Caleta Olla

WP 54° 56.6S 69° 09W

Situated on the north side of Brazo Noroeste, Caleta Olla is a safe and memorable anchorage except in E winds and is the last harbour before the northwest arm joins the main Beagle Channel. Winds are famously strong here having funnelled the length of the NW arm and it may prove a struggle to gain the anchorage, but once inside there is good shelter provided by tall trees and very good holding in mud. It would be possible to swing at anchor here. This is a popular anchorage and possibly the busiest you will come across, for most charter yachts make a visit here, the beach being a much-used barbecue spot.

Caleta Olla looking westward along the NW arm *Vicky Jackson*

A busy day in Caleta Olla *Tim Barker*

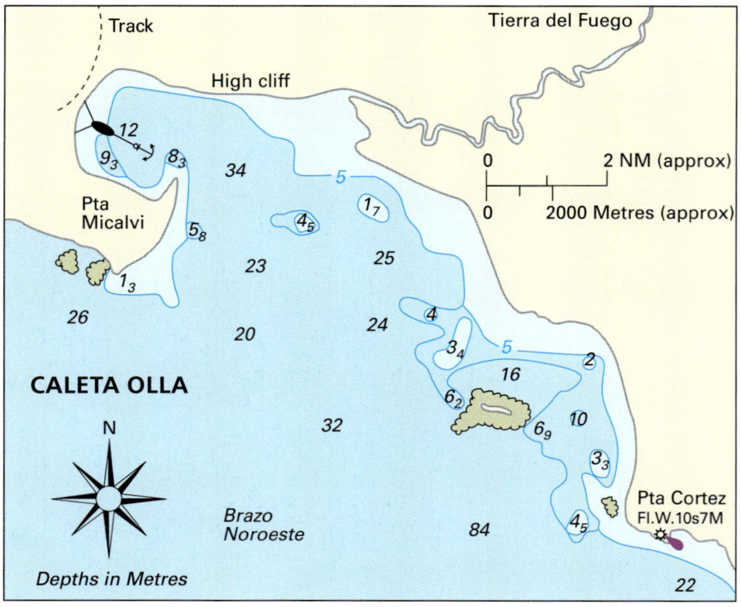

If approaching at night, you can confirm your position from the Ventisquero Holanda light on Punta Cortez, Fl.W.10s7M, a white GRP tower with a red band which stands to the SE of the anchorage.

Caleta Sonia

WP 54°58S 69° 01.4W

This is a useful anchorage and a convenient stopping place if making your way east or west along the Beagle. It lies just east of the Punta Yámana light tower Fl.W.12s12m7M, a white concrete tower with a red band. There is also a Chilean *Armada* station which can be called on VHF 16 (callsign *Alcamar Yámana*) although they will probably have called you first as you came into sight.

Round Punta Yámana and make towards the NE keeping watch for kelp creeping from the shore. You will see a small island ahead. To port you will see a beach with a ruined jetty. If possible anchor off the beach, good holding. It is possible that the officer in charge might direct you to the north of the island if the supply boat from Puerto Williams is expected. Access to the beach anchorage may be closed off by a rope.

Caleta Ferrari, Bahía Yendegaia

You may choose to make a stop in Bahía Yendegaia, a wide and impressive bay fed by a river whose silt-laden water gives the bay a milky colour. Ashore, at the head of the bay where the anchorage is good, you will see farm buildings where food may be available, or riding. Horses roam free here, they find dinghies a curiosity and will come and lick the salt off them.

Just beyond the eastern side of this bay is the Chile/Argentina border. If you are sailing eastwards from here you will have to sail on to Puerto Williams and check out of Chile before you can enter Ushuaia, temptingly close though it is.

Caleta Ferrari, Bahía Yendegaia
Paul Heiney

THE BEAGLE CHANNEL: SOUTHWESTERN ARM AND SOUTH SHORE EASTWARDS TO PUERTO WILLIAMS

The Brazo Sudoeste offers many opportunities for interesting navigation and exploration and the *Armada* has lifted some of the former restrictions.

If going from the NW to the SW arm west of Isla Gordon, your options may be limited. Almost certainly you will be told to use the Canal Thomson, to the west of Isla Thomson, which is well marked and surveyed and used by cruise ships – but it is exposed. It also lengthens the hop between the two arms by more than 20M and some sailors have chosen to ignore the *zarpe* and use Canal Borros Merino to the east. This presents no navigation problems, but be mindful of the fact the cartography hereabouts is imprecise and at times your plotter might show you taking an overland route. Eyeball navigation is needed here and the individual islands can be difficult to identify. The author found himself truly baffled and sailed up a dead end – very much in the spirit of a *Beagle* exploration.

Estéro Coloane

55° 05'7S 69° 48'6W
Charts Chile 1203, 1206, 13000, 12700

This is a lovely anchorage amidst towering mountains and two glaciers and it rates highly amongst the anchorages of the SW arm. Note that although the charts (which have minimal detail) show the entrance to be clear, there exists an island in the middle of the approaches to the inner bay. This is best passed to starboard on entering. There are then two anchorages to choose from:

Caleta Eva is a small cove in the NW corner behind a rock (also not shown on the chart) gives good shelter from all winds if anchored and tied to the shore.

Estéro Coloane looking SW over Caleta Sunstone
Vicky Jackson

Estéro Coloane *Paul Heiney*

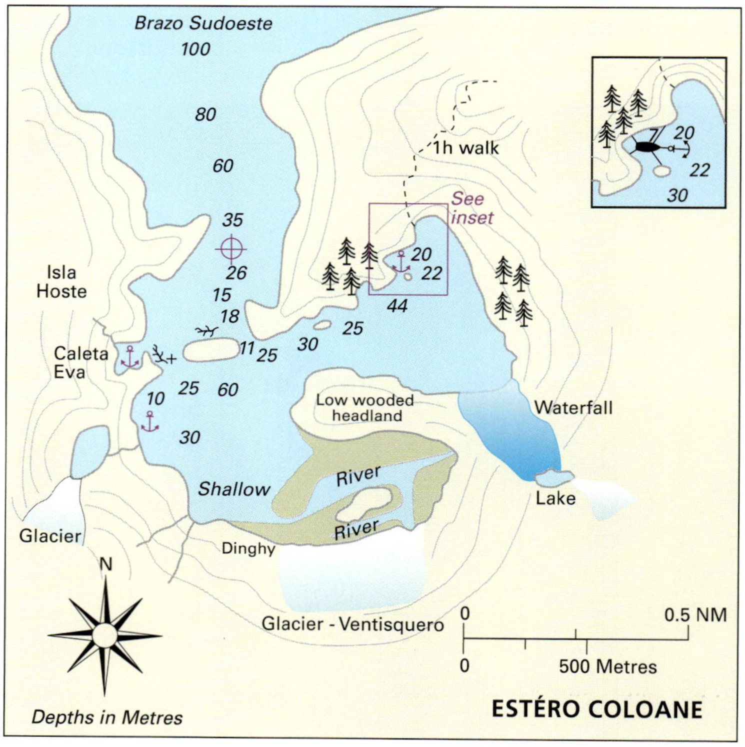

On the western side, just north of where a river runs into the sea, there is good anchorage on sand close enough to the shore to deploy a couple of lines to rocks. Take a moment to inspect the remarkable beaver dam where the river runs into the sea.

Both anchorages give you first class views of the glaciers. This is good place from which to launch hiking and walking expeditions.

Estéro Fouque

55° 02.9S 69° 32.7W (at the mouth)

This is a long narrow fjord with a good anchorage near its mouth, and opportunities to get close to glaciers, the first of which tumbles down to the sea. This is also good walking country.

A mile south of the entrance on the W side is a small cove, Caleta Lynch, protected from W winds by both land and trees. Observe the kelp carefully when entering as there may be foul patches. The N side of the cove is clearer. Anchor in good holding, mud, with lines ashore.

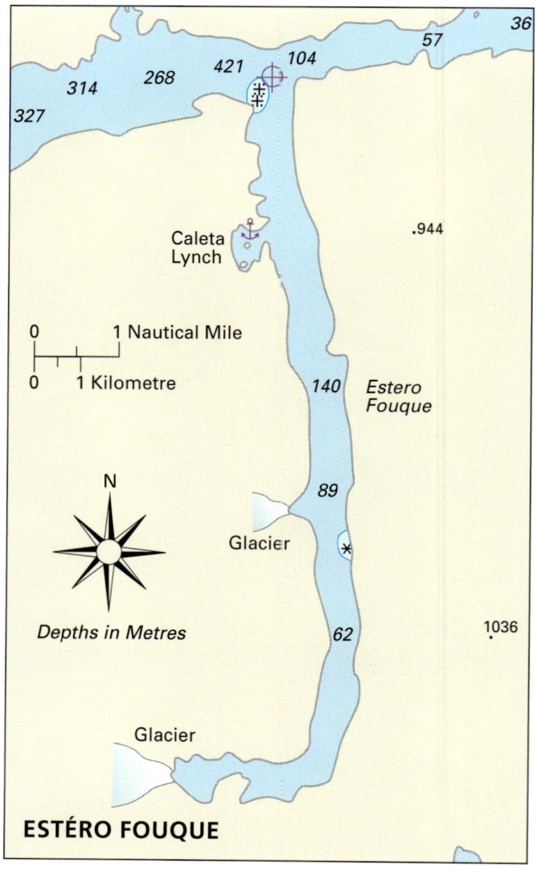

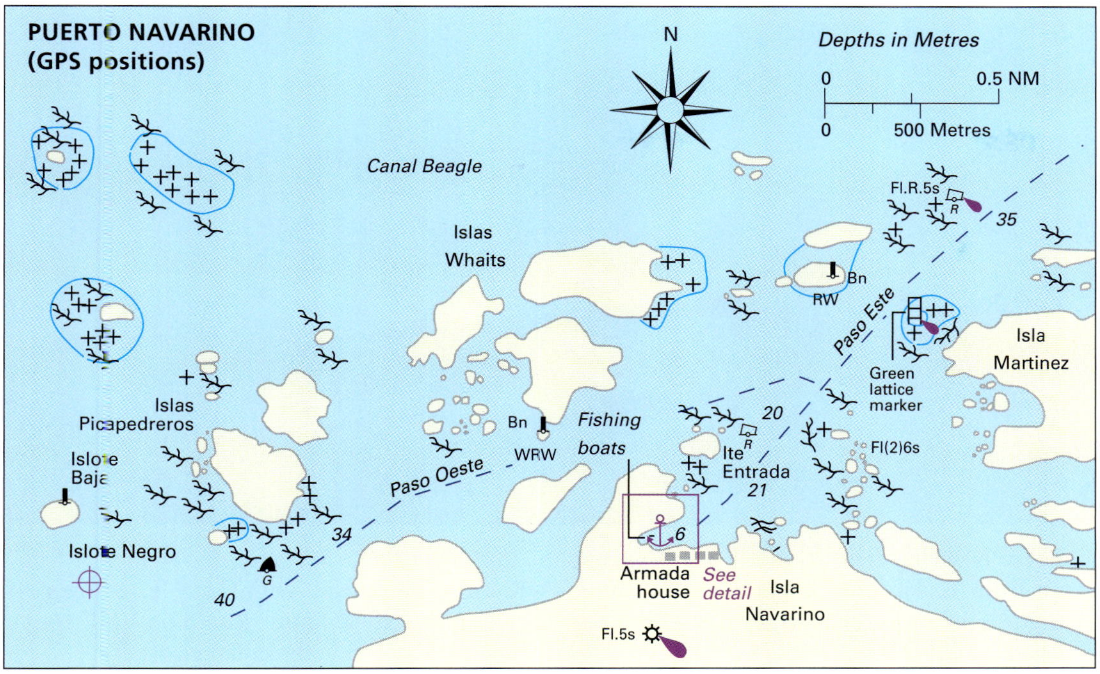

Canal Murray

It is a great pity that the Canal Murray remains out of bounds to yachts, and this restriction should be respected. It is frequently patrolled, and if you are caught there you will be towed to Puerto Williams and fines may result. Were it open it would provide a gateway to a wonderful cruising ground to be found to the S of Navarino Island, and at the same time provide much easier access to the Horn. The Chileans argue that they keep it closed for strategic reasons, though more likely for political ones as it emerges directly opposite Argentine Ushuaia.

Puerto Navarino

54° 55.4S 68° 19.3W

Charts BA 554, 1373 Chile 13100, 13131, 13200

There is a small *Armada* station here, said to be welcoming. It is directly opposite Ushuaia. The approaches are well marked (red, right, returning when leading into the harbour)

Anchor in front of the *Armada* building in 7m and take a line ashore to a small jetty. The mud is soft and the holding good.

There is also a large *Armada* buoy and permission might be given to lie to this, although it can be exposed.

Just to the west of Navarino, and again useful for providing a break is Caleta Martinez (54°54·8S 068°16·3W). Having identified Isla Martinez, pass between it and Islote Paty which lies to the east. The anchorage lies in the indented eastern tip of Isla Martinez which lies between Islote Paty and Islote Tito.

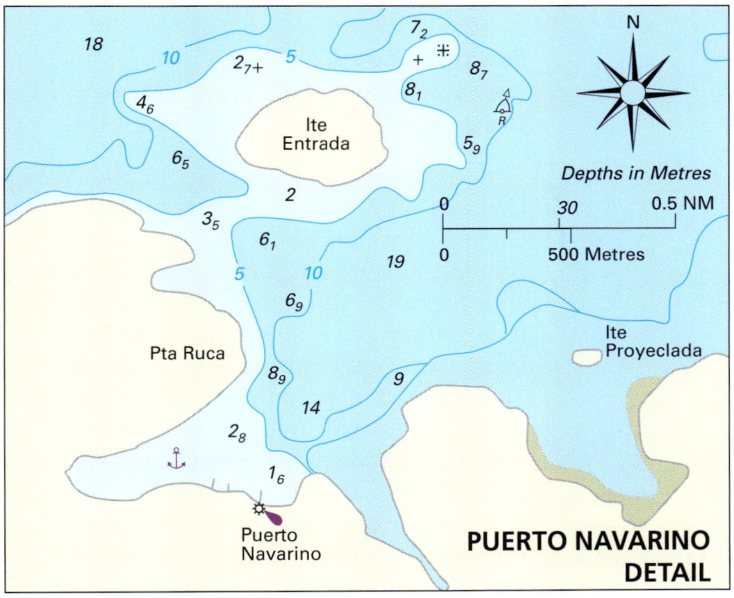

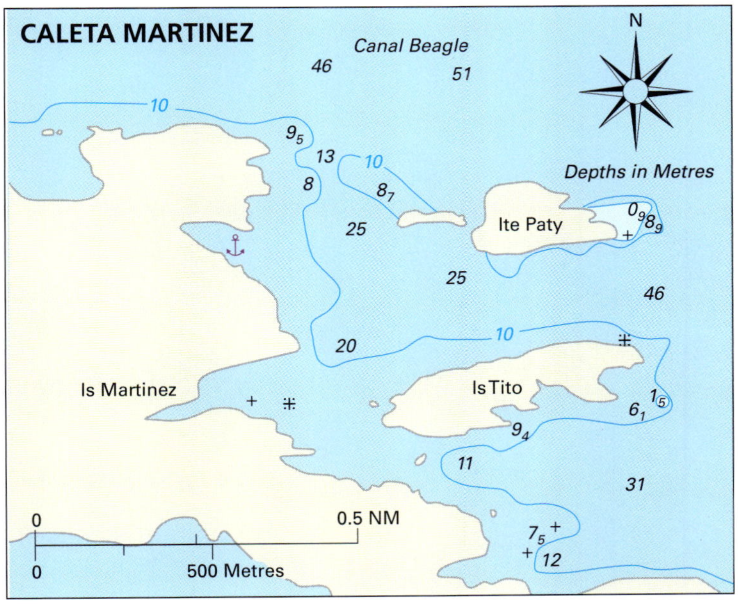

Looking N over Caleta Martinez to the Beagle Channel beyond
Paul Heiney

There is shelter here from all winds except those from E. Holding is good in 3m, mud. Swing to anchor, or drop and reverse into the cove with two lines ashore.

Radio ahead to *Alacamar Navarino* VHF Ch 16 for permission to lie here.

Puerto Williams

56°56'S 67°37'W
Charts BA 554, 1373, Chile 13100, 13142, 13200

This is the Chilean 'capital' of the Beagle Channel and the only place to conduct Chilean formalities if arriving from the Atlantic, the Pacific, or reaching the end of your trip south through the Chilean channels. It is principally a naval base and boasts of being the 'southernmost town in the world'. You will get a friendly welcome here, and although you will find the shopping far less sophisticated than in Ushuaia, few regret a visit to Puerto Williams and the *Micalvi* Yacht Club which declares itself the 'southernmost yacht club in the world'.

Approaches

Radio well ahead with your intentions by calling *Puerto Williams Radio* on VHF 16 – if they have not already called you.

Give your destination as *Micalvi* and officers will be there to meet you. Large yachts are sometimes given permission to anchor in the creek that leads to *Micalvi*.

Lights

Punta Gusano Fl(3)R.9s10m3M (red GRP tower) stands at the end of Peninsula Zanartu, which gives Puerto Williams its all important shelter from the west.

This is the only place in the Beagle Channel where you will have to tackle sandbank navigation; the Banco Herradura spit extends 1M NE from Punta Gusano and its outer limit is marked by a north cardinal mark Fl.Q. However, most yachts will find sufficient water to cut across the bank and, although shallow, it appears safe to cross when 50m beyond the Punta Gusano light.

Puerto Williams looking north
Vicky Jackson

Looking W towards the airport, note the spit extending to the north
Paul Heiney

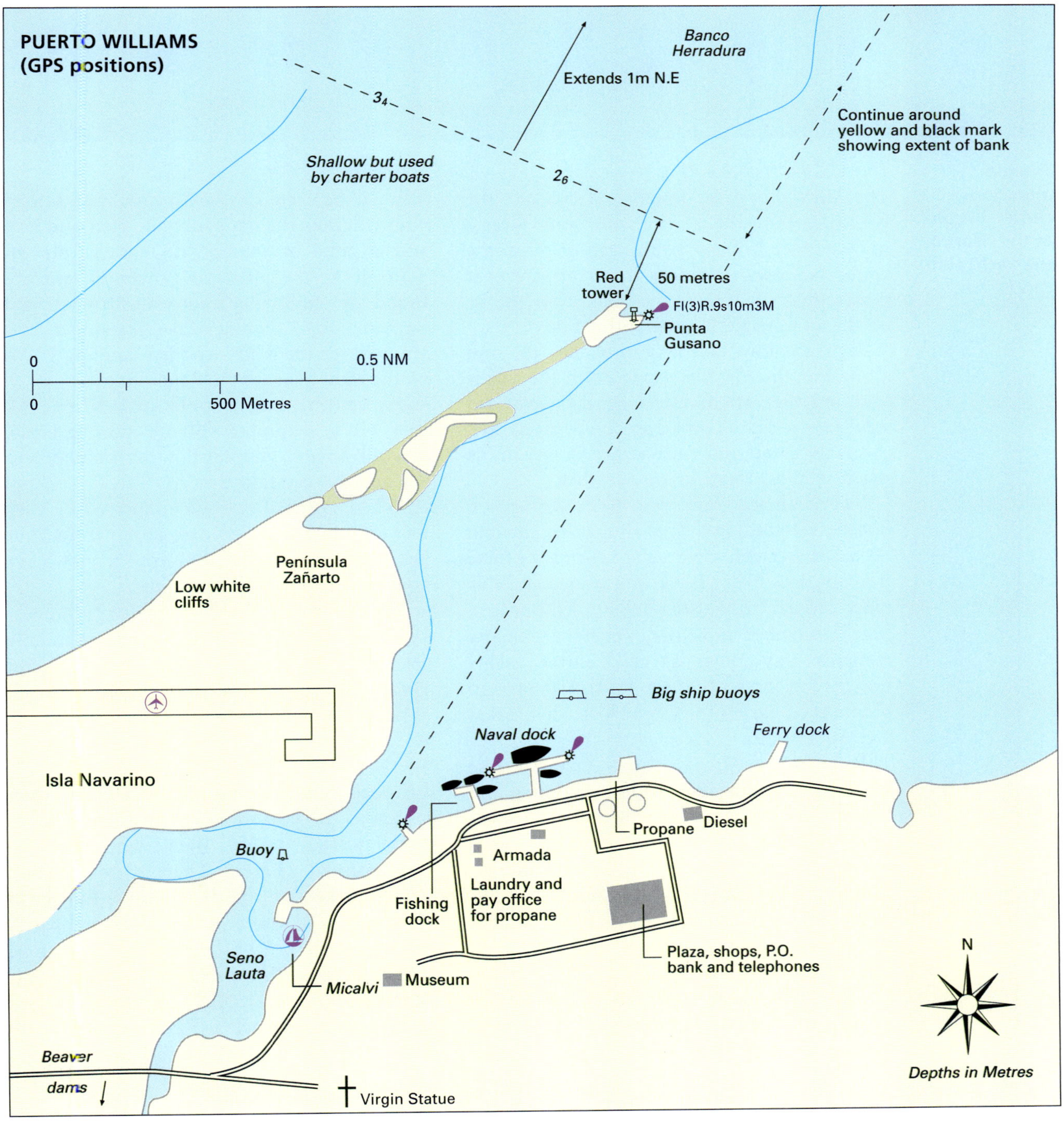

The old munitions carrier, *Micalvi*, at the heart of the yacht club
Paul Heiney

The *Micalvi* Yacht Club

The *Micalvi* is to be found in a creek to the west of the naval base and you should steer a mid-channel course being aware that the water shallows outwards from the spit that divides the two arms of the creek. At night, be on the lookout for large mooring buoys.

It is shallow in the approaches to, and alongside, the *Micalvi*, especially if the tide is low and the raft of boats on the westward side is more than 3 or 4 deep. Once alongside, this is the safest and most secure facility in the Beagle Channel, safe in any weather.

The Club secretary, who has an office on board, is helpful and English may be spoken; he will direct you towards the *Armada* office. It is not possible to book in advance and this place can get busy at the height of the season (late December onwards). There are many comings and goings as the charter yachts bring their crews across from Ushuaia to obtain their *zarpe*s for Cape Horn, the Drake, and Antarctica.

Between the *Micalvi* and the shore is the quieter side of the ship, with less coming and going; this is where you will find the longer term residents. If you are planning to leave your boat here, this is the side to choose. Check how much rise of tide you will need to get round there as there are shallow patches and a rock off the port bow of the *Micalvi*; best attempted at high water.

The Club is greatly welcoming, the charges modest, the fire always burning, and the pisco sours (Chilean national drink) flow freely.

Formalities

You will be visited at the *Micalvi* by an officer who will take the name of your boat and give you a time at which you should present yourself at the *Armada* offices. These are found by following the waterfront round until the road divides. Take the upper, and you will see the white wooden building 100m on the right beneath the flagpole.

Expect little English to be spoken here, but they will be helpful. If you are entering Chile, you will have to give a list of safety equipment etc, and this can take time.

When inspecting your paperwork, they will be looking for an exit stamp from your last port so it is vital that you do not leave your previous port without one.

There may be a small charge for light dues.

The passport and customs officers usually attend at the time of your appointment. Otherwise, you may have to present yourself at the town hall a short walk away.

Puerto Williams - the town

A much smaller and simpler place than Ushuaia. If you have a taste for more sophisticated foods then you will be disappointed here. There are several 'supermarkets', modest by European standards, and you will find all of the basics but little variety. All fish and meat seems to be frozen. It is worth wandering the back streets of the town for there are many smaller shops to be discovered, such as bakeries, which may offer things the bigger shops do not have.

The 'city centre' *Paul Heiney*

There is a small restaurant in what is called the Centro Comercial, but it is mostly of the fast-food variety. Good food can be had at a hotel to the east of the town.

The bank has an ATM which takes most cards. The *Micalvi* has WiFi.

Diesel is available in cans from a filling station on the seafront road beneath the *Armada* office. Most gas bottles can be generously filled.

There is a hardware store but opening times seem a little random.

This is a good base for walking expeditions on Navarino Island.

Leaving a boat in the Beagle

Puerto Williams is the only safe place to leave a boat unattended for any period of time and the Chileans are quite accustomed to it.

A useful contact is Denis Chevallay (fuegia@usa.net) who acts as Mr. Fixit. Swiss born and speaking French and English, he lives at the east end of town and can arrange most things from gas to laundry. If asked, he will open up your boat while you are away to let some air through. He will also act as caretaker and attend to your boat if it needs to be moved to allow others to leave. His charges are modest. Denis may also appear on your deck, unannounced, having picked some fresh herbs from what is the best tended garden in Puerto Williams. It is possible that he is the most southerly strawberry grower in the world.

If you are leaving your boat in his care, there is a small formality to be gone through to legally assign care of your boat to him. This requires the signing of a form – which Denis prints out – and then together you must go to the town hall where it is presented to a notary, entered in a book, and a few dollars taken off you. It is quite possible that once this has happened Denis owns your boat until you return. It's best not to ask.

EASTERN APPROACHES TO THE BEAGLE CHANNEL

The Le Maire Strait

This narrow passage between Staten Island and Tierra del Fuego was discovered in 1616 by Dutchmen Jacob Le Maire and Willem Schouten, shortly before their discovery of Cape Horn.

Lights in the Le Maire Strait

Cabo San Diego 54°39.23S 65°07.35W
Fl(3)W.28s39m13M white, square concrete tower

Faro Le Maire 54°47.6S 64°42.67W
Fl(3)W.32s46m9M

Note the similar characteristics of these two lights

Also of use, though further south, is
Faro Buen Suceso 54°49.04S 65°13.5W
Fl(2)16s57m8M

Yachts which have sailed south from Argentina and are heading for the Beagle Channel will be seeking to position themselves for a safe transit of the notorious Le Maire Strait which lies between Cabo San Diego on the west, and Isla Los Estados (Staten Island) to the east. Although 16M wide, its deadly reputation is earned from the ferocity of the tidal flow which when set against the often strong prevailing winds can produce severe overfalls and standing waves. Waves as high as 10m have been reported and these would be survived by only the most skilfully handled and strongest boats. However, there are ways to avoid the most dangerous areas and detailed knowledge of the tides is essential if you are to make a safe and trouble-free passage.

Things to remember:

- *Make sure you know the times of HW at Bahía Buen Suceso (and double check it).*
- The flood tide runs north and slack water occurs at roughly HW and LW.
- The flow is regular in the middle of the channel, but can accelerate unpredictably in the shallow areas off Cabo San Diego

Eastern approach to the Beagle Channel *Paul Heiney*

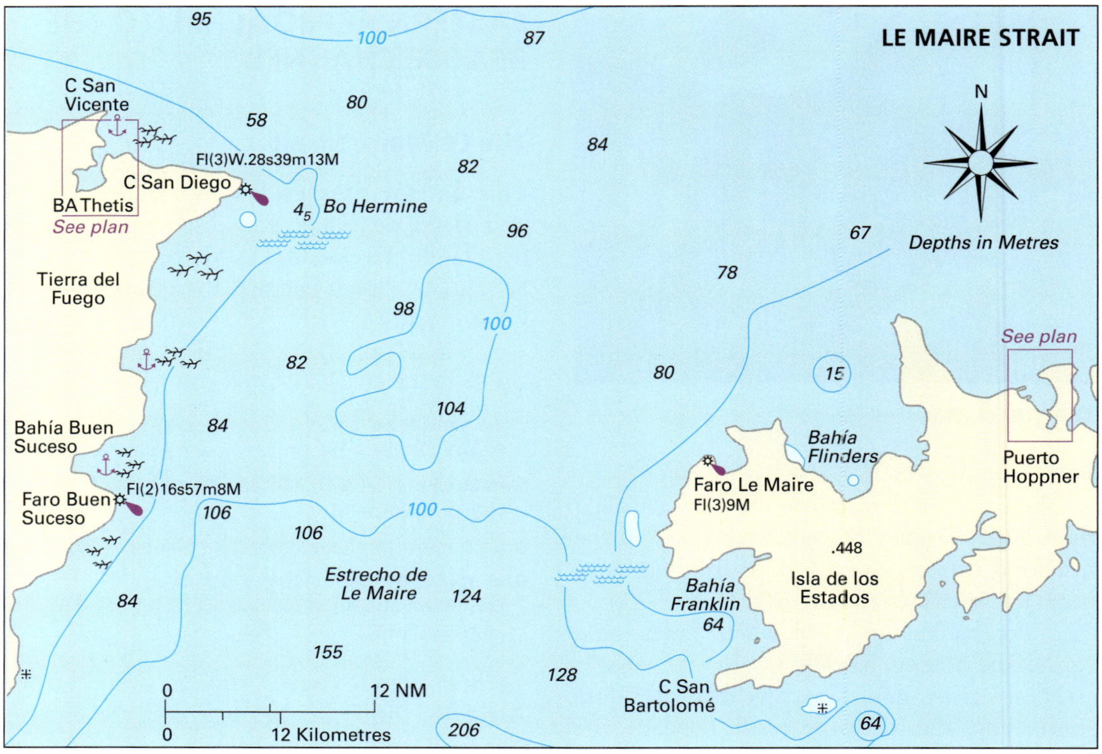

and the eastern tip of Staten Island – these are the most dangerous parts of the channel. Give San Diego a berth of at least 8M, and Staten Island 5M.

- In areas where turbulence is likely to be found, given good visibility the white water will be seen from quite a distance.
- The flow peaks 1 hour before HW and 5 hours after HW.
- You need a south-going tide to get through the Le Maire and if strong S or SW winds are forecast then you should wait.
- Fortunately, there are places where you can linger and wait for ideal conditions.

Staten Island

Puerto Hoppner

54°46'.9S 64°24'.5W
Charts BA 1373; Chile 13400

This is a most remarkable and memorable anchorage and a diversion here will be well rewarded. It is a good resting place after the long haul south, and it will give you inspiration to sail onwards to the Beagle Channel.

The 'harbour' consists of two parts. The entrance is found at 54°45'.2S 64°25'.8W but the centre of the outer harbour is generally too deep for anchoring. Instead, enter by passing Islote Montegrosso on either side and turn sharp to starboard south of Punta Ross; anchorage in Caleta Benitez can be found close to the shore with the possibility of taking lines ashore. This is a good place to wait for tidal conditions to enter the inner lagoon, which should be your aim.

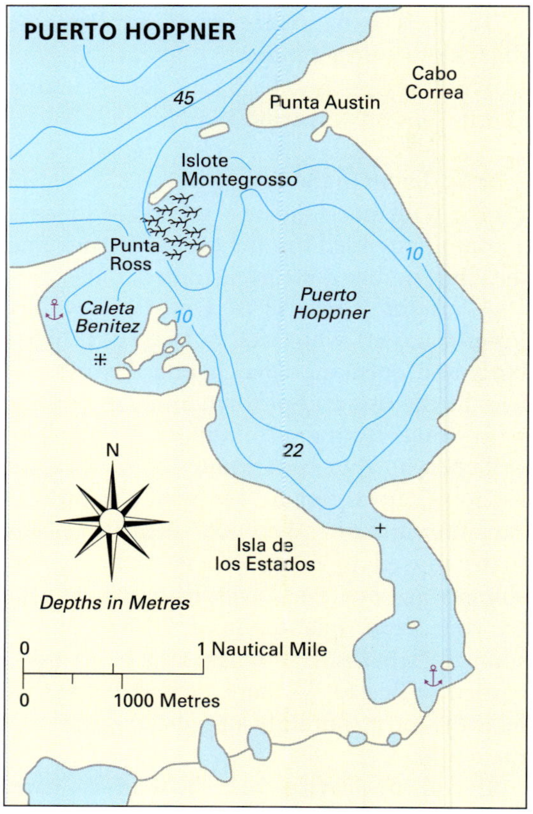

To enter the inner lagoon requires you to navigate around a rock in the middle of the channel at the narrowest part. It is easily seen at LW, but at HW it can be just awash. Leave the rock to port, keeping closer to the W shore. At LW, the minimum depth here is 2m.

***Wild Song* in Puerto Hoppner** *Paul Heiney*

Nasty rock in Hoppner inner lagoon entrance - leave to port when entering
Tim Barker

Because the flow can be up to five knots, HW slack is the time to enter (and leave) and this occurs at HW Buen Suceso +2.

Once through, keep over to the E shore to find a small wooded island ahead. It is possible to pass either side to anchor between it and the shore, but leaving it to port provides a safer passage. Anchor behind the island with lines ashore. This anchorage is said to be free from *williwaws*.

Staten Island is a national nature reserve and permission may be needed to land ashore although it is far from clear who might give it. Few visitors, though, are able to resist climbing the hills around from where the true splendour of this anchorage is revealed.

Isla Grande de Tierra del Fuego

Bahía Thetis

WP 54° 37'95S 65° 14'10W
Charts Argentina 95H, 417, 418, BA 1332, 1373, Chile 13000, 1340

This is the only safe anchorage along this tip of Tierra del Fuego and it lies between Cabo San Vicente and Cabo San Diego.

The outer bay gives shelter, but yachts which can take the ground or have very shallow draft can work their way towards the inner harbour for total shelter. The outer anchorage is used by ships, for whom onshore transit marks have been provided bearing 252°. Anchor tc find the best shelter, mindful of the kelp which is thick and

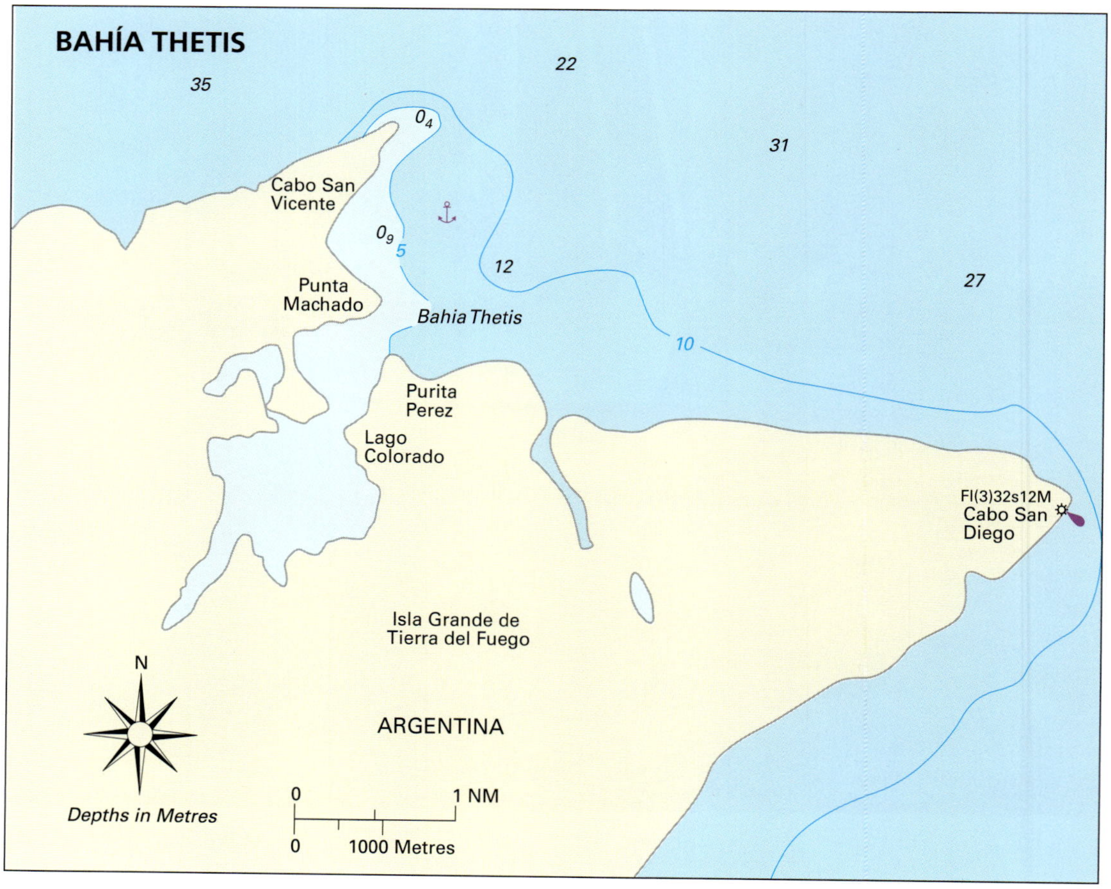

plentiful both here and in the approaches. Needless to say, any hint of a N or E wind requires a swift departure.

Note that if intending to round Cabo San Diego, a berth of at least 8 miles should be given to avoid the race and overfalls.

Bahía Buen Suceso

WP 54° 48'S 65° 15'W

Charts BA 1373; Chile 13400

Light Faro Buen Suceso (on the southern tip of the bay) Fl(2)16s57m9M (white tower with red bands)

Baliza Martíns Lopez (on the shore, to the south of the Navy hut) Fl.W.5s10m8M (red metal pyramid with white bands)

There is shelter to be found here in winds from N through to SW, and for good reason is it called the Bay of Good Success – although the name derives from the name of a ship that was part of a Portuguese fleet of 1618. It provides a convenient place on the western side of the Le Maire strait to wait for weather or tide, and it is an easy crossing to here from Staten Island if you have previously paid a visit to Puerto Hoppner.

This wide, open bay was visited by Darwin aboard the *Beagle*, and he wrote on 17 December 1832:

> *A little after noon we doubled Cape St Diego and entered the famous Strait of Le Maire. We kept close to the Fuegian shore, but the outline of the rugged, inhospitable Staten land was visible amidst the clouds. In the afternoon we anchored in the Bay of Good Success...The harbour consists of a fine piece of water half surrounded by low rounded mountains of clay-slate, which are covered to the water's edge by one dense gloomy forest...At night it blew a gale of wind, and heavy squalls from the mountains swept past us. It would have been a bad time out at sea, and we, as well as others, may call this Good Success Bay.*

You will find no Fuegians here today; instead there is a small outpost of the Argentine navy in a wooden hut on the shore which will call you on VHF 16 as soon as you hove into view or appear on their radar.

This lonely outpost is manned mostly by young recruits who spend 40 days at a time here and become ever more anxious about the arrival of their relief boat from Ushuaia – their only way out. They are famously hospitable and a run ashore is well rewarded.

There is a good anchorage on sand on the N side of the bay, and although landing can be difficult if there is any swell running, it can usually be achieved towards the northern side of the bay where a river runs into the sea.

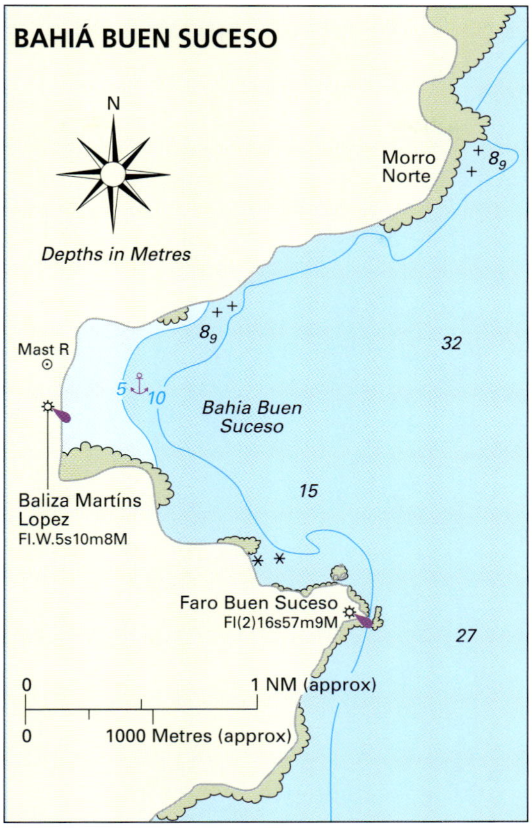

Cabo Buen Suceso

Although the Beagle Channel is now within your grasp, there are still a few remaining challenges. In particular, Cabo Buen Suceso, which you must round before heading westwards and can prove troublesome in headwinds. There is a permanent easterly tidal set here driven by the wind, and it can attain rates of up to 3 knots. It is impossible to make headway against it in any headwind. If a strong SW wind is blowing, it is better to wait in Buen Suceso for it to drop or change direction before attempting to make westwards. The flow can change quite suddenly: the author found it impossible to round this headland against a SW wind of force 5 and adverse current, but the next day motored round in lighter airs and found no adverse current at the same time of day.

It is a good 80M from here to the first decent harbour on the northern shore of the Beagle Channel, at Harberton, and you should be certain of the weather forecast for the next 36 hours before leaving Bahía Buen Suceso.

Remember, until you have cleared into Ushuaia, and then into Chile, all Chilean harbours on the south side of the Beagle Channel are forbidden.

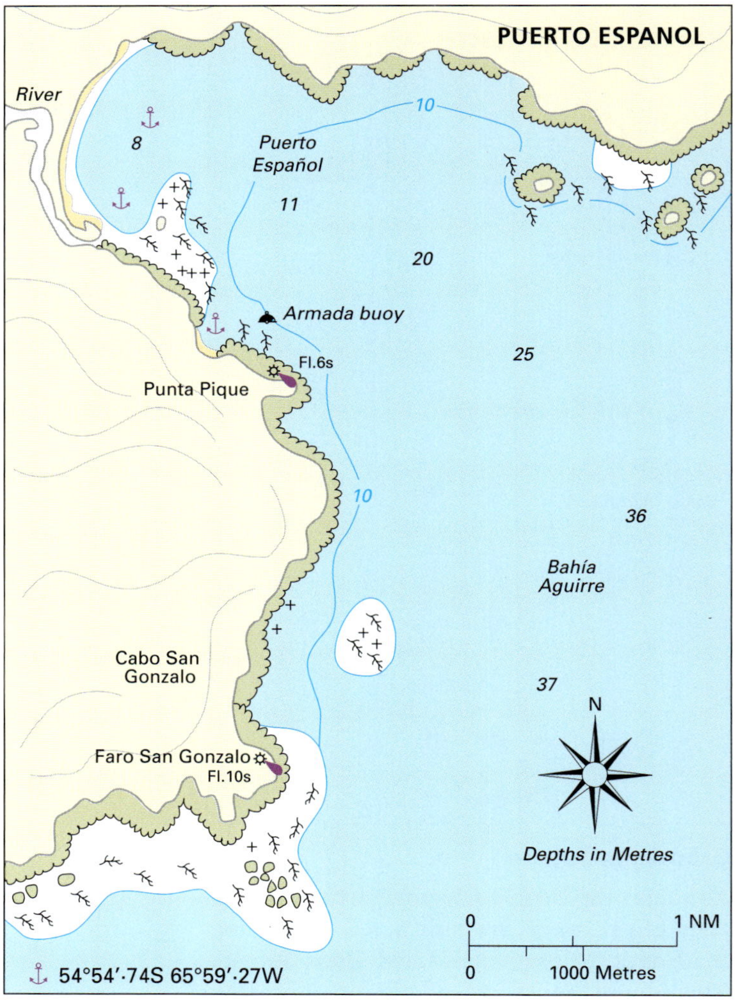

Puerto Español

54°54'50S 65°58'9W

Charts UK 559, 1373, Chile 13000, 1340

Lights

Faro San Gonzalo on Punta Kinnaird Fl.10s38m7M
Baliza Punta Pique Fl.6s9m6M (white conical tower)

At the western end of Bahía Aguirre is the useful anchorage of Puerto Español where the long haul westwards from Buen Suceso can be broken.

There are two lights to help you identify the bay.

This anchorage could safely be approached at night with the steep cliffs giving good radar reflections, and two lights to guide you. The light structure on Punta Kinnaird gives good guidance by day. Give a wide berth to the rocks lying between Punta Lobos and Punta Kinnaird.

This bay has two anchorages which provide shelter from W winds although some swell may enter. The first is just north of Punta Pique where an *Armada* buoy may be in place. It is possible to anchor close under in 3m sand with good holding, but beware of *rachas* which tumble down the mountain to your south.

An alternative would be in the NW corner of Puerto Espanol which would give more shelter in strong NW winds.

There is a certain romance to this place, and a morbid feel too. The estancia, or estate, was founded by a young Yugoslavian who came here in search of gold. Failing to find any, he took labouring jobs for 14 years until he had money to buy a piece of land at the head of the bay where the farm buildings and houses still stand. His girlfriend was true to him, and waited until he had collected enough money and then came to join him. His children eventually took over, but the place was abandoned by the family in the 1970s. It is about as remote a place as you could wish for. It might take a week to reach Ushuaia from here, and that would be by horseback.

A sadder story is that of the missionary, Allen Gardiner who, traumatised by the loss of his wife, came to Patagonia to establish a floating mission which would travel the bays and islands, spreading the Good Word amongst the native people who were a wild and uneducated race. Fleeing for their lives from natives intent on killing them, Gardiner and his men were overtaken by bad weather and blown into Puerto Español, where they took shelter in caves. In need of food, Gardiner sailed back to Caleta Banner on Isla Picton some 30M to the west, the harbour from which he had been evicted. It was a piece of considerable seamanship. Caleta Banner was named by Gardiner from Psalm 60: *'Though hast given a banner for those that fear thee, that it might be displayed because of the truth.'*

A cache of food had been buried there and he quickly secured it as the natives gathered once again, clutching their spears and intent on murder. Optimistically, Gardiner left a note for any friendly passer-by – 'You will find us in Spanish Harbour.' He set off and made it back to Español. But no rescue came, the food soon ran out, scurvy and starvation followed. Gardiner died in the cave which you can see if you choose the anchorage behind Punta Pique.

Puerto Harberton

54°52.7S 67° 19'5W
Charts Chile 13000, 1301, 1318

This is an easy harbour to enter with good shelter and a beacon on Punta Harberton to aid identification. The shelter is good in everything except SE, the only drawback being that the holding is patchy due to large areas of kelp and an anchorage must be chosen with care. By applying for permission to the *estancia*, it is possible to lie alongside the jetty. There is a large mooring buoy in the middle of the harbour which is unlit and should be identified if entering at night.

This is a major tourist attraction hereabouts and there will be many tripper boats arriving from Ushuaia in the summer season. You will find your first restaurant and tea shop for many miles. You will be welcome to dine, but supplies cannot be bought. However, the owners are helpful and welcoming and will do anything they can to aid you.

This is the site of the first *estancia* to be established on Tierra del Fuego in 1886 by Thomas Bridges, a missionary held in high regard by the government of the day. The house that still stands bears close examination for it is built entirely of wood and was brought out, piece by piece, from Harberton in Devon, UK – the world's first flat-pack house. An English garden has been created and has the only British daffodils to be found in Tierra del Fuego.

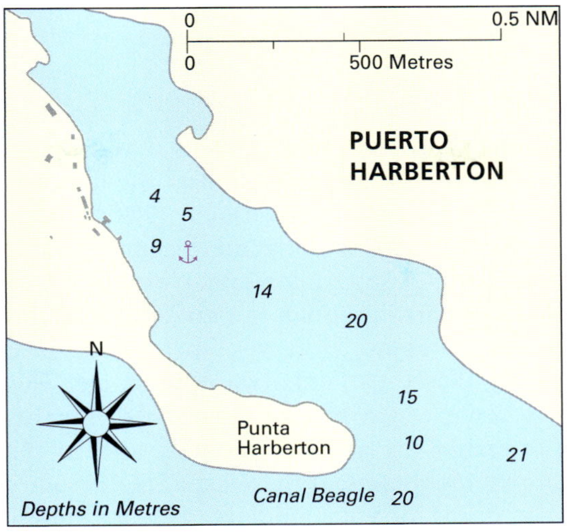

The story of the Bridges family is a captivating one and you should not cruise here without a copy of *Uttermost Part of the Earth*, by E Lucas Bridges, Thomas's son. This is a highly readable account of life amongst the Fuegians in the late 19th century.

There is a bookshop here and *Tierra del Fuego* by R Natalie P Goodall, the present heir to the Bridges family and resident at Harberton, gives an encyclopaedic insight into the culture, flora and fauna of this unique part of the world.

Harberton and the heads (right) *Paul Heiney*

Ushuaia

54°50S 6816W

Ushuaia, in the Yaghan language, means 'bay facing east'. Remember this as a warning if there is any strong east wind in the forecast, although this is rare and usually fleeting.

Most yachts cruising the Beagle Channel will call at Ushuaia for either provisions or small repairs, although the range of facilities is very limited. However, there is food a plenty, diesel, gas and a warm welcome. This is a town which presents two faces: towards the sea in the summer months, and to the snowy mountains in the winter. The result is that if any of your cold weather clothing is lacking, then this is the place to re-stock. Remember the local wisdom that it can snow here on any day of the year since you are only 500M north of the Antarctic peninsula and a southerly wind can rapidly bring cold air towards you, even in summer.

Approaching Ushuaia

The approaches present no problem. If arriving from the E and staying close to the N shore to stay in Argentine waters, be aware of the isolated Rocas Lawrence and the rocks surrounding it roughly halfway between Ushuaia and Gable Island:

54°52.7S 67°52.4W
VQ(6)+LFl.W.10s9m8M

Identify the Islote Les Eclaireurs lighthouse

54°52.44N, 68°05.04W
Fl.WR.5s22m10M (red conical tower with white band)

after which there are no hazards if a course is made directly towards the town.

Formalities

You should give the *Prefectura* 30 minutes notice of your arrival by calling on VHF 16. The callsign is *L3P (Lima, Tres, Pappa)*. They will not answer to any other callsign. You will be asked again the questions with which you will now be quite familiar – name of boat,

flag, persons on board etc. You will also be asked at which club you intend to land – either AFASyn, or Club Náutico. For an initial visit, AFASyn has more facilities and the dock is in better condition with electricity alongside and a Club secretary who speaks English (2014) who can offer advice on any matter.

Once alongside, you will be visited by a *Prefectura* officer who will examine your passports but you will still have to attend the *Prefectura* office – he will advise. All crew must attend. To find the office, you will need to walk the dusty track towards town, along the way you will notice the whereabouts of the supermarkets, the filling station to which you must bring a can for diesel (no diesel alongside), and also the customs office which is at the root of the commercial pier (unlikely that any English will be spoken here). If you get lost, there is a tourist office near the entrance to the pier.

It can snow any day of the year
Paul Heiney

The *Prefectura* is found by walking northwards the full length of the waterfront until the town starts to peter out. On your left, set back from the road and halfway up a hill, is a large, pine-clad building flying the Argentine flag. This is the *Prefectura*. Some English is spoken here and the service is courteous. Next you must go to the Customs office (*aduana*) which you will already have

Evening in Ushuaia
Vicky Jackson

identified. Expect customs to be slow as they also deal with cruise ships and commercial traffic, and if you have not already done so at a previous customs office you will be asked to provide a list of all equipment (radios, gps, radar etc.) and personal possessions (camera, ipads etc). It would be wise to prepare this in advance, including serial numbers.

A word of warning about the Customs here. Relations between the Ushuaia customs and visiting yachts have been difficult in the past. Private yachts are unlikely to encounter problems, but any suspicion that you are a charter yacht and trying to conceal the fact may result in endless delays, and possibly fines. Such yachts have been impounded here. Honesty is the only policy.

Current legislation (2016) allows yachts to stay in Argentine waters for up to 8 months, after which you must leave the country. If you have been making a slow cruise south from the River Plate, Ushuaia allows you an easy opportunity to drop across to Puerto Williams, in Chile and then return to Argentina having 'reset the clock'.

Anchoring

Anchoring in Ushuaia is not recommended, even if a space can be found; the harbour is quite shallow and the holding poor.

Club AFASyN

Pasaje Fique s/n, 9410 Ushuaia
✆ +54 2901 437 842/435 805 *Fax* +54 2901 443 404
VHF 16 0900–2100
clubafasyn@speedy.com.ar
Open 1500-1700 Mon-Fri, 1300-1600 Saturday

Charges to lie alongside at AFASyN are quite modest and have the advantage of electricity and water, as well as a single shower and toilet in a block at the pier head. The Club itself is a major centre of diving, kayaking, dinghy sailing and all watersports. There is a strong community atmosphere alongside, especially amongst the charter skippers who take on passengers here. There is also a small workshop which might be available for a small fee. The club can also be used as a postal address, and offers WiFi. After a while you may tire of the long walk to the town, in which case it is quite usual to take the dinghy across the harbour and tie up at Club Náutico's pier.

It might be possible to use the slipway to haul shallow draft boats given a suitable rise and fall of tide, or to dry out at the root of the pier.

The Club Náutico, which lies to the north, is not really a club at all, more of a restaurant. It is nearer the town but closer to the traffic. There are no facilities other than those provided by the jetty but cruisers report a warm welcome alongside. It is a useful alternative.

Services

The town will provide pretty much everything you could ask for, including gas and laundry. It is reported that most gas bottles can be filled.

Although there are no dedicated facilities for yacht repairs, there are countless workshops and diesel engineers who can give help and the best advice will be found through the secretary's office at AFASyN.

Most banks have ATMs. WiFi is commonplace now in the cafes and bars.

The two largest supermarkets are close to AFASyN, but there are many smaller shops and bakeries to be found by exploring the back streets. If sailing onwards into Chile, you should certainly stock up here as this offers the widest selection, certainly of fresh food, you will find for another thousand miles.

On larger yachts you may see the carcass of a lamb hanging from the rigging. This is now becoming something of a local custom for visiting yachts, and butchers in Ushuaia can supply them to order. Because of the generally low humidity and cool temperatures, the meat stays fresh for quite a while and joints are hacked off over a period of a week or so and prove very useful for boats without fridges or freezers.

Charts can be ordered from the *Prefectura*.

Support

For logistical support and advice, Ushaia Logistics, **http://rvdiaz.com**, is a very experienced and effective organisation and you should contact the dynamic Roxanna Diaz who seems able to fix most things. She offers her services as Port Officer (free) to members of many clubs including the Ocean Cruising Club and the Seven Seas Cruising Association (SSCA).

Club AFASyN *Paul Heiney*

Ushuaia *Vicky Jackson*

Stocking up in Ushuaia
Vicky Jackson

Crew changes in the Beagle Channel

You would think that getting from Ushuaia to Puerto Williams was simple but there is no regular transport link and travelling between the two, other than on your own boat, needs careful planning. The option of a light aircraft flight between the two airports, mentioned in some pilot books, no longer exists (2015). The author left his boat in Puerto Williams one November and had to hope that a yacht might arrive to take him back to Ushuaia from where his flight was booked. In fact, it is not unusual for yachts to be used for this purpose and you may get several requests for a lift to the other side while you are alongside in Ushuaia. The authorities have no problem with this providing all the immigration and emigration procedures are gone through.

There is a seasonal high speed tourist ferry which crosses daily (depending on weather) between Ushuaia and Puerto Navarino on Navarino Island 6M due south. It departs from the main pier in Ushuaia where the tourist boats are found. At Puerto Navarino, you will be met by a truck which will take you on a pleasant if bumpy ride to Puerto Williams (about an hour) where you can conduct formalities. The truck will then take you to the *Micalvi*. This is not cheap at $115 per person (2015). Sometimes, the truck ride is charged separately and for this you will need Chilean pesos, but Argentine pesos to pay on the ferry. US dollars may or may not be accepted. There may also be other small amounts to pay for 'port tax'. Make sure you have both currencies with you. Again, US dollars can be useful too. Remember that getting a hitch on a yacht is the cheapest option.

Because of the complexity and uncertainty of travel between these two harbours, you might want to consider flying out of Puerto Williams if leaving your boat there. There are regular, and spectacular, flights to Punta Arenas from where there are connections to all the main hubs in Chile. Similarly, flights from Ushuaia airport will fly you to Buenos Aires and further connections. In extremis, it is possible to fly out of Puerto Williams to Punta Arenas and then take a six hour bus ride back to Ushuaia, an exhausting and expensive way of travelling 25M.

It is not possible to leave a boat unattended for any period of time in Ushuaia. Although perfectly safe in winds from south through north and as far round as north east, any strong easterly wind, although rare and often short-lived, will blow directly into the harbour and can raise a nasty, short sea.

Depending on the time of year, a direct service may be running between Ushuaia and Puerto Navarino. Consult the websites below to check times and dates:

http://islanavarino.com/2013/10/05/by-boat-from-ushuaia/

www.fernandezcampbell.com/navegacion_ushuaia_puerto_williams.html

CAPE HORN

The name of this infamous headland comes from the town of Hoorn in the Netherlands from whence the Dutch adventurer, Schouten, set off to make his first voyage to the Horn in 1616. Cape Horn itself is a grim, black granite headland 400m high but physically less imposing than many others; there are far more impressive ones to be found around the coasts of Europe. But it has a fearsome reputation all of its own, and with good reason. The Southern Ocean has had an unhindered passage all the way around the globe at this latitude leading to ever-growing swells fuelled by strong westerly winds. These winds can blow with violence, and weather systems come through at speed making for dangerously changeable conditions as a result of a never ending meteorological battle between the cold Antarctic air and the warmer winds of the Pacific. Add to this the shallowing of the water where the Drake narrows between the Horn and the Antarctic peninsula and you have a recipe for a true maelstrom.

Be cautious about claiming you have 'rounded the Horn' for you have to have achieved more than just sailed past it in order to claim that distinction. The International Association of Cape Horners say that a proper 'rounding' is defined as a passage from 50°S on one side of South America to 50°S on the other – about a thousand miles. 'Doubling the Horn' is an expression frequently heard and is defined as above.

Although it is unlikely to be a problem in the days of GPS navigation, you should beware of 'false Cape Horn' if approaching from the west. This stands at the S end of

Sapphire of London **rounds Cape Horn**
Vicky Jackson

Hoste Island in 54°43'S 68°03'W and is where countless ships have foundered having thought they had rounded the Horn, only to find themselves on the lee shore of the Wollaston Islands dead ahead.

The Chilean navy has a station on Cape Horn which includes a chapel and a lighthouse and a large memorial featuring the silhouette of an albatross in memory of sailors lost in these waters.

If you are expecting a statuesque lighthouse befitting its iconic position, you will be disappointed – the light is a mere 4m fibreglass tower. It is also worth noting that there are two lights here, as the chart will reveal, only one of them on Cape Horn itself. If you are able to land on the Horn (see below) you will find a plaque beneath the albatross memorial, in Spanish, which translates

I am the albatross that waits for you
at the end of the world.
I am the forgotten soul of the
dead sailors lost rounding the Horn
from all the seas in the world.
But they did not die in the wild seas.
Today they fly on my wings towards eternity
in the high cry of the Antarctic winds
Sara Vial

Planning for Cape Horn

It is but a small step from Puerto Williams to Cape Horn, roughly 70M, but it calls for some planning and an awareness of the difficulties.

A first glance at the chart will reveal an easy passage to the west of Isla Navarino, south through the Canal Murray and then in the lee of Isla Hoste pretty much all the way to the Horn. Sadly, this is forbidden. As long as yachts have been sailing here, permission for passage through the Canal Murray has been denied except in the rarest of circumstances. This is said to be for 'strategic' reasons, and you do not have to be much of a strategist to realise that allowing vessels free passage through these Chilean waters would provide an easier access to Ushuaia from the south. There is an uneasy territorial truce here.

For cruisers, this means that the *Armada* will dictate your route down to the Horn and a rich and complex cruising ground will be closed off to you.

You must apply for your *zarpe* before leaving, do not go without one. Your permitted route will be clearly stated. If you want to try and negotiate, take a chart with you. You will get a 'yes' or a 'no', further argument is pointless. Their reasoning is that they wish to know where you are likely to be in case you need rescue; in these waters this argument has some force.

A warning about charts. You will most likely be navigating on Chilean charts *13600* and *13200*. The accuracy of the cartography outside the main shipping channel must always be questioned and it is far from clear to which chart datum they are drawn – there is no indication on the chart itself. Transferring of positions from GPS to chart cannot be relied on. This is a place where, again, eyeball navigation must play a large part, and those old hand-bearing compass skills will once again prove invaluable.

Your most likely route will be eastwards from Puerto Williams, turning south at the eastern end of Isla Navarino, through the Paso Picton, and then the Paso Goree passing between Navarino and Lennox.

Once clear of Paso Goree, a course roughly S for 30M will take you to 55°47S 67°07W and you will be between the N end of Isla Deceit and the eastern tip of Isla Freycinet.

From here, shape a course for the Paso Mar Del Sur (this will be listed on your *zarpe*) to find a rather feeble light marking rocks halfway between Isla Herschel and Isla Deceit at the narrowest part of the passage. This is the Isolete Carrasco, Fl.5s30m4M. Note that this light does not appear in the *Admiralty List of Lights*. You can pass either side but the E passage is the most commonly used.

Once clear of the rocks, you can make directly to the west or south, depending on the wind, and thence make a passage round the Horn. However, the passage to the north of Isla Hornos may be more problematical than it appears for there can be a considerable tidal flow through here and you will most likely be facing a headwind. Given that you are also vulnerable to Pacific swells, many yachts have found this short 10M passage to be challenging.

However, there is some satisfaction when you arrive at a point where, in a W wind, you can bear away and make a quick run down to the Horn. The western side of Isla Hornos is more jagged and intimidating than the chart would lead you to expect. Be aware of isolated rocks Ra Robinson and Ra Bascuñan shown on both charts.

Another permitted route likely to appear on your *zarpe* allows you to take the Canal Franklin north of Isla Herschel and then take the Paso Suazo heading south for the Horn from there. It should be noted that although the Canal Franklin appears to be a simple passage, which is lit and apparently sheltered, it has often been the case that yachts have

struggled against wind, swell and tide and had to retreat to await a change in the conditions.

It is worth stating again that conditions in this area can change suddenly for the worse and the weather does not always bear any relation to the forecast. It is better to set off for the Horn in hope rather than expectation.

Anchoring off the Horn

Caleta Leon, Isla Hornos

55°58′S 67°13′W

It is possible to anchor in the lee of the Horn where landing is possible if the swell allows but there is much kelp which forces you to

Toro
Adventure 2013

anchor further off than you would wish, in areas where the depths might be as much as 15–20m. The *Armada* have cut a pathway through the kelp to assist landing. Because the holding can be poor, a yacht should not be left unattended. Some yachts have chosen to heave to while crew members take turns to go ashore.

If you are able to land, you can take the steps to the *Armada* station where a VHF 16 call ahead is recommended. Logbooks and passports can be stamped and souvenirs bought.

Alongside and at anchor, Puerto Toro
Máire Wilkes

Harbours and anchorages to and from Cape Horn

It would be as well to familiarise yourself with one or two harbours of refuge before you leave Puerto Williams so that you can get to shelter if conditions turn against you. There are several useful places on the way to the Horn. The most important are as follows.

Puerto Toro, Isla Navarino

55°04'S 67°04'W
Charts 13200, 13300
Light Fl.5s.7m6M white GRP tower, red band 4m 150°-vis-301°

There is a friendly *Armada* station here in what is one of the original settlements in Tierra del Fuego. There are many claims to being 'the most southerly' hereabouts, but you can say with some confidence that this is the most southerly village in the world.

If entering from S, be aware of shoal water extending from the headland beneath the light tower, which has two drying rocks. There is good protection here from all but E and NE winds, and the ground around is high. The bay is deep but it is possible to tie to the pier which is in good condition, although in the crab season this is a major centre for the

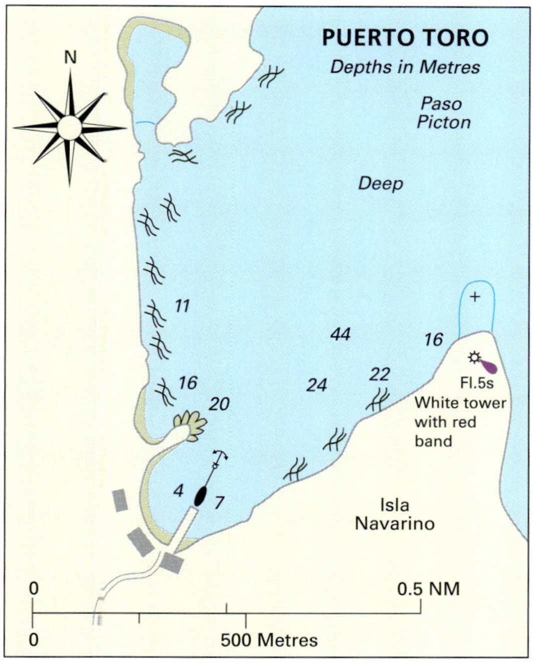

centolla-catching industry which makes use of a rough road between Toro and Puerto Williams to get the mighty crabs to market. The crab season is July to November.

The village is modest, and for no clear reason is home to a police training centre. There is a small shop which sells local crafts, and coffee may be available.

Caleta Martial, Isla Herschel

55° 49S 67°18W

This may be the only anchorage that your *zarpe* allows you to use on your way to or from the Horn. It provides good shelter and holding in all but E winds when you should call Cape Horn and request permission to move to Puerto Maxwell (below).

The approach is easy to identify as you will see a yellow sandy beach at the head of the bay. There are no dangers in the approach.

Of the two anchorages, the N one is better in N to W winds, and the southern in SW winds. Beware the force of the wind here when fronts are passing over.

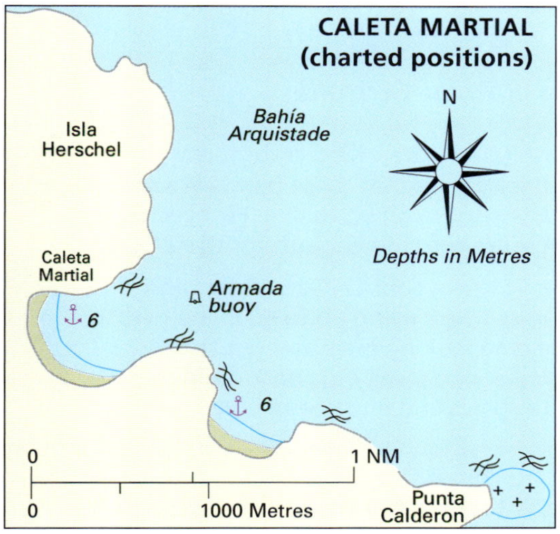

Caleta Martial anchorage, Isla Herschel
Vicky Jackson

Puerto Maxwell, Isla Hermite

55°49S 67°30W

This is the best anchorage in the area although with a fetch to the NE. Winds can be very strong here, but the *rachas* are infrequent. Take lines to the W shore and enjoy good walking.

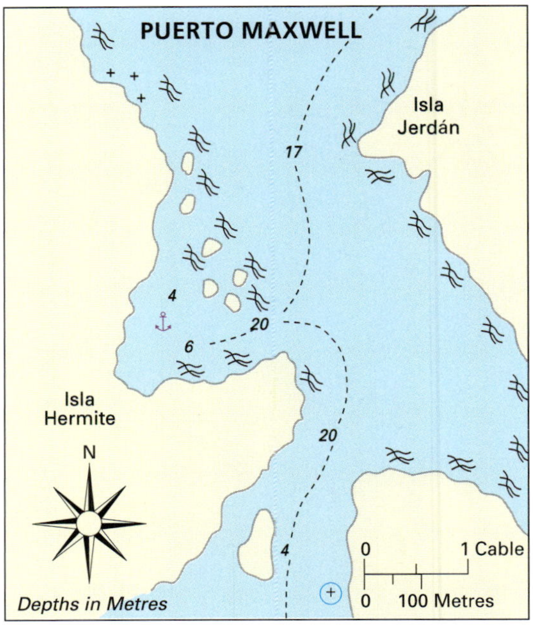

Cooking a King crab, or *Centolla*

Fishermen might well trade their King crabs for wine and other goods, but beware that these beasts are of considerable size and can weigh up to 4kg. Few yachts are equipped with saucepans big enough for these!

The *centolla* loves the deep, cold Chilean waters and it thrives on the rocky sea bed, living up to 600m below the surface. A fearsome looking creature, not the sort of thing you would want to meet on a dark night, it is well armoured with spikes and must be handled with care.

The meat of the King crab is said to be the sweetest of all the crabs, and the finest part is the *merus* section which is the upper part of the leg nearest the body. A knife inserted into the body and a deep, swift cut made towards the head will ensure a quick kill. Then remove the legs.

You need to come up with an arrangement whereby you can cook the legs in steam, rather than boiling water. With a large pan, a few inches of boiling water in the bottom and a tight fitting lid would do the trick. Put as many legs as you can in the pot, fasten the lid, and allow the legs to steam for up to eight minutes. A good tip: once you can smell the crab cooking, it's ready to eat.

Most yacht ovens are too small, but you might try baking them in a hot oven over a baking tray with little water in it. Make a parcel of the crab legs with foil to hold in the steam. About ten minutes should do it.

Eating King crab is no small task as the legs are spiny and the shell is tough. You may try a hammer, pincers, nutcrackers, or whatever else the toolbox provides. Your reward will be some of the finest crab you have ever tasted. It needs no more than a little butter, and possibly a squeeze of lemon if you have it.

King crabs - fearsome but delicious *Tim Barker*

5 THE FALKLAND ISLANDS AND SOUTH GEORGIA

THE FALKLANDS

A yacht that has sailed the 350M to the Falklands from the mountains and fjords of Patagonia will find far less drama in the Falklands landscape, and the little that there is diminishes the further east you sail, to be replaced by something far more subtle. The south and east coasts can be featureless making navigation based on observation more difficult. On the west coast, where rocky and craggy headlands are more easily identified, the sailing is said to be reminiscent of the Highlands of Scotland. The high and imposing headland on the western tip of New Island, Landsend Bluff (51°41′S 61°19′W) would be hard to miss. As would Cape Meredith (52°15′S 60°39′W) at the southern tip of West Falkland, which gains a height of 220m.

However, by the time you are well on your way to Stanley and sailing the eastern edge of East Falkland, you might feel you are amongst the high moors of England. It is hilly rather than mountainous, and this barren landscape of peat bog, moorland and tussock grass, interrupted by high, craggy outcrops, has been described as 'Dartmoor surrounded by sea'. However you choose to describe the landscape, the word that returns is 'enigmatic'. It is easy to relish the majesty of the mountains but to fully appreciate the landscape of the Falklands requires a different eye and perhaps a bit more effort. The rewards, though, are huge. To see the tall marsh grasses swaying in the wild wind, and the isolated white houses bathed in the orange glow of a setting sun, is to know that you have arrived in a place quite like no other.

There will be those who dismiss the islands as bleak, barren and windswept. When Darwin arrived here in March 1833 onboard the *Beagle*, he was also somewhat uncertain of the charms of the Falklands:

> *[The islands are] … remarkably easy to access to persons on foot; but half-concealed rivulets and numerous bogs, oblige a mounted traveller to be very cautious. There are no trees any where, but a small bush is plentiful in many vallies. Scarcely any views can be more dismal than that from the heights; moorland and black bog extend as far as the eye can discern, intersected by innumerable streams, and pools of yellowish brown water.*

Don't be put off by Darwin who was possibly having a bad day. For the navigator there can be no doubt that the estimated 15,000 miles of coastline make the Falklands one of the richest cruising grounds imaginable, with shelter and safe anchorage from any wind and weather, and enough creeks and anchorages to satisfy the most curious of sailors. Taken with a famously hospitable population and the overwhelming sense of true isolation, it is little wonder that those who have made the considerable effort to sail this far rarely find disappointment.

Goose Green, East Falkland
Tim Barker

The Falklands climate

The islands are cool and temperate with winds mainly from the west. The highest January temperature recorded is 24·4°C, the highest July temperature is 10°C (measured between 1929 and 1970). The record lows for the same months are –1·1° and –11·1°. These are extremes, however; average temperatures over 24 hours would in fact be 9°C in January and 2°C in July.

Swimmers should note that the sea temperatures in the summer hardly ever rise above 11°C due to the Antarctic Coastal Current which flows eastwards round the Horn before diverting northwards to form the chilly Falklands current. The islands are south of the northern limit for icebergs.

It is also worth remembering the significance of wind chill, which is an ever-present danger. Even in summer when walking on the shore, a combination of high winds and heavy rain can turn a pleasant ramble into a survival exercise. It is likely to be less of a problem while under sail since you tend to be expecting it and are suitably dressed. So, although the summer temperatures might not seem too challenging when seen on the page, it is generally safe to assume that it will 'feel cold'. Even in summer, a cabin heater will be welcome, if not strictly essential.

Rainfall is surprisingly low given that the islands lie in the paths of the depressions which have already rattled across the Southern Ocean, but much of their moisture has been dropped on the distant Andes which give the Falklands some beneficial rain-shadow effect. However, there is considerable variation in rainfall along the 150M length of the islands; the western islands being much drier than the east. Stanley, on the east coast, will expect an annual rainfall of 63cm per year (the same as the Midlands of England) while the island of Westpoint, 100M to the west, will receive half of that. The west is also reckoned to be blessed with more sunshine. Taking low rainfall together with the drying effects of the strong winds, parts of the islands can be described as semi-arid. Snow is possible in the winter months; in fact snow has been recorded in every month of the year, but snowfall here is rarely long-lasting.

The hours of daylight are long in the summer at these latitudes, but cloud cover restricts the warming effect of the sun. The average duration of summer sunlight is only 6 hours per day - those relying on solar panels to charge their batteries should take note.

Since wind is probably the most significant of the elements as far as sailors are concerned, there are some words of comfort. Given their latitude and position, the Falklands might not be as windy as you would expect. The prevailing wind, throughout the seasons, is from the west. For 60% of the time the wind blows at less than 17 knots and the average wind speed taken over a whole year is remarkably constant at just above 16 knots. For 25% of the time the wind blows from 22 to 33 knots, and for the remainder of the time it blows at speeds above this.

Although the winds tend to be strongest by day, sometimes falling to calm at dusk and dawn with light winds overnight, the strength

of the wind can change very quickly, and unpredictably. Northerly or northeasterly winds, although less frequent, are trickier and can arrive, blowing hard, without warning. In these situations the wind speed can rise to a full gale in a matter of minutes. These winds often produce fog on northern coasts in the summer months.

There are two bits of weather lore worth noting:

'When the wind fills in 'fore eight, you know 'twill be a day you'll hate.'

'When the Magellanic oystercatcher whistles, this is a sure sign of northerly wind and rain.'

It is also worth remembering that the locals here don't talk about 'having a good day,' but instead pin their hopes on 'a good hour or two'.

A word about woollies: this is the local name for *williwas* which sailors arriving from Patagonia will be already familiar with. They occur in strong westerly winds and are found most frequently under the lee side of Falkland Island Sound and in some of the narrow passages between the western islands. One of those passes is named Woolly Gut, for reasons that can be imagined.

The one advantage of this windy climate and its subsequent impediment to the growth of trees – which rarely stretch above ground level – is the lack of bug, insect and termite populations. The absense of creatures that feed upon decaying wood means that there is many a well preserved wooden hulk to be found littered around the islands. In fact, the Falklands are said to house the finest collection of wooden tall ships in the world, even if they are mostly wrecks.

Falklands time

The islands have adopted daylight saving, and used to move from UTC –4 hours to UTC –3 on the first Sunday in September, the clocks reverting on the 3rd Sunday in April. In 2011, the government agreed a trial to keep summer time all year round (UTC –3), but you should check to see if this has been maintained as local opinion on these matters can be strong.

The history of the islands

There were claims of sightings of the islands as long ago as the early 16th century by the French and the Portuguese, and maps exist from that century. But not until 1690 is it reckoned that the first landing took place by John Strong of England, master of HMS *Welfare*, on 27 January in that year. It was not a planned landing. His true mission had been to capture Spanish treasure contained in a wreck off the coast of South America.

His log records:

..this morning we weighed and stood unto an harbour on ye west side and there came to ane anchor and sent our boat on shoar for fresh water and did kill abundance of geese and ducks but as far as wood there is none.

He had successfully navigated the sound between the west and east group of islands, and named it the Falkland Sound after Viscount Falkland, a Scottish nobleman and English politician who, at the time, was an Admiralty Commissioner held in low esteem by Samuel Pepys. The name's use was later expanded to cover all the islands.

The strategic significance of the islands was quickly grasped by George Anson, an Admiral of the Fleet famous for his circumnavigation begun in 1740, when he noted:

> *Even in time of peace [the islands] might be of great consequence to this nation, and in time of war would make masters of the seas.*

Strong was only just ahead of the French who landed in 1701 but did not settle on East Falkland until 1764. They called the islands Iles Malouines since the expedition had left from St Malo, and from this the Spanish derived the name Malvinas. The Spaniards were successful in expelling the British in 1774, after which the islands were Spanish for the next sixty years. It was when the Argentinians became independent from Spain in 1816 that they laid claim to the Falklands, which they took in 1820 only to be evicted by the British in 1833. Arguably, the present dispute between the two countries stems from that time. Many attempts have been made to find a legal resolution but little progress has been made, and in 1965 the United Nations urged the two countries to negotiate, but with little success.

For a compact collection of 770 islands covering less than 5,000 square miles, the Falklands have packed in a lot of history. Much of it has been as turbulent as the waters that surround them. To understand their significance, you have to look at how strategically placed the islands are.

The Panama Canal did not open until 1914 and until that time all sea trade between the Atlantic and Pacific Oceans had to pass either through the Drake Passage south of Cape Horn, or through the Magellan Strait. Whichever route was chosen, and in whichever direction, the Falklands were perfectly placed to provide refuge, repair and re-stocking. It was also clearly valuable as a base for naval operations. Those who held the Falklands could claim to be the doorkeepers between the two great oceans.

Commercial and strategic significance

With the opening of the Panama Canal came a rapid change in the commercial trade routes, and the passage round the Horn was (with doubtless the thanks of many a seaman) consigned to history. However, as the century progressed the Falklands found a new importance. Advancing fishing techniques led to industrialisation, and as the catching of fish became ever more efficient and sophisticated, new fishing grounds were eagerly sought. In recent decades the waters around the Falklands were found to be rich in highly-prized squid, and in the 2010 season – considered a poor one – a considerable 12,000 tonnes were harvested. The squid have only appeared around the Falklands in recent years; before the 1980s they were hardly found and now they are abundant.

The waters are also rich in finfish (as opposed to flatfish) but species such as rock cod are of low value so the catches had to be large if the fishing was to be profitable. This led to over-fishing in the 1970s and only a fishing ban prevented the extinction of some species. A recovery has now taken place and the Falkland waters are rich fishing grounds once more.

But advanced engineering methods now mean that the holy grail of all economies, oil production, is becoming possible in the deep and stormy waters of the South Atlantic with a growing belief that beneath the waves may lie as many as 60 billion barrels of oil. For that reason the Falklands have been called the new 'treasure islands'. Tax revenues of $10 billion are talked about in the next 25 years. The Falklanders may have heard such talk before.

Taking oil and the flourishing fishing together, the Falklands have found a new strategic significance in the 21st century. For navigators this means that a sharp lookout needs to be kept, particularly for the Japanese squid-fishing fleets which consist of large factory ships often working in close formation. Oil exploration vessels are also likely to become more common in the coming years.

The Falklands war of 1982

The spark that ignited the Falklands war, leading to the landing of 500 Argentinian troops on 2 April 1982, may have been something as apparently insignificant as the retirement of a Royal Navy ice patrol vessel, HMS *Endurance*, from waters around the islands. It was the view of its then Captain, Nicholas Barker, that this sent a signal that Britain no longer cared much about the Falklands. Argentine domestic politics played a part too when their leader, General Galtieri, saw an opportunity to give support to his failing regime. 1983 marked the 150th anniversary of the British invasion (and the Argentine eviction), what better date for the Argentinians to retake the islands?

The conflict started in a modest way. A group of scrap metal workers landed at Leith Harbour on South Georgia, a bleak outpost

Reminders of the war can be found across the islands *Sandy Duker*

some 750M to the east of the Falklands. Amongst them were Argentine marines who planned to hijack a legitimate scrap metal business and use it as a cover for an invasion. HMS *Endurance* was despatched to remove them. This was the modest beginning of a conflict that led to the loss of 655 Argentine troops and 255 British, the majority of those British losses sustained in the bombing of the landing ships *Sir Galahad* and *Sir Tristram*.

On 3 April 1982, the British Prime Minister, Margaret Thatcher, despatched a task force to recover the islands, and at the same time introduced a 200M exclusion zone. It was while steaming out of this exclusion zone in early May, following a pincer movement on the British task force by the Argentine Navy, that the Argentine destroyer, *General Belgrano*, was sunk. 386 lives were lost in the most controversial event of the war.

British troops began landing in San Carlos water on 21 May, and after fierce fighting in the difficult conditions to be found on the ground, the Argentine troops finally surrendered on 14 June. Shortly after, the South Sandwich Islands were retaken, South Georgia having been recaptured as early as the end of April by Royal Marines.

Increased attention has since been given to these remote islands by the British government with the building of new military bases, in particular RAF Mount Pleasant which is home to 2,000 military personnel and lies 30M southwest of Stanley. It is equipped with the Eurofighter Typhoon, and C130s, as well as aircraft for in-flight refuelling. There are also Sea King helicopters for search and rescue although it is not clear if these would be deployed on civilian rescue. The base has been fully operational since 1985 and is designed to send a powerful signal to anyone contemplating another invasion.

The above summary cannot do justice to a bitter, if brief, war. See the appendix p. 206 for suggested further reading.

Who are the Falkland islanders?

The population of the islands is almost 3,000. 75% live in and around Stanley, 12% in the area known as 'camp' which refers to those parts of the islands outside Stanley (see below), and 13% are based around the airport. The military presence varies, but there are generally reckoned to be about 1,300 personnel operating 4 Typhoon fast-jet aircraft, a VC 10 tanker, Hercules transport, Rapier missiles and a Falklands patrol ship. Also in attendance might be a Type 45 destroyer.

There is a strong sense of identity with 57% defining themselves as Falkland Islanders, 28% as British, the remainder made up of 9% from St Helena and a handful from Chile.

If the human population seems small, then by contrast the sheep are numerous, with a total population of nearly half a million, outnumbering the humans by 167 to 1. To put this in perspective, despite its fame as a sheep-keeping country, the ratio in New Zealand is just 7 to 1.

The main employer is the government who provide work for 28% of the population. Agriculture and tourism provide a further 11% each. Fewer than 50 people are employed in the fish industry, and 20 only in oil and gas, though this number may well grow. The possibility of oil exploitation is now taken so seriously that the Argentine government has threatened financial sanctions against companies involved in exploration.

Source: The Guardian Datablog

What is 'Camp'?

The word is derived from the Spanish, *campos*, meaning countryside. On the Falkland Islands it applies to anywhere outside of Stanley, including both East and West Falkland. There is no other town as large as Stanley, and most settlements tend to consist of nothing more than a handful of houses. The largest proportion of the population in Camp live on East Falkland. The camp constituency elects four members to the Legislative Council and seems to have,

Ewen Southby-Tailyour and the Falklands

Ewen Southby-Tailyour's book, *Falkland Island Shores* (Nautical 1985), was the first book to be written about small boat navigation in the Falkland Islands. It is doubtful there will ever be a better one. Although now quite dated, there is little that will have changed when it comes to navigation, and the general advice remains as valid as the day it was written.

Some details have been amended by Pete and Annie Hill in 1996. These are available here:

www.rccpf.org.uk/publications/south-atlantic/falkland-islands-shores-a-supplement.

It would be a foolish navigator who did not have both these onboard, as well as a copy of the latest 2011 pilotage notes here

http://iron-bark.blogspot.co.uk/2011/10/falkland-island-pilotage-notes.html

The story of how Southby-Tailyour came to cruise the Falklands Islands, and accidentally help win a war by doing so, is one of the great yachting tales of recent times.

He joined the Royal Marines in 1977 and found himself stepping ashore in Stanley from HMS *Endurance* to begin a routine year's tour of duty. As a cruising yachtsman, he was quick to spot that the intricate waters in and around the islands had never been properly surveyed from a yachtsman's perspective. The Admiralty Pilot did a good job from a big ship's point of view, but this gave none of the detail that a cruising sailor aboard his own small craft could exploit.

While on patrol in a converted 150-ton fishing vessel, Southby-Tailyour took the chance to spot interesting harbours and anchorages of use to cruising sailors. He took notes, drew charts and gathered advice from Captain Jack Sollis who was reckoned to have a more precise knowledge of Falkland Waters than any Admiralty chart could provide. When his year long tour of duty came to an end he had collected over 1,000 photographs, 200 sketches, 150 pages of notes and many watercolours of the landscape and seabirds.

It was never his plan to do more than share this information with the very few yachts that ever visited the Falklands, and it came as no surprise that no publisher back home saw this as a commercial proposition. His folio stayed tucked away in his bottom drawer.

In early April 1982, as Margaret Thatcher prepared for the sending of a Task Force to retake the islands after the Argentinian invasion, he took a phone call from the Royal Marines base in Poole. This he first dismissed as a late April Fool's joke. It was only when confronted by the Brigadier in charge at Royal Marines Commando HQ that he realised how vital his pilotage information had suddenly become, especially for troops now part of the Task Force heading south and expecting to land on the Falklands' inhospitable shores. At first he was asked to lend his charts and drawings, but when he made it clear that he wasn't going to be parted from them, an invitation to join the Task Force swiftly followed.

While heading south, he took upon himself the role of evangelist for the islands, and seized every opportunity to brief his colleagues. He did not confine himself to navigation, but made sure that all onboard were familiar with the seabirds, the whales and the wildlife, using the valuable space on the ship's noticeboard to introduce a little ornithology and ecology.

It is difficult to be certain how large a part his pilotage notes played in Britain's ultimate success. Suffice it to say that many regarded it as fundamental.

When the war was over, publishers who had originally shunned his book as having no commercial importance, now found a new interest in it. That it was published and has remained in print ever since, and that its accuracy has never been questioned, has been hugely to the benefit of increasing numbers of yachts which now sail to these intriguing islands.

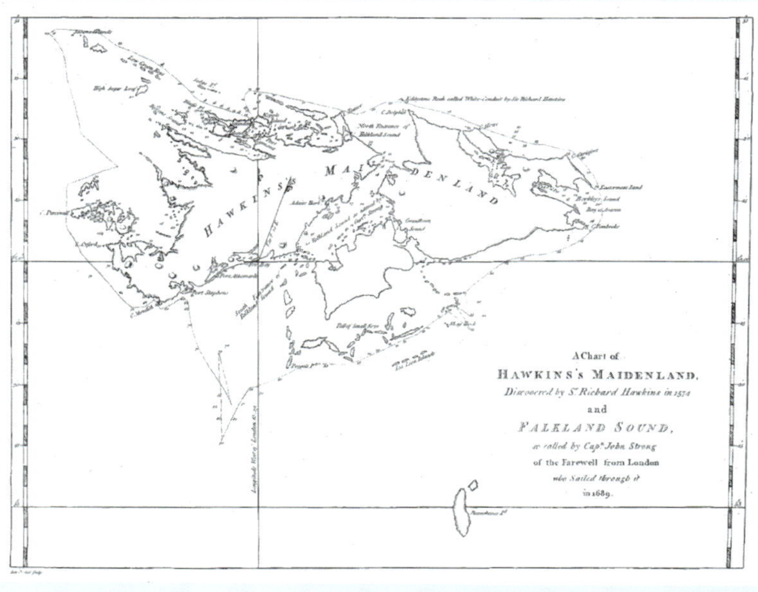

The landscape of East Falkland
Tim Barker

on occasions, a mind of its own; for a period there was an hour's time difference between Camp time on West Falkland and Stanley less than a 100M away.

Lafonia, part of Camp, is a large peninsula which forms the southern part of East Falkland; if you are heading for Stanley from the south west, you will skirt its coastline. The landscape is low and undulating, much of it peat based, giving it a moorland feel. Viewed on the chart, it looks like a letter 'E' which has partly toppled over. The connection to the remainder of East Falkland is by a narrow strip of land on which sits Goose Green to the east (see p. 132 for sailing directions) – an early battle site in the 1982 conflict during which 100 local residents were imprisoned in the village hall. At the northern end of this isthmus, north of the small settlement of Darwin, can be found both a British memorial and an Argentine military cemetery. Darwin and Goose Green, together, form the largest settlement outside Stanley.

Sheep are by far the most numerous inhabitants of Lafonia. For them to be brought easily to Goose Green for annual shearing, the famous Brodie suspension bridge was constructed. Built in 1925 from a kit shipped from England, it closed in 1997 but can still be seen. It is the most southerly suspension bridge in the world.

Do not expect to travel easily in camp. Until quite recent years the only way to travel was by horse, although four wheel drives have now taken over. However, do not expect any tarmac roads, and hold on tightly as you bounce through ruts in the peat tracks. Motorbikes are popular with some locals.

At all times when travelling ashore you should be aware of minefields, many of which may still be live see p. 122. Do not ignore any warning signs.

Falkland Island birds and wildlife

There can be no more authoritative book than *Birds and Mammals of the Falklands Islands* by Robin and Anne Woods. (Princeton University Press 2006) which can be found at

http://press.princeton.edu/titles/9799.html

It outlines all 227 species of seabird to be found in the islands.

See also **www.seabirds.org/data.htm** for comprehensive descriptions of habitats, birds, seals and sea lions as well as whales, dolphins and plant species.

Three unusual delicacies

I mention these because they can be found in the wild and may be a useful supplement if fresh provisions such as fruit and vegetables are scarce/expensive, which they can be on the islands. The climate only allows for slow growth of vegetables, and even then the variety is restricted. Imported fresh fruit and vegetables can come at an eye-watering price.

The root of the tussock grass is said to be delicious. It can be found along much of the coastline and off-lying islands and also around the settlements. It is not the grass stalks themselves that are the delicacy but the bulbous root found at the end. It looks a bit like the end of a spring onion. It can be chewed raw but is said to have a chestnut taste when boiled. Locals eat them regularly.

Fruit does not grow wild in the islands, but two types of berry are of interest. The Diddle-dee berry is a small red berry growing on a kind of low-lying heather, in and around small rocks. In summer, the berries can be eaten raw. They are sharp, and the taste is described as similar to Campari. Look out for something the size and colour of a red currant. The locals make wine with them. The Tea berry, meanwhile, is red and white and the size of a wild strawberry, but smooth. You will find them in the same places you come across the Diddle-dee. Baked Tea berry pies are considered a delicacy.

When to sail to and from the Falklands

If leaving from Tierra del Fuego the westerly wind will be blowing at all times of year and, although the passage might be a rough one, winds between NW and SW are to be expected. Be aware of a favourable set provided by the Falklands Current which may give you a lift of 20–30M a day.

If coming down the South Atlantic, from Brazil for example, it is best to sail early in the year, between December and April, when the winds off the Brazilian coast are typically from the NE and the south-flowing Brazil Current gives assistance. Be aware that this current can set up unpredictable eddies and you can find the flow against you for no obvious reason. This is more noticeable south of Rio.

If leaving the Falklands for a northbound passage to the area of the River Plate, the summer months of December to March are the best time to enjoy the help of the prevailing westerlies and the Falklands current. If planning to sail further north from the River Plate, a pause can be taken until May when winds along the Brazilian coast are more likely to be fair.

For detailed passage planning see:
World Cruising Routes Jimmy Cornell (Adlard Coles Nautical)

Visas and permits

Entry

Stanley is the only port of entry in the islands and should be your first stop. Yachts are required to report in advance of arrival by VHF (Ch 16 or 10). See Stanley, p 126, for arrival details.

Customs will allow you to make short stops on the way to Stanley in the event of bad weather, providing they are kept informed of your movements and you do not go ashore. Likewise, if leaving the Falklands having checked out of Stanley, permission can be obtained to allow you to make stops on the way as you leave.

Permit and visa requirements

If you are not a Falkland Islander, or have no residency rights in the Islands, you will require a visitor's permit to enter the islands. Nationals of some countries will require a visa in addition to a visitor's permit.

Visas can be obtained in advance from Falkland House in London.

www.falklands.gov.fk/self-governance/london-office/

Expect to pay something in the order of £70.

In countries other than the United Kingdom a permit may be obtained from, and processed through, a British Embassy or Consulate.

Visas must be obtained before arrival.

You do not require a visa if you have a passport issued by the United Kingdom, the European Union, Argentina, Australia, Brazil, Canada, Chile, New Zealand, Norway, South Africa, Switzerland, the USA, Uruguay.

Further advice can be obtained from **admin@customs.gov.fk**

Visitor's permits

A visitor's permit will only be issued for an initial period of one month although this can be extended by application to the Immigration Officer after arrival in the islands. You will have to show that you are able to support yourself financially. If you want to extend your stay beyond a year, then an application must be made to the Governor and good reason will have to be shown.

You should not expect to be automatically granted a work permit if you want to find employment. However, jobs crop up from time to time and if there is no Falklander to fill the vacancy, then you might be considered. It is only permitted to work for three months out of any twelve.

Immigration

Clearance procedures for both customs and immigration are carried out by an officer who will visit your yacht as arranged. These are reported to be friendly encounters, quick and efficient, which may come as a relief if you have been dealing with the South American authorities during your voyage south.

Arriving from Argentina

This can get complicated, and expensive if proper procedures are not followed.

On leaving any Argentine harbour, you will be asked to sign a document stating that you do not intend to sail to the Falkland Islands (Malvinas) without permission, and that you will incur a fine of several thousand dollars if you do. This should be respected. If you return to Argentina and the *Prefectura* have the slightest suspicion that you have paid an unauthorised visit to the Falklands, life can become very difficult.

However, it is possible to apply for permission - a *permiso* - at the *Prefectura* but it must be applied for 10 days or more in advance of departure. Yachts making applications have found no trouble obtaining permission, but it can be slow.

Argentina regards the islands as their territory and any visit will be included in your 3-month visa. They will not stamp your passport on leaving for the Falklands and you should return to Argentina and then clear out of the country within the 3 months. Disregarding this law has heavy financial penalties; fines of $25,000 have been reported.

It is possible to apply online for permission to visit the Falkland Islands without first clearing into Argentina. When applying, remember to use the Argentine names i.e. Islas Malvinas and Puerto Argentino (Stanley), otherwise the form will be returned as incorrect.

Use this form to apply for permission to sail the the Falklands (Malvinas):

www.prefecturanaval.gov.ar/web/es/html/ordn_swf/2-2010-1.swf

If you visit the Falklands without first obtaining permission from Argentina, it is reported that you may be arrested and fined on entering Argentine territorial waters, including approaches to the Magellan and Le Maire Straits, even though these are international waterways.

Most other South American countries, except Chile, will impose similar conditions before giving clearance. This leads to the bizarre situation of a yacht clearing from Puerto Williams (Chile) for the Falklands needing to get a permit from the Argentine authorities first.

Aside from the legal objections to this, there are the delays and costs of having to deal with the Argentine bureaucracy in Buenos Aires.

Arriving from Chile

The *Armada* in Puerto Williams and Punta Arenas will give clearance for you to sail to South Africa with no questions asked. This allows a yacht to sail from Chile and make a stop at the Falklands. However if a yacht subsequently enters an Argentine port for any reason, including an emergency, the penalties for having visited the Falklands without having first signed the declaration are draconian.

All these regulations are politically charged and for that reason can vary unpredictably and at short notice.

Customs

Import restrictions exist for cigarettes and alcohol but visiting yachts have reported no problems with customs provided that only small quantities for personal use are found on board. At the time of writing the regulations state that the following are permitted:

200 cigarettes or 50 cigars or 100 cigarillos or 250 grammes of tobacco.

1 litre of wine or spirits if more than 38.8° proof (22° Gay-Lussac) or 2 litres of maximum 38.8° proof (22° Gay-Lussac) and 2 litres sparkling wine or still table wine; 10 litres of beer or cider or similar beverage.

Check the latest information here:

https://falkland-islands.visahq.com/customs/

Bringing food to the Falklands

The islands are free from any serious plant diseases and, unsurprisingly, they want to keep it that way. You should not, therefore, arrive with large quantities of fresh food on board. Fruit and vegetables bought outside the islands should be placed in the yellow sack provided on arrival along with any uncooked meats, fish and dairy products. If you have walking boots, ensure they are clean. The packaging from any of the above foods could also be contaminated and should be put into a yellow sack along with organic waste.

Health insurance

You are strongly advised to have full medical cover if you are cruising the islands. Holders of UK passports are given the benefit of a reciprocal arrangement between the Falkland's health service and the UK's National Health Service. The islands have well-equipped medical and dental facilities.

Stanley - a little bit of old England
Vicky Jackson

However, in the event of a serious medical emergency you will have to cover the costs of any air ambulances which might be required to take you to South America.

Money and banks

The local currency is the Falklands Pound which is given in exchange for sterling on a one for one basis. US dollars and Euros are also accepted in the shops but a better exchange rate might be obtained in Stanley's only bank, the Standard Chartered Bank, which is in the centre of town near the Post Office. Note, though, that the bank is reluctant to accept any US or Euro notes which are not in mint condition. If your notes have spent a while in salty water, they may be refused.

There are no ATMs anywhere in the Falklands (2016).

If trying to get money on a credit card, the results at the bank can be variable with some cards rejected, often at random. The charges can be high. However, the same card will often be gladly accepted for payment in some shops.

Shopping and leisure

One attractive tradition is the mid-morning tea or coffee break, and this is known as a *smoko*. It's a time for sitting and chatting and it is a word widely used in the English-speaking southern hemisphere in Australia, New Zealand and the Falklands, especially amongst the sheep shearers. It is thought that the word originated in the British merchant navy to describe a 'smoking break', and this might well be how the word came into use in the Falklands, picked up from the crews of the 19th century ships which visited.

As far as shopping in the Falklands is concerned, you can expect to find as wide a selection of non-perishable items as you might in Europe. However, the prices can be up to 50% higher due to the cost of transport and handling. There are two main supermarkets; West Store (owned by the Falkland Islands Company) in the middle of Stanley, and the Chandlery which is out towards FIPASS (Falkland Interim Port and Storage System). Both accept credit cards.

As well as groceries, West Store has an in-store bakery, wines and spirits, medicines, office supplies and, behind the café, clothing. Next door is an electrical and entertainment store. There is a builder's merchant called Home Builder which might be useful for obtaining parts for onboard plumbing and domestic repairs.

Cold weather gear and fishing tackle can be obtained from the branch of West Store across from the airport. Here you can also purchase the Falkland Islands newspaper, the *Penguin News*, published every Friday.

The Chandlery supermarket, on Airport Road, imports from Spain and Chile as well as stocking Sainsbury's branded items. It has a large delicatessen section. Fishing and outdoor gear can also be bought here. Open weekdays and weekends.

There is no dedicated pharmacy and prescriptions are made up at the dispensary in the King Edward Memorial Hospital.

The difficulty comes when trying to obtain fresh food. Milk is always available and, as you might expect, meat, especially local beef and lamb. Eggs can be scarce at certain times of year and while long-lasting vegetables such as potatoes, onions and carrots (imported from Chile or the UK) are generally available, they can be of poor quality. The secret seems to be to gather intelligence as to when the next fresh supplies are due to arrive either by sea or air, and be ready to pounce. You need to be fast; shelves can empty quickly. In the summer, look out for garden-grown vegetables sold over the garden gate.

If trying to shop in Camp, outside Stanley, the larger settlements of Fox Bay, Port Howard, North Arm and Goose Green have small shops offering limited supplies.

As regards leisure time, the warnings about temperatures might make the Stanley Leisure Centre's 25m heated indoor pool and gym facilities a more tempting option than a dip in the sea. Dancing is popular and the local dances are similar in style to Scottish country dancing. If you're lucky, you might catch a show given by the Falklands Islands Operatic and Dramatic Association who organise a well-supported local talent show every July. All island events can be found in the *Penguin News*:

www. penguin-news.com

Eating out

There are no fewer than five pubs in Stanley and in most of them anyone coming from the UK will feel instantly at home. They are the Victory Bar, the Globe Tavern, Rose Hotel, The Upland Goose, the Stanley Arms and Deano's Bar. Most serve food, including fish and chips.

Restaurants close early but some serve up some fine cooking. The Malvina House Hotel (3 Ross Road, Stanley) is famed for its seafood. Michele's Café near the public jetty is famous for its fish and chips. Most restaurants will be found as part of hotels, and cafés and snack bars can be found in the supermarkets.

Out in Camp, you'll get a warm welcome and good food at Darwin House in Darwin, Lafonia and at the Galley Café in Goose Green, which offers what is reputed to be the best breakfast on the Falkland Islands.

Mail

All post arriving in Stanley arrives via the British Royal Air Force. The service can be slow and unreliable. It should take two weeks for letters to arrive from the UK but they seldom do. It has been reported that one parcel took no less than four months to make the journey.

Vital items should be sent via a courier service such as DHL, where the service will be reliable and traceable.

Internet, broadcasting, and communications

Internet is provided via satellite and data charges can be expensive. In fact, it is said that internet usage is the most frequent cause of family rows here. However, there are WiFi hotspots at many locations in Stanley and also at Mount Pleasant, Darwin, Carcass Island and Sea Lion Island. These can be accessed using WiFi cards available from retailers.

Any queries on communications can be answered by dialling 131 from an island telephone.

There is a mobile phone network and roaming services are available with most suppliers. Check your contract carefully before using it as roaming charges can be extremely high. If you have an unlocked mobile phone, you can purchase a local SIM from Cable & Wireless or the West Store.

To call the Falklands, use the prefix +500.

Countryside Code

If venturing ashore, the Countryside Code must be observed.

1 Always ask permission before entering private land.
2 Keep to paths wherever possible. Leave gates open or shut as you find them.
3 Be aware of the high fire risk throughout the Islands. Be extremely careful when smoking not to start fires. Take cigarette butts away with you.
4 Do not drop litter*. Take your rubbish home with you.
5 Do not disfigure rocks or buildings.
6 Do not touch, handle, injure or kill any wild bird or other wild animal*.
7 Never feed any wild animals.
8 Always give animals the right of way. Remember not to block the routes of seabirds and seals coming ashore to their colonies.
9 Try to prevent any undue disturbance to wild animals. Stay on the outside of bird and seal colonies. Remain at least 6m (20ft) away. When taking photographs or filming stay low to the ground. Move slowly and quietly. Do not startle or chase wildlife from resting or breeding areas.
10 Some plants are protected and should not be picked*. Wildflowers are there for all to enjoy.
11 Whalebones, skulls, eggs or other such items may not be exported from the Falkland Islands*. They should be left where they are found.

* Such actions (with a few special exceptions) may constitute an offence in the Falkland Islands and could result in fines of up to £3,000.

Landowners MUST be contacted prior to landing on any islands and the lighting of fires for any reason is strictly prohibited unless permission has been given in writing by the landowner.

There are four broadcasting networks; FIRS, the Falkland Islands Radio Service; KTV Radio Nova, and KTV Radio Nova Saint FM (these two provide, on subscription, TV and radio channels, including some UK channels). There is also BFBS Radio, the British Forces Broadcasting Service.

Cable & Wireless are the internet and telephone providers.

Weather forecasts

The FIRS provides weather forecasts throughout the day with information taken from the UK Met Office.

A full weather forecast, including shipping forecast, is broadcast after the news at about 0800, 0900 and again (updated) at 1700 and 1815 with a weather summary at 1215 (which does not contain a shipping forecast). All times are Local (UTC–3).

Landmines

It is vital that you do not land anywhere by dinghy without having first ensured that you are not about to wander into a minefield. It is a real danger and must be taken seriously. The landscape may appear benign but this is a hidden and dangerous legacy of the 1982 war.

The major minefields are near Stanley, Goose Green, Fox Bay and Port Howard, and have been fenced in and warning signs erected. Mine removal was abandoned after serious injuries were sustained by those carrying out the clearance.

For up to date information and guidance, the bomb disposal office is located on Ross Road and they will have the latest information. Even so, when landing on Camp, it is worth taking advice from the local community in advance who will know where any minefields are located.

There are also firing ranges on the islands. Firing times are announced on the radio each day (see above for frequencies).

If you think you have found an item of unexploded ordnance take the following actions:

- DO NOT TOUCH
- Mark its position on the ground
- Make a note of its size, shape, colour, markings, condition and quantity
- Report it to Joint Services Explosive Ordnance Disposal (JSEOD) or contact Stanley Police ✆ 27222

There are 117 minefields in the Falkland Islands, all clearly signed and fenced. It is extremely dangerous and illegal to:

- Enter a minefield
- Damage a minefield fence or remove minefield signs
- Throw items into a minefield

There are several FM frequencies:

Location	*FIRS*
Mt Sussex	97·2
Byron Heights	97·4
Mt Alice	97·6
Mt William	97·8
Stanley	88·3

FIRS also broadcasts on 530MW, which has a range of several hundred miles depending on propagation conditions. This can be useful when making an approach to the islands.

The Shipping Forecast for open waters is also broadcast each day at 0830 Local on HF Frequency 4066.1 KHz by the Fisheries Department, preceded by any local navigational warnings. Whenever possible the Shipping Forecast and Navigation Warnings will also be broadcast in Spanish.

Do not ignore *Tim Barker*

Flights to and from the Falklands

It is possible to arrange a crew change at Stanley. International flights land at the Mount Pleasant military complex, 37M from Stanley. If you are using a search engine to locate suitable flights, the international airport code is MPN.

www.falklandislands.travel

gives advice on flights, and claims to be able to offer the best fares.

If planning your own travel, there are two carriers: LAN, a group of South American airlines based in Chile, and the UK Ministry of Defence 'airbridge' flights.

LAN flights connect with flights from Europe and USA in Santiago, then take you onwards via Punta Arenas in the Magellan Strait, stopping once a month at Rio Gallegos, Argentina.

The MOD operates non-commercial flights directly from the UK from the RAF base at Brize Norton in Oxfordshire. The flight is 20 hours and includes a refuelling stop on Ascension Island where you can break your journey. The Falklands Islands London office can supply details:

travel@falklands.gov.fk

CRUISING THE FALKLAND ISLANDS

Admiralty Charts

The following Admiralty Charts cover approaches to the islands, entry to Stanley harbour, and cruising East Falkland:

2505 Approaches to the Falkland Islands

2512 The Falkland Islands

2536 Port William to Choiseul Sound

2547 Port Salvador to Port William

2550 Plans in East Falkland Island

2558 Falkland Sound Northern Part

2559 Falkland Island Southern Part

1614 Stanley Harbour and Approaches

Charts of West Falkland

2513 Eagle Passage to New Island

2514 New Island to Pebble Island

2545 Port Egmont to Port Purvis

2543 Anchorages in West Falkland Island

2559 Falkland Sound Southern Part

2558 Falkland Sound Northern Part

Some of the above are required for close navigation. 2517, 2518, 2519, 2520 show approaches to the islands from the NW, NE, SW and SE. You may decide that charts from the above list give sufficient information for making a safe landfall.

Electronic charts

The following electronic charts provide coverage of the Falkland Islands but check before buying as this advancing technology is subject to change.

C- MAP MAX SA-M500 (Costa Rice, Chile, Falklands)

NAVIONICS Platinum Plus South America West

MAXSEA TIME ZERO
Chart reference: WVJSAM501MAP6.1
Gulf of Paria to Cape Horn

Tides

Tidal ranges are not large ranging from about 1·6m at springs to 0·5m at neaps.

The tidal flows in Stanley harbour itself are generally weak but can reach 1·5 knots in the Narrows where wind over tide could make for an uncomfortable, but not dangerous, passage.

The flood tide off the south of West Falkland runs towards the west but flows to the north at the southern entrance to Falkland Sound. Off Port Edgar the flood sets to the west, but off Calista Island it sets to the north. The tide splits off Fox Bay resulting in minimal tidal streams thereabouts.

Which way round the Falklands?

I have chosen to list the harbours in a clockwise direction around both the East and West Falkland Islands. However, when it comes to planning a cruise around these coasts the decision on which way to go is not quite so simple.

If leaving from Stanley and going north (anti-clockwise), heading, perhaps, for the Tamar Pass, there are a couple of lengthy passages to make, but the sea area from

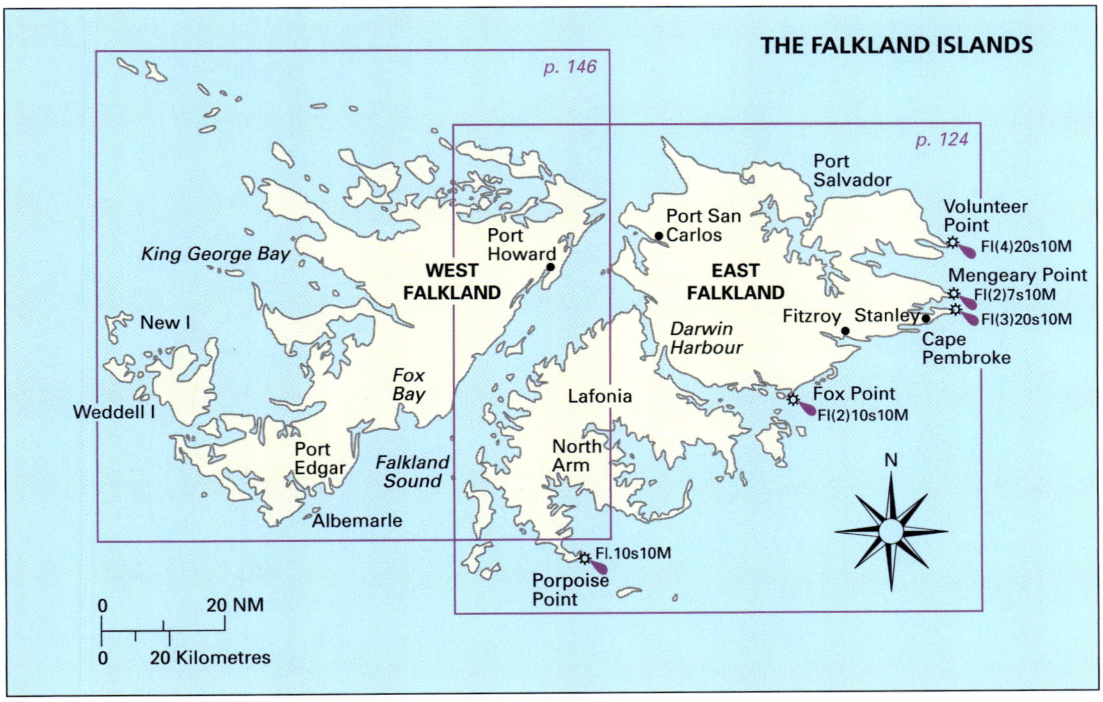

Pebble Sound all the way round the west coast to Weddell Island, though windy, is surprisingly sheltered from SW/WSW ocean swell and can make good sailing.

South-about has the advantage of plenty of shelter on the way but to achieve this passage under sail requires cunning to make use of pre-frontal winds (eg from the north), hoping to get to shelter before the wind backs. If unlucky with the weather, you may end up doing a lot of motoring.

A careful and up to date check must be kept on a yacht's position due to unexpected tidal sets. The direction depends on local weather conditions. Wind-induced streams can reach 2 knots.

STANLEY AND EAST FALKLAND

Approaching Stanley Harbour

51°39'S 57°40'W

A reporting line exists between Volunteer Point 51°30'·8S, 57°44'·4W, Fl(4)W.20s10m, and Cape Pembroke 51° 41'S, 57°43'·2W.

Call *Stanley Port Control* on VHF 16 or 10 (24 hours) or HF 4066.1Khz (office hours) when crossing this line inward or outward bound. Out of office hours, VHF watch is kept by Cable and Wireless South Atlantic Ltd who will take routine reports and alert harbour staff in case of an emergency.

In an emergency you can also call *Stanley Police* on VHF 16.

You are required to keep a VHF radio watch at all times while navigating in Stanley Harbour.

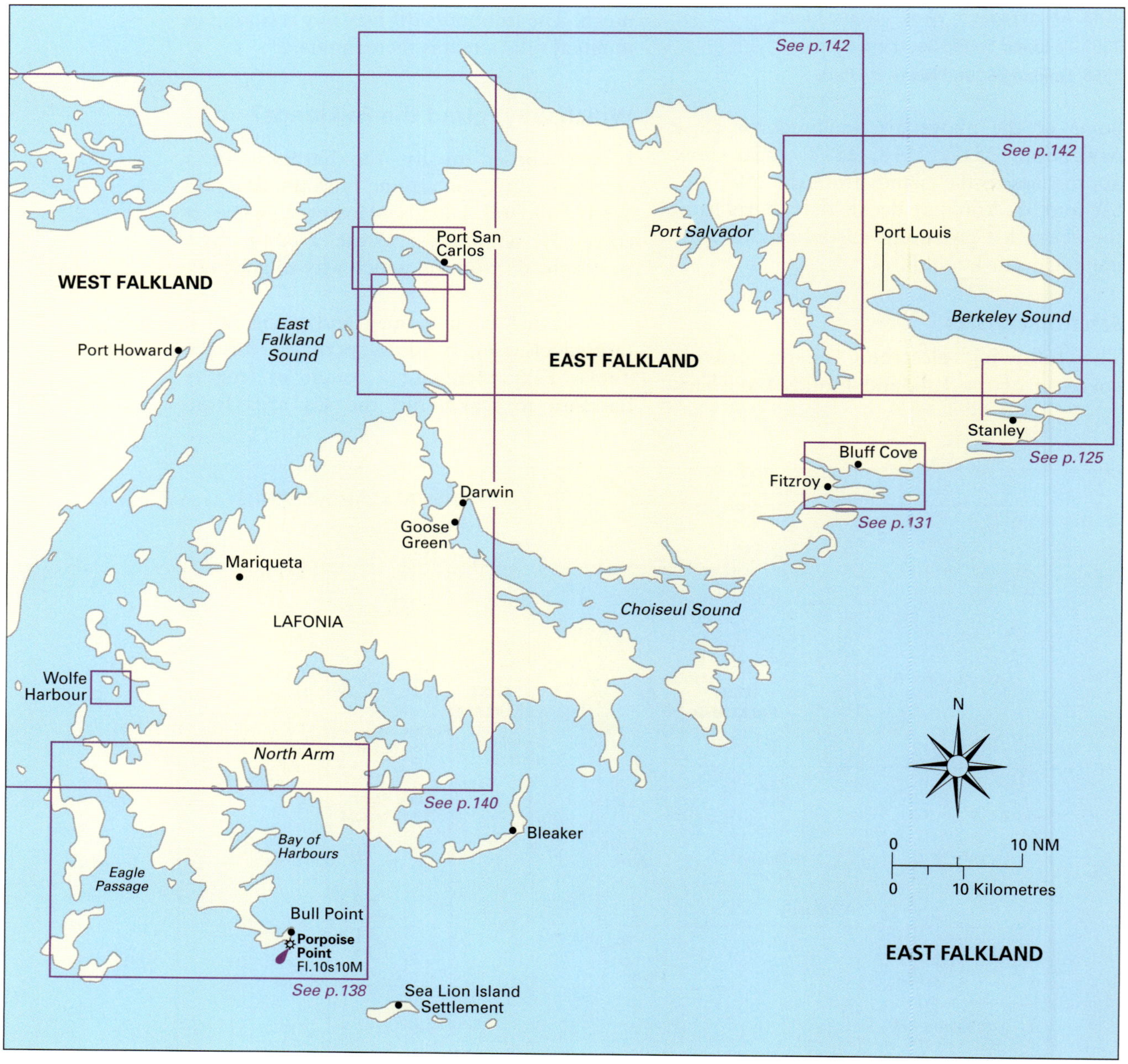

Approaches to Stanley
Sandy Duker

The Narrows

51° 40'S 57° 49'W

Make a course to pass halfway between Mengeary Point and Cape Pembroke, to enter Port William. This large expanse of water is clear of dangers north of the Tussac Islands although it is an anchorage used by large ships and trawlers and care must be taken at night.

A safe leading line can be found on the north shore of Port William, west of Navy Point at Blanco Bay where a white metal column has been established (Fl.WRG.2s.7·5M). The narrow white sector leads 260° until the lights either side of the Narrows on Navy Point and Engineer Point have been identified. The leading lights, both FR, will then be seen through the Narrows on the far side of the harbour.

Care should be taken when approaching the Narrows not to stray east of a line joining Tussac Point and Engineer Point where the Forth Shoal has been reported to have depths of less than 5m and is not marked by kelp.

If entering Stanley at night, note that there are unlit ship mooring buoys, one in particular in the middle of the harbour a little to the W of the Narrows.

For temporary anchorage, the inner part of Port William is fine west of Navy Point with good holding in thick, black mud. Except in prolonged easterly weather, the bay tends be free from swell making it an ideal day cruising ground for a yacht based in Stanley.

The shores of Port William look inviting, and the charts show many possible anchorages in settled weather, however, some beaches are mined (see p. 122) and present a considerable danger to anyone venturing ashore. DO NOT land anywhere unless you have been given the all-clear by the authorities in Stanley.

www.falklandsailing.com/html/information.html

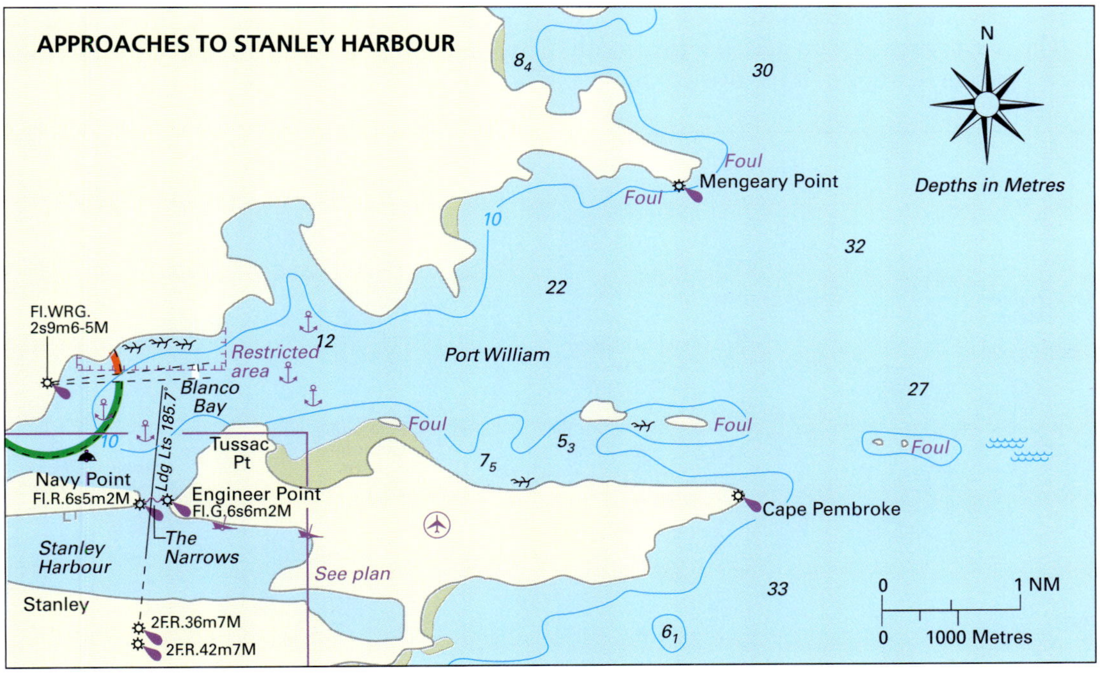

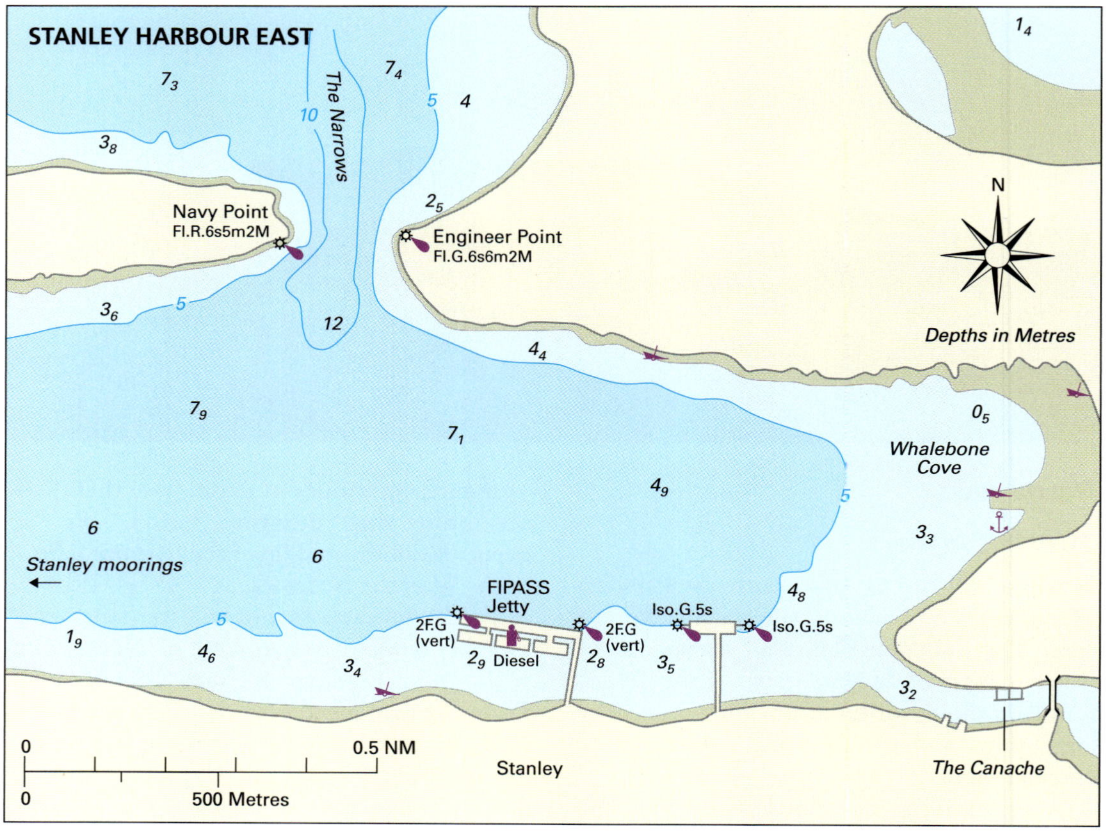

Stanley Harbour

Local dialling code +500

Harbourmaster ✆27260 /21867 (out of hours) / 52867 (mobile)

Customs ✆27340 / 51618 (mobile)

Police ✆28100

Bio Security Officer ✆27355

Berths and mooring

There are three places where a yacht can lie alongside in varying degrees of comfort. Consult the harbourmaster by VHF for guidance when first arriving.

The Government jetty, shown on some charts, has now been removed.

The East jetty is situated on the south shore of the harbour. It is owned by the Falkland Islands Company. There is 3·7m of water at its head and it is convenient for the town but the water can be rough and the berth is exposed.

The Public jetty is used for landing passengers from cruise ships but you can lie alongside here without charge unless a cruise ship is expected, in which case you will have to leave by 0700 on the day of its arrival. The head of the jetty should no longer be used.

The Public jetty is the best option when it is available; otherwise anchor 50m off and use the pontoons to land your dinghy (having got permission from the security officer first).

There is good protection from westerly winds but it is open to the northeast and dangerous if there is any strength in the wind

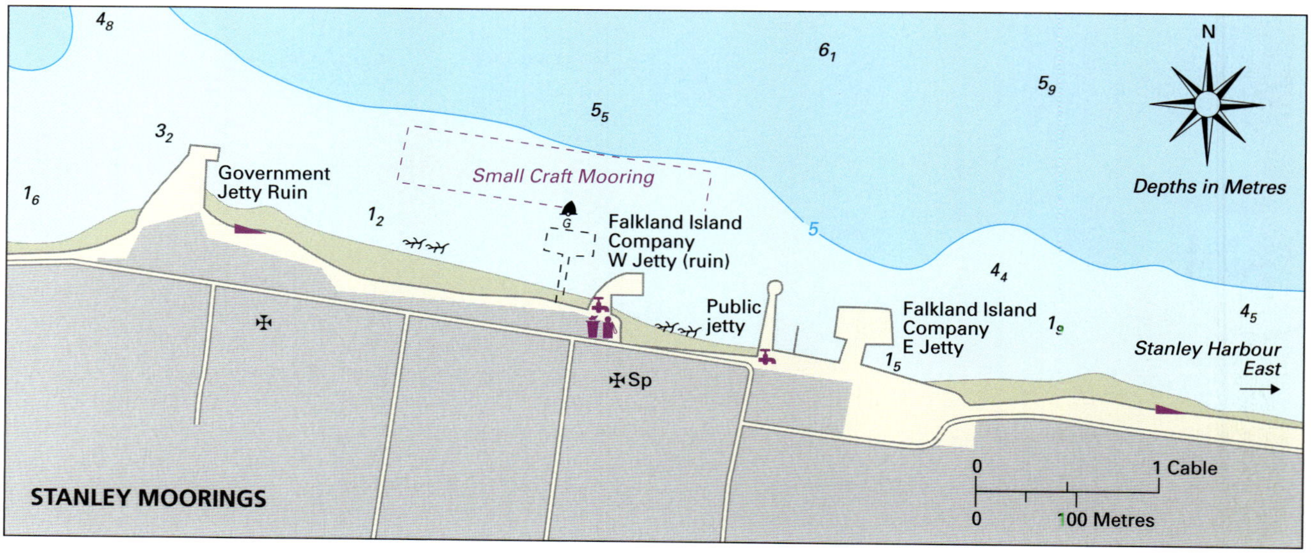

***Kiwi Roa* on the Public jetty, Stanley** *Peter Smith*

***Moonshadow Star* uses *Pelagic Australis* as a fender, East jetty, Stanley** *Sandy Duker*

Land or lie alongside here unless cruise ships are expected - Public jetty, Stanley
Sandy Duker

from that direction. Northeast winds are usually well forecast so you should have time to clear out if necessary. There is a water tap at the foot of the public jetty. A new pontoon has been established on the east side and this can be used by yachts if no tourist launches are expected.

You may find visitors' moorings off the town E of where the old Government jetty once stood (still shown on some charts) although these have been reported as missing or unreliable.

FIPASS (Falkland Islands Port and Storage System) operates a substantial jetty on the south shore of the harbour to the east of the Narrows. There is never less than 6·5m of water here. Yachts can moor on the east side, and there is a charge. Diesel and water are available along with a rubbish skip. This is reported to be a rather uncomfortable berth, noisy, and rough in strong SW winds. It is also over a mile's walk to Stanley, although you can always get ashore from here whereas it might be difficult from a mooring or at anchor. If you were contemplating leaving a boat unattended here, this would be your only safe choice. Undercover storage might be possible, though it would require crane hire and the removal of masts.

The Canache *Pete Smith Kiwi Roa*

The Canache is at the eastern end of Stanley Harbour and consists of privately owned moorings, some of which might be available for a long term stay.

Anchorages

The best anchorage will be found at the western head of the bay towards Moody Brook where it can be shallow but with sufficient depth in places to provide an anchorage. The best spot can be found by continuing westwards until abreast of a scrap metal landfill site (now overgrown) on the S shore. A little to the E of this is a small area of beach (covered at high water) which has been cleared of rocks to create a landing place for a dinghy. Anchor abreast of here in 2m, thick mud. There are no facilities. It is protected from SE through W to N. As a rough guide, if the weather is good enough to row ashore at Moody Brook then it will probably be safe enough to anchor off the Public jetty and dinghy ashore saving a two-mile walk into town.

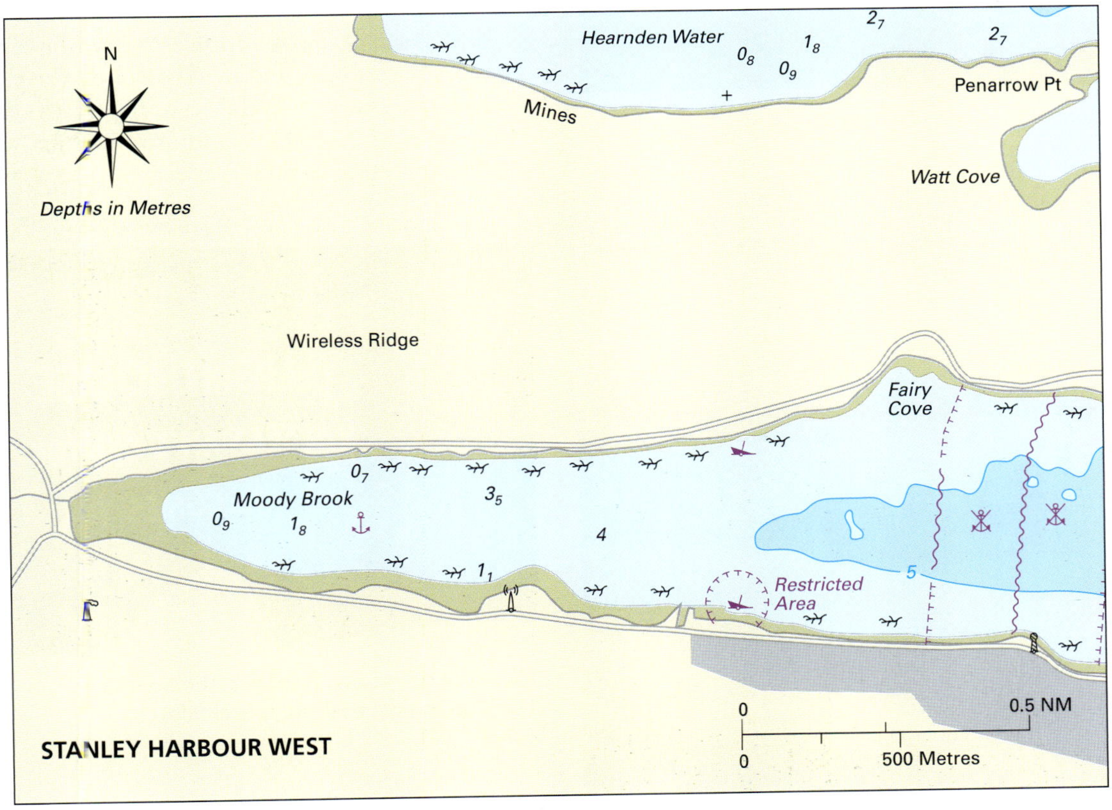

STANLEY HARBOUR WEST

Winds in Stanley Harbour *Pete Smith*

Curlew *National Maritime Museum Cornwall*

The landing at the western end of the Stanley harbour was created by Tim and Pauline Carr for the benefit of fellow sailors who might find it of use. The Carrs are sailors of the highest order having spent ten years making world cruises in their Falmouth Quay Punt, which they lived aboard for 30 years. For a period they were full time residents of South Georgia. *Curlew* is now in the care of the National Maritime Museum, Cornwall, in the UK

If in need of shelter from easterly winds, anchorage can be found in Whalebone Cove, east of the Narrows, in the lee of the wreck of the *Lady Elizabeth*, said to be in a remarkable state of preservation.

The wreck of *Lady Elizabeth* *Pete Smith*

Near the commercial wharf, the Seaman's Mission makes everyone welcome
Sandy Duker

Services in Stanley

Fuel

Stanley Services Ltd on Airport Road has a filling station where jerry cans can be filled. You will also find solid fuel. Stanley Services can also provide diesel in bulk from a tanker. It may be possible to fill gas bottles at their depot next to FIPASS.

Diesel is available alongside at FIPASS.

Repairs

There are no dedicated facilities for yacht repairs in Stanley but this is a maritime community and there will be many engineers, welders and electricians, who have the skills you require. Enquire at FIPASS, where advice will be given as to who you might contact.

There are no chandlers, and any weighty spares may take months to arrive. If you have an engine problem, it is possible to find a skilled engineer but he is very unlikely to have the necessary spares for your engine. For this reason your spares list must be comprehensive.

It might be possible to haul-out using a railroad pulley system onto a sloping beach. Reports say that, although costly and far from ideal, it is a useful option in the event of problems.

Other options for drying out in the islands include against the jetty on Weddell Island, or at Beaver Island on spring tides.

Anchorages in East Falkland (clockwise from Stanley)

Only the major harbours and anchorages are given here. You might call them 'bolt-holes' but the locals know them as 'catch-ups'. They have been chosen as places where the entry is less complex, and where shelter can be found.

The islands abound with bays and creeks and the adventurous will be richly rewarded. For those wanting to carry out more detailed cruising, then *Falkland Island Shores* - referred to here as *FIS* - and its supplement should be consulted.

Leaving Port Stanley

Chart 2356

On leaving Stanley, yachts bound south will pass north of the Tussac Islands where there are no dangers and little tidal stream. The safest course is then to pass between the Billy Rock and the Seal Rocks where the flood runs to the north. To ensure you remain clear of the notorious Billy Rock (51°40'30S, 57°42'42W) from north of the Tussacs, do not bear away to the south until Cape Pembroke light bears 225°. The coastline from here to the southwest becomes low and uninteresting and there is little with which to fix your position by observation. Also, the thickness of the kelp beds can give a false radar echo and you can appear, by radar, to be much closer to the coast than you are. For all these reasons, it is clearly not a place to be caught out in heavy weather.

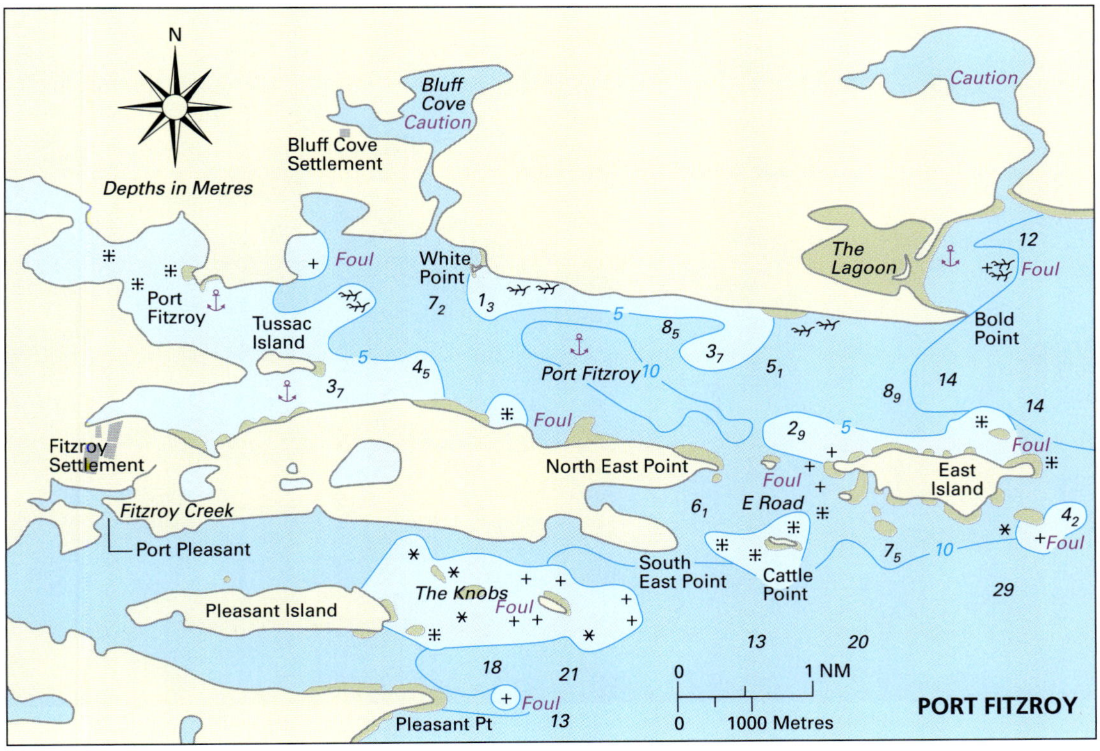

War memorial, Fitzroy, Falkland Islands *Vicky Jackson*

Fitzroy settlement *Vicky Jackson*

Port Fitzroy

51° 46'S 58° 03'W

The approaches to Port Fitzroy from the NE are marked as 'unsurveyed' so proceed with caution from Seal Point onwards using kelp for guidance. If making from Cape Pembroke, a course of 247° will clear all dangers. Incidentally, if you are planning to visit the Fitzroy settlement, then note that this lies not in Port Fitzroy but in Port Pleasant, the next bay south.

Those visiting Port Fitzroy are usually heading for Bluff Cove on the north shore. The chart shows a thick bed of kelp running east of East Island so a course should be made to pass midway between East Island and Bold Point before proceeding westwards into Port Fitzroy, watching for kelp lying off the north shore, north of the gap between North East Point and East Island. (*FIS* gives entry directions using leading marks in the event of electronic navigation failure). Bold Point is easily identified by its low cliffs beneath low land which sweeps down to a broad beach. East Island is the breeding ground for the Falkland flightless steamer duck.

Port Fitzroy is a beautiful, sheltered stretch of water where dolphins are to be found, along with Jackass and Gentoo penguins.

Anchorages can be found to the north of Bold Point, off The Lagoon, be mindful of a couple of rocks shown on chart *2536* which will be betrayed by kelp. A swell can run into this anchorage making landing difficult. If you manage to make it ashore, you will find the legendary Sea Cabbage Café with home-baking and live music and the Bluff Cove Museum, which tells the story of farm and Falkland life.

If seeking shelter, a good anchorage can be found further to the west in Port Fitzroy between Tussac Island and the south shore of the bay, east of Fitzroy. Anchor in 8m in thick mud.

Bluff Cove

51° 46'S 58°10'W

Bluff Cove has always had a reputation as a safe small boat haven. White Point must be rounded no closer than 3 cables off, and the anchorage will be found 2 cables 190° from the narrow entrance.

It is possible to enter the cove and anchor in the pool 075° from the landing point. As the entrance is narrow with sheer cliffs, winds can accelerate here and it might be advisable to anchor a yacht fore and aft. There is no navigable water beyond the pool, except by dinghy.

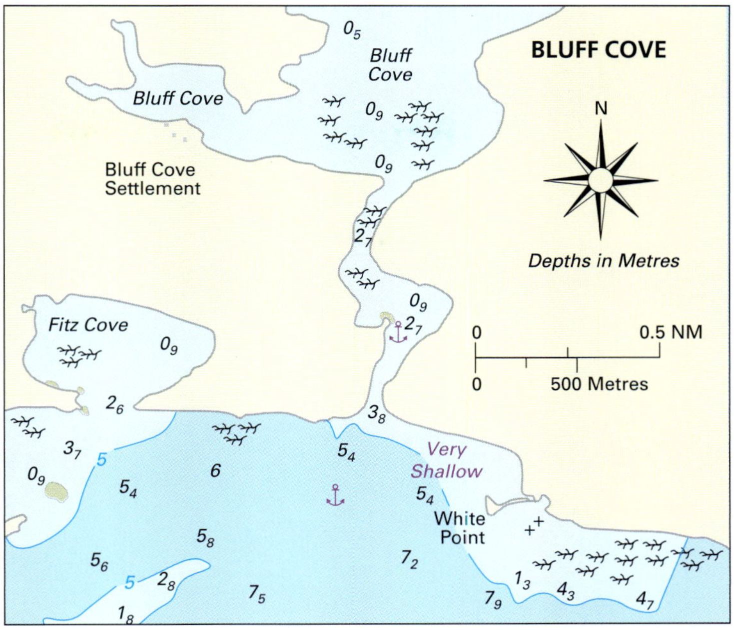

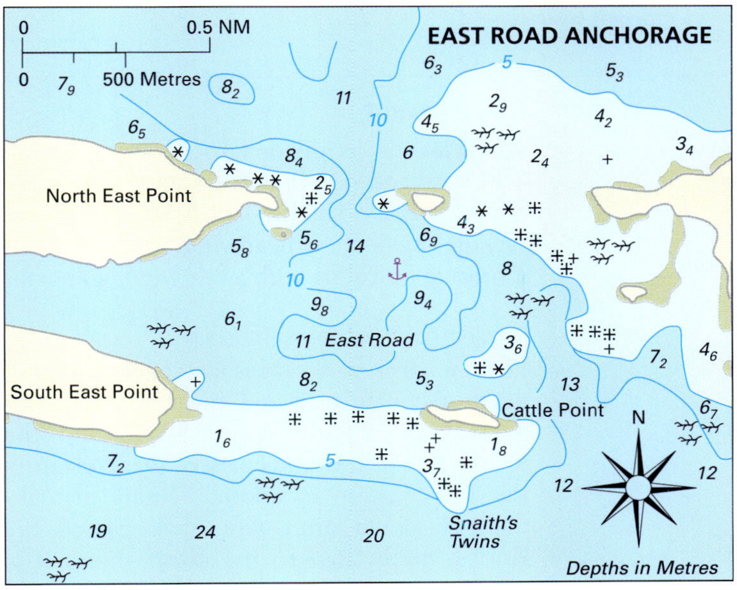

East Road

East Road anchorage lies between North East Point and East Island on the south side of Port Fitzroy. This also provides a passage between Port Fitzroy and Port Pleasant to the south.

Enter East Road 1½ cables to the east of North East Point. The chart shows a mass of kelp, but there is a z-shaped passage through which can be clearly seen from a yacht. There is a wide, clear area 5 cables by 3 in the centre. If the weather is calm and there is sufficient moonlight, the kelp marks this channel so well that it would be possible to make the transit at night. The anchorage is in 7–12m over thick mud.

A tussock-covered island lies 7 cables to the east of South East Point (known locally as Cattle Point), it is easily identified. There are rocks 2 cables to the south of the island and you should not turn to the west until the kelp shows that you are clear of them.

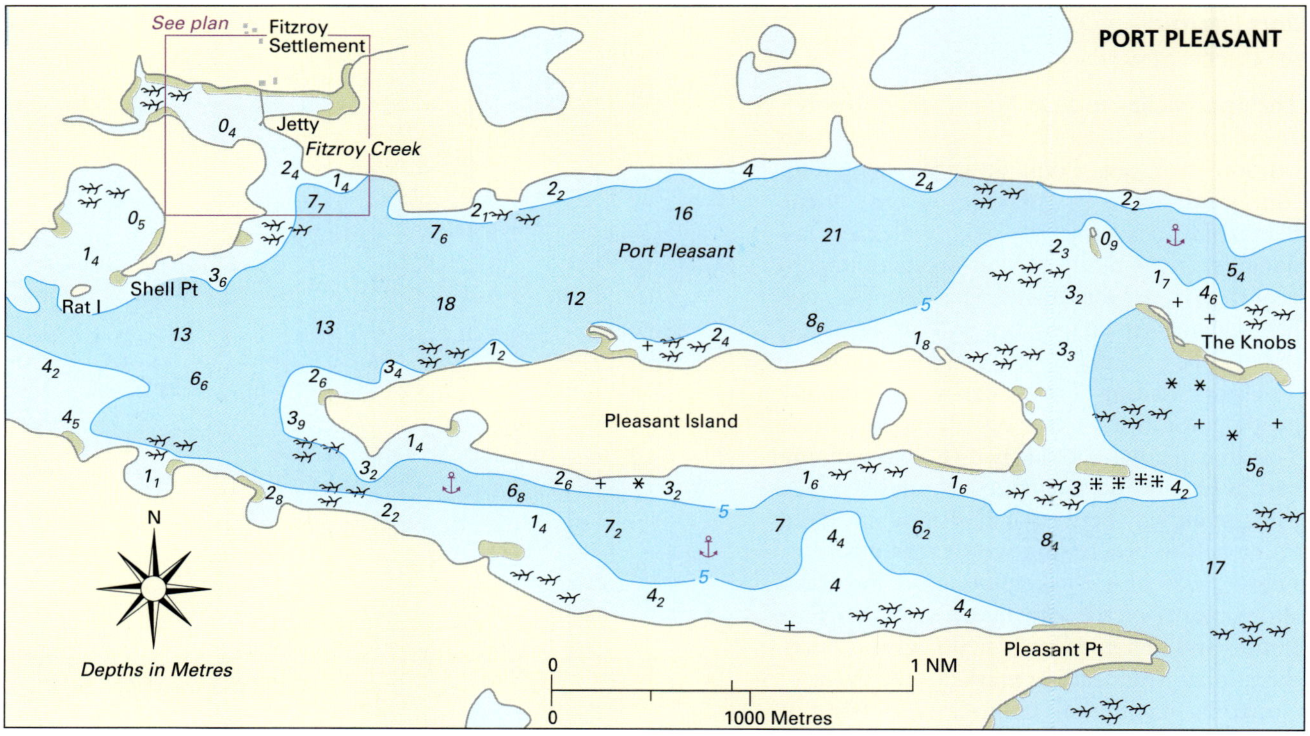

Port Pleasant

Port Pleasant is divided by Pleasant Island. The northern side is narrow and deep while the southern is shallow and wide. If you are tacking against a headwind, go south. If motoring or sailing with a fair wind, go north.

Passing north of Pleasant Island

Having cleared the tussock-covered island, make a course to avoid the kelp off South East Point. Identify Outer Knob and the Knobs and pass to the north of them, clearing the kelp. There is another small tussock-covered island after you have passed the Knobs, quite close to the north shore. It is vital you identify this and pass to the north of it. Chart *2536* shows a yellow beacon marking this island. There is no passage to the south. If you stay a cable from the north shore you will be in safe water.

Passing south of Pleasant Island

After clearing the small tussock island which lies to the south of East Road, continue southwards until the length of the island opens up. Alter course to find the kelp that runs east from outer Knob Island. Follow the line of the kelp until southeast of Pleasant Island and cross the bar at its northern end, nearest to the island. The edges of the channel are now quite steep-to and any dangers are marked by kelp so a yacht can tack in safety.

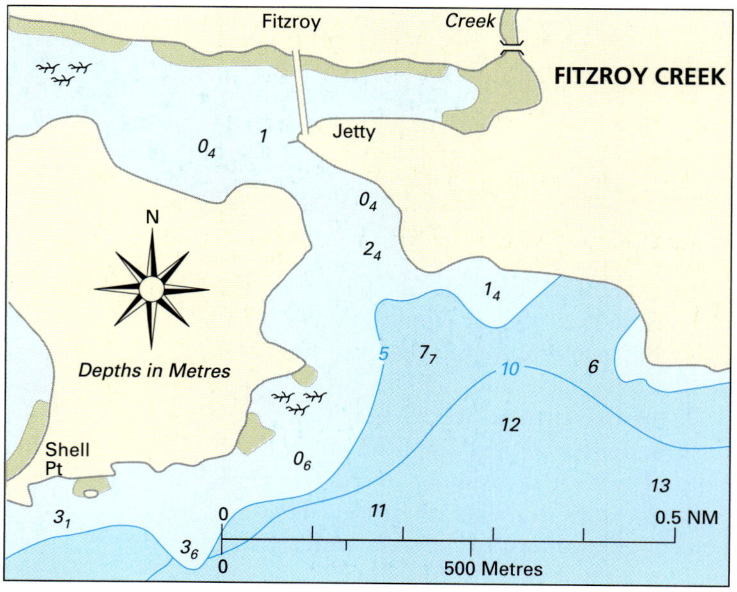

Fitzroy Creek

51° 48'S 58° 13'W

N or NW winds can funnel here but holding is good in 2·5–3m thick mud with little kelp. The cove immediately west of the creek has better protection but is open to the SW. The lagoon north of the narrows is too shallow for navigation (the bridge leading to the jetty mentioned in *FIS* is derelict).

You will find a small and friendly community here.

Further exploration seems possible well inland towards Island Harbour. Pete and Annie Hill's supplement describe it as a

> *pleasant sail with room to tack all the way…and an anchorage off Rabbit Island in 3m, mud. In strong W winds a more sheltered spot can be found N of Knob Point.*

Fitzroy takes its name from Captain Fitzroy of HMS *Beagle* who, together with Charles Darwin, landed here in 1833.

Memories of the War

It is impossible to sail to Fitzroy and Bluff Cove without reviving memories of the 1982 war. The names of so many of these hitherto innocent harbours are now ingrained in the minds of people old enough to remember the conflict as it unfolded on television screens back home. Fitzroy and Bluff Cove in particular will be remembered by British visitors as the scene of their greatest loss. This was where two British supply ships, *Sir Galahad* and *Sir Tristram*, were bombed in a surprise and skilful raid by Argentine airforce pilots. The attack came before air defences could be put in place making the two ships sitting targets. *Sir Galahad* was towed out to sea and sunk as a war grave.

Choiseul Sound and Mare Harbour

This is a glorious stretch of water which cuts into the heart of East Falkland, and for a cruising yacht provides safe anchorages, creeks aplenty, and rivers for exploration. At the head are the two settlements of Goose Green and Darwin, and closer to its eastern mouth excellent anchorages in Mare Harbour. It marks the northern edge of Lafonia. At the entrance to the sound on the northern shore is Bertha's Beach Bird Area consisting of 3,300 hectares of wetland of great importance to migrating birds. 77 species of wildflower have been recorded here. Peale's dolphins can be seen playing in the surf.

Warning

This area was the scene of much military activity in 1982 and there may still be unexploded bombs, missiles or ammunition. Areas around Darwin and Goose Green may still be mined. It would be unwise to venture far ashore without local advice.

Approaches to Mare Harbour

Both the north and south shores are low-lying grassland and radar images will be poor and unreliable. The beaches consist of boulders leading to cliffs no higher than 2/3m. All the dangers, however, are marked by kelp and the tidal flows are of no significance. However, at the north end of Lively Sound spring rates may reach 2 knots, and there can be tide rips on the ebb and flood off Pyramid Point. In the Darwin Narrows and off the entrance to Mare Harbour the spring rate can also reach 2 knots.

If navigating by magnetic compass, unpredictable variations have been reported in 51° 51'.5S; 58° 11'W.

Mare Harbour

51° 56'S 58° 28'W
Chart 2506

This is reckoned to be one of the safest anchorages in East Falkland with excellent holding and no swell. The entrance is clear of dangers and the kelp patches, which reduce the width of the entrance to 3 cables, easily seen.

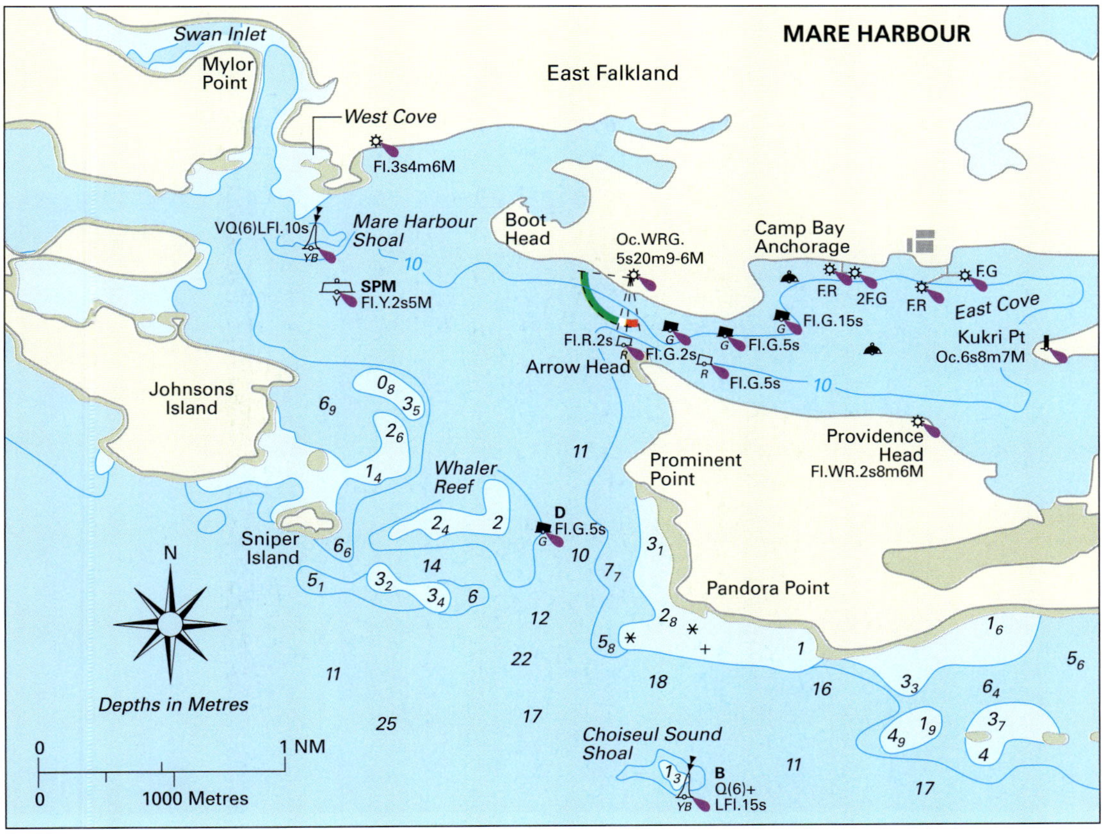

The landscape here is low and undulating, and the beaches are mostly shingle and boulder. The depths in the centre of the harbour reach 17m and a yacht can seek an anchorage in one of the many arms.

The harbour is used as a base for British Royal Navy ships patrolling the South Atlantic and Antarctica and is a port facility for RAF Mount Pleasant 5M to the north. You are likely to meet tankers, container ships and RoRo vessels.

This is a military area under the control of the Queen's Harbourmaster.

Because of the naval and commercial activity, a yacht is afforded the luxury of lights and buoys, rare in these islands.

Entrance

After identifying and passing south of the Choiseul Sound Shoal buoy (Q(6)+LFl.15s) course can be altered to the NNW to find the G Whaler Reef buoy Fl.G.5s. To the NNE will be seen oil storage tanks and by night a light on the shore Oc.WRG.5s20m9-6M the white sector of which will cause you to leave Arrow Head to starboard. Tidal streams in the entrance are less than 1 knot.

The best anchorage if seeking shelter is in East Cove and you should continue NNE, following the white sector of the above light until the narrow Hecate Channel opens up and the light beacon on Providence Head (Fl.WR.2s8m6M) can be identified. The entrance channel is narrow but marked by red and green channel markers.

For best shelter make a course towards Camp Bay in the NW corner and find an anchorage well sheltered from the W in 5m, thick mud.

With Chart *2506*, a yacht will be able to find many more anchorages. In West Cove the entrance to the Swan Inlet is said to be beautiful and trout can be caught on a spinner.

Darwin and Goose Green

Charts 2561, 2550

From a position mid channel north of Middle Island, the passage to Darwin and Goose Green is, for the most part, straightforward with deep, clear water to be found as far as Scott Island. The north shore of the Sound provides useful anchorages, particularly Mackinnon Creek north of Sea Lion Island which is sheltered from all quarters and has good holding in stiff mud.

Goose Green Quay
Tim Barker

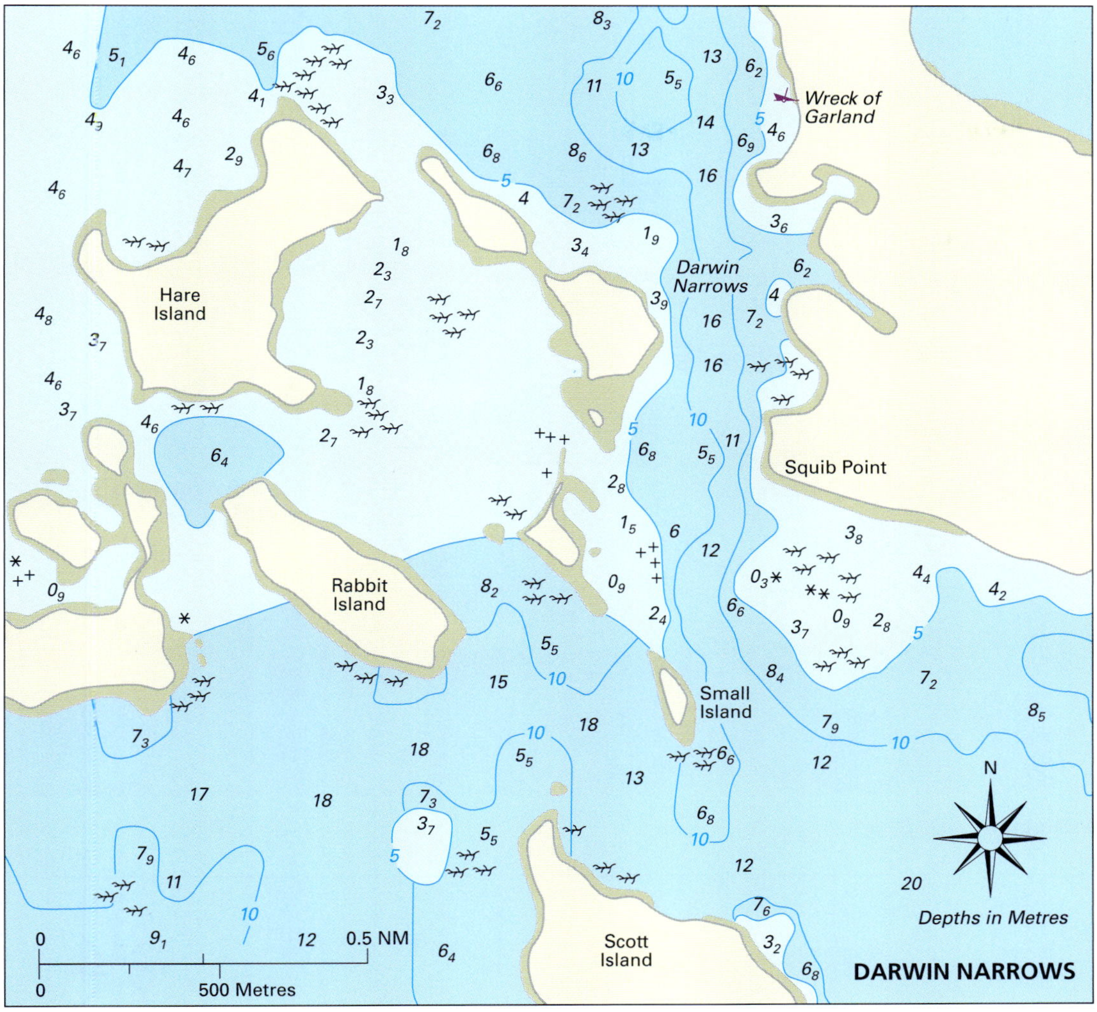

The Darwin Narrows

Chart 2550 - Plans in East Falkland Island

These present the only navigational challenge before reaching Darwin. The spring flood in the Narrows can run at up to 1 knot and kelp may run under and not be seen.

Stay close to the north shore, about 3 cables off. Scott Island should be left 2–3 cables to port. Identify the first small, low island (5m) to the north of it. This island, known as Small Island but not named on the chart, marks the port hand side of the entrance to the Narrows. From Small Island, the best course is 345°, but be sure to avoid kelp. From here, *2550* shows a clear passage in a roughly N direction until the bay widens. Observe the wreck of the *Garland* on the starboard side, and do not alter course for Goose Green until it bears due E, ensuring you do not get snared in the kelp north of Hare Island. With the *Garland* abeam, a course of 285° takes you directly to the jetty at Goose Green. There is more than 2m of water at this jetty and yachts can lie alongside.

If proceeding next to Darwin, take care to avoided the charted patch of kelp surrounding a small island which is directly in your path. The kelp is reported to be more widespread here than charted, so a wide berth should be given leaving it to port if heading north.

The combined settlements of Darwin and Goose Green represent the largest settlement outside of Stanley and, typically, you will be made welcome. Consult the settlement manager before undertaking any shore-side excursions. This is the site of the first major land battle of Falklands War and there may be unexploded ordnance. It is not thought the beaches were mined, but check.

The quay at Goose Green with the historic wreck of the *Vicar of Bray*
Tim Barker

The Goose Green Settlement *Tim Barker*

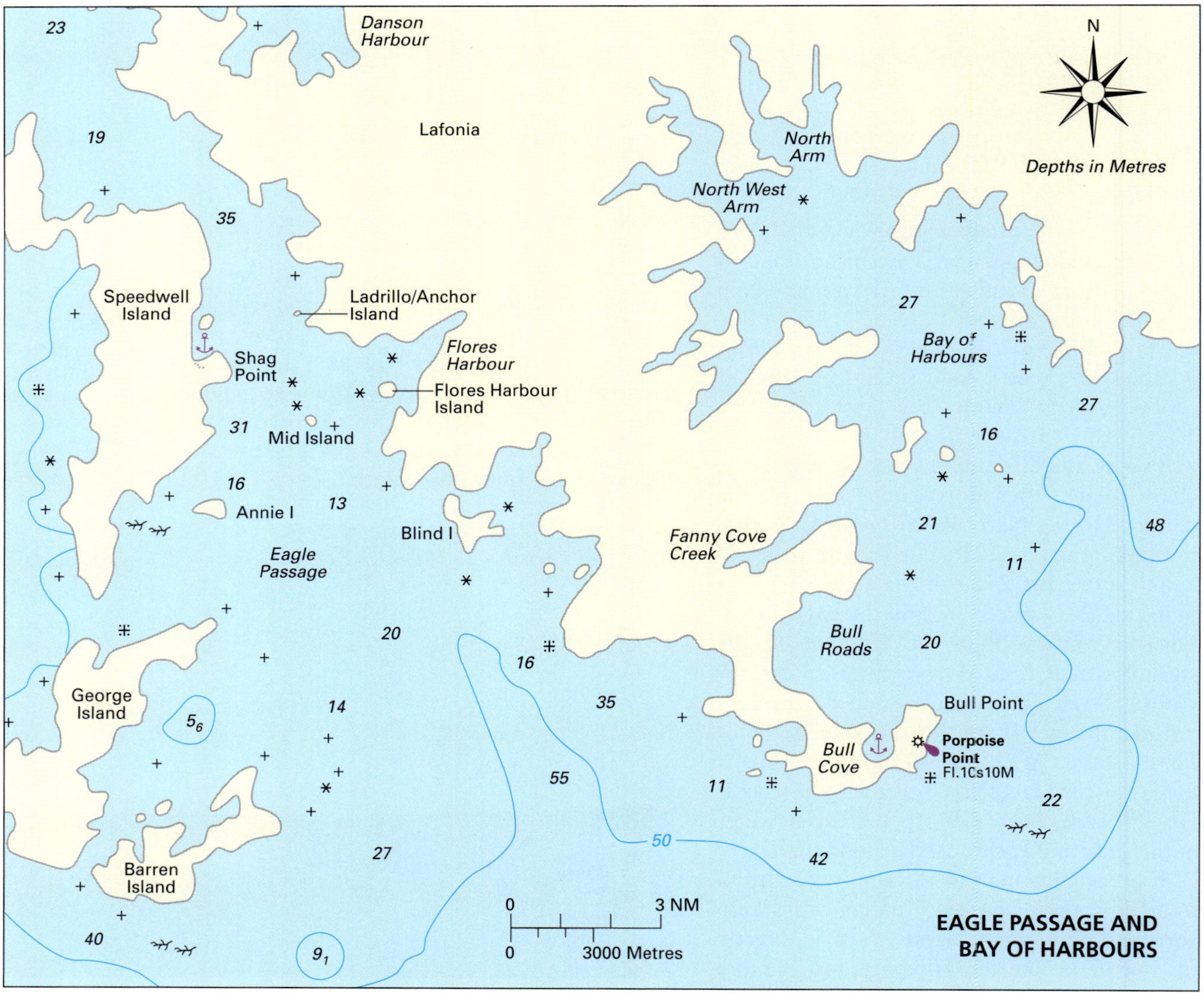

The south coast of East Falkland Island

Most yachts do not find this a place to linger. The coast is featureless and navigation by observation is difficult. Of passing interest might be Low Bay and Adventure Sound which could provide useful anchorages, but the land here is low lying and gives little protection from the wind. In Low Bay, many of the anchorages are filled with kelp and uncharted rocks and southerly winds can produced a nasty swell.

Note that a strong SW wind against tide kicks up a nasty race off Bull Point and Porpoise Point making progress slow, if not dangerous.

Bay of Harbours

Chart 2560

Bull Roads (52°20′S 59°19′W), at the southern end of the Bay of Harbours, provides a useful sheltered anchorage in which to break a passage around the southern shores of the island.

Bull Cove lies on the southern side of Bull Roads and would appear to provide a near perfect anchorage, were it not for the extensive kelp which fills the bay. From Bull Point navigate to avoid the kelp and then nose your way into Bull Cove where it is possible to see areas of clean bottom through the clear water; anchor in the narrow neck of the cove.

Be aware that to seaward of Bull Cove, on the south side, the kelp is reported to be extending; if heading westwards a berth of at least 2M should be given.

6M further north an anchorage in Fanny Cove Creek (52°15′S 59°20′W) would give good shelter in N winds. As in much of Lafonia, the low shoreline provides little shelter from the wind, but the 'woollies', at least, will not trouble you. Between here and Bull Roads you will see a Gentoo penguin colony said by some to be the home to two million birds, although the numbers may be greatly exaggerated.

Eagle Passage

Chart 2560

Eagle Passage lies between Lafonia and the smaller islands of Speedwell, Barren and George Island which lie off the SW coast of East Falkland Island.

Eagle Passage tides

The flood tide runs north through the passage at up to 3 knots, giving rise to wind over tide conditions; these are most frequently found off Mid Island and Ladrillo Island, known locally as Anchor Island. Also be aware that a tide race can be found off the NE point of Speedwell Island.

After rounding the light on Porpoise Point (Fl.10s.10M) heading westwards, give the shore a berth of at least 2M to avoid rocks and kelp. Streams off the point run W/E at up to 3 knots. Be aware of a strong set after prolonged westerly weather; it has been the cause of many shipwrecks along this coast.

FIS notes anchorages on Barren, George and Speedwell Islands, but only the latter is of great interest. To enter, identify Shag Point halfway along the E coast of the island, 8 cables NE of a distinctive white beach. Follow the coast round to Halfway Cove, passing to the south of yet another tussock island. Tie up alongside the jetty where the least depth is 1·2m. You will see the settlement which consists of ten white houses, and from here there is a walk to a Gentoo colony south of Kits Creek.

The northern end of Eagle Passage presents no difficulties, but be aware that after passing Stinker Island (the breeding ground of the Great Petrel, known locally as 'The Stinker') it would be unwise to turn to the north until a clearly charted large area of kelp to the east of Ruggles Island has been passed.

East Falkland Sound

Chart 2559

If you are making a passage of it and want to transit the Falkland Sound without stopping, then navigation is far simpler if you take the western shore. The eastern shore is sheltered and has pleasant anchorages, but be prepared for rock hopping and eyeball navigation.

North of Ruggles Island anchorages can be found in Ruggles Bay, Findlay Harbour and Wharton Harbour although there is some exposure to strong westerly winds and the 'woollie' effect of the higher land of West Falkland might be felt.

Wolfe Harbour

52°01′S 59° 39′W

Wolfe Harbour off the NE of Wolfe Island is described by one local as 'one of the finest anchorages in the Falkland Islands'. Anchor in 7m over thick mud just clear of the kelp.

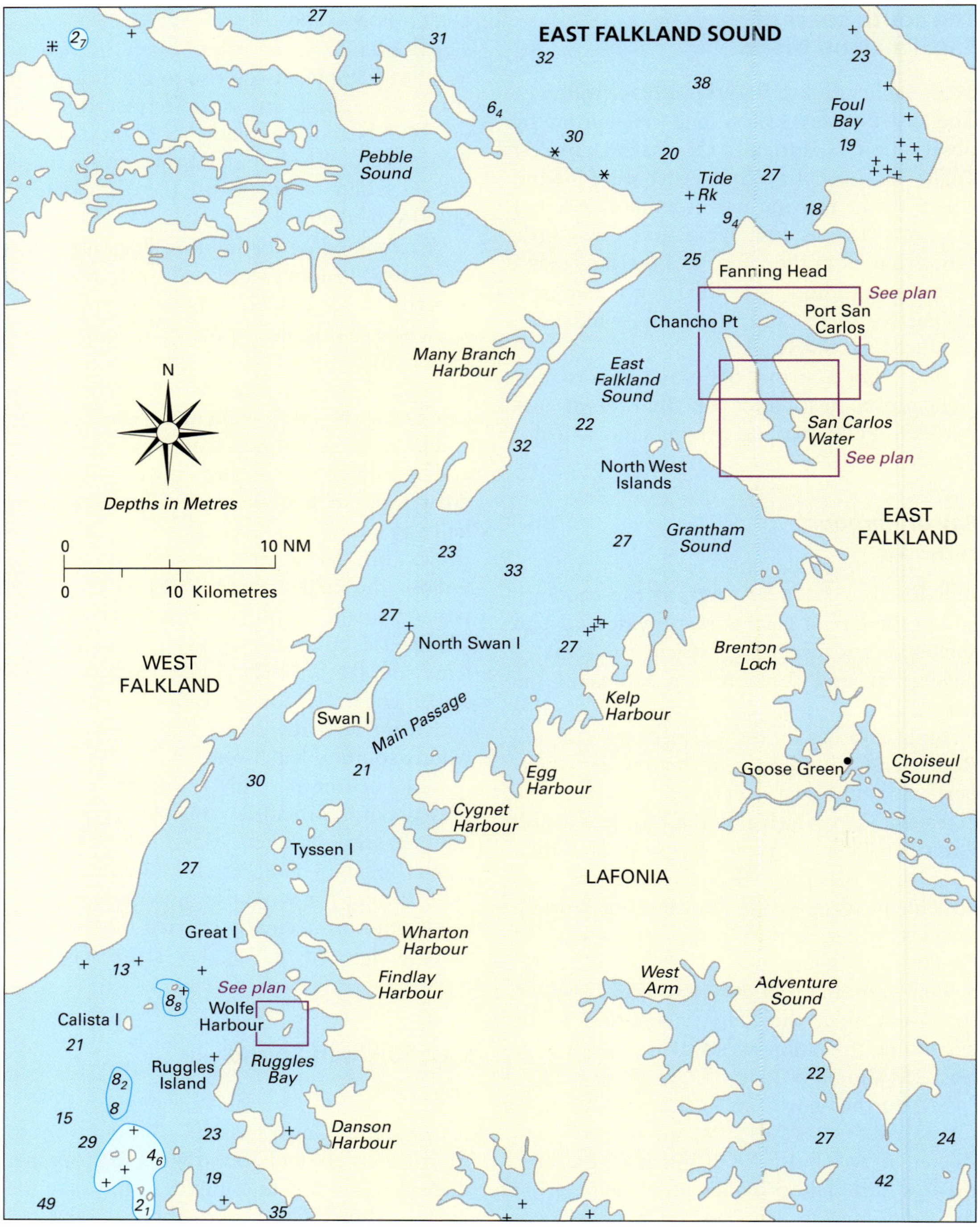

To enter, leave Flat Wolfe to the south, and note the charted rocks off the NW of Wolfe Island.

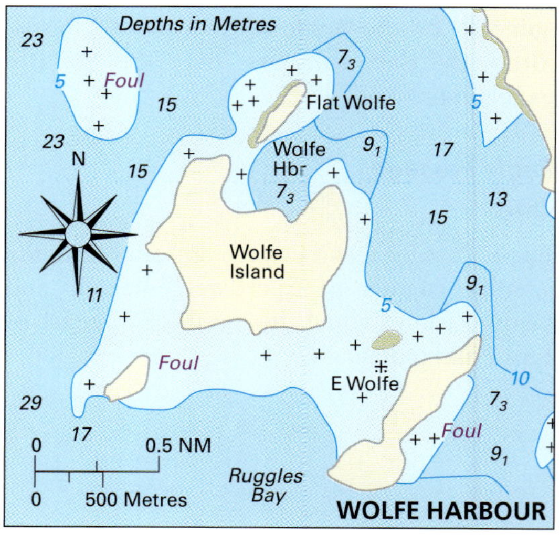

Port San Carlos and San Carlos Water

51°29′S 59° 08′W

This consists of two long bays; Port San Carlos to the north, and San Carlos Water to the south.

San Carlos Water is a large, sheltered area 9M long and 1M wide offering a wide choice of anchorages giving shelter from all wind directions. The tidal range is between 0·9m at neaps, 1·6m at springs. There is a settlement in each of the bays, and both have 'camp track' connections to Stanley, one passing via Darwin on what is reported as a 'reasonable road'. The other leads from Port San Carlos, round the north of the island and is reported to be 'poor and slow'. Both settlements have substantial jetties. These inlets were of great strategic significance in the 1982 war, and known as 'bomb alley'. It was in San Carlos Water that British forces established a bridgehead from which to mount an assault on the Argentine forces holding Stanley.

Both bays are free of dangers providing notice is taken of kelp markers. Southerly winds can produce quite a chop in San Carlos Water when the best anchorage will be found in Seaview Creek (see plan below). 'Woollies' can be experienced in westerly weather with considerable gusts, mostly along the western shore.

Fanning Harbour, the first bay on the port hand if entering either Sound is quite deep for a yacht anchorage, but the holding is good and is shown as a ship anchorage. If heading for Port San Carlos, notice the rocks off the end of Fanning Island, after which the water leading to Port San Carlos will be seen. However, the Careening Cove and the settlement will not be seen until you are within a mile of them. The banks here are steep-to.

There is a good anchorage close to the shore south of the stony beach at Careening Cove. Follow the edges of the kelp patches in the entrance. The jetty is T-shaped and substantial with plenty of depth alongside. This has a reputation for being a truly hospitable place, and given the near perfect shelter you may find that you linger here.

An added attraction is the San Carlos River which is navigable for the first couple of miles. Chart *2558* shows some detail, and *FIS* contains EST's sketch map used in Commando operations.

San Carlos Water anchorages

Chart 2582 is useful, although 2558 has sufficient detail for safe navigation

Ajax Bay

51°33'S 59°04'W

This provides a good anchorage southeast of an old refrigeration plant. Expect 'woollies' tumbling off Campito Hill in westerlies, and a choppy sea in easterlies. There are shingle beaches either side of the old jetty for easier landing. It would be unwise to approach the jetty as a sunken barge lies off the end of it with only 6 feet of water.

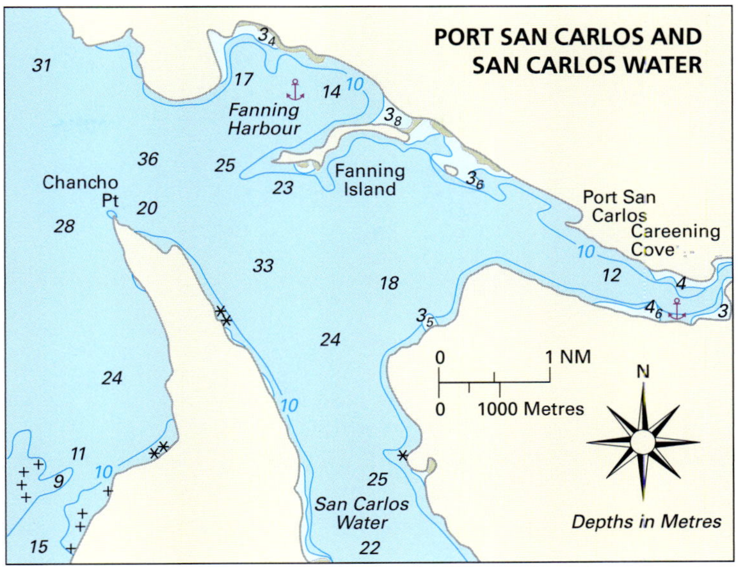

Fern Valley Creek

51°33' S 59°02'W

Anchor on the edge of the kelp in the SE corner. Safe in all winds except E when subject to 'woollies'.

The Upper Reaches

Note - there is more kelp off Poker Point than shown on the chart, and also off Little Rincon.

Bonners Bay

51°34'S 59°02'W

This is the closest anchorage to the Port San Carlos settlement. The anchorage is one and a half cables to the SE of the jetty in 4m, thick mud. This jetty could be useful if attempting underwater repairs. At low water, the end of the jetty has 1·2m with a hard sand bottom. It would be possible to lean against the jetty and dry out here.

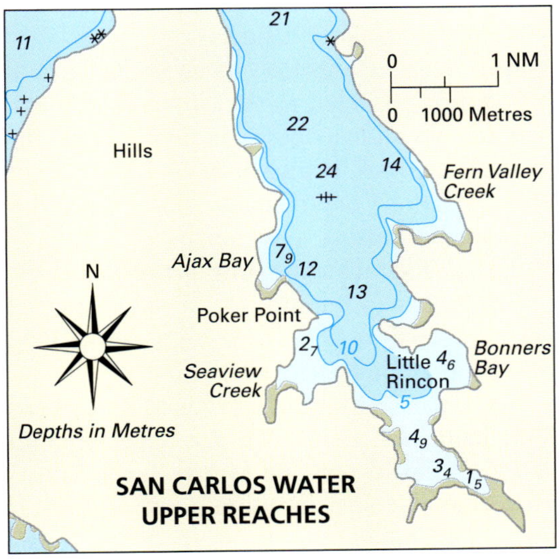

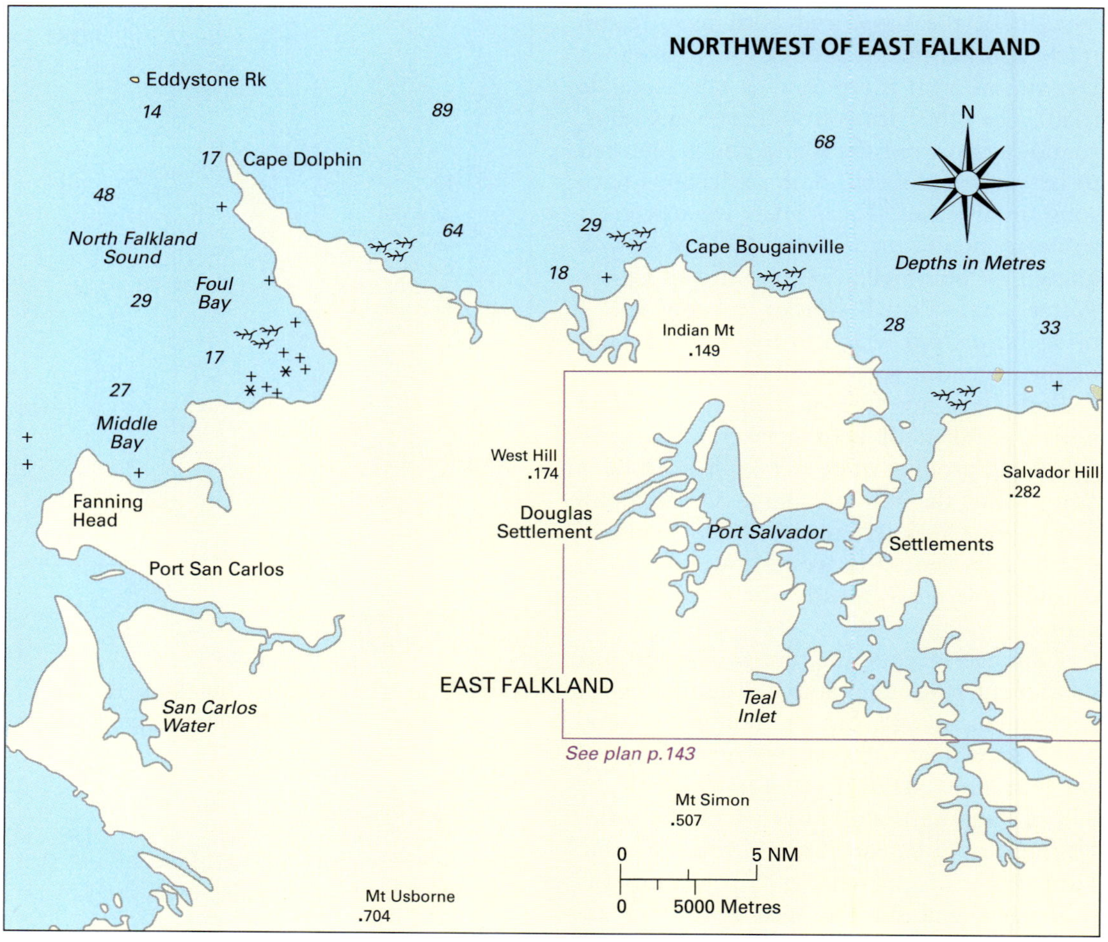

The North Falkland Sound and northwest coast of East Falkland

Chart 2507

The tides run more strongly here than anywhere else in the Falklands and the kelp can run under making it less useful for navigation. North of Fanning Head, both Middle Bay and Foul Bay are places where a yacht could become embayed. The chart may not show all the dangers due to sparse surveying. Fanning Head is steep to with kelp showing any inshore dangers.

Tide Rock (51°25′15.5S 59°09′16.4W) should be identified and left to port if heading north. Aim to pass midway between the rock and the shore. This rock is awash at high water but gives a good radar echo. Locals do not recommend passing to its north.

There is a race extending 4 cables off the north of Cape Dolphin. However, in settled weather, it is possible to pass inside the kelp patch shown on chart *2507*.

Eddystone Rock (51°11′20.3S 59°03′14W) 44m high, lies to the NW of Cape Dolphin and is a breeding ground for the Fur Seal. It is a considerable structure and a useful mark if making a landfall on the north Falkland coast.

From Cape Dolphin eastwards lies an inhospitable coastline with no safe harbours and a yacht should not consider a passage with a forecast of a strong onshore wind. Northerly winds in wintertime produce big seas and dense fog. The tides run parallel to the coast and can reach 2–3 knots in places.

Port Salvador

51°21′S 58°17′W
Chart 2546

This is a large area of landlocked water which can provide weeks of cruising and exploration. It is only 50M from Stanley and could be reached in a day. There are settlements of interest to yachts at Salvador, Douglas, Rincon Grande and Teal Inlet. The *FIS* supplement provides a sketch chart for attempting Douglas Creek. To detail all the possible anchorages in Port Salvador is beyond the scope of this book, so only those close to the settlements are described.

Tides can run very strongly in the entrance, up to 8 knots on the ebb and 6 knots on the flood. The best time to attempt entry or exit is one hour before the start of a favourable tide when the water will be slack and the kelp won't run under. The tides turn one hour after low and high water, but this can be subject to weather. There are eddies on both sides of the entrance with the fastest running tide down the eastern shore.

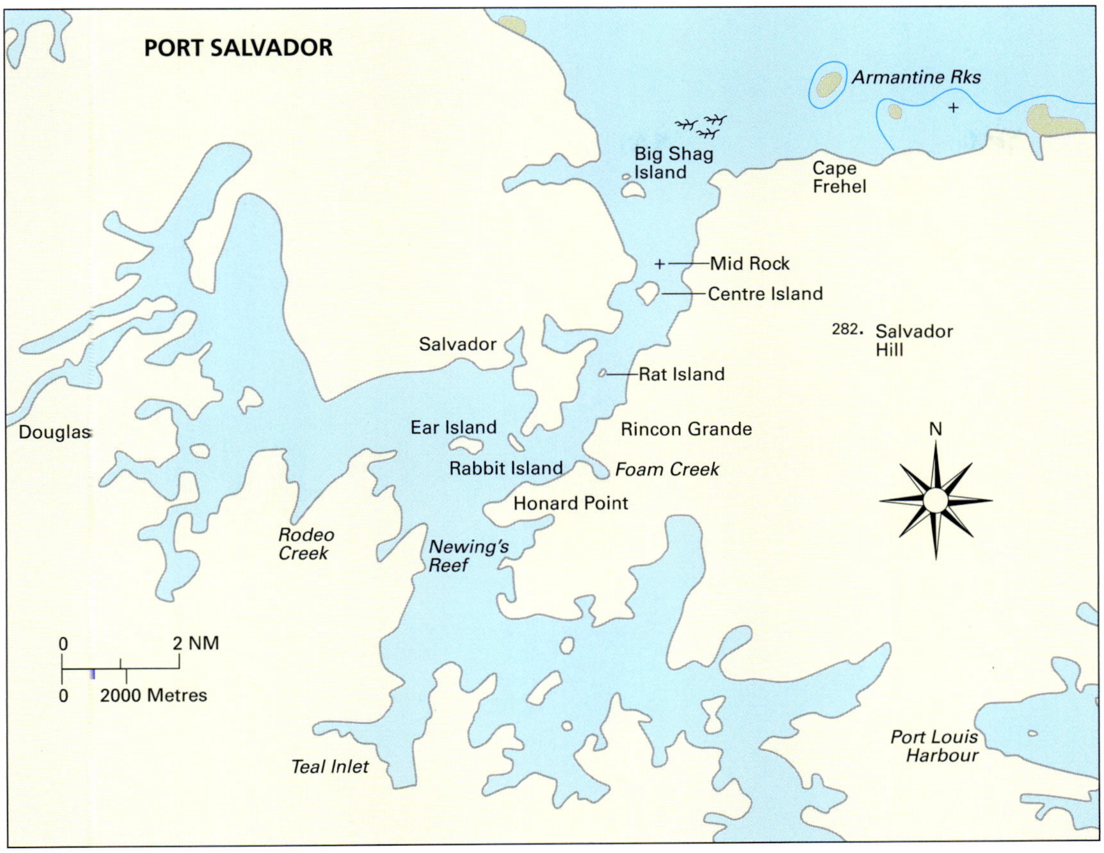

Approach to the broad entrance should be clear of the charted kelp which extends a considerable distance from each shore. From Big Shag Island, a course of 193° takes you to the west of Centre Island, but be careful to avoid Mid Rock, which is kelp covered and always causes a disturbance on the surface. Leave it to port. EWS reports that a fast flowing tide around this rock can create surface turbulence while the water over the rock itself may appear smooth. You can easily be misled.

Once past Centre Island, you are in clear water until Rat Island, which should be left to starboard.

Foam Creek

This good anchorage is on the E side of the entry channel to the E of Rabbit Island. Anchor off the jetty in soft mud. This is the closest anchorage to the Rincon Grande and Foam Creek settlements.

Salvador

If bound for Salvador Settlement, pass south of Rabbit Island where the shore is steep-to then make a course to the north. This anchorage gives good shelter from WNW through N to SE but there is a lot of kelp here and holding may be poor if the anchor is not well set.

It is very exposed to the SW and should the wind come on from that direction shelter should be found in Punta Frio Bay (Rodeo Creek) opposite, 2½M away. Anchor in the middle of the bay off the rock outcrop which divides the beach (not shown on the chart). There is a spring just behind the beach, to the S of the outcrop.

Teal Inlet

After passing Honard Point, the channel is littered with rocks close to Newing's Reef. Their position is uncertain. Make a course 180° due south from the western end of Ear Island until west of Honard Point and continue on that course, bearing in mind that the rocks and the kelp may extend further westwards than the chart suggests. The entrance to Teal Inlet has no dangers.

In prevailing winds, the best place to anchor is in the bay to the W of the jetty. If seeking more shelter, particularly from the NW, it is possible to go further into the bay which gradually shoals to less than 1.5m.

There is a road from here to Stanley, an hour's drive away.

The *FIS* supplement (Pete and Annie Hill) gives good pilotage for many more anchorages in Port Salvador.

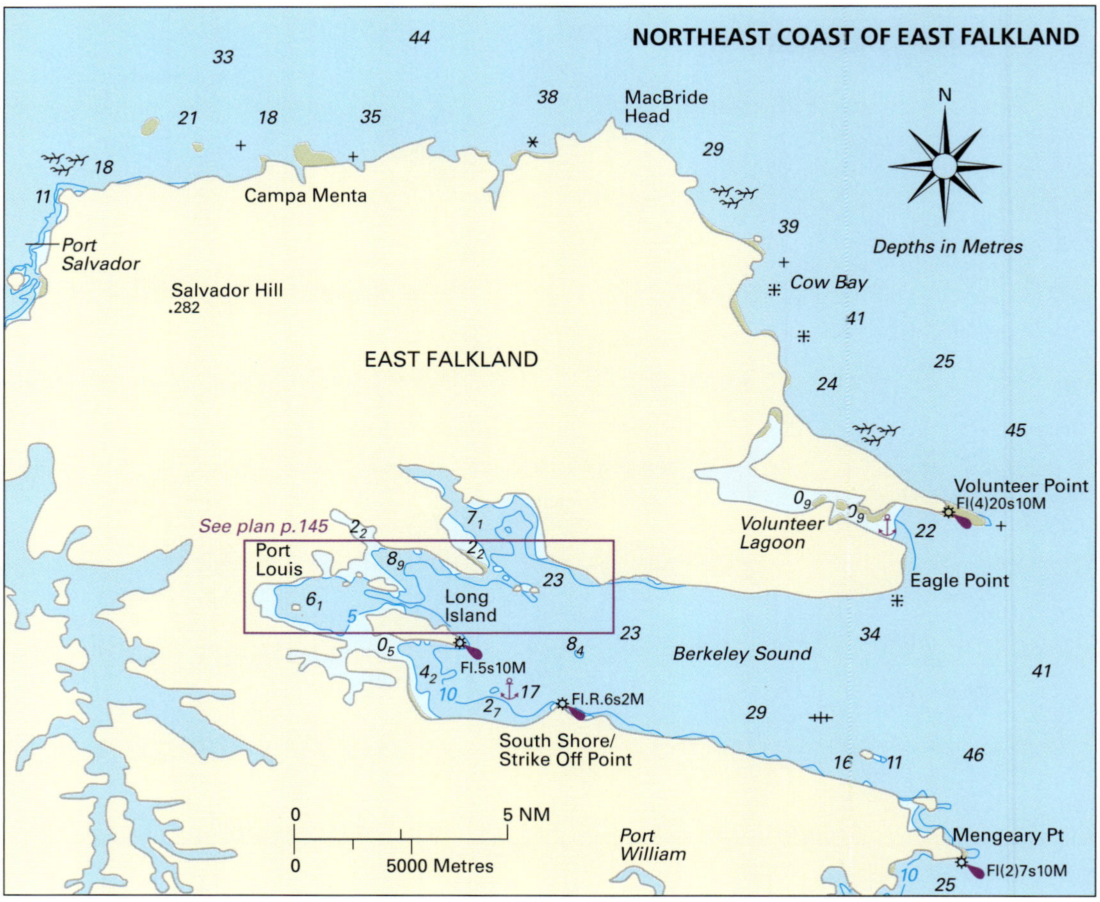

The northeast coast of East Falkland

Chart 2547

If heading for Stanley, the rounding of the north coast is a 30M passage, open to winds with any north in them. Easterly winds can bring fog. It is a coastline fringed with cliffs up to 50m high, and topped with grass. This coastline has not been surveyed since the middle of the nineteenth century.

The flood tide runs to the west reaching a maximum of 2 knots.

Northerly winds on this coast will occur when the glass is falling fast and an approaching depression passes between the islands and the South American mainland. Listen for the whistle of the Magellanic Oystercatcher which is said to be a good sign of northerly winds.

There are three anchorages on this north coast which might be useful in an emergency, or to provide a break. None are safe in all weathers.

Campa Menta Bay

51°23'S 58° 08'W)

Half a mile long and recognisable by the white sand at its head. Considerable kelp is found on both shores but this gives protection from wind and swell from both W and E. The anchorage is open to the N but comes recommended as a landing place for a good walk ashore.

(Note: there are no reports of any of the north coast beaches having been mined but this is no guarantee of safety.)

Cow Bay

Cow Bay (51°26'S 57°51'W) provides a very good anchorage with shelter from all directions other than those with E in them. The bay is distinctive for its wide sweep of white sand and Jackass penguin burrows. Anchor in sand as close in as the depth allows. There are rocks and kelp off both the northern and southern limits of the bay and the best advice is to steer south until the head of the bay bears west before turning in.

Volunteer Bay

The only King penguin breeding ground in the Falklands, this bay is a dedicated nature reserve. Sadly, the kelp makes it a poor anchorage and it is best to anchor in Cow Bay and take a walk south if you want to see the penguins. Another possibility is to anchor W by S of Volunteer Point at the entrance to Volunteer Lagoon (51°31′S 57°46′W) where you can anchor in sand, 3m.

By dinghy you can enter the lagoon and make your way to the northern branch and see the penguins from there.

Berkeley Sound and Port Louis

Lights
Volunteer Point Fl(4)W.20s
Mengeary Point Fl(2)W.7s
Long Island Fl.W.5s
South Shore (Strike Off Point) Fl.R.6s
Charts 2550, 2507

Berkeley Sound is a large expanse of water, 15M long and 3M wide and it is rare for swell to be felt here. It is a favourite anchorage for fishing vessels and factory ships.

At the head of the bay lies Port Louis, the first French settlement and the oldest on the islands, later becoming the capital under the Spanish who renamed it Puerto Soledad. The administration, under the British, was moved to Stanley in 1845.

Entrance to the Sound presents no problems, it is clear of dangers and both coasts are steep-to.

Port Louis

51° 32′S 58° 03′W

The passage into Port Louis harbour leaves Peat Island and Hog Island to starboard and Celery Island to port. Care must be taken to avoid a charted kelp patch off the NE of Long Island, otherwise pilotage is by observation of the Sea Lion Rocks, Lamarche Point on the N coast of the bay, and Monkey Point on the N shore to the E.

Once inside Port Louis harbour, anchorage can be found in 4m, 1 cable off the entrance to the Careenage.

There is also a settlement at Green Patch on the south side of the harbour, but the jetty is not recommended for a long stay.

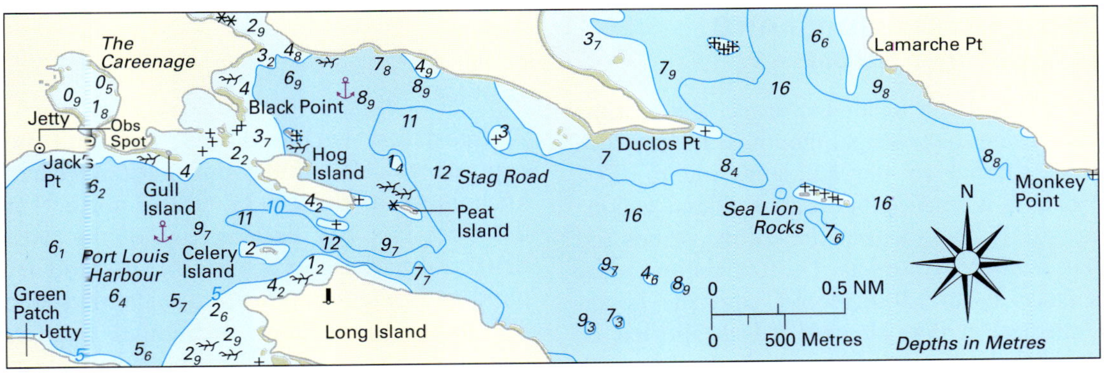

BERKELEY SOUND & PORT LOUIS

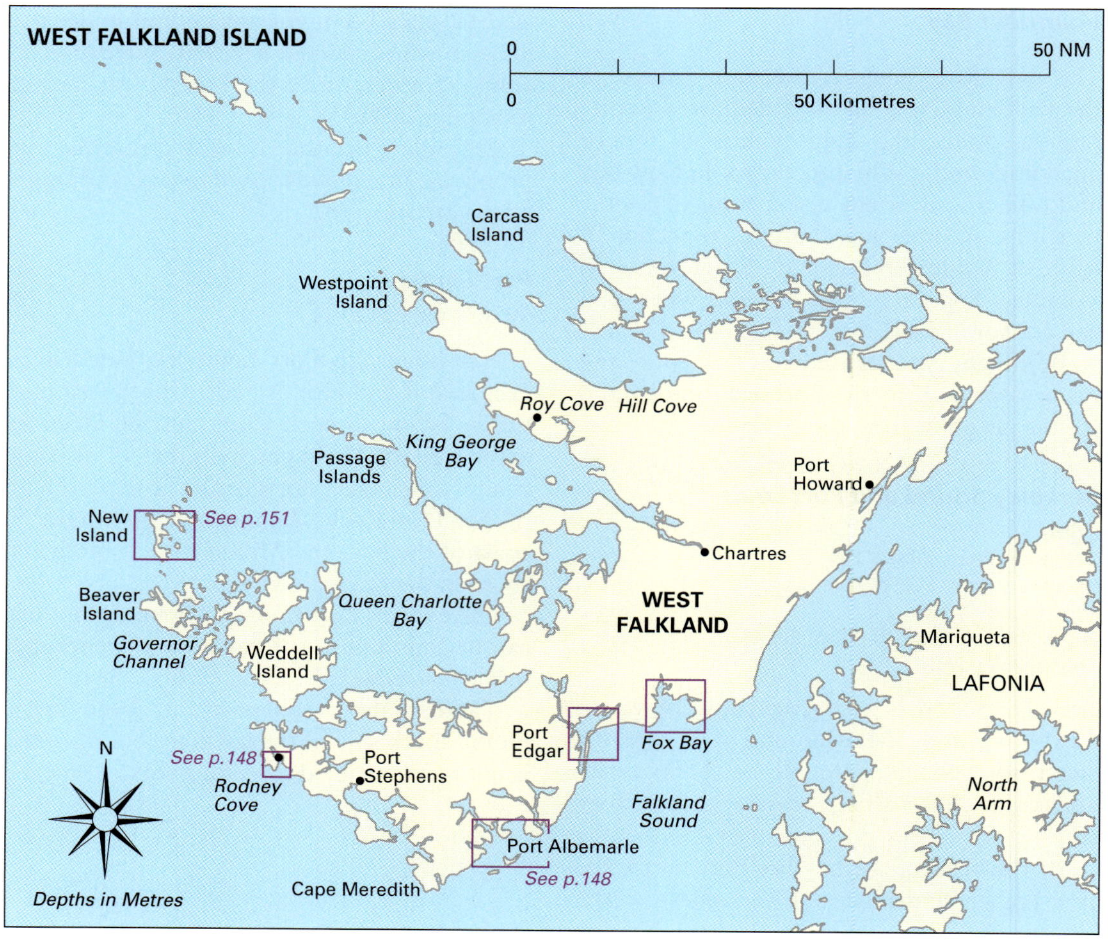

WEST FALKLAND ISLAND

Clockwise from Fox Bay

This is a much hillier landscape, the Hornby Hills being the principal mountain range which runs parallel to the Falkland Sound. West Falkland is smaller than East Falkland making up just 37% of the total area of the islands and has a 800M coastline. The population is far smaller at just 200 people, with the largest settlement at Port Howard, which also has an airstrip. As a rule of thumb, high cliffs with seabird colonies are found on the south side, sandy beaches and dunes to the west, these much enjoyed by elephant seals. The island was once home to a small wolf called the Warrah which has been extinct since 1880, but is remembered in the name of one of the island's rivers (which has excellent sea trout fishing). It was the islands' only native land mammal. Charles Darwin, on his 1833 visit, found them on both east and west Falkland but couldn't decide if they were different species. The poor wolf's downfall was its apparent trust of humans and so it was easily lured with meat and then killed to extinction. The name translates from the Latin into 'foolish dog of the south'.

Fox Bay

52°00'S 60° 03'W
Chart 2543

A large natural harbour open to the south and exposed to SW swell, but with excellent anchorages in the creeks to the north. *FIS* describes Fox Bay East as 'one of the most delightful settlements to visit.' At its head are good anchorages in quiet and sheltered spots. The passage to these anchorages appears complex but a 'highway' through the kelp is well defined and, due to the small tidal flow, the kelp never runs under.

Note: there is the possibility of uncleared mines along all these shores.

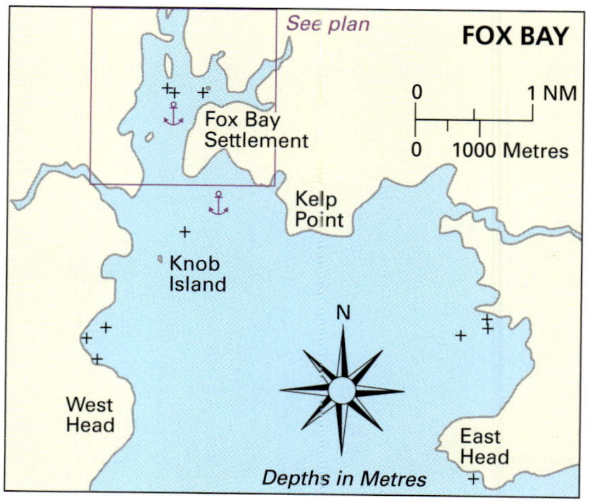

From a position in the middle of the bay halfway between East Head and West Head, identify and make a course towards Knob Island, which is a low, flat tussock island. Note firstly the kelp extending from the appropriately named Kelp Point, and also the charted kelp to the NE of Knob Island which has an unnamed obstruction causing sea to break. Use the kelp to guide you to a position with Flat Island on your beam, to port. When Knob Island and West Head are in transit, alter course towards the right hand edge of Packes Island. Continue until Fox Bay East pier is abeam. Unless the surface of the water is being kicked up by the wind, it is perfectly possible to achieve all the above by paying close attention to the edges of the banks of kelp.

The best berth for a yacht is undoubtedly in the pool at the entrance to Doctor's Creek, southwest of Dip Point in 5–7m, soft mud and good holding. However, there may be a sunken mooring hereabouts so buoy the anchor. Swinging is limited and it may be advisable to moor. Yachts have dragged ashore in strong winds, although *Iron Bark* reports surviving sustained winds of hurricane strength 'with dubious help from the engine'.

In a southerly blow, the best anchorage is 1½ cables NNW of Flat Island in 3m over thick mud. In settled weather, 2 cables NW of the Fox Bay East jetty is a good anchorage.

This is a place to experience real 'camp' life in a friendly and dynamic community. There is a well-stocked Co-op open Monday and Thursday evenings.

The jetty has been rebuilt and is substantial but exposed to the west and used by the supply vessel, *Concordia Bay*. Ask permission before using.

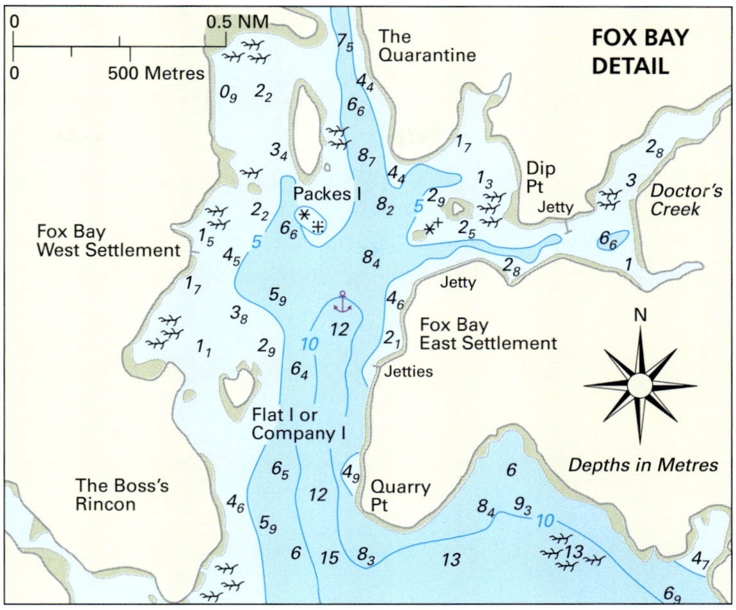

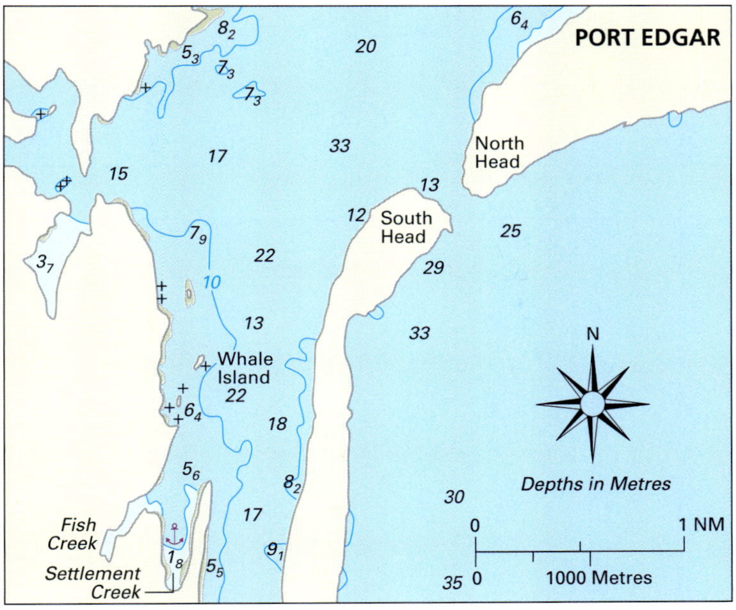

Port Edgar

52° 01'S 60° 12'W
Chart 2543

This was once considered the finest anchorage for the British fleet in the whole of the southern hemisphere. For yachts it provides good anchorage, although the entrance is narrow at only one cable with the deepest water being slightly to the south. It is open to southerly swells and the entrance should not be attempted in strong southerly winds. The entrance is often not seen until you are abreast it and the water can be seen beyond it.

Settlement Creek (52°03'S 60°17'W) provides the best anchorage for yachts. Having rounded South Head, a course should be made roughly SW until Whale Island is identified. A course can then be made to the anchorage, guided by the visible kelp. Follow the kelp down the western side of Settlement Creek towards a small two-storeyed shepherd's house at the head. The anchorage is in 2m, mud, off a small sand beach by the house.

Port Albemarle

52° 11' S 60°W
Chart 2543

This is part of a complex of estuaries, rivers and bays surrounded by hilly countryside and off-lying islands. It is a lonely spot - but the wildlife is abundant.

From the position shown, it is an easy entrance with no dangers. The tides run up to 2 knots offshore. If approaching from the south, Albemarle Rock (52°13'01S 60°23'10W) must be identified.

The best anchorage will be found in the West Arm off an old sealing station. An exploration of the northwest arm might also reveal some useful anchorages

Chaffers Gullet, north of Lucas Point, (52°10'S 60°22'W) is a beautiful river with well sheltered anchorages. If there is any swell running, the entrance is identified by a dramatic 'blow hole' in low cliffs on the northern entrance. There is kelp in the entrance, but it can be navigated. The best anchorage is off a small sand beach where the river divides.

There is a drying sand spit about 1¼M from the entrance, not marked by kelp but visible in most light.

Tim and Pauline Carr reported that they anchored 'in a little nook ESE of the Little Mollyhawk (238m high), with lines ashore (52°07'S 60°23'W) describing it as 'the ultimate hurricane hole' however, in 2010, *Iron Bark* reported few suitable rocks to tie lines to.

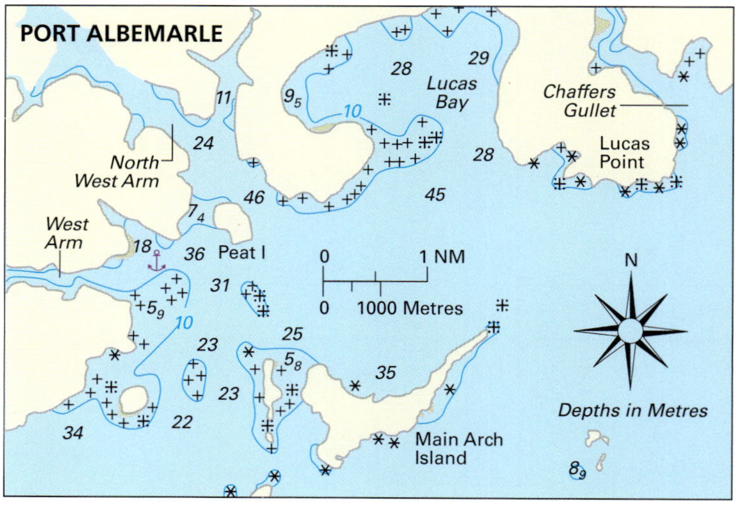

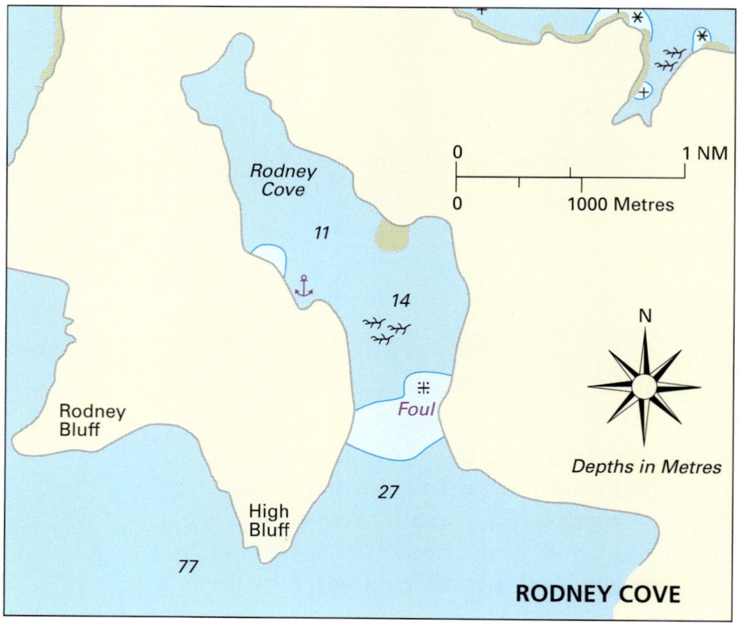

Cape Meredith

52° 15' S 60° 39'W

This is steep-to and can be passed at 2 cables. Passing close inshore also avoids the overfalls and a reported shoal 5 cables south of the Cape. The tides off the Cape reach 3–4 knots at springs and create overfalls in wind over tide conditions.

Rodney Cove

52° 04'S 61° 00'W

This is a useful anchorage if sailing the SW coast of West Falkland Island as it offers good shelter and is a convenient spot to break the passage. In good conditions, the land can be closed in safety as it is very steep-to and high. The entrance has much kelp but you can find a clear lead through a little to the east of the centre, with just enough room to tack if you had to.

The best shelter (in SW winds) is off the sand beach on the W side of the cove tucked in behind a small headland and outside the kelp, 6·5m. In a northerly wind, shelter can be found towards the head of the cove. The N partly dries out at low water.

The passage NW from Cape Meredith to Cape Percival should be approached with the greatest caution unless you are confident that a wind shift is not going to make this into a dangerous lee shore. It goes past a number of tricky passes through which the tide races faster than anywhere else in the islands, attaining speeds of up to 8 knots or more in certain conditions. There are no harbours or anchorages which could be described as bolt holes. By way of compensation, the scenery is stunning. One feature to note is the distinctive Horse Block Rock, 67m high (51°56'27·1S 61°06'54·3W). If it doesn't look like a horse to you, try imagining a Scottie Dog.

Note: there is no passage between Tea Island and Staats Island.

Horse Block Rock *Tim Barker*

The Governor Channel to Beaver Island

51°53′S 61°13′W

The Governor is considered safe except in the strongest onshore weather, although the kelp will run under in the strength of the tide. There are no unmarked dangers. Do not attempt to pass between Governor Island and Beaver Island.

The Stick-in-the-Mud passage runs to the east of Governor Island and is not named on *2513*. It has a tussock island in the middle which should be passed to the west. The navigation is straightforward, but great attention should be given to the tide which can run at up to 8 knots and the slack is very short-lived. Slack water is at 2¾ hours after HW Beaver, after which the NW flowing ebb starts. The rise and fall here provides the greatest range of anywhere in the islands.

The shore can be kept close to when rounding the north of Governor Island since it is very steep-to.

Pass between Rookery Island and Rat Island to its SW, (not named on chart *2513*). Fish Creek and the settlement will be seen ahead.

All dangers are marked by kelp and this is a very sheltered anchorage where a couple of moorings may be found, otherwise anchor off the jetty on the north side of the creek in 6.5m making sure not to drop on one of the many kelp patches. In a strong SW, there is quite a fetch from the head of the creek and it could become uncomfortable.

Beaver Island farm is the home of well-known sailors Sally and Jerome Poncet who are veterans of high latitude sailing and are widely referenced in the Antarctic section of this book.

Beaver Island northwards

Retrace your steps between Rat Island and Rookery Island and be sure to identify Stinker Island and Stinker Point which lie ahead. Pass 1 cable south of Stinker Point to avoid an isolated rock and kelp. The flood tide sets quite strongly westwards across this reef and allowance must be made. Pass close to the east side of Stinker Island and aim to sail between Beaver Island and the Channel Islands (now bird sanctuaries) in water free of obstructions. The Colliers - two fingers of rock easily seen and rather dramatic - lie ahead (51°47′25S 61°13′15W). From here, a course can be made for the anchorage off New Island, although be aware of the streams running in and out of the Grey Channel to the west which can reach 8 knots at the narrowest part. The stream runs W here 3 hours before HW New Island.

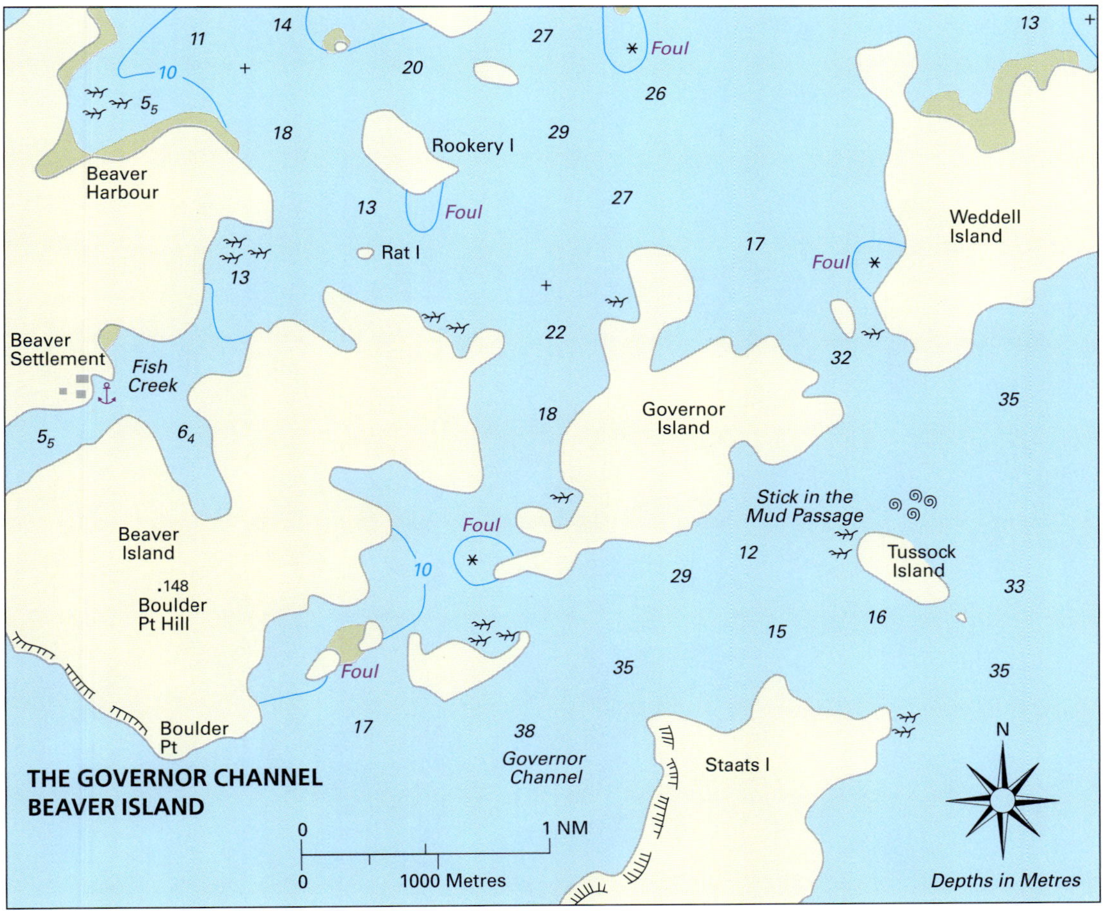

Beaver Island looking SE *Pete Smith*

Anchorage off New Island *Tim Barker*

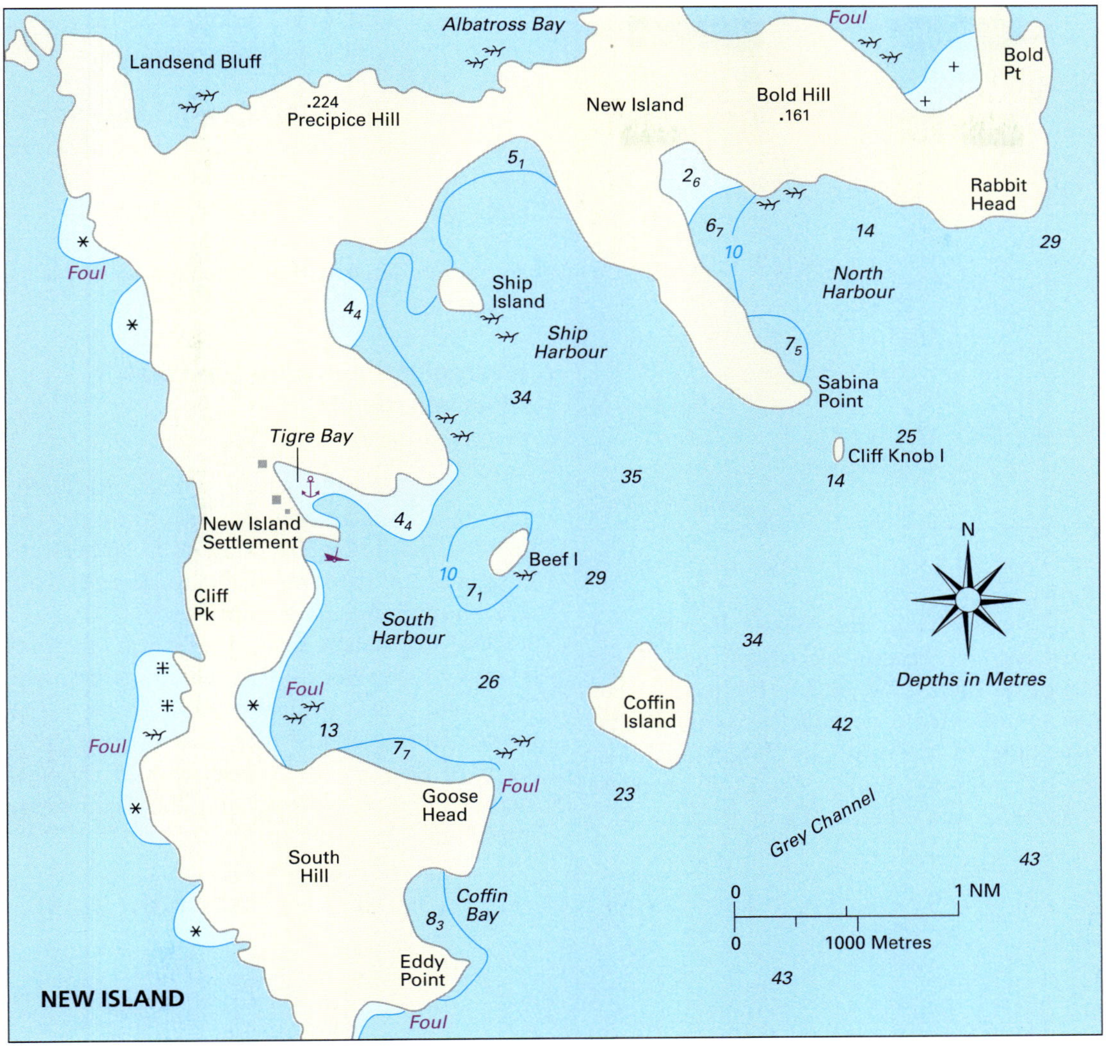

New Island

51° 44′S 61° 13′W

This island is home to vast colonies of Black-browed albatrosses and Rockhopper penguins. Despite its exposed position, New Island can provide a snug anchorage, although open to the SE.

If approaching from the direction of The Colliers, Coffin Island (122m) should be identified, then Beef Island behind it. The settlement will be seen in a cove in the NW corner of South Harbour, charted as Tigre Bay. Anchor ½ cable off the jetty, but do not be tempted to lie against it as it is in poor shape and dries at LW. Good anchorage will be found by heading towards the Protector, an ex-Canadian minesweeper said to be 'laid-up' at the head of the cove.

Strong winds from E will cause a swell to build here, and SE winds are worst for this anchorage. For shelter in SE winds, head towards the southern side of South Harbour and tuck yourself close under about 7 cables due north of South Hill. Good mussels and squid are reported on the rocks here. Also beware of the rooks which will get their beaks into any of your possessions.

(For detailed navigation around Weddell Island and Queen Charlotte Bay, as well as the Smylie Channel, consult FIS and, most importantly, its accompanying supplement)

The Passage Islands

This string of four islands is easily identified and divides Queen Charlotte Bay to the south from King George Bay to the north. Of the passages between them, Whale Passage is the widest, but all are safe to use except False Passage which is not navigable. The tide flows swiftly enough through the passes to run the kelp under. The flood tide runs to the south here and can reach 5 knots at springs.

Roy Cove

51°35′S 60° 30′W

Said to be 'one of the most beautiful estuaries in the Islands' and reminiscent of an English south coast river estuary. It has a protected

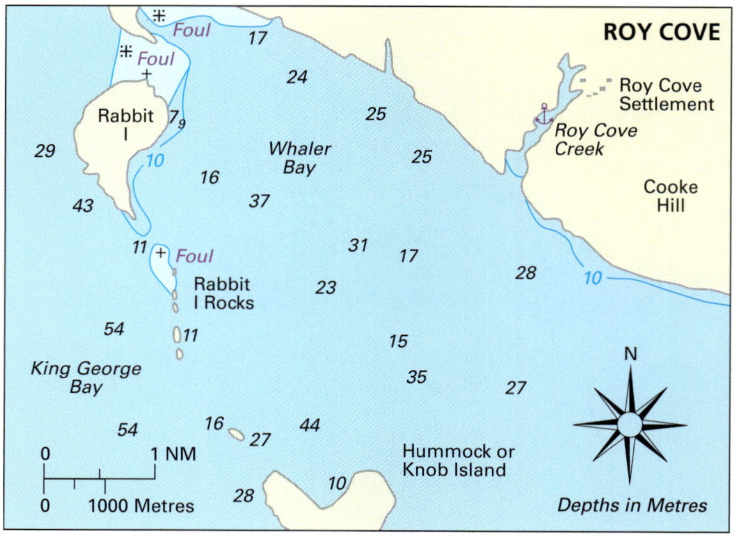

entrance in a largely sheltered expanse of water.

If coming from the Whale Passage, you must identify Hummock Island, and Rabbit Island to the NNW of it. Hummock Island has an unnamed rock 4 cables to the NW, and extending to the south of Rabbit Island are the Crouching Lion Rocks, sometimes charted as the Rabbit Island Rocks. Those who have seen them report that they look more like lions than rabbits. Pass south of the rocks.

The entrance to Roy Cove (51°34′S 60°24′W) is not easy to spot but it will suddenly open up. You should keep to the middle of the inlet and clear of the kelp fringes. The cove is narrow but the sides are steep-to, and there is a concrete jetty at the settlement with plenty of water to lie alongside.

Westpoint Island (also known as Albatross Island)

51° 22′S 60° 40′W

This is a beautiful island which, unusually, has some trees and an excellent harbour. The waters round here are home to Commerson's dolphins and there are walks to albatross and Rockhopper breeding colonies.

The approach from the south requires transit of the Woolly Gut which, as its name suggests, is subject to strong and unpredictable winds. Although the passage is clear of dangers, the tides run very strongly and, combined with the woollies, can cause problems.

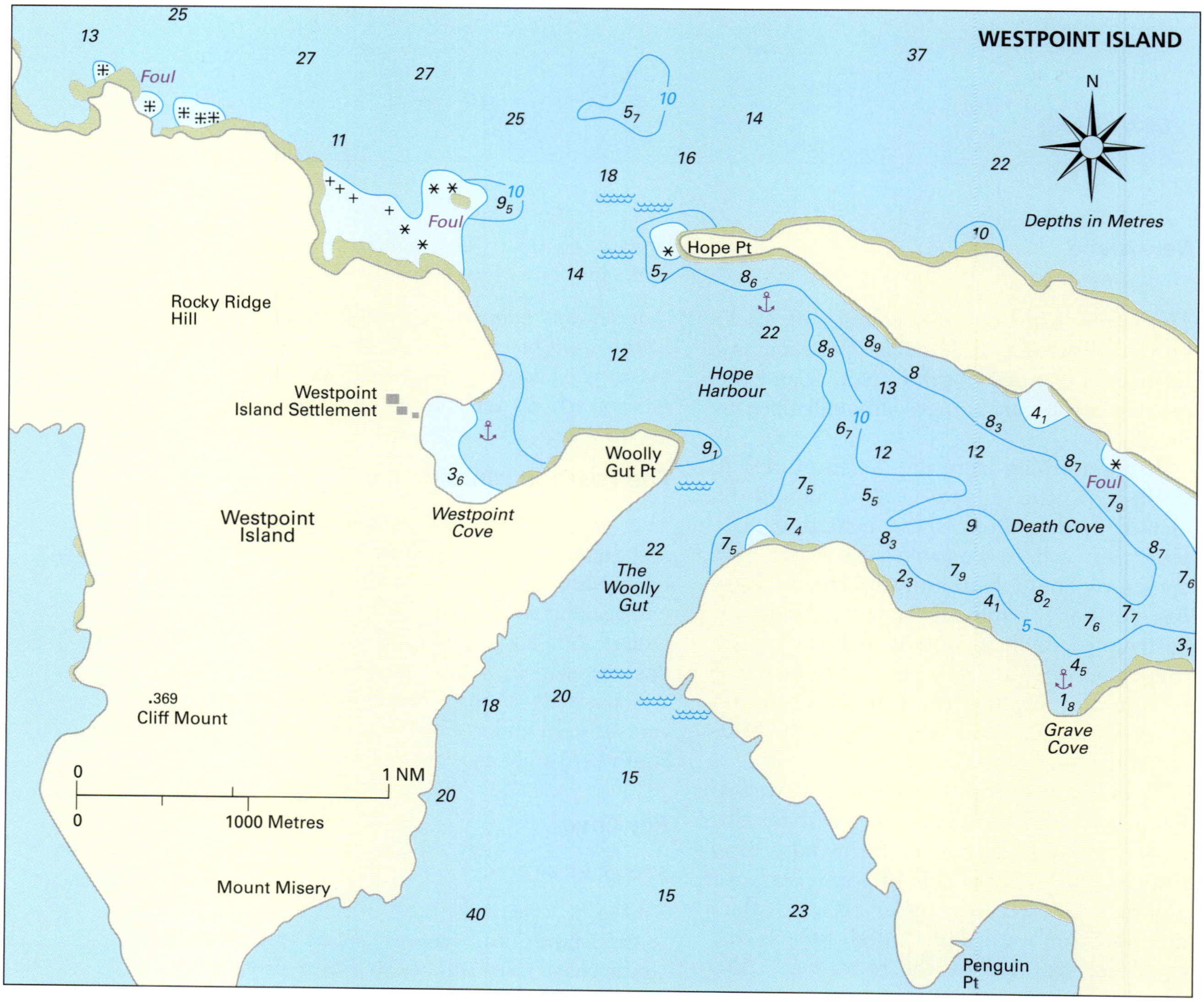

The flood tide sets to the south at up to 8 knots. Slack water can last for less than 15 minutes and the tide can reach maximum speed very quickly. To the north of Woolly Gut, the flood tide divides NE of Hope Point and sets W past Cape Terrible before turning SW across Gibraltar Reef where 15 knot tides have been reported. From Hope Point there is a less strong flood tide which runs E into Byron Sound.

Woolly Gut should be approached with a fair tide and winds of less than gale force. SW winds produce fewer woollies. Following the western coast, the settlement will eventually be seen to the W as Hope Harbour opens. Anchor 1 cable off the stone jetty in 5m, mud and sand. There are kelp streamers in the harbour but these can be sailed through. Woollies can blow through here in W winds. Good mussels and clams on rocks on the eastern side of the harbour.

The anchorage in Grave Cove, on the south side of Death Cove (not the gloomy place its name implies) has a very remote beach with a large Gentoo penguin colony.

Carcass Island

51°19'S 60° 32'W

This island is less than 5,000 acres but has rich wildlife and scenery, consisting of cliffs, sandy bays and dunes, which is hardly bettered anywhere in the islands. The owners are Rob and Lorraine McGill who have been here for 40 years, and it is a regular stopping place for the Antarctic cruise liners. The settlement is at Port Pattison, which is known for its gardens (with trees and hedges) and its small grocery shop. The island has no rats or cats so birdlife flourishes. There is good hiking and walking to be had, as well as a warm welcome. You will find Elephant seals, Magellanic penguins, short-eared owls and black-crowned night herons known in the Falklands as 'quarks'. There are several freshwater ponds providing good habitat for waterfowl. This is an ornithologist's and photographer's paradise.

There are no dangers on the approach or inside Port Pattison although if approaching from Westpoint Island, the Carcass Reef must be identified. The tides are a little complex and split off the NE coast of the island; so the flood sets in from the NE and sets SW past the northern end of the island, turning south and then eastwards past Port Pattison, towards Byron Sound. At the Needles at the SE tip of the island, the flood sets S before joining the E-flowing stream. Other than close to the headlands, the streams do not exceed 2 knots.

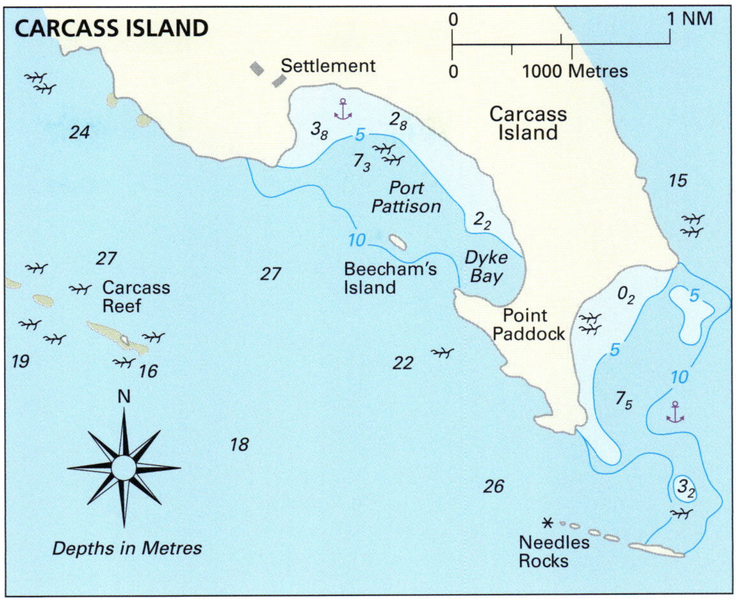

North of the island, the flood turns 2 hours after HW Port Egmont.

For Port Pattison, pass west of Beecham's Island steering clear of the kelp off Point Paddock. Anchor in 3·5m off the settlement over hard sand where you will see a rocky ledge which can be used as a dinghy landing. A stone jetty will also be seen, but this dries out and is not suitable for lying alongside.

Should the wind come from the S or E, a good anchorage will be found in the SE corner of the harbour in Dyke Bay, ½ cable off in 3m, hard sand.

Keppel and Pebble Sounds, Port Egmont and Port Purvis

The waters of Keppel Sound, Pebble Sound and Port Egmont and Port Purvis provide opportunities for anchoring with varying degrees of shelter and full details are beyond the scope of this book (see *FIS*). Keppel Sound provides the poorest anchorages and is open to the NW. The entrances to Pebble Sound can be tricky because of the tides and narrow passages.

Port Egmont was the first formal British settlement in 1765, and Commodore John Byron declared, 'The whole navy of England might ride in perfect security from the winds.'

Jersey Harbour

51°26'S 59° 13'W

This is surprisingly sheltered, even in NE winds, and is the only port on the W side of Falkland Sound that is completely sheltered from westerly gales and woollies. White Rock Bay, with Jersey Harbour in the SW corner, is entered between White Rock to the N, and Jersey Point to the S.

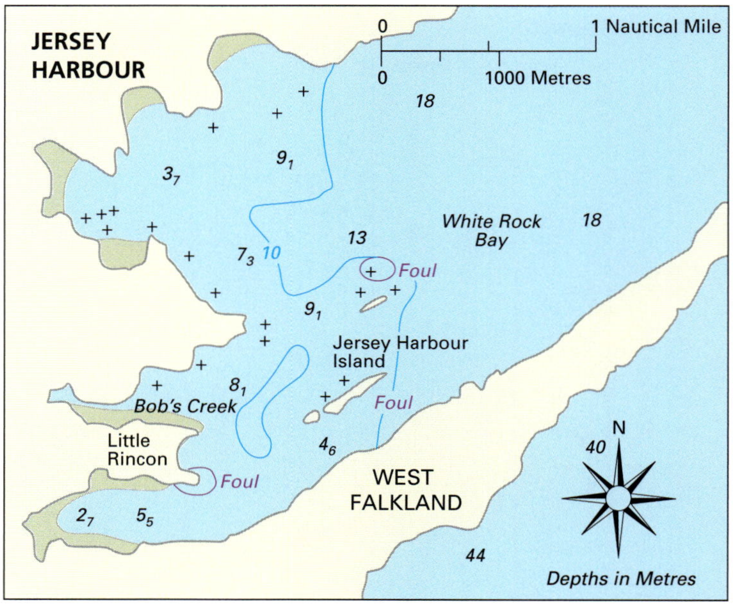

The flood tide past these headlands sets south at rates up to 5 knots.

Keep 2 cables off White Rock (51°24'S 59°11'W) if coming from the N. The north shore can then be followed as close as 3 cables, mindful of the kelp. Once the two Jersey Harbour Islands have been identified (no passage between them) make a course for the anchorage off Little Rincon, south of Bob's Creek. Kelp extends for at least 2 cables in all directions from the Jersey Harbour Islands but the tidal flows are slight and the kelp does not run under. Anchor in 10m.

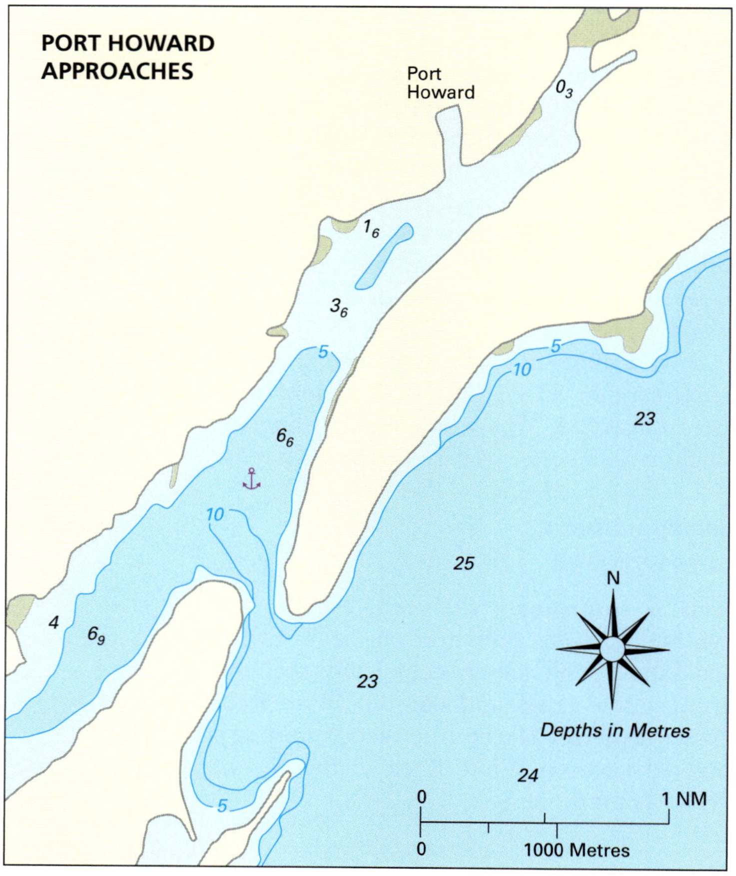

Port Howard

51°39'S 59°31'W

An excellent harbour set against a background of rolling countryside with even the occasional hedgerow to be seen. There is a substantial jetty serving the settlement ashore and the water is deep and safe, although woollies will have to be watched for.

This is the largest settlement on West Falkland (if you count Fox Bay as two distinct settlements) with 20 residents, an airstrip with flights to Stanley and a terminal for the E–W ferry. If you are lucky, you might be here for the West Falkland Games, held every three years, with serious horse racing and much festivity.

The entrance is narrow but safe although to the south there is a shoal, well marked by kelp. If coming from the north there are no off-lying dangers.

Off the entrance, the flood tide sets south at up to 2 knots.

Anchorages can be found the full length of Port Howard, with good holding. The settlement is towards the northern end of the harbour and you should anchor close NE of the jetty in 3·5m, sand. Strong SW winds can funnel the length of the harbour, making the anchorage uncomfortable. In a strong blow, it might be a good idea to secure a line to the jetty.

There is a hotel, a small grocery shop and, rather surprisingly, three golf courses.

SOUTH GEORGIA

This island comes with the warning that while the many bays and fjords provide a variety of anchorages, there are none on South Georgia which can be considered safe in any weather. Utmost confidence in craft and crew is needed here.

It is worth noting the advice of Pete Smith (*Kiwi Roa*) who wrote, whilst anchored at Elsehul South Georgia, and experiencing 'wind bullets of 60 knots' that 'stronger winds of a more consistent 80 knots were experienced. Conditions endured for several days, typical of the area'.

It is a week's voyage of 750M from the Falkland Islands to South Georgia and a landscape far removed from the one you have left behind. The high mountains, the tallest being Mount Paget at 2,900m, can create problems for sailors who may find themselves subject to strong *williwaws* and *katabatic* winds. These can make apparently safe anchorages, at times, untenable. It is essentially an alpine landscape in miniature.

This is an awe-inspiring island by any measure, the southern end distinctly Antarctic in appearance. The coast is indented with numerous fjords; 75% of the landmass is covered by glaciers and in the winter (July to September) the snow line will fall as far as sea level. Have a look on Google Earth and see these icy highways snake their way to the cold sea. A landfall here can be spectacular.

The island has been described as 'long and narrow, shaped like a huge, curved, fractured and savage whale bone'. It is 106M long and averages about 15M wide. The SW facing coast takes the full violence of the weather and offers little shelter for any kind of vessel.

The Admiralty Pilot describes the SW coast as 'little visited', which is not surprising given that there are few harbours and it is a perpetual lee shore with a big swell, limited surveys, and many uncharted rocks and reefs. It makes the NE coast sound distinctly relaxing.

Only anchorages on the more sheltered NE coast are given here.

The richness of the wildlife is breathtaking. South Georgia is home to three million penguins of varying species, a million fur seals, 360,000 elephant seals and also a large number of Wandering albatross which come here to nest. Breeding birds enjoy the rodent free islands, and the authorities go to great lengths to make sure it stays this way (see Biosecurity below).

The islands are a UK overseas territory, governed from the Falkland Islands, and there are no permanent residents, although two British Antarctic research stations are manned in the summer months when the population also includes government officers based at King Edward Point. However, in the days of whaling, at the height of the season the population might have expanded to 3,000.

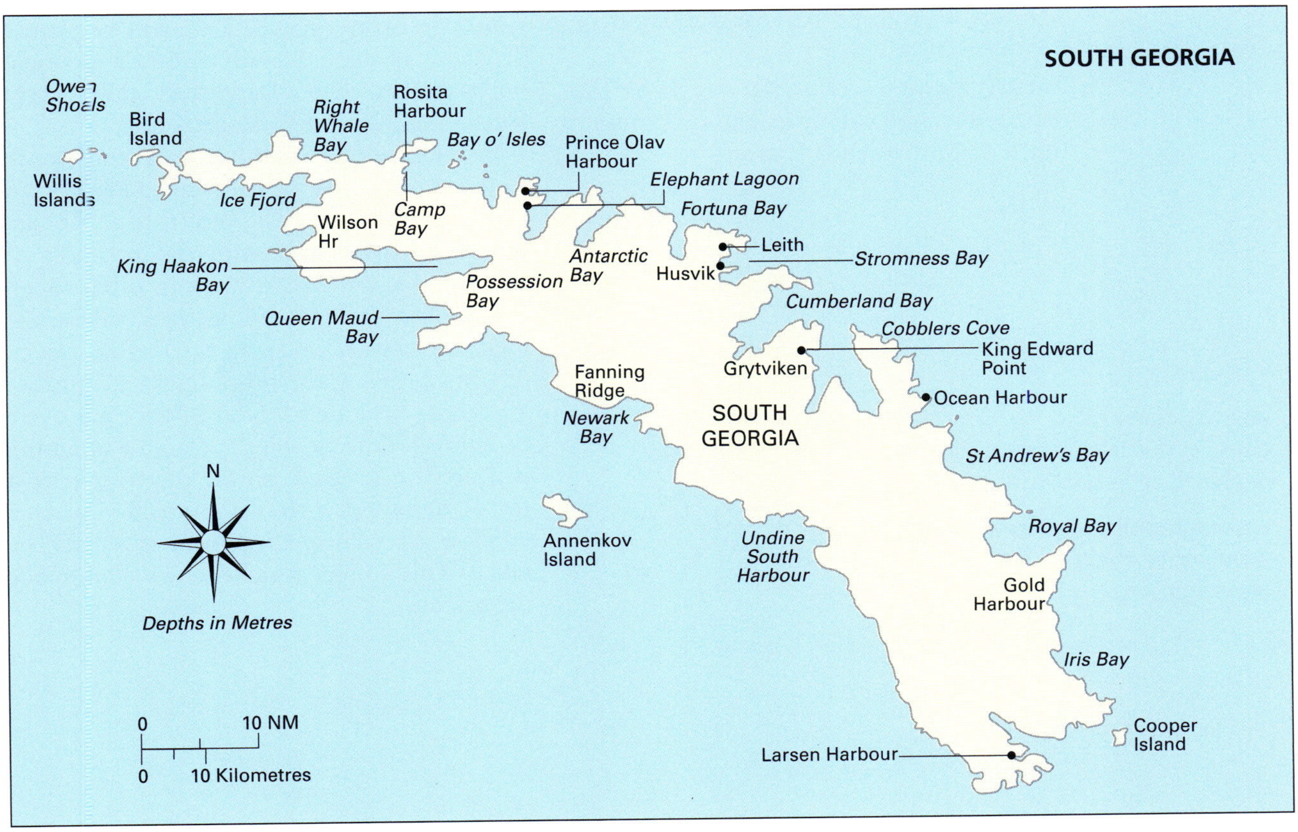

The forbidding north coast of South Georgia, towards Grytviken
Sandy Duker

Before coming to South Georgia you should appreciate and prepare for the following:

- There are no rescue services
- There are no medical facilities
- There are no repair facilities
- You must be self sufficient in food and fuel
- There is no airfield
- There is no transport to the Falklands or South America
- There is a postal service, but largely for the benefit of stamp collectors and it cannot be relied on for obtaining spares.

www.sgisland.gs
gives detailed information, mostly for cruise liner tourists, but much of it of great value to sailors

www.sghtonline.gs/South-Georgia-books
www.sgmuseum.gs
www.sght.org

Getting to South Georgia

Most yachts will make the passage from the Falklands, which is by far the easiest port of departure from an administrative point of view. Remember, if you leave for South Georgia from Ushuaia, the Argentine authorities will not consider you to have left their territory and will not, therefore, give you a departure stamp. This will not cause problems in the Falklands or South Georgia, but may elsewhere. Departing from Puerto Williams, Chile, is less bothersome.

The journey to South Georgia from South America is likely to be a downwind ride, even if a boisterous one. The return trip, though, presents a challenge, with the prospect of considerable windward work in often rough conditions. Yachts heading back to Europe might consider taking a leg to Uruguay (see p. 32) and bringing the prevailing wind further aft. Those heading for South Africa are likely to enjoy following winds. Careful attention will need to be given to the forecasts over a period of days prior to departure, and when a window is seen the opportunity must be taken. This applies whichever way you make the passage.

The history of South Georgia

Was Amerigo Vespucci the first man to sight South Georgia? In April 1502, while sailing in the latitude of the island, he encountered 'a high, gloomy rough land where human life was rendered impossible by severe cold'. That might describe South Georgia quite nicely, but historians are not certain what Vespucci saw.

More certain is the discovery by the Englishman, Anthony de la Roche, in 1675. He was rounding the Horn eastbound, intending to make northing, but strong weather forced him hundreds of miles to the east where he eventually took shelter on the south side of the island. It became known as Roche island.

The first landing, though, was by Captain James Cook who surveyed and mapped the islands and renamed it 'Isle of Georgia' after his King, George the third. Cook wrote: 'The wild rocks raised their lofty summits until they were lost in the clouds, and the valleys lay covered with everlasting snow. Not a tree was to be seen, nor a shrub even big enough to make a toothpick'. The southwest point of the island is called Cape Disappointment. Cook was not taken with this place.

On 17 January 1775, three musket shots were fired and a British territory was declared. That date remains a public holiday on the island - Possession Day.

In the early 20th century, South Georgia became a major whaling station based around Grytviken, and the grave of the great explorer Sir Ernest Shackleton (died 1922) can be found here. His remarkable open boat voyage in the *James Caird* ranks as one of the greatest small boat voyages of all time (see reading list in the Appendix p. 206). After the loss of their ship, *Endurance*, Shackleton set sail from Antarctica in a 23 footer, eventually reaching South Georgia. He then trekked across the island's mountainous interior to reach the settlement from which he could organise a rescue operation to recover the men he had left on Elephant Island.

More recently, South Georgia hit the international headlines when Argentina again made claims to the island and used a scrap-dealing operation as cover to launch an attack on the Falklands. This is said to have precipitated the Falklands War of 1982.

There is an active museum on South Georgia (see website opposite).

A Scandinavian flat-pack church sent out from Norway in 1913
Sandy Duker

A full size replica of the *James Caird* in the excellent South Georgia Museum, Grytviken
Sandy Duker

Administration

Useful phone numbers

The Government of S Georgia, Stanley
✆ +500 28200
info@gov.gs

Govt Officer King Edward Point (seasonal)
✆ +870 382 359 033
go@gov.gs

British Antarctic Survey King Edward Point (seasonal)
✆ +870 382 359 031

Permits

No visas are required for a visit to South Georgia. An excellent and comprehensive set of documents and advice can be found at:

www.sgisland.gs

This gives all the information you need to make the necessary applications for a visit (and also to the South Sandwich Islands). Much of it is written for the operators of ships, but yachts get a mention too and it is quite easy to understand the general principles which apply to all vessels.

In brief, all visitors should apply for a permit, for which there is a charge, prior to arrival. This is easily done if you are leaving from the Falklands. If you intend to make payment on the island, then you must have Sterling, US dollars or Euros. Cash or travellers cheques are accepted, not credit cards.

A 200M Maritime Zone is in place around South Georgia, and if you are able you should make contact with the island's government officer when you enter that zone by using the following contacts:

go@gov.gs

✆ 00870 382 359 033 (Inmarsat) or
✆ 0044 1223 221781 (VOIP)
Iridium ✆ 00881 631831394

South Georgia north coast
Martin Thomas

Arrival

Your first port of call must be King Edward Point/Grytviken where a government officer will carry out Immigration, Customs and arrival briefings. Contact Channel 16. A bio-security check may also be carried out and you should closely read the advice. It is unlikely that any yacht would carry rodents, but the environmental damage done by an accidental release could be considerable.

Ice and weather

South Georgia lies south of the Antarctic convergence and 'enjoys' the frigid ENE flow of Antarctic waters which can contain icebergs of considerable size, which at times can be clustered. The outer limit of the ice is 400 miles in the direction of the Falklands so, if making from Stanley, an appropriate lookout must be kept and icebergs expected when that line is crossed.

It is rare for the Antarctic winter pack ice to reach the south coast of the island, but it does on occasions. The N coast remains ice free.

The best weather is to be found on the NE coast between Cooper Sound and the Bay of Islands. The NW and SE tips tend to be more overcast and the weather unsettled.

Charts

Admiralty charts:
3596 Approaches to South Georgia
3597 South Georgia
3585 Harbours and Anchorages in South Georgia
3587 Harbours and Anchorages in South Georgia
3592 Stewart Strait

It should be noted that there may be variations between charted positions and those shown by GPS. The positions given here are GPS derived, and may not always coincide with some older charts. Certainly the chart datum should be examined carefully before conducting any navigation here which is entirely GPS dependent.

Electronic charts

MaxSea TimeZero MegaWide chart MWVJSAM504MAP6.1 covers the whole of S America (both coasts) and includes South Georgia.

C-Map has global coverage

Digital suppliers are constantly upgrading their catalogues so check for any updates.

Pilot books

Admiralty Sailing Directions - Antarctic Pilot NP9 has good information on South Georgia.

www.rccpf.org.uk/publications/southern-islands-a-antarctic-peninsula/south-georgia has detailed notes by Andy O'Grady and Ulla Norlander (2005), and Pete and Annie Hill (1995). Much of the anchorage information below has come from these sources, the authors in turn drawing partly on the experience of Jerome Poncet, Tim and Pauline Carr, Mark and Fraser Carpenter, and Roger Wallis.

See also Annie Hill's website **www.annie-hill.blogspot.co.uk**

The anchorages and harbours shown below are only a selection of those available and they have been chosen on the basis of ease of access and safety. For a more detailed exploration of South Georgia the above sources should be carried onboard and consulted.

The Pilotage Foundation would be extremely grateful for any further information or updates from this remote area. Contact info@rccpf.org.uk.

Biosecurity

The Government of South Georgia has a waste policy designed to prevent the introduction of pests and diseases that could upset the delicate wildlife balance. For example, parts of the island have become infested with rats and mice which have done great damage to albatross nesting sites in particular. Intensive eradication programmes have taken place. Even if you have brought no rodents with you, you may inadvertently collect them as you move from place to place on the island and you should be aware of the possibility and take steps to avoid it.

Any breach of biosecurity legislation will be regarded as a criminal offence. It is worth studying the document below in some detail.

www.sgisland.gs
South Georgia and South Sandwich Island Biosecurity

Biosecurity rules in outline

- No plants, animals or soil must be brought ashore
- Boots should be cleaned and washed after each new landing
- Check your clothing and bags for traces of organic material (seeds, for example, in your hood)
- No fresh meat, vegetables, fruit or unpasteurised dairy products, especially poultry and eggs, to be brought ashore
- Food should not be stored on deck
- Yachts must deploy bait stations in areas likely to be rat infested (these obtained from Stanley before departure)
- All hatches must be kept closed at night if a yacht is left unattended
- Closed areas are put in place to assist with conservation and the locations can change. The best advice is to consult www.sgisland.gs before leaving Stanley. Permits can be obtained to visit closed areas if approved landing sites are used
- Hunting is not allowed.

Fur seals

Fur seals are a great attraction, but a major pest to visiting yacht crews. They can attack and bite without warning and, to make it worse, seem to have no fear of humans. However, those who have been brave enough to face up to them say they will back off.

Their breeding season is November to January and they are likely to be more aggressive at this time. The bulls defending their females are the ones to watch. For defence, you can try sticking out your boot or brandishing a stick, which needs to be 4 feet long - a boat hook or oar would do; a shout or a growl may work, or even clapping your hands or banging stones together. Often, a light tap under the chin will show them who's in charge - if you dare get that close.

If the worst should happen and you get bitten, then infection seems inevitable and antibiotics are a must. Tetracycline and metronidazole are recommended.

Fur seals occupy almost all the beaches and in many places landing may call for some courage.

Grytviken
Sandy Duker

Grytviken - smaller cruise ships will anchor here
Sandy Duker

Cruising South Georgia

King Edward Cove and Grytviken

54°17'S 36°29'W
Chart BA 3587

King Edward Cove is found in Cumberland East Bay and leads to Grytviken which might be considered the 'capital' of the island. This is where you deal with entry formalities and it should be your first port of call.

Call on VHF 16 as you approach and mooring or anchoring advice will be given.

The wooden jetty may be in poor condition, and the best place to moor may be alongside the old whale catcher, the *Petrel*, at the south end of the whaling station. This was used for several years, including in winter, by Tim and Pauline Carr. Face the bow offshore and take a breast line ashore to the wooden jetty to the N so that you can pull off in event of an E wind.

It is also possible to tie up at any of the wooden wharves, but deploy an anchor to ensure you can haul off in the event of easterly weather.

The wharf at King Edward Point is exposed in SW weather and not available to yachts except by permission of the Marine Officer. This is where you will find the post office - the stamps are collectors' items.

There is a very good whaling museum here, and a shop selling souvenirs. This is also the place where Sir Ernest Shackleton died; a conspicuous white cross above King Edward Point is his memorial.

This is reckoned to be the safest place in the islands, but strong winds still occur.

Grytviken
Sandy Duker

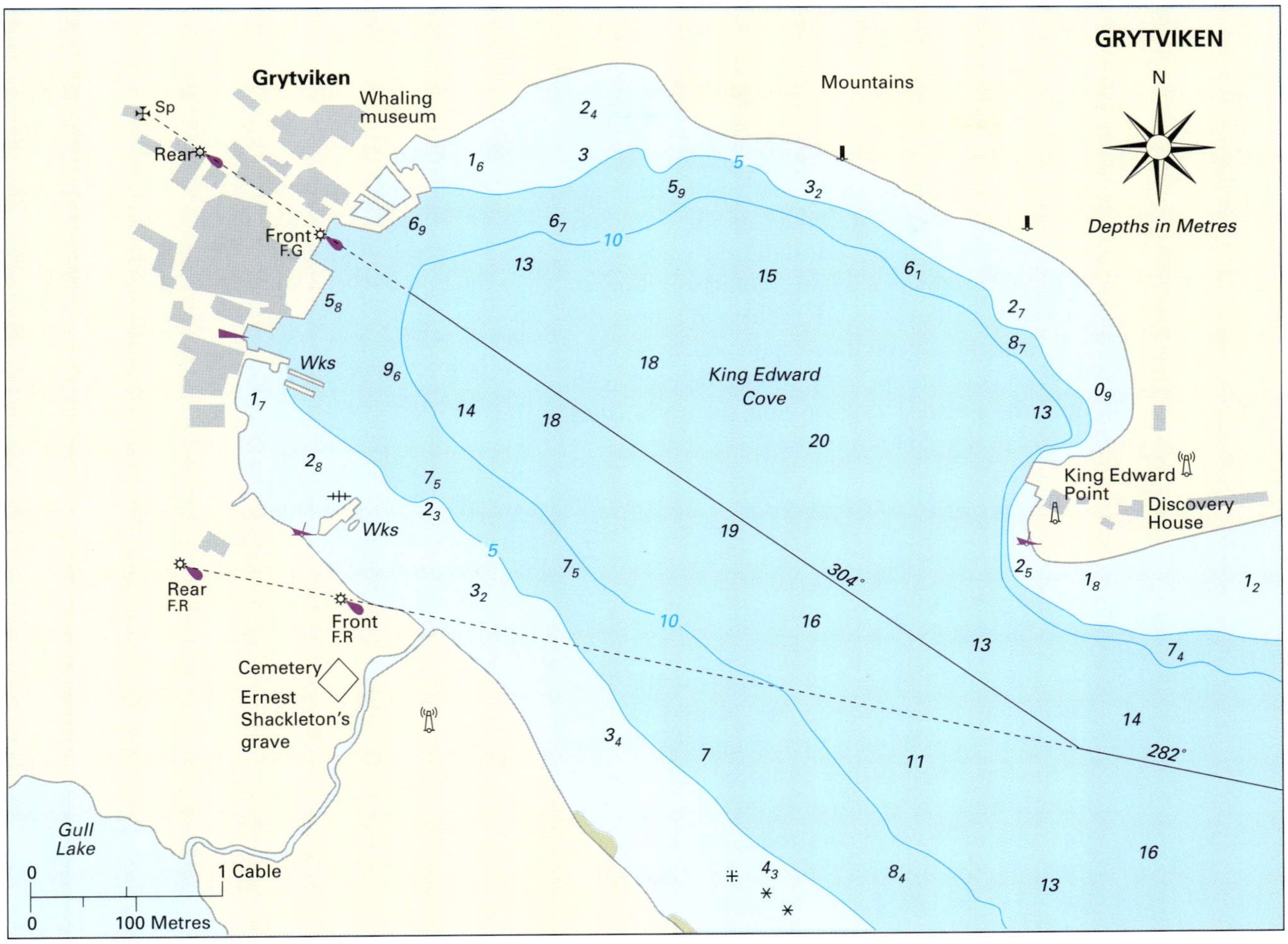

Shackleton's grave, where visitors pay their respects *Sandy Duker*

The 'new' jetty, Grytviken *Sandy Duker*

Anchorages along the NE coast

Old whaling stations and jetties

None of the jetties and structures have been maintained since the whaling business ceased, therefore they are all in poor or very dangerous condition. Many of the buildings ashore have been vandalised, and what remains of them may be dangerous due to asbestos residues, etc. For these reasons, the government accepts no responsibility for any of these structures. They should be used with only the greatest caution and the authorities would prefer you not to use them at all.

Anchorages W of Grytviken

Elsehul

54°01'S 37°59'W
Chart BA 3585

Anchor in the inner bay in 10m, sand. This anchorage is exposed to the N and can be affected by swell but if tucked into the W side of the inner bay shelter from the NW can be found. There is reported to be less swell on this side of the bay, and the gusts less fierce than on the E side. There is a freshwater stream in the NW corner of the inner bay

The fur seals here are reported to be exceptionally aggressive.

Right Whale Bay

54°00'S 37°40'W

There are two good anchorages giving shelter from nearly all directions, although marginal in E/NE winds.

Anchor in the inner part with good holding in 8–10m off the N end of Binder Beach.

If caught in E winds, shelter may be found to the E in Barber Cove (54°00'30S 37°39'00W).

Rosita Harbour

54° 00'S 37° 21'W
Chart BA 3585

Generally considered the best anchorage in the Bay of Islands, Rosita Harbour is virtually an all-weather anchorage, and is a useful place for visiting Albatross Island and Salisbury Plain. Even in E winds, shelter has been found here with the dense kelp flattening the seas.

Of the two anchorages here, the N cove is preferred and although there is a lot of kelp, a path can be found between it. Anchor in a clear patch close to the shore in 5m. Good holding in sand, especially safe if shore lines are deployed and the boat is pulled close in.

South of this anchorage, on the far side of a kelp-covered reef, is an anchorage in 4·5m, clear of kelp.

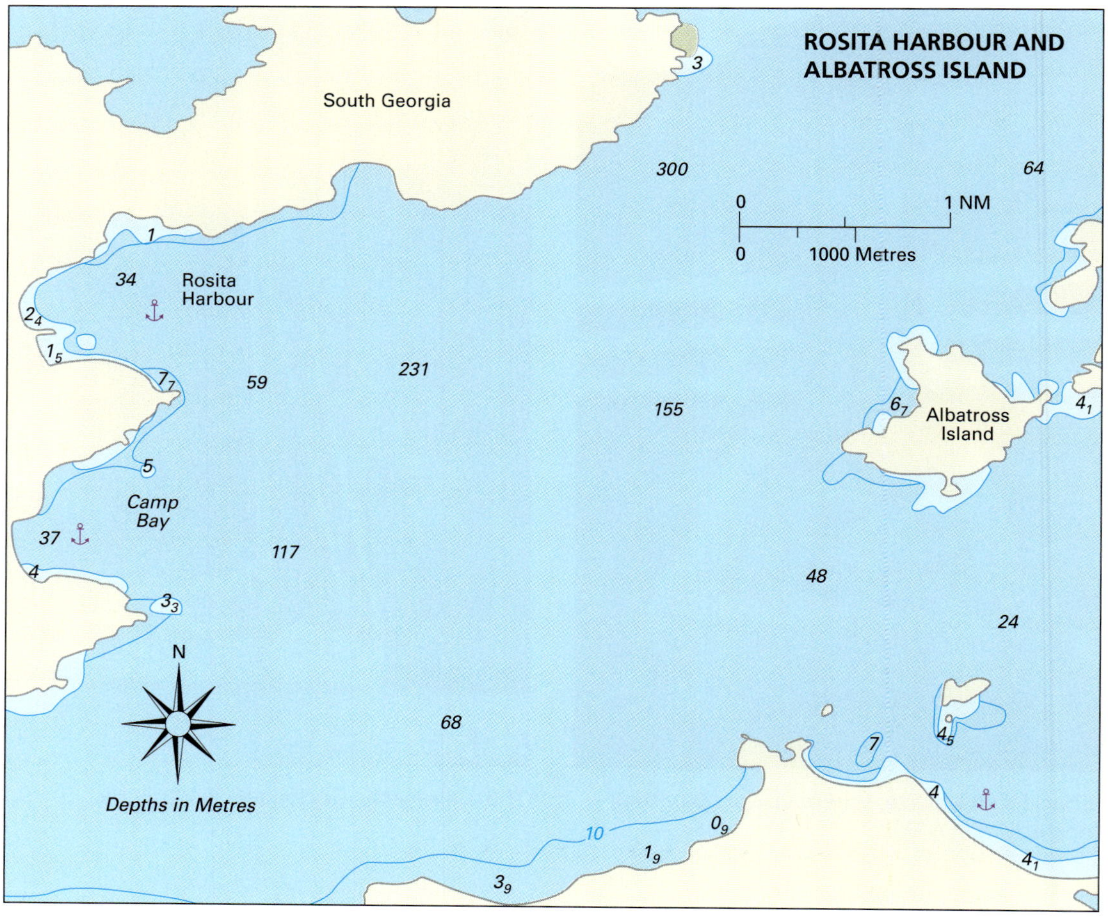

Camp Bay
54°02′S 37°27′W
Chart BA 3585

Immediately south of Rosita Harbour with anchorage in 7m clear of kelp in the SW corner off a small waterfall. The Admiralty pilot says that the wind appears less strong in this bay.

Albatross Island
54° 01′S 37° 20′W
Chart BA 3585

There is no secure anchorage, but for a short visit a shingle beach at the head of a cove can be found at the S end of the island. A reef extends from the SW tip of the island marked by thick kelp. Approach this anchorage from the SW and anchor off the beach in 7m, clear of kelp.

This is a nesting ground for the Wandering albatross and some Giant petrels.

Prince Olav Harbour
54°03′S 37°08′W
Chart BA 3582

A reasonably secure anchorage off an old whaling station abandoned in 1946. Good holding can be found in 7-8m, thick mud. Enter by passing N of Brutus Island (marked Saddle Island on old charts). You should then thread your way through the kelp towards the old jetty.

You will have to make a judgement on whether the jetty is strong and safe enough to tie to (see above). The bay is small enough to anchor and for lines to be taken ashore, which might be a safer, more secure, option.

Elephant Lagoon
(centred at) 54°04′S 37° 08′W
Chart BA 3585

This is an almost totally landlocked lagoon with a very narrow approach best taken on a rising tide as the narrows have a least depth of 2m at LW. Once in the lagoon, there is excellent holding in 5–8m thick mud. It has been reported that in strong winds the *williwaws* which affected south and east bay (to the east) were felt less in the lagoon, so although this is undoubtedly a windy anchorage, it is a secure one. There is good walking on the hills above. The fur seal population may be smaller on the S side, making landing easier.

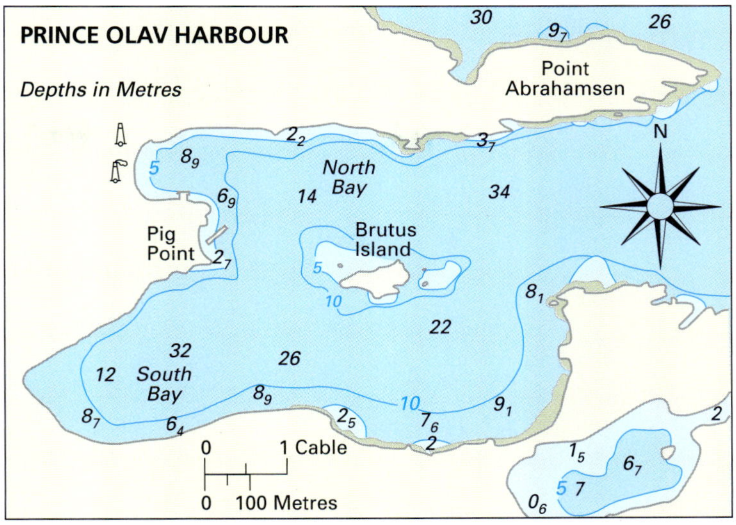

Leith Harbour
54° 08′S 36° 41′W
Chart BA 3587

This harbour is famous as the place where, in 1982, the Argentine scrap dealers ignited the Falklands War (see p. 114).

Apart from this historical connection, there is little to recommend it. There is a perpetual swell and although the small bay would appear to offer some protection, it has in fact been reported to be a dangerous place, not only because of swell and wind strength, but also due to the debris that flies from the dilapidated buildings. The dock itself is small making manoeuvring difficult. It should not be attempted by yachts longer than 15m. It would be a dangerous place in a E or NE blow and W winds are diverted to the NW and can blow very strongly.

There is a minumum depth of 6·5m alongside the main dock.

The harbour has been described as 'the worst eyesore on the entire island'.

Husvik Harbour
54° 10′S 36° 41′W
Chart BA 3587

This is an old and dilapidated whaling station abandoned in the 1950s and, as with all such places, the jetty is in very poor repair and should not be regarded as any kind of facility. To reach the anchorage you must navigate through a mass of kelp. The Bar Rocks (marked by a beacon) are the southern limit of the kelp. The easiest approach is S of these rocks.

If anchoring S of the jetty, the bottom may be littered with debris (reported to now be covered with shifting sand) so the anchor should be buoyed. If tying to the N side of the jetty (recommended) an anchor might be

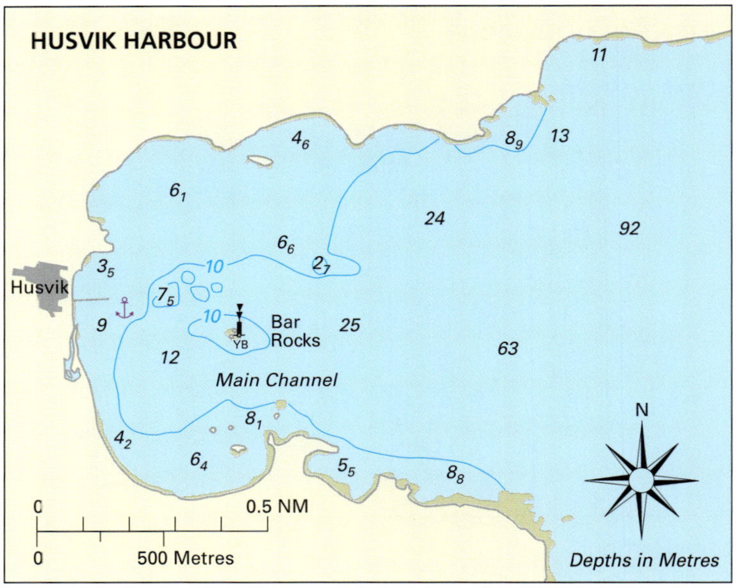

deployed to hold the vessel off should the wind come from the north. Do not attempt to walk the old railway line, it is now considered dangerous.

Although this harbour appears open to the E, the outlying rocks and kelp reduce the swell considerably and yachts have ridden out E gales here.

The walking and wildlife make this one of the best spots on the island.

Anchorages E of Grytviken

Cobbler's Cove

54°17S 36°17'W
Chart BA 3587

This Cove (known as Pleasant Harbour on old charts) offers complete shelter from the sea, although the land rises sharply to the NW which may induce *katabatic* winds when the wind is blowing from that quarter.

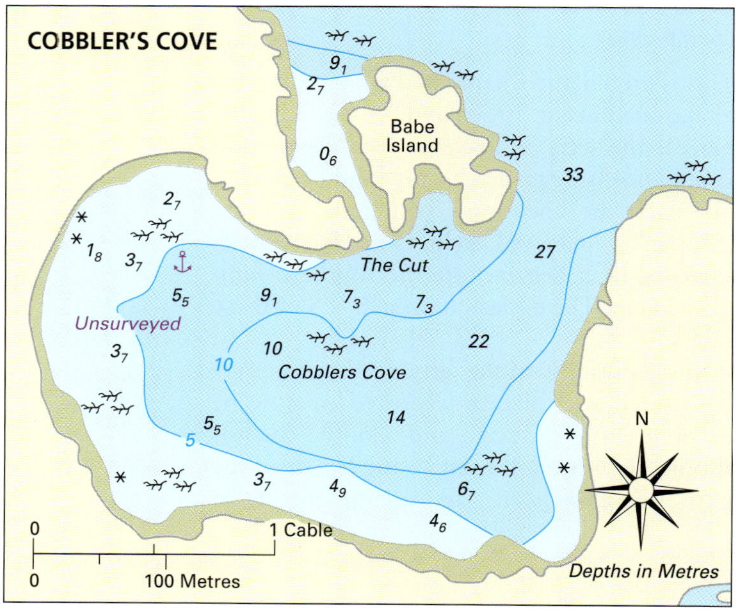

The entrance is straightforward and by taking a sweep to the S, once through the narrows, much of the kelp is avoided.

Anchor in the NW corner in 6–8m sand. Lines ashore will be required to hold the boat in position and head to any swell. It is reported that a yacht sat out a NE gale here largely untroubled.

Ocean Harbour

54°20'S 36°15'W
Chart BA 3589

Good shelter and good holding here in 5–8m sand between the wreck on the S shore and the head of the bay. NW winds can be strong, and swell in E winds or calm may be uncomfortable, however this remains one of the best anchorages with good walking and wildlife. This was the site of a whaling station closed in 1920, little remains.

Gold Harbour

54°37S 35°56'W
Chart BA 3582

This may not be the best of anchorages, open to the E and subject to swell, but the situation is spectacular.

Anchor off the beach just N of the Bertrab Glacier between the rocks off the beach and the first stream. There is good shelter from W in 9m, sand.

Larsen Harbour

54°50'S 36°01W
Chart BA 3585

This is a spectacular harbour, with good protection from the sea, but its E/W orientation means that is can be subject to accelerating winds. It cannot, therefore, be considered a safe anchorage in all weathers.

Anchor to the E of the Fairway Rock off Bonner Beach in 4·5m, mud in a clear patch free from kelp. If it appears that more shelter would be found off the N shore, then anchor with lines ashore in a basin below a small mossy cliff due north of the Fairway Rock. This anchorage can be found at 54°50'·3S 36°01'·2W. Note that this does not accord with pre-1962 charts.

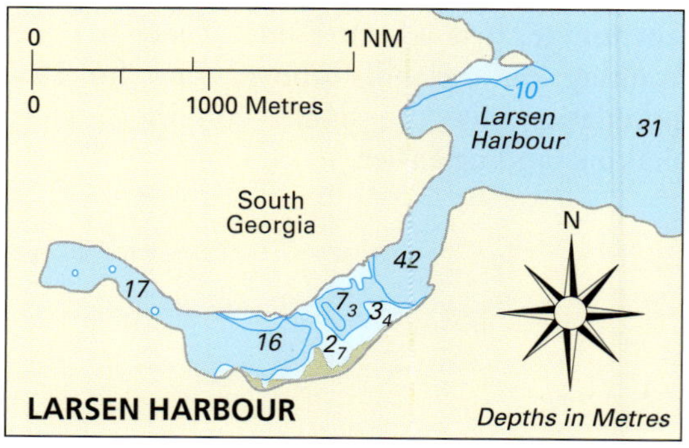

Wreck in Ocean Harbour *Sandy Duker*

A typical South Georgia penguin colony *Sandy Duker*

THE SOUTH SANDWICH ISLANDS

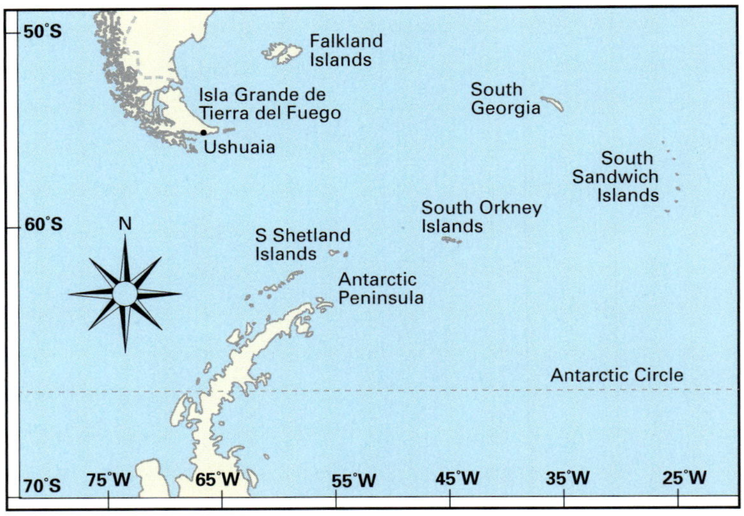

Captain Cook first discovered most of these islands in 1775 as part of his search for what was believed to be a great southern continent. He did not paint a good picture of them:

> *'Thick fogs, snowstorms, intense cold and every other thing that can render navigation dangerous.'*

They consist of 11 volcanic islands lying in an arc 240M long. In the winter they are hemmed in by pack ice but are ice-free in the summer. They lie 400M SE of South Georgia and are mostly snow covered except for those areas where penguins have made colonies.

We can offer no guidance for yachts wanting to visit these islands.

The Admiralty pilot advises that all the islands lack harbours but most of them have anchorages where ships may find shelter. Landing is impossible because of swell in even the best weather, and the shores are steep-to and rocky. However, some of the more adventurous cruise liner operators land their passenger in good weather using large, tough Zodiacs.

There has been no proper survey of the islands and uncharted dangers are likely to exist.

It is possible to circumnavigate the islands safely at a distance of 1½M offshore as the waters are clear of dangers at that distance.

The Pilotage Foundation would be pleased to hear from any yachts that have sailed in these waters. Golden Fleece Expeditions led by the veteran Antarctic sailor Jerome Poncet, has taken sailing expeditions and may advise.

www.goldenfleecexp.co.fk

The Russian yacht *Apostol Andrey* spent New Year's Day 2005 off the islands. Skip Novak's *Pelagic* offers the South Sandwich Islands as one of its destinations.

www.pelagic.co.uk

The islands are administered by the Governor of the Falkland Islands and are a British Overseas Territory.

6 THE ANTARCTIC PENINSULA
including the South Orkney and South Shetland Islands

Before even considering sailing to Antarctica, it is worth noting the guidelines issued by the UK government for yachts crossing the Drake

> .. *most of the commercial yachts regularly operating in these waters have been knocked down, and several have been rolled through 360°. Any skipper should be mindful of this when preparing a vessel for the area.*

This book has already offered many warnings of the difficulties and dangers of high latitude sailing, but you should be fully aware that once you set off for Antarctica you are hugely escalating the risk to life. This is a dangerous and unpredictable continent.

'Sailing into uncharted waters' has become a much-used expression, and here it can be taken literally. The Antarctic landscape is, of course, hugely inspiring but it also brings considerable stresses, strains, risks and dangers, which must be seriously considered before even thinking about heading for these waters.

Antarctica covers 5½ million square miles and is the size of the USA and Europe combined, with 14,000 miles of 'coastline'. It is the world's highest, driest, and coldest

Half Moon Island
Adventure 2013

For more information on permissions relating to your country of origin, consult the following websites

Argentina
www.dna.gov.ar

Australia
www.antarctica.gov.au/about-antarctica/tourism/environmental-approvals-for-tour-and-expedition-organisers

Brazil
www.mar.mil.br/secirm/proantar.htm

Canada
www.ec.gc.ca/gdd-mw

Chile
www.inach.cl

France
www.taaf.fr/Acces-a-l-Antarctique

Germany (German)
www.umweltbundesamt.de/themen/nachhaltigkeit-strategien-internationales/antarktis/antarktisreisende

Netherlands (Dutch)
www.hetlnvloket.nl/xmlpages/page/lnvloket/actueel/document/fileitem/18768

(English)
www.hetlnvloket.nl/xmlpages/page/lnvloket/actueel/document/fileitem/18770

New Zealand
www.mfat.govt.nz/Foreign-Relations/Antarctica/3-New-Zealand-Procedures-for-Visitors-to-Antarctica/index.php

United Kingdom
www.gov.uk/government/policies/protecting-and-developing-the-overseas-territories/supporting-pages/antarctica-and-the-polar-regions

United States
travel.state.gov/content/passports/english/country/antarctica.html

continent and contains 90% of the world's ice. Its icebergs, glaciers and snowfields contain the majority of the world's freshwater. There are no trees or native mammals. The largest native animal is the *Belgica antarctica*, a wingless fly.

However, much of this bleak mass of rock and ice is of no concern to cruising folk. When sailors talk of cruising Antarctica they really mean the Antarctic Peninsula (shown as Graham Land on some maps). This includes the South Orkney and South Shetland Islands, places that have been described, tongue in cheek, as Antarctica's 'Banana Belt'. The Peninsula is a 'mere' 600M hop from Cape Horn, or 700M from the Falklands. Departure can be taken from either Ushuaia (Argentina) or Puerto Williams (Chile) as well as from Stanley (UK). The Peninsula itself is charted in more detail than other parts of the continent, although total accuracy cannot be relied upon.

The Antarctic Circle lies at 66°33'S, where the sun does not set on 22 December. It is doubtful if many yachts will venture this far south.

Who owns Antarctica? The answer is nobody and everybody, or rather the 28 nations who have signed the Antarctic Treaty. This may be the reason that it is one of the few places on earth where there has never been a war. It is 'a natural reserve, devoted to peace and science'.

Everywhere below 60° south is governed by the aforementioned treaty, first signed in 1961 as an agreement by the twelve countries who were active there at the time. No individual country has any territorial rights (although some may make claims) and when you see a national flag flying from one of the scientific bases, it simply denotes the nationality of the scientists working there. This can cause difficulties for skippers who are keen on correct flag etiquette; for example, when anchored off an Argentine base, it has been known for the skipper to be questioned as to why he was not flying an Argentine courtesy flag. Of course, they had no right to demand it, but an Antarctic foreshore with the prospect of some warm hospitality may not be the best place to argue the case.

The treaty bans all forms of military activity and promotes international cooperation in science. It sets aside the potential for any sovereignty claims, and provides for inspections to ensure the terms of the treaty are kept to. It is, in fact, a remarkable and unprecedented piece of international cooperation.

From the sailor's point of view, we have a duty to respect it and stand by its principles. Possibly the most important of which, from a cruiser's point of view, is the requirement to give notice of our 'expeditions' and obtain permission from our national governments. For the purpose of the treaty, any visit to the continent, even by no more than a couple of people on a yacht, is considered an expedition.

Strict penalties may apply to any expedition proceeding below 60ºS without permission and each country is responsible for the regulation of visits by its nationals. This is an important point: you *must* have permission from your government before you set off. You will not be able to obtain it anywhere en route.

An informative resource is the Antarctic Treaty Secretariat:

www.ats.aq

Getting permission

This can be a lengthy process and the sooner you start, the better. Nine months ahead would be ample time, less than five months might cause you anxiety. Do not expect permission to be automatically granted. You will have to satisfy the authorities that you are capable of the voyage and that you have planned it thoroughly. Expect testing questions. You will be required to show you have considered environmental aspects of your intended expedition, completed risk assessments, sorted insurance, and planned for health and safety as well as rescue and medical care, including evacuation.

A post-visit report must be filed within 90 days of the expiry of the permit (UK).

As the continent is owned by no individual country, a visa is not needed to make a visit.

You should note that Chile controls the entire sea area south of the Horn and much of the Antarctic peninsula. In addition to any permissions you may have obtained before leaving home waters, you will have to apply to the *Armada* in Puerto Williams, Beagle Channel for a *zarpe* which allows you to set sail for Antarctica. This is no substitute for permission from your national government, without which the Chileans will not issue you with a *zarpe*. Both permissions are an essential requirement.

Additional guidelines for yachts sailing to Antarctica have been produced by the UK Foreign and Commonwealth Office. These guidelines are very useful even if you are securing an authorisation or permit from another country. They can be found at

www.highlatitudes.com/antarctic-yachting-guidelines.pdf

The US Department of State is the lead agency to notify regarding any planned yacht expedition to Antarctica. Contact Alfred Schandbauer, Senior Advisor for Antarctica.

For US-based or US-flagged yacht operators, please review the Guidelines for US Yacht Expeditions to Antarctica.

UK citizens should start here:

www.gov.uk/government/publications/2010-to-2015-government-policy-uk-overseas-territories/2010-to-2015-government-policy-uk-overseas-territories#appendix-3-antarctica-and-the-polar-regions

You are advised to discuss your plans informally with the UK Polar Regions Department (part of the Foreign and Commonwealth Office) before you begin the application process.

The application forms can then be downloaded here:

www.gov.uk/guidance/visits-to-antarctica-how-to-apply-for-a-permit

The Polar Regions Department can be contacted on ✆ 020 7008 1639 or at PolarRegions@fco.gov.uk

Be aware that once your application has been made, the FCO will make it publicly available.

Since 2010, a simplified application form has been available for use by yachts carrying fewer than 20 people.

Getting to Antarctica

If you are sailing from Chile or Argentina you do not need customs clearance as both countries consider Antarctica to be part of their territory, but you must carry a *zarpe* from the Chilean *Armada*, or clearance from the Argentine Prefectura.

You will not get permission from either if you are not in possession of the necessary permits from your home country.

If clearing out of Ushuaia (Argentina) be careful not to stray into Chilean waters in the Beagle Channel, and keep to the northern shore until well east of Islas Lennox, Picton and Nueva. If you do pass into Chilean waters, you may be asked to leave and the name of your boat will be taken, which could cause complications later. The same rules apply in reverse if leaving from Puerto

Williams (Chile). It may be a condition of your Chilean *zarpe* that you report to Chilean bases in Antarctica in person or by radio. If you do not do so, you may have to explain why on your return. You will also be expected to file your passage plan before leaving, indicating the places you intend to visit. You should attempt to report any changes to your itinerary as you progress.

Crossing the Drake Passage

The Antarctic Circumpolar Current is the largest in the world by volume and transports 5,000 million cubic feet of seawater per second - roughly 1,000 times the flow of the Amazon - and is at its fastest around 60°S. All of this water has to pass through the narrow Drake passage which is no more than 600M wide and made more treacherous by the rising seabed which joins the Antarctic peninsula to South America.

Most yachts making passage through the Drake will pay what is known as the 'Drake Tax', reckoned to be a tax on a boat's preparedness, the hardiness of the crew, and the skill of the skipper in getting them safely through one of the worst 600M stretches of water in the world.

Leaving from the area of the Horn is easier than making the return passage. Departing from the Beagle you will be able to judge the likely development of weather systems and time your departure to suit a weather window. Coming the other way, it is less certain what conditions you will eventually meet off the Horn.

On average, a depression rolls across the Horn every three/four days and if you depart from the area just as a blow has gone through, you can make good progress and be more than two thirds of the way there before the next is upon you. After that, the weather tends to be easier the further south you go but there are no guarantees. Using cunning like this has enabled many yachts to pass through the Drake without experiencing any severe conditions, although you must always be prepared for it.

When returning to the Beagle from Antarctica, the decision on when to depart is more difficult. If you are planning a five day crossing, you are working at the limits of reliable forecasting in this volatile region. Consequently, the weather window you thought you had might suddenly disappear when you are half way across and you may experience the worst winds in the worst possible place, off the Horn.

The Antarctic Convergence

Only when you are south of the Antarctic Convergence, a line which rings the entire continent between 45°S and 60°S, can you truthfully consider yourself to be in Antarctica. Your arrival will be clearly marked by plummeting temperatures, a change in the sea colour, and sightings of new wildlife. The change in temperature as you pass through can be as large as 6°C. The boundary between the warmer and colder air masses is known as the polar front.

When cold, north-flowing water meets the 'warmer' water of the south Atlantic and sub Antarctic; the colder water sinks, mixes with the warmer, and rises, resulting in a rich marine feeding environment where shrimp-like Antarctic krill, and similar crustaceans, flourish. These are much loved by Blue and Fin whales, Emperor penguins and seals. The Convergence itself is 20–30M wide and represents a barrier for sea life – crabs and lobsters, for example, will not be found anywhere to its south. Its existance explains why Antarctic waters are rich in wildlife, when you would expect the cold to prevent it flourishing.

The Antarctic Divergence

The Divergence is found at around 60–65°S, and, like the Convergence, it rings the entire continent. This narrow band of water marks the line between the east-flowing Antarctic Circumpolar Current, found in the Southern Ocean and Drake Passage, and the west-flowing current to be found closer to the Antarctic land mass driven by prevailing easterly winds. Where the two meet, an upwelling occurs and with it comes a sharp change in the ocean salinity, resulting in yet more changes in wildlife.

The Antarctic Peninsula

It is of the upmost importance to understand that most of the pilotage information given here has been gleaned from notes and sketches made by visiting yachts over the last two decades. Some of these will have been compiled on the basis of the sailor's own experience, or may have been taken from notes written by yachts that went before them.

There is much scope for error. All anchorage information should be treated with great caution.

Electronic charting cannot be relied upon as the data will have been taken from the elderly surveys on which the original paper charts were based, and these too can prove inaccurate. This is a place for traditional navigational skills where your eyeball is the most reliable instrument you have on board, and even your magnetic compass cannot be relied upon (see below).

We can offer no guarantee of detailed accuracy in the charts which follow - use them for guidance only.

Yachting in Antarctica is a modern phenomenon. Not until 1973 did the first yacht, *Damien*, reach the Antarctic Peninsula and sail below the Antarctic Circle. Now there are many charter expeditions and increasing numbers of private yachts departing regularly from the Beagle Channel. Some cruisers first take a charter in order to familiarise themselves with the terrain, its dangers and geography, before committing to taking their own boats across. An internet search will come up with packages offered by yachts of all shapes and sizes and you should check each of them carefully. If possible, check with others who have been before and make your choice on the basis of recommendation. The Antarctic charter fleet is quite small and protective of its good reputation; word would spread quickly if any operator was thought not to be up to the mark. Poor operators will not last long.

As a starting point consult IAATO, the International Association of Antarctic Tour Operators, **www.iaato.org**, and search their list of members. The majority of vessels will be cruise ships, but several yachts are listed. A trip in the company of one of these highly experienced yacht skippers will yield a vast amount of invaluable information.

A list of their yachting members can be found here:

www.iaato.org/service-providers-and-operators

High Latitudes offer expedition support, advice and training, and can arrange charters.

www.highlatitudes.com

Skip Novak was a pioneer of Antarctic sailing and few know these waters better than he does. His two yachts, *Pelagic* and *Pelagic Australis* have high reputations.

www.pelagic.co.uk

The IAATO website is also a vast resource of information on Antarctica and, although more concerned with tourism than adventurous cruising, there are many areas of overlap. In particular, the 'Visitors to Antarctica' guidelines lay down simple rules for visitor behaviour ashore when encountering wildlife.

The basic rule on refuse is 'if you bring it in, take it out.' This includes fitting holding tanks for grey and black waste and certainly no oily bilge water should be discharged, so do not leave bilge pumps on 'auto'. If emptying holding tanks, you should do so as far offshore as you are able, and while travelling at speed to aid break up of the waste. Remember, at these low water temperatures sewage takes far longer to disperse than in warmer waters.

If going ashore, remember that weather conditions can change very quickly, ice can fill an anchorage, and you may not be able to return to your boat. Take emergency supplies with you in case you are stranded ashore. If staying in one anchorage and planning several visits ashore, it might be worth planting a tent and stores ashore in case it becomes impossible to get back to the boat.

Only take items from emergency huts in life-threatening situations.

This is a sailing, and not a walking/climbing/hiking book, but anyone going ashore should be aware that glaciers and ice fields can be littered with hidden crevasses

IAATO 'Visitors to Antarctica' guidelines

- Do not interfere with wildlife. Observe their behaviour and back off if you sense you are not welcome
- Do not feed wildlife or leave food scraps
- Always give wildlife right of way
- Do not land on moss beds or lichen-covered rocks. Any damage you do will take a very long time to repair
- Follow tracks if there are any; if not, take the most direct route and avoid vegetation
- Do not introduce any plants or animals
- Wash your boots, bags, clothes, tents, walking sticks etc before coming to Antarctica. Boot treads, Velcro fastenings and pockets can contain seeds (Cruise ships are strict on this point and yachts should be too)
- Be aware of ASPAs (Antarctic Specially Protected Areas) and make sure you have a permit to enter
- Get snow and grit off your boots before entering any historic area
- If visiting stations, get permission well in advance and reconfirm well before arrival. Most stations will answer calls on VHF 16 or 12
- Do not leave litter
- If you smoke (in designated areas) arrange to remove the ash from the continent
- Do not wash yourself or your equipment in lakes or streams
- Do not paint your boat's name anywhere
- Ensure all rubbish is wrapped in such a way that it cannot be spread by wind or plundered by wildlife.

The above is a summary only, please read the rules in full on the IAATO website.

Poling off the ice floes
Adventure 2013

and should not be crossed without proper equipment and training.

Keep your distance off icebergs and ice cliffs, which can collapse without warning.

This is the experience of one Antarctic sailor, Tim Barker, who took *Mina²* to Antarctica in 2012

The risks you take when sailing in ice depend on your experience, your judgement, your vessel, your crew and your luck. So far as hull construction is concerned the chances of hull damage caused by impact with ice in a glass fibre boat is much greater than if in a custom-built steel high-latitude expedition yacht. But in all cases one has to be careful and prepared, not just to minimise the risk of damage by ice, but also prepared to deal with the consequences. Contingency planning will include the ability to stem quickly the ingress of water caused by impact with ice.

When I sailed to the Antarctic Peninsula in 2012, it was no coincidence that we went in January – it was because in January you still have light 24 hours of the day. When sailing in open water, icebergs and larger bergy bits can be picked up on radar. However, it is very difficult to spot a growler amongst white horses, so watch-keeping has to be particularly vigilant particularly in the South Shetland Islands that are prone to foggy conditions. To minimise the probability of sailing amongst growlers, wherever possible sail to windward of icebergs; on the leeward side you will find a greater density of ice that has broken off the berg.

The cruising season

The west coast of the Antarctic Peninsula is where the ice tends to clear first, particularly at its northern end, and the cruising season here is reckoned to be December, January and February. Summer ice conditions here are more favourable than in any other part of the continent. Even so, the Argentine Islands at 65°15'S are as far as yachts should venture, and even then not alone.

Sailing in ice

A lot of the time you will be motoring because often there is insufficient wind to sail (offset by those occasions when there is far too much wind) and it is easier to manoeuvre through ice under power. For this reason, you must have a completely reliable engine, sufficient spares, plenty of diesel, and if one of your crew happens to be an engineer, so much the better.

Only experience will tell you at what speed it is safe to motor through ice and it will depend on the type of ice, its density and the strength and composition of your hull. You are likely to start off nervously trickling through any type of ice, but by the end of a couple of weeks on the peninsula you may have sufficient confidence to go through brash ice at a reasonable lick. Growlers and bergy bits, however, should always be avoided.

Impact with the hull, as well as the rudder and propeller, can cause damage. When motoring through brash ice in a straight line, all the ice will have been divided by the hull and will not make contact with the rudder or propeller. However, if changing course sharply, your stern could find itself running over ice with the possibility of the ice going under the stern rather than round it. Particular care needs to be taken when going astern as there is a much higher probability of contact between ice and the rudder or propeller. Preparation for sailing in ice should include contingency plans to deal with potential damage to the rudder or propeller.

Following ice leads

Ice leads are channels which open up to allow the passage of a boat. They can be quite narrow, sometimes hardly more than a boat's beam. To spot them, a crew up the mast can be useful. The danger in their use is the potential for the leads to change rapidly, possibly trapping a yacht by closing up ahead and behind. The yacht can then become beset. If the ice concentration is ³⁄₁₀ or less then careful navigation can usually enable progress. The risk of becoming beset rises rapidly above that figure.

The dangers of icebergs

As every schoolchild knows, most of the ice in an iceberg is below the waterline, meaning that current has a greater impact upon its movement than wind. Bergy bits (see definition p. 177), on the other hand, tend to be more greatly influenced by wind.

Because the visible portion of an iceberg is eroding under the influence of wind and sun, its stability can be subject to substantial change. This is why an apparently stable iceberg can suddenly capsize. If a yacht is close to one, the danger is obvious. But even at a distance the effect can be felt, as a substantial wave, similar to a tsunami, is propagated. This wave may become steeper as it approaches shallows and can bend round headlands and enter anchorages.

Because bergy bits are under the influence of wind, the safest side on which to pass an iceberg is to windward. Bergy bits can be difficult to spot if the sea surface is flecked with white water.

If sailing near the foot of glaciers, do not approach closer than 200m.

Anchoring in ice

A safe and sheltered anchorage can fill with ice with very little warning. A shift in the current or wind can happen at any time and it is not safe to assume that because you have anchored in clear water, it will remain that way for the rest of the night.

If you have the slightest suspicion that conditions may change, an anchor watch is the only safe option. Small floes can be shoved aside with a pole, but larger ones may become lodged on the anchor chain. You will not be able to move these, nor raise the anchor because of the weight of the ice. In this circumstance the only option is to buoy the anchor chain and let it go, hoping you can retrieve it later on.

Much of the advice given by Andrew Wilkes in the Arctic navigation section of *Arctic and Northern Waters* (Imray) also applies in Antarctica. However, detailed and up-to-date ice charts, such as those which can be obtained for Greenland waters, are not available in Antarctica although ice edge charts are available here:

www.natice.noaa.gov

Cold work keeping lookout
Adventure 2013

Manoeuvring in sea ice

It is said that hitting new ice is like hitting solid wood, and hitting old ice is like hitting iron. Old ice can be distinguished by its blue tint, it is harder and more eroded and, therefore, flatter, than newer ice. Collision with either is to be avoided, although small floes may be gently pushed aside using engine power. Long ice poles are useful for deflecting smaller floes.

The opening and closing of leads can take place quickly and suddenly and it should not be underestimated how quickly floes can move under the influence of wind and current.

It can be dangerous to navigate through any clear water that lies between the shore and moving ice. An onshore wind shift will eventually force the boat aground, trapped in behind the ice.

The effect of pack ice is to greatly reduce the sea state. If sailing out of ice, far tougher conditions may be encountered once you leave the ice.

If approaching ice from a distance, ice blink and fog can be useful indicators of the presence of ice. Once seen, the ice can appear as a continuous white line with no prospect of any passage. It is only when you approach it more closely that the leads become apparent.

Sea ice

Sea ice begins to form in March as winter approaches and the advance can be as much as 3km per day until mid September when it will be at its greatest extent and extend N of 60°S.

Sea ice can break into ice floes or consolidate into pack ice. The density of the ice is measured in tenths, as follows:

Open water with little pack ice	1/10 to 3/10
Open pack with some rafting	4/10 to 6/10
Dense pack ice	7/10 to 9/10
No visible water	10/10

It is generally reckoned that yachts can navigate safely only in less than 2/10 ice cover.

Ice comes in many forms, depending on the stage of its development, and brings with it its own vocabulary.

The various types of sea ice are carefully defined and many of the subtleties are beyond what a sailor needs to know. The following descriptions are kindly supplied by the Australian Government's Antarctic Division:

www.antarctica.gov.au/about-antarctica/environment/icebergs-and-ice/sea-ice

Frazil ice
Fine spicules or plates of ice, suspended in water. Frazil ice formation is the first stage of sea ice growth. The frazil crystals are usually suspended in the top few centimetres of the surface layer of the ocean and give the water an oily appearance. The crystals may be stirred to a depth of several metres by wave-induced turbulence.

Grease ice
This comes after the Frazil ice has formed when the crystals have coagulated to form a soupy layer on the surface. Grease ice reflects little light, giving the surface a matt appearance and behaves in a viscous, fluid-like manner, not forming distinct ice floes. Grease ice will support the weight of a seabird.

Shuga ice
An accumulation of spongy white lumps, a few centimetres across; they are formed from grease ice or slush.

Nilas ice
A thin elastic crust of ice, easily bending on waves and swell and under pressure, thrusting in a pattern of interlocking 'fingers' (finger rafting). It has a matt surface and is up to 10cm in thickness. There is dark and light nilas ice. Dark nilas is less than 5cm thick and very dark in colour. Light nilas is 5–10 cm thick and reflects proportionately more light than dark nilas, depending on its thickness.

Pancake ice
Circular pieces of ice from 0·3–3m in diameter, and up to 10cm in thickness with raised rims due to the pieces striking against one another. It may be formed on a slight swell from grease ice, shuga or slush.

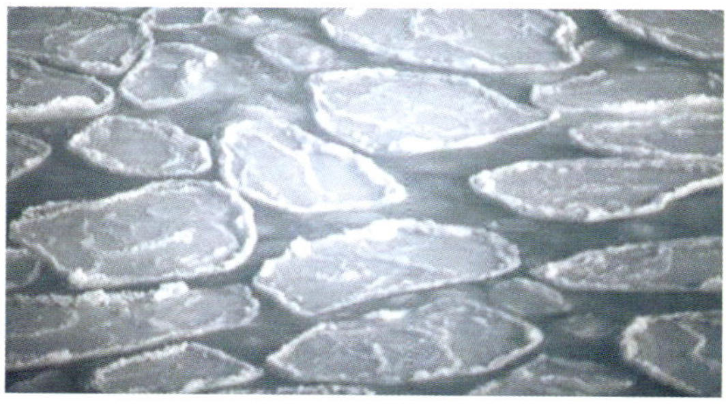

Pancake ice *Sibéal Turraoin*

Young ice
Ice in the transition stage between nilas and first-year ice, 10–30cm in thickness. May be subdivided into grey ice and grey-white ice.

Grey ice
Young ice 10–15cm thick. Less elastic than nilas and breaks on swell. Usually rafts under pressure.

Grey-white ice
Young ice 15–30cm thick. Under pressure more likely to ridge than to raft

Rafting is the process whereby one piece of ice overrides another and is most common in new and young ice. Ridging is the pressure process by which sea ice is forced into ridges.

New ice
A general term for recently formed ice which includes frazil ice, grease ice, slush and shuga.

First-year ice
Sea ice of not more than one winter's growth, developing from young ice; thickness (typically) 0·3–2m. May be subdivided into thin first-year ice/white ice, medium first-year ice and thick first-year ice.

Fast ice
Máire Wilkes

Second-year ice
Old ice which has survived only one summer's melt. Because it is thicker and less dense than first-year ice, it stands higher out of the water. In contrast to multi-year ice, summer melting produces a regular pattern of puddles. Bare patches and puddles are usually greenish-blue.

Multi-year ice
Old ice up to 3m or more thick which has survived at least two summers' melt. Hummocks (hillocks of broken ice that have been forced up by pressure) even smoother than in second-year ice, and the ice is almost salt-free. Colour, where bare, is usually blue. Melt pattern consists of large interconnecting irregular puddles and a well-developed drainage system.

Other types of ice you will encounter

Brash ice
This is an accumulation of floating ice made up of fragments of not more than 2m wide which are the wreckage of other forms of ice. Brash is common between colliding floes or in regions where pressure ridges have collapsed.

Fast ice
Sea ice that forms and remains attached to the shore, an ice wall, an ice front, or between shoals or grounded icebergs. It may extend a few metres or several hundred kilometres from the coast. Fast ice may be more than one year old and may then be prefixed with the appropriate age category (old, second-year, or multi-year).

Floe
This is a flat piece of sea ice 20m or more across. A giant floe is over 5.4M across, a vast floe is 1·1–5·4M across, a big floe is 500–2,000m across, a medium floe is 100–500m across, a small floe 20–100m.

Bergy bit
A large piece of floating glacier ice, generally showing less than 5m above sea level but more than 1m and normally about 100–300 square metres in area. It is smaller than an iceberg but larger than a growler. A typical bergy bit is about the size of a small house.

Growler
A piece of glacier ice smaller than a bergy bit, often transparent but appearing green or almost black in colour. It extends less than 1m above the sea surface and its length is less than 20 feet (6m). A growler is large enough to be a hazard to shipping but small enough that it may escape visual or radar detection.

Sastrugi
Sharp, irregular ridges formed on a snow surface by wind erosion and deposition. On mobile floating ice, the ridges are parallel to the direction of the prevailing wind at the time they were formed.

Floe ice
Máire Wilkes

Cuverville Island *Nick Coleman*

ANCHORAGES IN ANTARCTICA

The melting of the sea ice in the summer is unpredictable and you can never be certain that any of the anchorages mentioned below will be free of ice. What's more, an anchorage which is ice-free when you drop the hook may fill with ice due to a shift in the wind, making it easy for a yacht to become trapped, not only by the density of the incoming ice but by bergy bits and growlers, which may cover your anchor and prevent a speedy escape.

Many of the anchorages mentioned below are covered by the ATS (Secretariat of the Antarctic Treaty) website which gives much useful information regarding wildlife and geographical features which will be invaluable if venturing ashore. Suggested landing places to minimise wildlife disruption are shown.

www.ats.aq/e/ats_other_siteguidelines.htm

The *Admiralty Pilot* warns:

> *Waters covered (in this pilot) are only 15% surveyed and of that just 10% to modern standards. Within the 200m contour 60% of the area has never been systematically surveyed.*

Remember, coordinates are given here only as an aid to identification, and not navigation.

South Shetland Islands

There are over 20 islands in the South Shetland group with more than 150 outlying islets, skerries and rocks. There are four distinct groups: Clarence and Elephant islands in the NE, King George and Nelson Islands are just NE of Robert, Greenwich, Livingston, Snow and Deception Islands. Smith and Low Islands are at the SW end of the chain.

Coming from the direction of the Horn, you may choose to make a stop here as the South Shetlands are the first islands you will meet and you will now be only 75M from the Antarctic Peninsula, 450M from the Beagle Channel and 600M from the Falklands.

The 20 or so islands are considered part of Antarctica and the rules and permits apply here in the same way as in the rest of the continent. There are several research stations, 16 at the last count, most of them on King George Island where there is also an airstrip (at the Chilean base, Eduardo Frei), as well as cafeteria, bank and comfortable housing for the staff of the Chilean research station on the Fildes Peninsula on the SW of the island.

The weather is generally cloudy and damp with a prevailing strong W/NW wind; as these islands often lie in the depression track, easterly winds can be experienced as well. In a good year, cruising might be possible in early

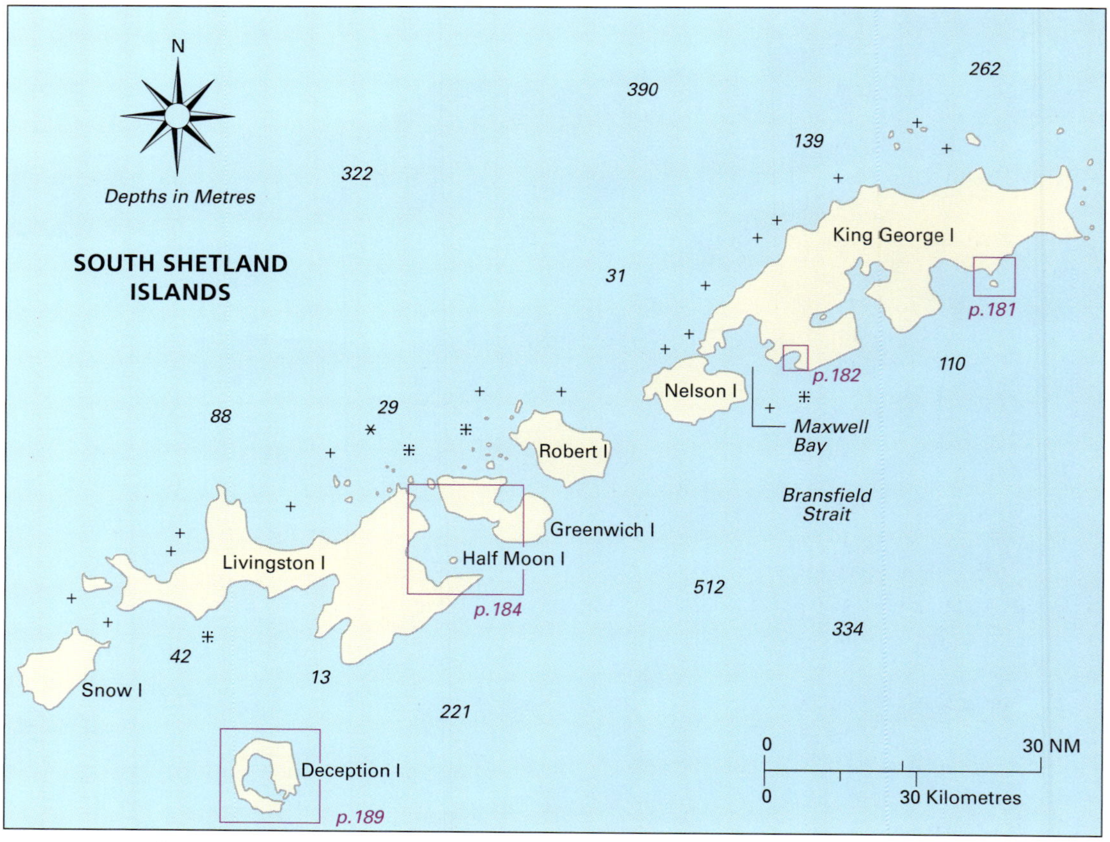

Penguin Bay anchorage
Pete Hill

December although late December is a safer bet after sufficient melting of the ice. January and February are the warmest months, July the coldest. The sunniest weather is associated with very cold weather brought on a southerly wind.

Given the many sheltered anchorages here, and the relative ease of access, visits by yachts are frequent (by Antarctic standards). Although the western coasts of the islands have many small islands and rocks which make navigation difficult, if not dangerous, the south side is reckoned to have few such dangers.

It is worth noting that the tides around the islands are unpredictable and the rise and fall cannot be relied upon and will vary according to weather conditions. If engaged in close navigation, a sharp lookout should be kept for any unexpected tidal set.

A reminder that although some coordinates are given here, they should NOT be used for navigation and are given only to help with identification of anchorages and features.

The anchorages below have been chosen as places where you can plan for shelter in adverse weather. For detailed exploration, consult Pete Hill's notes (a free download from **www.rccpf.org.uk**) together with the *Admiralty Pilot* NP9.

King George Island

This island is less typical of the Antarctic landscape than any other and has the mildest climate of any place in Antarctica. Amongst the hardcore visitors to Antarctica, King George Island is considered a 'bit of a beach holiday'.

The terrain is quite low with the coastline broken into many bays and fjords. It is also the least isolated with many countries having research stations here. 90% of King George Island is glaciated.

Mersey Spit and Penguin Island

62°05S 57°55W

Found on the S side of King George Island, Mersey Spit and Penguin Island form the east side of King George Bay. If passing to the east of Penguin Island the approach is straightforward. Anchor NE of Mersey Spit in 7m.

There is shelter here from W and NW, but with any S in the wind, ice moving from the Bay can cause problems. In which case anchorage can be found in 9m, off the north end of Penguin Island, opposite a shingle beach.

Because a large part of the land around Mersey Spit is ice free, there is good walking ashore here and on Penguin Island. Expect to share your walks with cruise ship passengers – this is a popular stopping place.

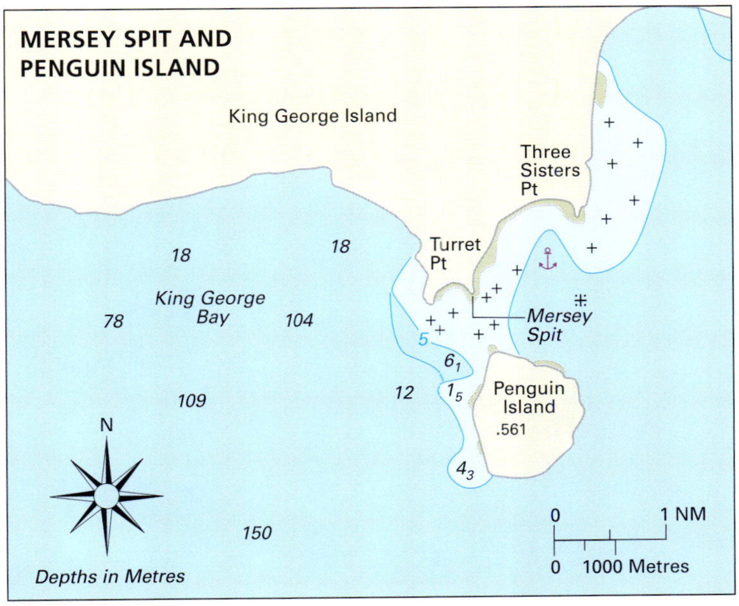

Maxwell Bay approaches

Approach by identifying the Three Brothers peak (196m, 62°15'S 58°41'W) which stands on the E side of the entrance (noting rocks and shoals if approaching from E). Enter midway between either side of the cove to avoid rocks off the W headland. If entering from the SW, note the rocks off Duthoit Point, the western edge of Maxwell Bay.

The Carlini Station (formerly the Jubany Base) (Argentina) lies on the S shore and in winds E to WSW it is possible to anchor off here in 5m.

If the winds are from N, there is an anchorage off the northern shore of the cove, but beware of glacier ice, which can be a problem here, and drying rocks just to the S. Sound carefully before anchoring.

The hinterland behind the Carlini Station is a SSSI (Site of Special Scientific Interest) and should not be crossed.

The station was named in memory of the biologist Alejandro Carlini in 2012 but older books and charts will use its previous name, Jubany Base. It is a substantial encampment with 15 buildings providing housing for up to 60 people. It is believed to house Antarctica's only cinema.

Note: there is a substantial glacier at the head of Maxwell Bay with reports (unconfirmed) of an uncharted pinnacle some way off it.

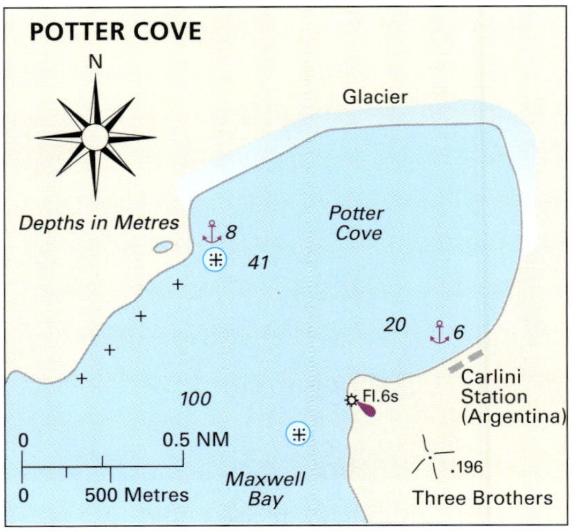

Potter Cove, Maxwell Bay

65°15S 58°42W
Chart Inset on BA 1774

The best and safest anchorage in the islands, with shelter from all wind directions. Excellent shelter in the bay with good holding in 10–15m behind the point on the E entrance in front of the Argentine Carlini base, (formerly known as the Jubany base). Access is straightforward. Enter favouring the western shore in order to clear foul ground on the eastern side. Ice is not a problem here except in periods of sustained NW winds.

Ardley Cove, Maxwell Bay

62°12S 58°57W

Ardley Cove lies in the NW corner of Maxwell Bay, on the Fildes Peninsula.

The anchorage is found by passing N of Ardley Island and identifying Becerra Island, marked by a yellow pole with no top mark. Identification is helped by the presence of

Research stations at Ardley Cove *Pete Hill*

Russian Orthodox church, Bellingshausen Station *Pete Hill*

Chilean and Russian research stations, and an airfield with a 1,300m runway from which it is possible to organise a flight to Punta Arenas. There is also a Post Office. Land on the shore at the head of the bay.

Note the spit that runs from Becerra Island to the shore in a NW direction. Anchor north of this spit in 3–4m.

Note that in early April 2012, a substantial Brazilian motor yacht, *Endless Sea*, became trapped in ice driven into Maxwell Bay by winds reported to be 120km/h (104 knots). The four crew were rescued but the yacht sank. The wreck has since been removed.

There are two bases here belonging to Chile and Russia. The Bellingshausen Station (Russia) was one of the first to be established on Antarctica and has the distinction of having the only Orthodox Church, with full time priest and complete with bells, on the entire continent. Most places of worship on the continent are somewhat utilitarian, but this church has been decorated in high Orthodox style having been built in Russia out of Siberian pine and then shipped out to King George Island.

In 1992, the area around this base was judged to be Antarctica's most polluted but 1,350 tons of waste were removed in 2002 making for a great improvement.

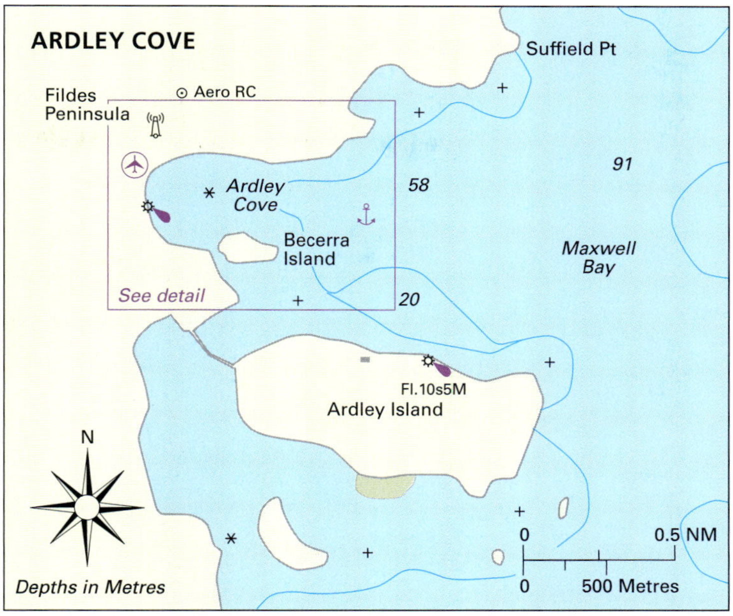

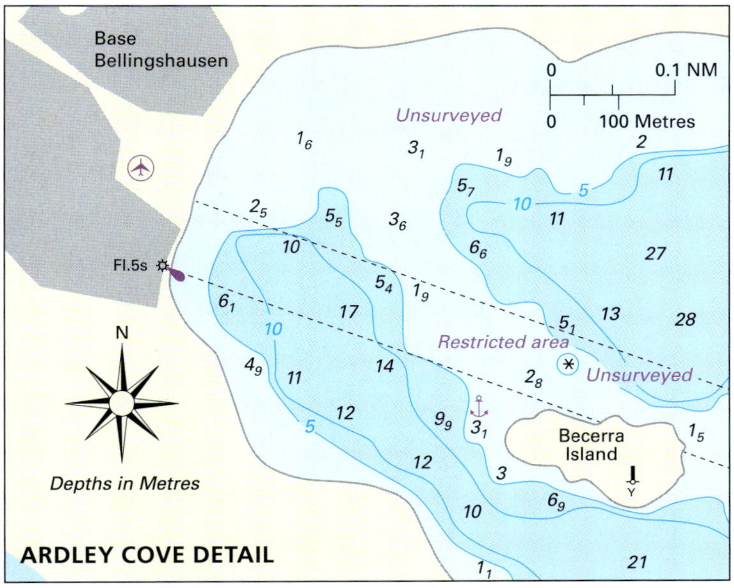

Livingston Island - Half Moon Island

62°35S 59° 54W

This anchorage is found on the east shore of Livingstone Island in Moon Bay and provides excellent shelter except from the E. It is a popular stop with cruise ships and a visit is recommended.

Half Moon Island *Pete Hill*

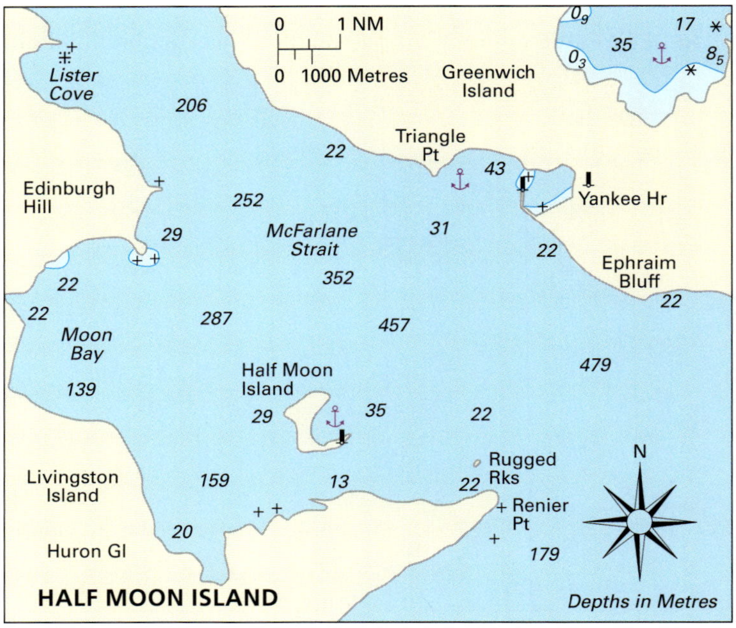

When approaching, take care to avoid rocks off each tip of the crescent. Identify the base (Argentina) and anchor W of it in about 5m. It is possible to land at the pebble beach in front of the base.

The chart shows a beacon on the SE end of the island, and a light may be exhibited, but neither can be relied upon.

Deception Island

63°00'S 60°40'W
Chart BA 3202 – note that outdated charts may not show a revised shoreline following volcanic activity.

The island consists of a massive volcanic crater lake, said to be amongst the most remarkable in the world, and was the original centre of commercial activity and exploration in the Peninsula area. There is still volcanic activity.

Enter through Neptune's Bellows; a notable entry by any standards because of the high rise on either side and the colourful strata which can be seen. As the name would suggest, expect strong and unpredictable gusts of wind against which it may be impossible to tack.

Avoid Raven Rock in the middle of the channel with 2·4m over it. The northern half of the passage is deeper. The red sector of the Collins Point light also marks the rock (Fl.W.5s10m6M white GRP tower with red band).

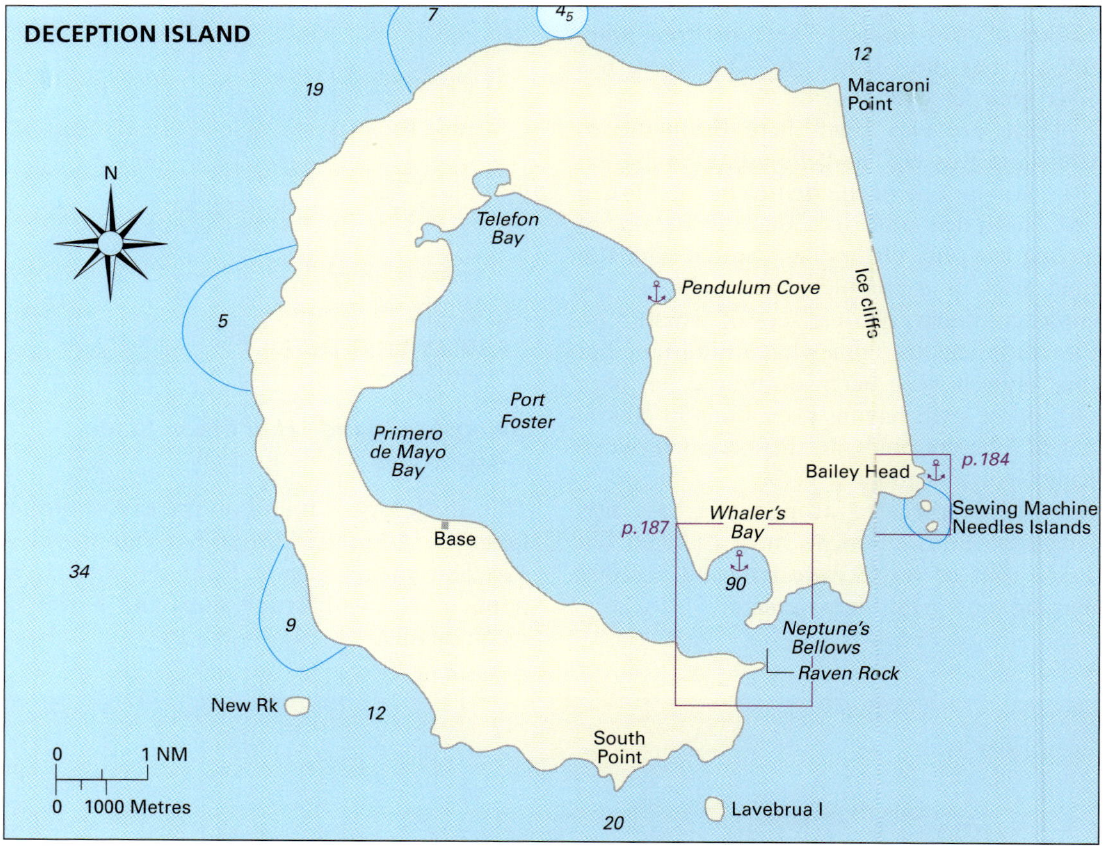

Neptune's Bellows
Adventure 2013

Deception Island *Adventure 2013*

Approaching Deception Island
Nick Coleman

The W-going tidal stream in the Bellows begins 10 mins after LW, the E-going stream at 10 minutes after HW with a spring rate of 1·2kn.

Once past Fildes Point, there are no further obstructions and you should head into Whalers' Bay.

Whalers' Bay, Deception Island

62°59S 60°32W

An open anchorage with good holding. Although it is well-sheltered from the sea, the wind can whistle down from the surrounding mountains. The sea-bed shallows well offshore so anchor in about 20m in case of a wind-shift. You will see the remains of whaling and scientific stations. There is a good walk up to 'Neptune's Window'.

In settled weather, anchor off the head of the bay to the west of the old whaling factory in about 4m; be aware that the bottom rises steeply here. Land on the beach.

Ashore, you will find the remains of an old British Antarctic Survey base with hangar and plane abandoned after an eruption in 1969.

This is a popular stopover for cruise ships.

The Antarctic Treaty Visitors' Guide offers the following advice:

Do not go beyond the western end of the airplane hangar in order to avoid entry into ASPA 140.

Approach oil and fuel tanks with caution. The foundations are vulnerable to erosion and the tanks are at risk of collapse. Do not enter buildings or tanks or sit or climb on the boats. Maintain a reasonable distance from any structures to avoid injury from collapsing debris.

Maintain at least 20m distance from seismic monitoring equipment and other types of scientific equipment, which normally will be marked with a red flag. Do not touch or disturb other types of scientific instruments, markers, or field depots.

Maintain a precautionary distance of 5m from wildlife and give animals the right-of-way. Increase this distance if any change in behaviour is observed.

Do not dig bathing pits.

Hiking between Whalers Bay and Bailey Head is discouraged as it can damage important vegetated areas, in particular Antarctica's largest recorded stand of Antarctic pearlwort.

All visits must be planned taking into account the significant risk posed by the threat of volcanic eruption. Real time information can be obtained from the stations operating on the island.

All the buildings on this site are in physically poor condition and there is an ongoing risk that parts of these buildings may collapse or sections be blown off. Entry to any of the buildings is unsafe at all times and a good distance should be left when walking adjacent to buildings. Beware of sharp objects and flying debris in windy conditions. In high winds the whole area should be avoided because of the risk of flying debris.

Whalers' Bay
Pete Hill

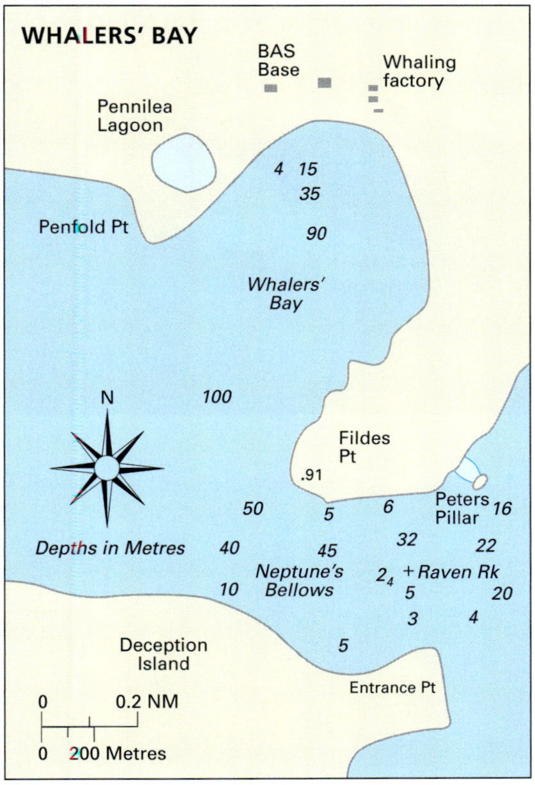

Argentine base, Deception Island *Tim Barker*

Remains of the British Antarctic base, Whalers' Bay *Pete Hill*

Whalers' Bay *Nick Coleman*

Pendulum Cove, Deception Island

62°56S 60 36W

Four miles north of Whalers' Bay, Pendulum Cove offers more shelter and good holding. But swinging space is limited. Shore lines or a second anchor should be used in unsettled weather.

The anchorage is named after an experiment conducted by Henry Foster of the Royal Navy in 1829 in which he erected a pendulum in an attempt to measure the force of gravity, with the intention of determining the earth's true shape.

Antarctic swimming in warm, volcanic water *Tim Barker*

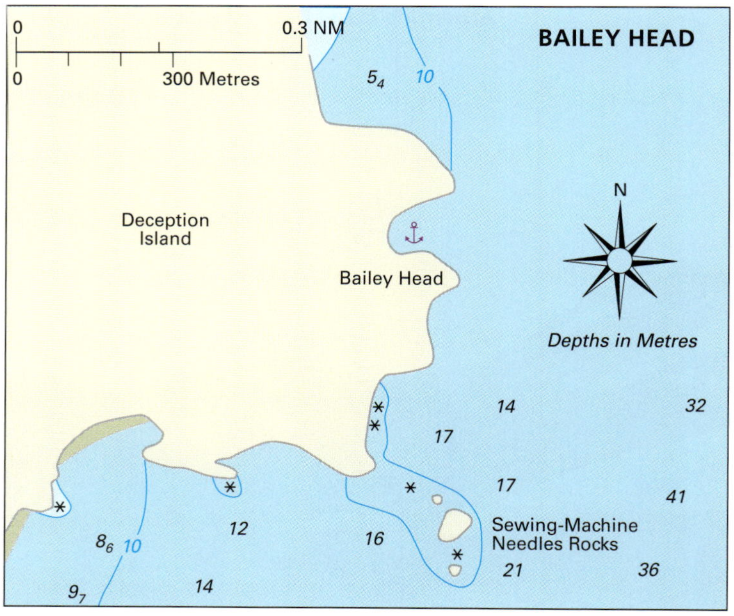

Bailey Head, Deception Island

This anchorage provides good shelter from W winds and an easy approach.

Bailey Head and the Sewing Machine Needles rocks to the S are conspicuous.

Anchor off the shingle beach in 9m. In strong W winds, *williwaws* can be created around Bailey Head but these can be avoided by anchoring ½M to the north of the headland.

Land near a stream found on the beach in the corner created by the headland. Territorial fur seals may make landing difficult.

If you are anxious to boast of having swum in Antarctica, Deception Island is the place to do it since the waters around the island are reckoned to be the warmest on the continent - but not by much!

Bailey Head *Pete Hill*

Emma Cove *Pete Hill*

Elephant Island

Elephant Island is the most northeasterly of the South Shetland island chain.

Those who have read Shackleton's account of the loss of *Endurance* and the subsequent epic small boat journey of 1916 in the *James Caird* towards South Georgia, will want to call at Elephant Island. It was here that twenty-two members of the expedition wintered for four months in 1916.

Landing is not easy as the 'beach' is strewn with boulders and many have reported that the best way to see this island is to remain offshore in a Zodiac, or similar. Landing can involve a carefully timed leap between surf, and if attempting this a wet suit, or at least waders, are advised.

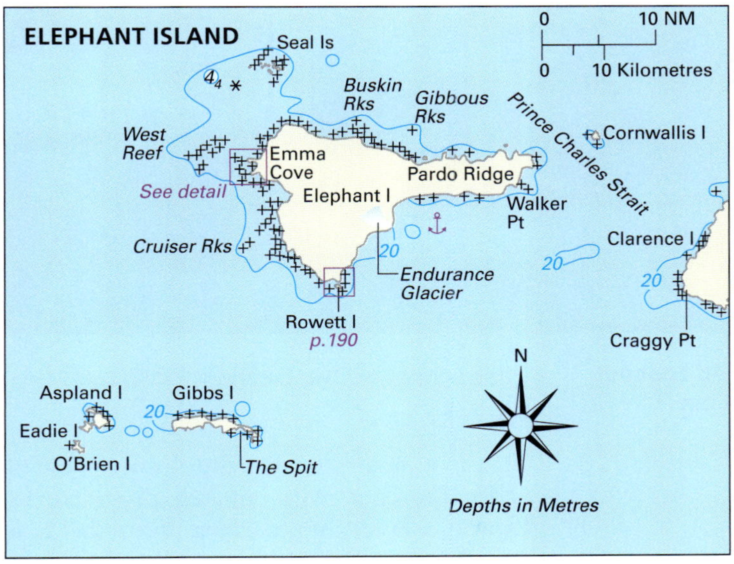

Emma Cove, Elephant Island

61°07S 55°28W

This bay is fully open to W, but there is good shelter from NNW, through E to SSW.

If approaching from W avoid the West Reef some 4M offshore and 2M wide. Rocks extend W from Cape Lindsey and should be avoided if entering from N. The southernmost arm, which forms Emma Cove, also has rocks extending off it for half a mile.

Enter the cove midway between the two points and head towards a small stream running down a scree slope on the S side of the cove. Anchor off this stream (being careful not to confuse it with a stream further N) in 8m, good holding.

The black scree cliffs which surround this anchorage can give it a glum feel.

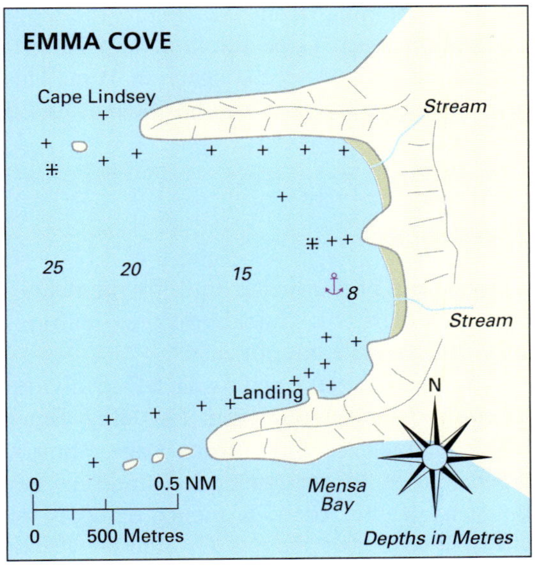

Lookout Cove
Pete Hill

Off Lookout Cove *Pete Hill*

Cape Lookout Cove, Elephant Island

61°17S 55° 12W

This is a small and delightful cove west of Cape Lookout with shelter provided by Rowett Island. Approaching from the E is straightforward, but pass south of Rowett Island if coming from W. Enter the cove midway between Cape Lookout and Rowett Island and anchor off the beach in 10m. This is a small cove and lines can be taken ashore if required.

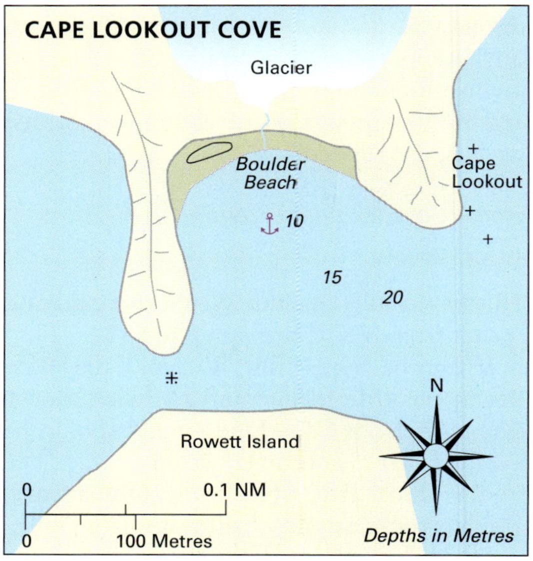

Point Wild, Elephant Island

61°06S 54°52W

This the site of the shelter built by the twenty two members of Shackleton's expedition. Access is possible but not easy.

The hut lies on a peninsula which divides West (or Glacier) Bay from East Bay. Enter West (Glacier) Bay from due north. Anchoring is not recommended, and may not be possible, but there is plenty of space to circle slowly in the bay in 15–20m level with the gap between Penguin Hill and Gnomon Island - this is shown on the official chart as a rock but is, in fact, 79m high. A shore party can then land while the boat circles. A suggested landing space is shown on the chartlet.

The site is not easily spotted from seaward and is wedged more closely between high rock and a cliff than might be expected if you are familiar with Frank Hurley's famous photographs.

Lookout Cove anchorage
Pete Hill

The Melchior Islands
Tim Barker

Islands off the Antarctic Peninsula

The northwest coast of the Antarctic Peninsula is littered with islands, amongst them Brabant Island, the Melchior Islands, Anvers Island, Hovgaard Island and many others. There is anchorage to be found on most of them, some even providing complete shelter.

The Melchior Islands

These islands are a popular landfall/departure point for those who have crossed the Drake, or are about to return. The height of Melchior Island makes it visible at a great distance and helps in making a landfall. Although open to NE swells, some shelter can be found in most conditions. The islands have a reputation for fair weather and it is reported that conditions here can be calm even while a gale may be blowing at sea.

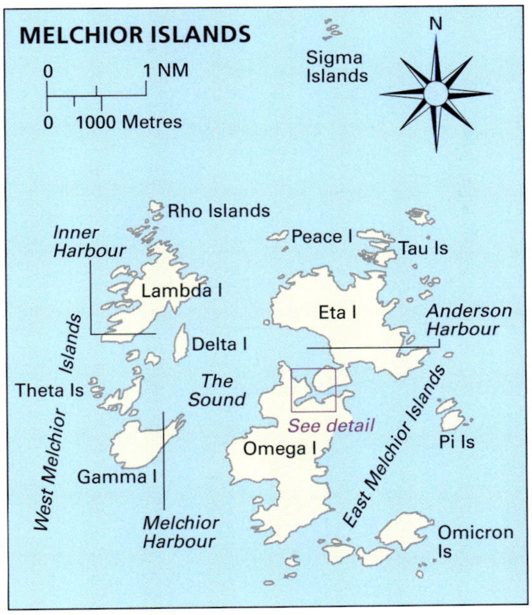

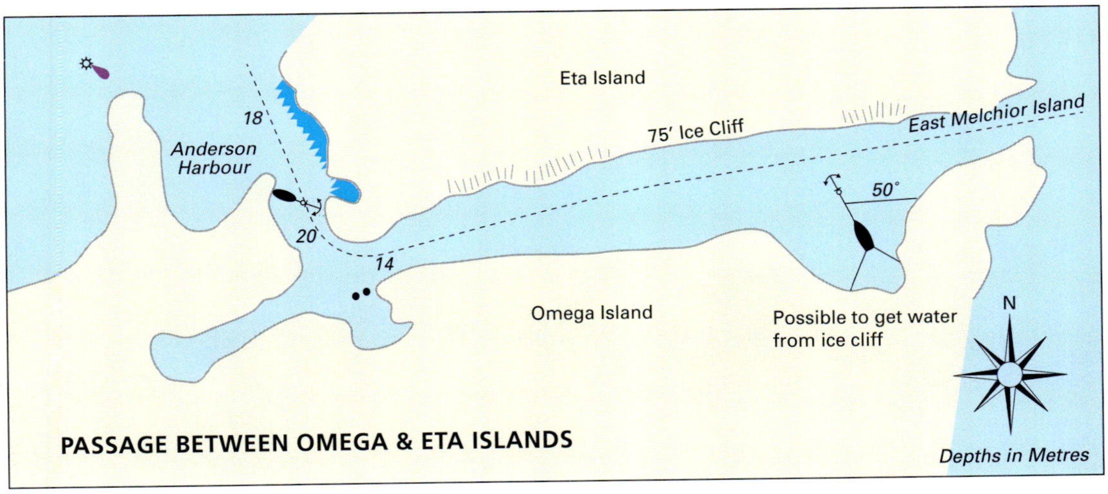

ENTERPRISE ISLAND

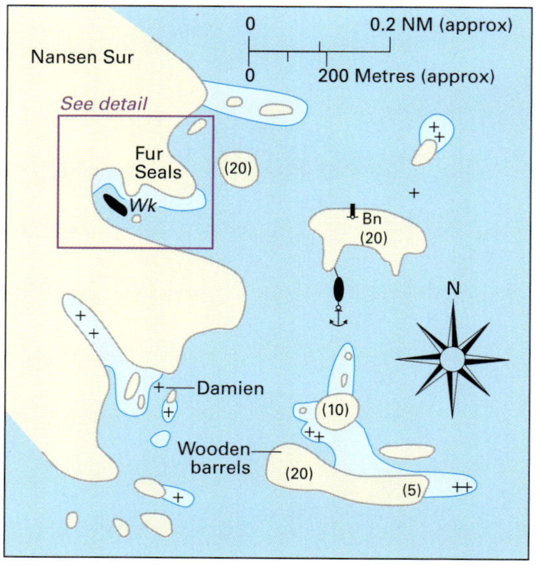

ENTERPRISE ISLAND DETAIL

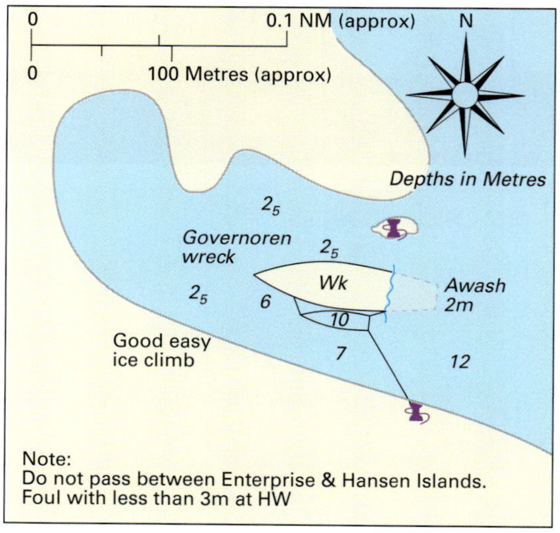

Omega Island, Melchior Islands

64°19S 62°55W
Charts BA 3219

The passage between Omega Island and Eta Island from the east is straightforward between high ice cliffs.

There are two possible anchorages. Anchor off the dock in front of the Argentine base in 8–10m. The creek is narrow between rocks and four shore-lines are recommended. Water is available from a stream off a snow bank at head of inlet. The scenery here is stunning.

In a NE wind, shelter can be found in Anderson Harbour, as shown. The tidal streams in the channel can be strong.

Enterprise Island

64°32′ S 61°59.9′ W
Charts BA 3566 DMA 29122

An excellent, all-weather way-station in the Gerlache Strait. Approach from just S of E and tie alongside the decaying hulk of a whaling ship, the *Governoren*, in which old harpoon heads can still be seen at low water. Make fast with lines to the bollard and/or rocks on shore. There is limited walking on the beach. Good protection from all winds but ice can be a problem in the cove.

Being alongside the old hulk is said to be the nearest you will get to a marina in Antarctica.

Alongside *Governoren*, Enterprise Island *Adventure 2013*

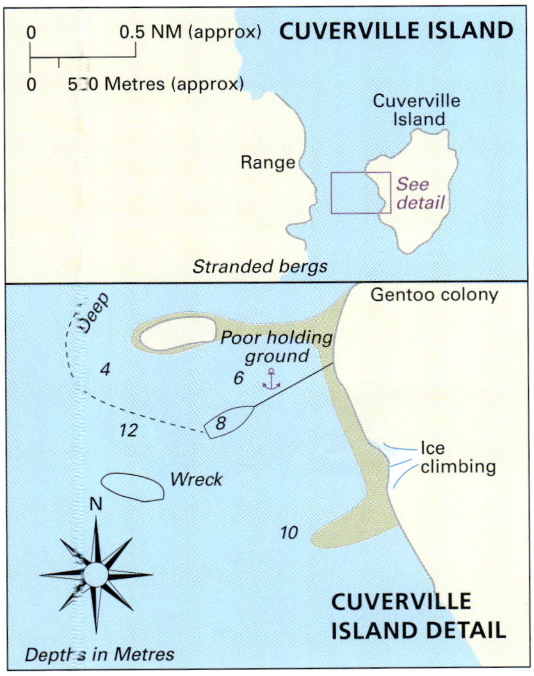

Cuverville Island

64° 41′ S, 62° 38′ W
Charts DMA 29122

Settled weather only. There is shelter here amongst the low, rocky islets, but not a lot of it. Grounded bergs can be a problem. Holding is not good. Lines can be taken to the eastern shore but the islets to the west are too far.

This is home to the largest Gentoo colony on the peninsula.

Cuverville Island *Nick Coleman*

***Minak* off Cuverville Island** *Tim Barker*

The US base, Palmer Station
Tim Barker

Anvers Island

Palmer Base, Arthur Harbour

64°46S 64°04W
Chart BA 3213

This is a difficult place to find a sheltered anchorage, with only limited shelter in W winds. The charts show little detail and an approach in fog would be difficult. The charting here is at variance with GPS plotting.

This anchorage is to be used only if visiting the USA base, which must be agreed well in advance. Tie to the Palmer Dock on the north side of Bonaparte Point.

Weincke Island

Port Lockroy

64°49′ S 63°29′ W
Chart See inset plan on BA 3213 and DMA 29106

This is the only place on the Peninsula where you can lie to your anchor and not worry about setting lines ashore. Swell does not enter, and the holding is good. However, this is possibly the most visited of all the anchorages and if you are unlucky, and others have beaten you to it, swinging room may be hard to find. There can be considerable cruise ship traffic here, and there is good walking ashore.

S or W winds may block the harbour entrance with ice. This is the former site of a whaling station – be prepared for the possibility of your anchor hooking old whale bones.

Port Lockroy is the site of the much-visited former British base, Base A, now run during the season by the UK Antarctic Heritage Trust as a visitor centre and museum with a working 'EIIR' Post Office, the Penguin Post.

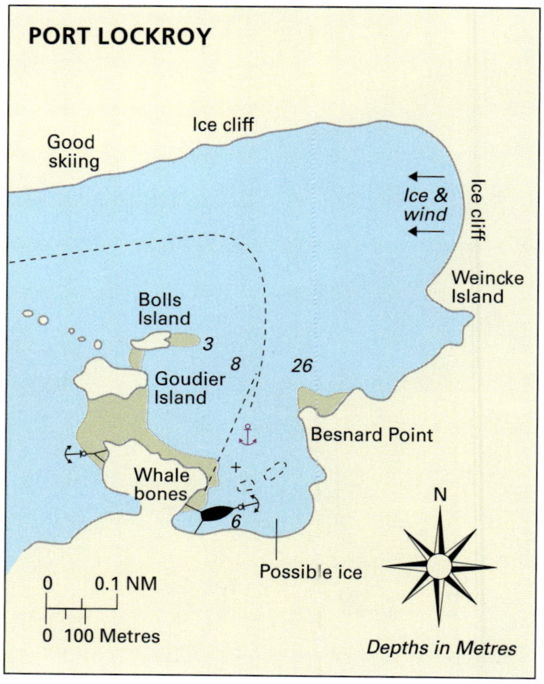

Cruise ship visits Port Lockroy
Tim Barker

To visit the station, go E of Goudier Island to the landing stage on the S side. Access is via the creek between the two islands, it is very rocky and involves tramping through a penguin colony. Contact the station in advance to arrange a visit if the cruise ship traffic is heavy.

In normal conditions it is easiest to lie at anchor in the middle of the well-sheltered bay, somewhere near where the chart indicates mud in around 20m.

For more shelter, depending on the wind direction, there is a well-used 'notch' in Alice Creek.

A tribute to Captain Oates presented by the Royal Cruising Club and placed by Tim Barker and the crew of *Mina*[2]
Tim Barker

Port Lockroy from above
Tim Barker

The Dorian Cove anchorage off Damoy Point *Mike Jacques*

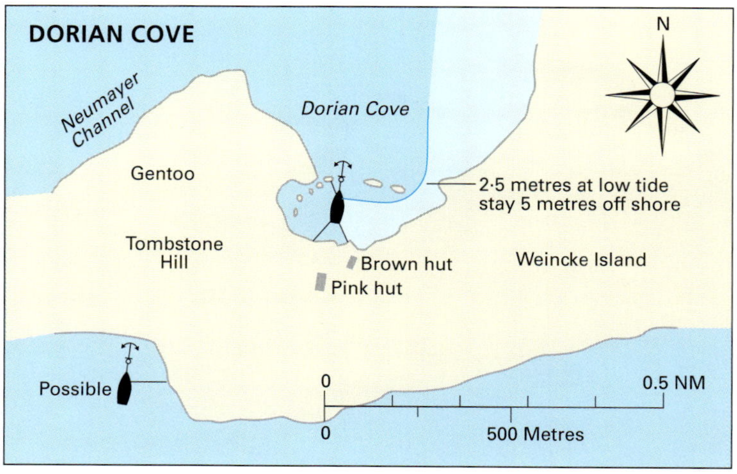

Dorian Cove

64°19S 62°58W

Anchorage can also be found outside the bay in Dorian Cove and E of Jougla Point.

Note the rock/islet towards the eastern side of the bay and the rocks extending from the W shore. You should enter E of it, staying very close to the ice cliff about 5m off the shore. The minimum depth here is 2·5m.

This can be a windy spot and should not be entered in strong N winds.

It is described as 'magical' with excellent hiking and skiing. Of the two huts to the S of the anchorage, the pink British one is said to be in good condition.

Fish Islands

Flounder Island

66°02′ S 65° 24.2′W

Chart Inset plan 'Prospect Point' on BA 3213 and DMA 29106

The inlet on the NW side is open to the sea but is deeper and better-protected than suggested by the chart. It is easy to set a secure four-point tie in depths of 5–10m. Depending on the state of the tide, water may be collected from the low ice cliffs.

Note: there may be a discouraging or prohibitive amount of ice, possibly moving rapidly. There is a snow-climb on the overlooking hills, and skiing.

Mutton Cove

66°00′S 65°39′W

Charts 3570, 3573 & 3213 (see chartlet)

This anchorage is formed by four small islands, Harp, Upper, Cliff and Girdler. Beer Island provides shelter from the west. There is not enough swinging room to anchor, so tie to the steep rock wall on the south side of the eastern end of the cove and run lines across to the north side.

Good shelter from all winds, but subject to drifting ice in a south wind.

The beacon on Shag Rock (an iron basket on a steel pole) about ¾M to the east is a good identification mark.

Detaille Island

66°52′S 66° 47′ W

Chart Inset plan on BA 3213 and DMA 29106

This former British base was abandoned in a hurry in 1959 and because the men were unable to take anything with them, the place has become something of a time capsule.

It is now in a dilapidated state pending a decision on whether to dismantle it or restore it as a museum site. In the meantime it offers a sad but fascinating visit. You will find a Hoover washing machine, jackets and long johns, a calendar from December 1957, survey books, astronomical observation logs, dozens of paint-size cans of Scotch oats, bottles of Heinz mayonnaise, and empty bottles of gin and whisky.

In conditions other than strong W or SW winds, anchor in 5–6m immediately below the base hut on the SW side, where there is good protection. Three lines can be taken ahsore at normal angles and a fourth can be tied to exposed rocks on the west side. In strong SW wind the anchorage in the bay N of the base, below a small hut, has been recommended (66°52′S 66°48′). But beware, the adjacent rock pools are shallow.

Ice conditions change rapidly.

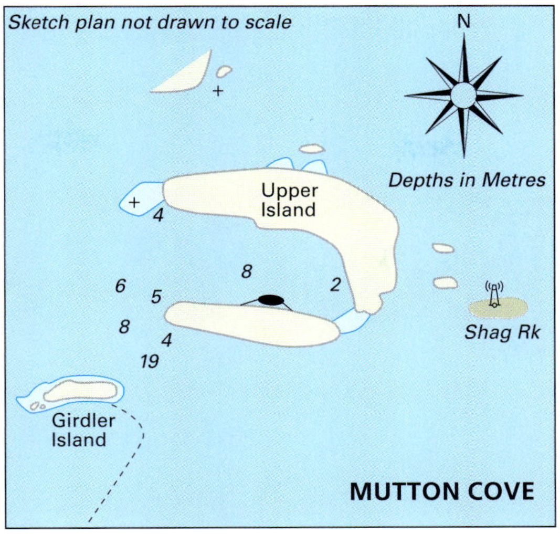

Hovgaard and Florence Islands

65° 07′ S, 64° 05′ W

Charts BA 3572 and 3575

The narrow gut between Hovgaard and Florence Island is well sheltered in almost any conditions, with plenty of places to take lines ashore. The E end is foul so enter from the west, passing S of the first rock shown into something of a pool and anchor in 5–6m. The shallowest depth found in the approach is 3m so the anchorage can probably be entered by most yachts at any stage of the tide.

The rocky islets off the W end stop larger icebergs from entering.

The passage shallows at the eastern end and leads to a 'bulletproof' anchorage in a basin at the south end of Plenau Island. The basin is shallow and should only be used by yachts with a lifting keel. It is not possible to pass between Pleneau and Hovgaard islands. The passage between Pleneau and Booth

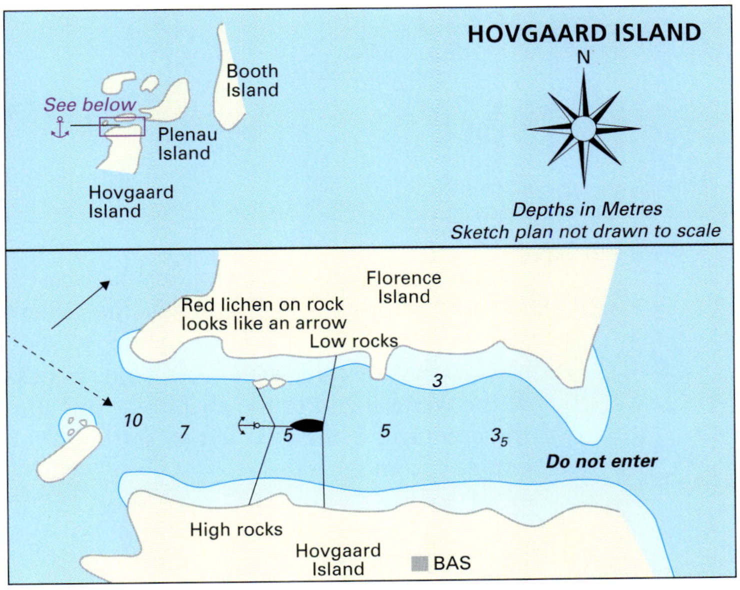

Port Charcot *Adventure 2013*

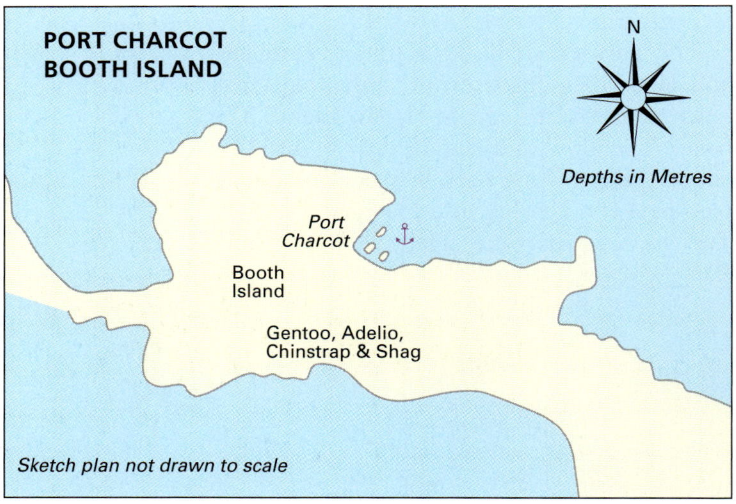

islands is often blocked by ice, in which case it is necessary to travel 5M down the eastern side of Hovgaard and back up the western side. In such circumstances, the band of rocks at the western end of the anchorage obscures the entrance. It must be left to starboard on entering from the west.

Port Charcot *Adventure 2013*

Argentine Islands

Verdansky Base

65°15′ S 64°15′ W
Chart BA 3575

Formerly the British Faraday base, which passed to the Ukrainians in 1998.

The approach is difficult, if not treacherous. Enter from SE through the Meek channel, turn south in front of rock with a signpost and curve round into the channel immediately by the landing dock on the S side of the base. In 2007 there were two orange plastic buoys marking the channel but there are still unmarked rocks to avoid. Proceed slowly and with great caution. Ice conditions can change very quickly here.

The favoured anchorage is in the secluded notch in Stella Creek. Otherwise in the E part of the bay by the station where it can be very gusty. Take lines from all four corners. Note that the rocks are crumbly.

The base can be called by VHF and it may be possible to arrange a tour of the former Faraday station. If you are lucky, you may get a sample of their home-brewed *garyelka* (a peppery vodka). They hold the key to the 'Wordie Hut', a restored British base built on winter Island in the 1940s, where the British Graham Land Expedition (1934–37) made its base before moving south to Marguerite Bay.

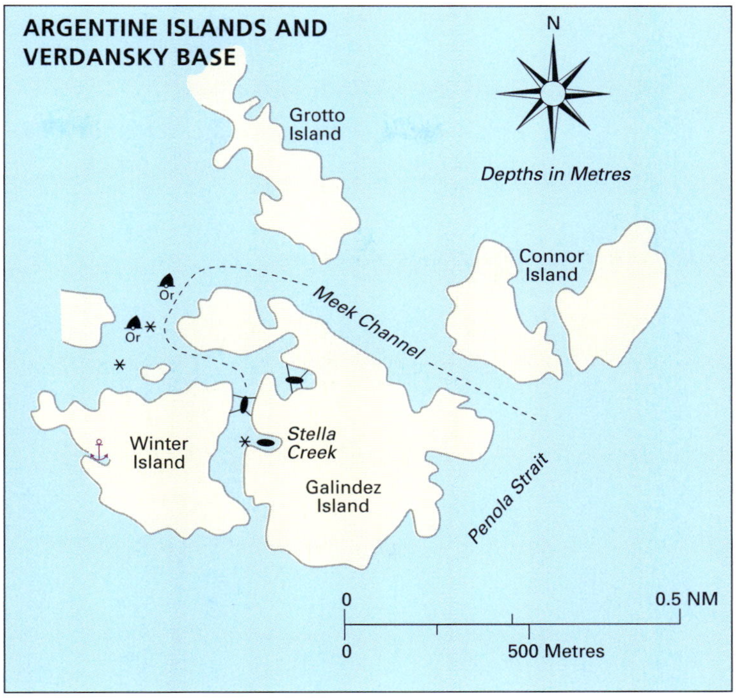

The Wordie House on Winter Island, Verdansky Base - named after Shackleton's chief scientist

Galindez Island

65°14′ S 64°15W.
Charts 3570 & 3575 (small chartlet)

This anchorage is close to the Verdansky Base and has been described as 'bullet proof.'

Anchor between Galindez and Winter islands with lines ashore. Interesting and delightful. Climb Woozie Hill for one of the best 360° views imaginable and then slide down to your boat.

Skua Creek, Argentine Islands *Adventure 2013*

Mainland Antarctic Peninsula

Less hospitable than the offshore islands, although one good harbour, Paradise Harbour, can be found at the southern end of the Gerlache Strait.

Waterboat Point, Paradise Harbour

64°49′ S, 62°52′ W
Chart DMA 29122

The name derives from the adventures of the British explorers Lester and Bagshawe, who, in 1921, spent a year in an upturned water boat, suffering extreme privations. When the first whaling ships arrived at the start of the new season, and offered rescue, it was declined because they did not consider their scientific research to be complete. They told the whaler to come back in a month's time. The base of the boat and their improvised shelter remains.

The harbour is home to the Chilean base, Gonzales Videla, which is reported to be very hospitable.

Approach from N and anchor well into the bay on the E side of the Chilean base, N of the isthmus, with two stern lines ashore. The bay on the southern side of the isthmus is reported to be secure in N or NE wind. The east side of the anchorage is part of the peninsula, making this one of the few sites at which visitors can walk on the Antarctic continent.

A large Gentoo penguin colony shares the base premises, apparently unconcerned.

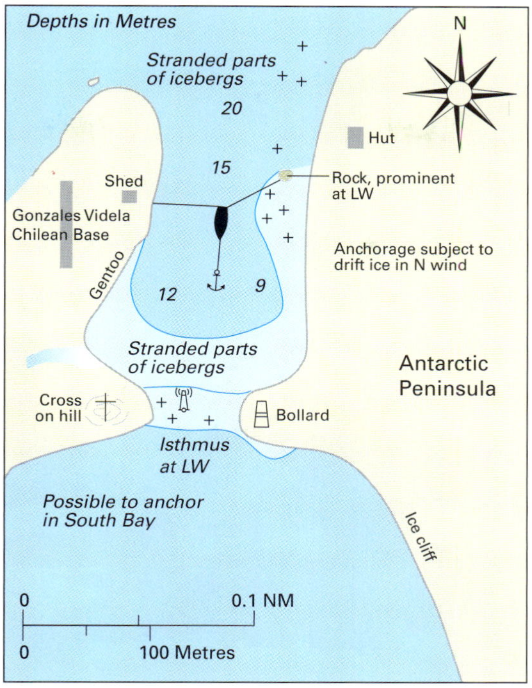

WATERBOAT POINT, PARADISE HARBOUR

The Waterboat Point anchorage
Tim Barker

Argentine Almirante Brown station
Tim Barker

Almirante Brown station, (South) Paradise Harbour

64°54′ S 62°51.47′W
Chart DMA 29122

One of the most spectacular bays in Antarctica, surrounded by a perfect circle of glaciated mountains tumbling towards clear blue water. Humpback, Minke and Killer whales may be seen here from late January to March.

The Almirante Brown station (Argentina) is found on the eastern shore of Paradise Harbour, and offers two anchorages on either side of an isthmus.

If entering the S bay, it is advisable to sound ahead with the dinghy as there is much shallow water at the entrance. Once inside, anchor in 20m, in good shelter.

Enter the N bay opposite Bryde Island south and east of the Argentine Base. Keep close to the prominent isolated rock on E side and anchor in about 10m in the middle of a pool surrounded on three sides by towering steep-sided glaciers. Use long lines to shore on the N side, and to a line of rocks to S. Sheltered from all directions.

Paradise Harbour off the Almirante Brown station
Adventure 2013

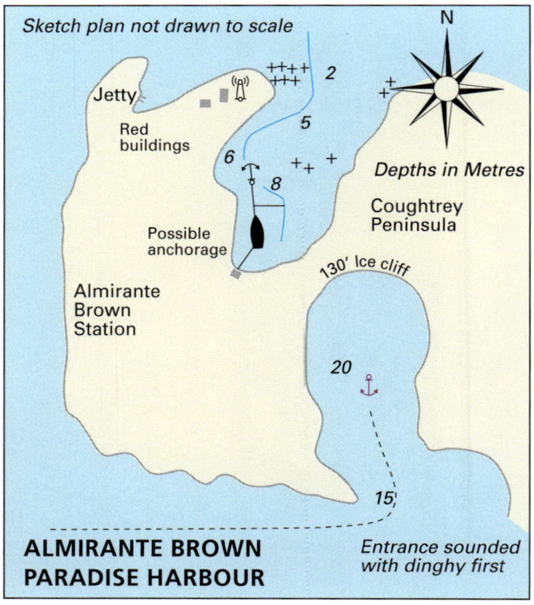

South Orkney Islands

These lie 420M SW of South Georgia and 240M E of the South Shetlands. As part of Antarctica, the same paperwork rules apply here as for visits to the Peninsula. There are four major islands; Coronation, Signy, Powell and Laurie.

The landscape is best described as grand but austere.

Visits by yachts are far more infrequent than in the South Shetlands, not being on a direct line from the Beagle Channel; but a yacht that had fallen foul of heavy weather and found it had made too much easting, might seek shelter here. Also, if coming to Antarctica directly from Stanley in the Falklands, the Orkneys lie closer to your direct route than the Shetlands.

The islands are uninhabited, but both Argentina and UK have research bases here: the Argentine *Orcadas* base is on Laurie Island and is one of the oldest bases in Antarctica, having supplied weather information since 1903 and been home to the first radiotelegraph on the continent. The British Antarctic Survey base on Signy Island was opened in 1947.

The seas around these islands are ice covered from late April to November, and in high summer the average temperature is 3·5°C although the recorded highest is 19·8°C. The summer also brings rain and low cloud, known as the infamous 'Signy mank'.

Be aware that much of the information given for the South Orkney Islands is based on notes and surveys by Pete and Annie Hill in 1994/5 and published in 2007. The possibility of changes to the topography, although likely to be small, should not be dismissed. Their surveys were made without the aid of GPS. Others have reported that the differences between WGS84 and Chart Datum can be considerable.

The accuracy of local charts should not be relied upon.

Because of the density of the water, echo sounders can be unreliable.

Their advice then, and ours now, is to employ eyeball navigation once navigating to within half a mile.

As the Hills said in their original notes, **'This is not simply the usual disclaimer made in Cruising Guides - it is very genuine.'**

Their original guide to the South Orkney Islands can be found at

www.rccpf.org.uk/passage-planning/satlantic

It is common to find icebergs stranded inside the 100 fathom line and this may be a useful guide when closing the islands. Icebergs can remain all year round and the remnants of pack ice can be expected at any time throughout the summer.

The islands are persistently windy and gales are recorded 60 days per year on average.

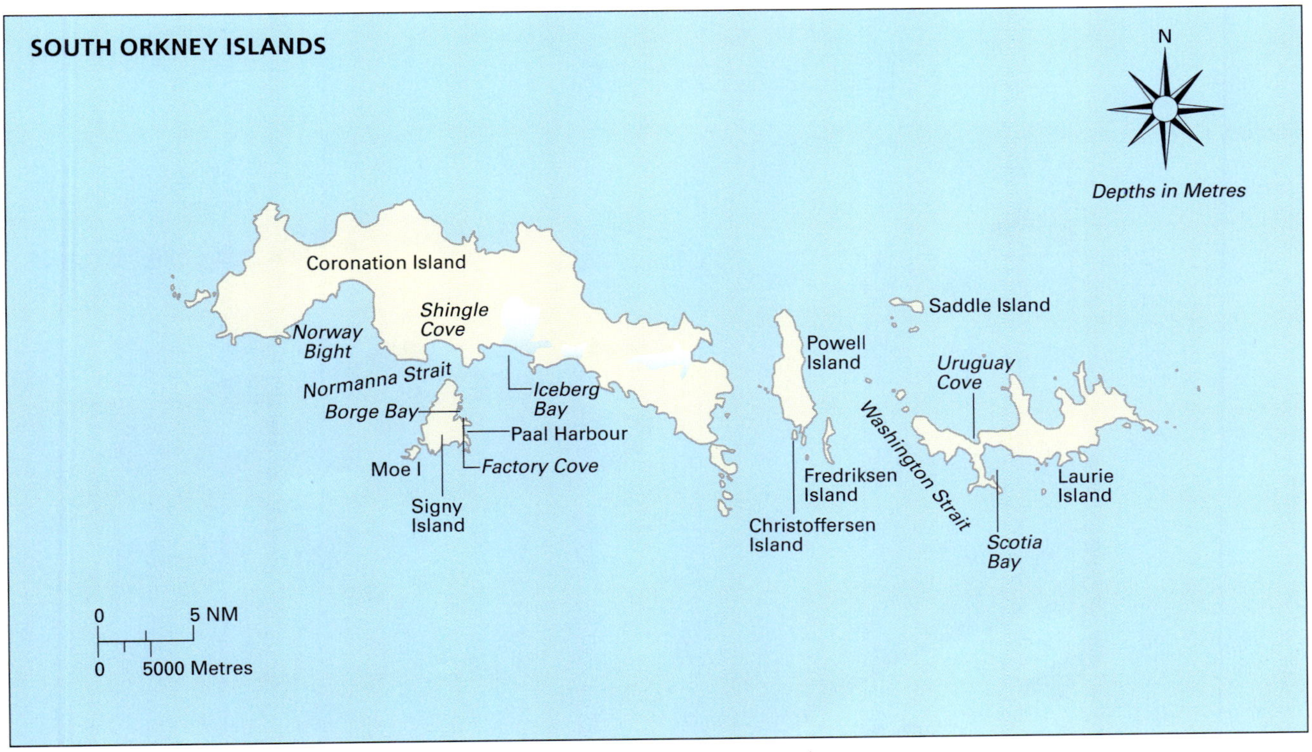

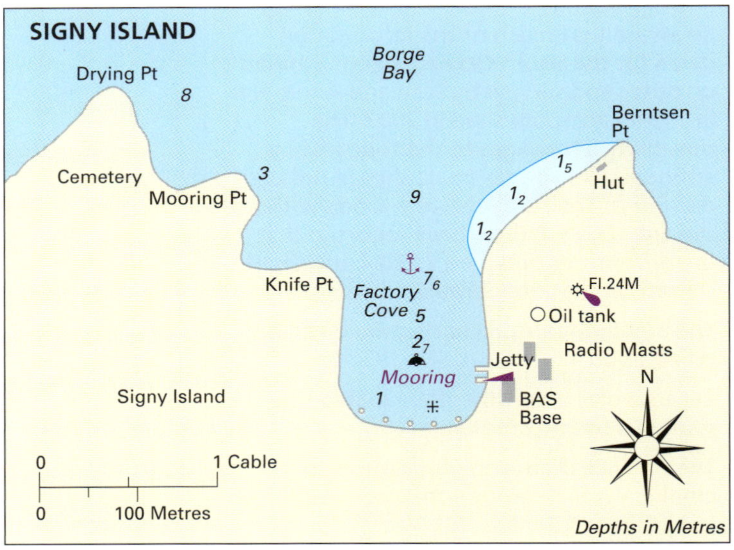

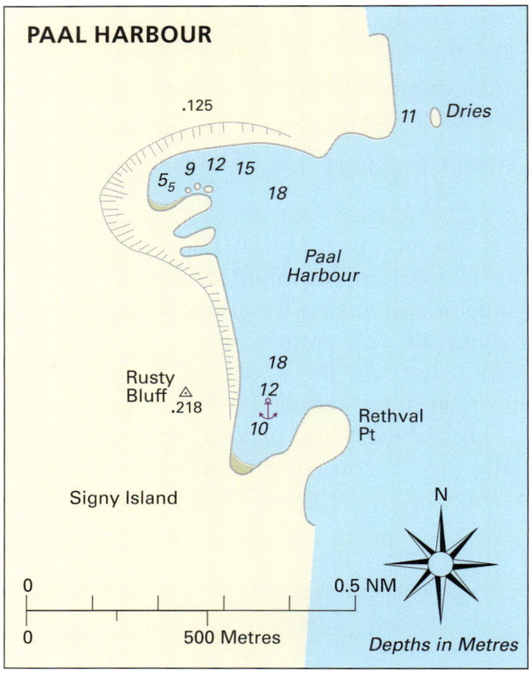

Signy Island

Chart 1775

There is less snow and fewer glaciers here than elsewhere in the South Orkneys, so there is good walking ashore.

Factory Cove, Borge Bay

60°42'S 45° 35'W
Chart 1775

The best anchorage on the island. This is the site of the British Antarctic Survey base, now a summer-only establishment.

Anchor E of Knife Point halfway across the entrance in 7·5m with good shelter from all but N and NE. Should the wind come from that direction, shelter might be found S of the Mirounga Flats or E of Balin Point at the N end of the bay.

Paal Harbour, Signy Island

60°43'S 45°35'W
Chart 1775

This is the next bay south of Borge Bay and is a good anchorage. There are high cliffs to the N and W and strong winds from those directions can create *williwaws*. The depths may be greater than the chart suggests.

The inlet at the NW of the harbour is small, but lines can be taken ashore.

At the S end of the harbour, anchorage can be found W of Rethval Point in 10m with room to swing to a single anchor.

Factory Cove
Pete and Annie Hill

Coronation Island

60°39'S 45°34'W

Shingle Cove

A popular stopping place for cruise ships. This anchorage is found off the W side of Iceberg Bay where you should anchor off the shingle beach in 4m, ensuring you have swinging room to clear underwater rocks to the N of the beach. There is a British Antarctic Survey refuge hut here.

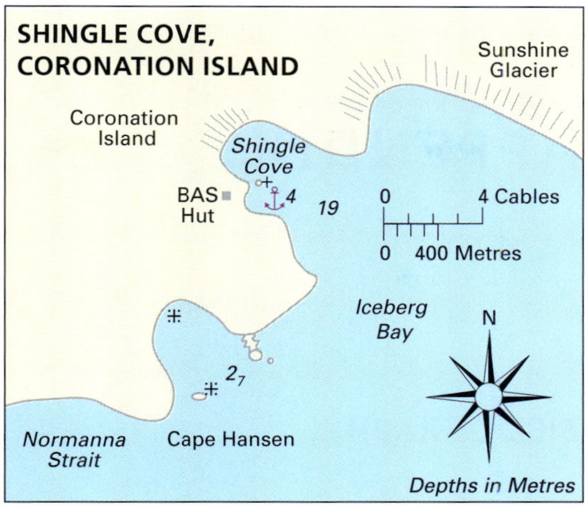

Powell Island

60°43'S 45°06'W
Chart 1775

The best yacht harbour in the South Orkneys. Christoffersen Island protects the bay from the W. There are two entrances: N of Christoffersen Island the minimum depth is 7m and the entrance 100m wide. Entrance can also be made from Ellefsen Harbour but with a minimum depth of 1·8m and less than 20m width. These shallow entrances prevent large pieces of ice from entering.

For best shelter, anchor in the N of the harbour when stiff mud can be found with room to lie to a single anchor, but check for rocks in the NE corner of the bay.

The land ashore is an SSI and permission must be sought to land.

If using Ellefsen Harbour, anchor on the E side off Michelson Island in 6m. There is good shelter from S although strong gusts were apparent in W gales.

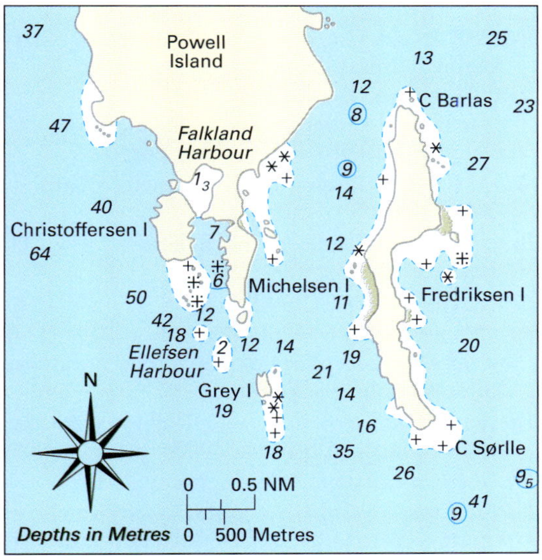

POWELL ISLANDS

Laurie Island

High and mountainous with many glaciers.

Scotia Bay

60°44S 44°42W
Chart 1775

The site of the Argentine Base, anchorage can be found in the W part of the inner bay in 8m under a high cliff. The holding here is poor and should not be used in the event of strong weather. A shore landing can be difficult in the swell.

In 1902, a crew of naturalists and explorers set off on the first Scottish expedition, seeking to establish a weather station. They encountered vast fields of ice and were forced to shelter here in Scotia Bay, which was named after their ship. They set about building a hut from materials found on the islands and named it Omond House after Robert Omond, the director of the Edinburgh Observatory. It was handed over to the Argentine government who maintain it, and is now known as 'Casa Moneta' after an Argentine explorer.

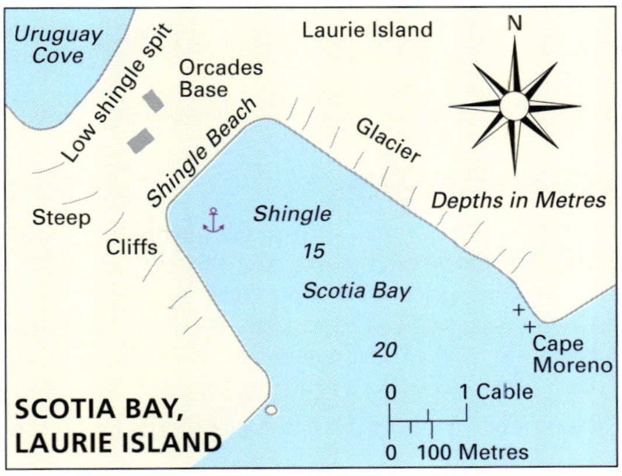

Scotia Bay, Laurie Island
Pete and Annie Hill

APPENDIX

BIBLIOGRAPHY

Pilot guides

RCCPF Atlantic Islands Anne Hammick & Hilary Keatinge (Imray, 2016)

RCCPF Atlantic Crossing Guide Jane Russell (Adlard Coles Nautical, 2010) Includes routes/timings and key ports.

World Cruising Routes, Jimmy Cornell (Adlard Coles, 2014)

Brazil Cruising Guide, Michel Balette (Imray, 2010)

Brazil, Pete Hill (RCCPF/ Kindle)

RCCPF Argentina by Andy O'Grady and Pete Hill (e-pilot from rccpf.org.uk and also in print from Imray)

Patagonia and Tierra del Fuego Rolfo and Adrizzi (Editrice Incontri Nautici, 2007)

RCCPF Chile, Andy O'Grady (Imray, 2016)

Pacific Crossing Guide 3rd edition, Kitty van Hagen (Adlard Coles, 2016) Includes routes to Puerto Montt.

Admiralty NP6 & 7 are comprehensive pilot books from which yachts can glean useful information. South America Pilot Volume 2 (NP6) covers the Chilean channels from 50°S to Cape Horn.

General interest

As well as pilotage information, you will need a stock of books to cover the history, geography, nature and culture of the places you visit and the seas you sail. This list is by no means comprehensive, but provides a good starting point from which to build a cruising library.

Rounding the Horn Dallas Murphy (Basic Books, 2004)

Cape Horn – A Maritime History Robin Knox Johnston (Hodder and Stoughton, 1995)

Cape Horn Felix Riesenberg (Robert Hale, 1950)

The Blind Horn's Hate Richard Hough (Hutchinson, 1971)

Patagonia - A cultural history Chris Moss (Signal, 2008)

Tierra del Fuego R Natalie P Goodall (Facsimilie, 1979). Can be bought in Ushuaia or Harberton.

The Voyage of the Beagle Charles Darwin (Penguin Classics)

Shackleton's Boat Journey F A Worsley (Pimlico, 1999)

South Ernest Shackleton (Penguin Classics, 2004)

Mischief Goes South, H W Tilman (TBS The Book Service Ltd, 1968)

In the Land of Fire: Fifty-six South Ben Pester (Seafarer Books, 2004)

Uttermost Part of the Earth E Lucas Bridges (Overlook Press, 2008)

Nature

Whales, Dolphins and Seals - A Field Guide to the Marine Mammals of the World Hadoram Shirihai and Brett Jarrett (A & C Black Publishers Ltd, 2006)

Whales of the World Lyall Watson (Hutchinson, 1981)

Penguins The Ultimate Guide Tui De Roy, Mark Jones, Julie Cornthwaite (Princeton University Press, 2014)

Penguins of the World Wayne Lynch (Firefly Books, 2007)

Some of the above may be out of print but can often be found through online second hand books dealers.

The Falklands

Battle for the Falklands Max Hastings (Pan Military Classics, 2010)

Falkland Island Shores Ewen Southby-Tailyour (Adlard Coles 1985)

The Falklands War 1982 Martin MIddlebrook (Penguin Classic Military History, 2001)

Marooned by Captain Barnard ed Bertha S Dodge (Wesleyan University Press, 1979). An account of his stranding on New Island, W Falkland in 1812.

South Georgia

The Island of South Georgia Robert Headland (Cambridge University Press, 1992)

Antarctic Oasis Tim and Pauline Carr (Norton and Company, 1998)

A Visitor's Guide to South Georgia Sally Poncet and Kim Crosbie (Princeton University Press, 2012)

GLOSSARY

From RCCPF *Chile,* courtesy of Andy O'Grady

The following limited glossary relates to the weather, the abbreviations to be found on charts and some words likely to be useful entering port. For a list containing many words commonly used in connection with sailing, see Webb & Manton, Yachtsman's Ten Language Dictionary (Adlard Coles Nautical).

General

aduana	customs
armada	navy
bahía	bay
caleta	inlet, bay
canal	strait, canal, channel
estero	sound
morro	headland
puerto	port, bay
seno	sound
surgidero	anchorage, roadstead

Weather

On the radio, if there is a storm warning, the forecast starts aviso temporal. If there is no storm warning, the forecast starts no hay temporal. Many words are similar to the English and their meanings may be guessed. The following may be less familiar:

viento	wind
calma	calm
ventolina	light air
flojito	light breeze
flojo	gentle breeze
bonancible	moderate breeze
fresquito	fresh breeze
fresco	strong breeze
frescachón	near gale
duro	gale
muy duro	strong gale
temporal	storm
borrasca	violent storm
huracán	hurricane
tempestad	borrasca, thunderstorm
chubasco	squall
racha	squall
ráfaga	squall
remolino	whirlwind

Note: We have not found a qualitative difference between *chubasco*, *ráfaga* and *racha*. *Chubasco* is a Chilean word; El Diccionario Enciclopédico 'La Fuente' defines *racha* as *ráfaga*. All three are commonly translated into English as williwaw, a word which used to be heard only in connection with the Magallanes.

visibilidad	visibility
buena	good
regular	moderate
mala	poor
calima	haze
fosca	haze
neblina	mist
niebla	fog
precipitación	precipitation
aguacero	shower
llovizna	drizzle
lluvia	rain
aguanieve	sleet
nieve	snow
granizada	hail
el cielo	the sky
nube	cloud
nubes altas/ bajas	high/low clouds
nubloso	cloudy
cubierto	covered, overcast
claro	despejado, clear

Names of cloud types in Spanish are based on the same Latin words as the names used in English.

sistemas del tiempo	weather systems
anticiclón	anticyclone
depresión	depression
vaguada	trough
cresta	ridge
cuna	wedge
frente	front
frio	cold
cálido	warm
ocluido	occluded
bajando	falling
subiendo	rising

Lights and charts – major terms and abbreviations

A	amarilla	yellow
Alt	alternativa	alternative
Ag Nv	aguas navegables	navigable waters
Ang	angulo	angle
Ant	anterior	anterior, earlier, forward
Apag	apagado	extinguished
Arrc	arrecife	reef
At	atenuada	attenuated
B	blanca	white
Ba	bahía	bay
	bajamar escorada	chart datum
Bal. E	baliza elástica	'elastic' (plastic) buoy
Bco	banco	bank
Bo	bajo	shoal, under, below, low
Boc	bocina	horn, trumpet
Br	babor	port (left, not harbour)
C	campana	bell
Card	cardinal	cardinal
Cañ	cañon	canyon
cil	cilíndrico	cylindrical
C	cabo	cape
Cha	chimenea	chimney
Cno	castillo	castle
cón	cónico	conical
Ct	centellante	quick flashing (50–80/min)
CtI	centellante interrumpida	interrupted quick flashing
cuad	cuadrangular	quadrangular
D	destello	flash
Desap	desaparecida	disappeared
Dest	destruida	destroyed
	dique	jetty, quay
Dir	direccional	directional
DL	destello largo	long flash
E	este	East
edif	edificio	building
Er	estribor	starboard
Est	esférico	spherical
Esp	especial	special
Est sñ	estación de señales	signal station
ext	exterior	exterior
Extr	extremo	end, head of pier, etc
F	fija	fixed
Fca	fabrica	factory
FD	fija y destello	fixed and flashing
FGpD	fija y grupo de destellos	fixed and group flashing
Flot	flotdora	float
Fondn	fondeadero	anchorage
GpCt	grupo de centellos	group quick flashing
GpD	grupo de destellos	group flashing
GpOc	grupo de ocultaciones	group occulting
GpRp	grupo de centellos rápidos	group very quick flashing
hel	helicoidales	helicoidal
hor	horizontal	horizontal
Hund	hundida	submerged
I	interrumpida	interrupted
Igla	iglesia	church
Inf	inferior	lower
Intens	intensificado	intensified
Irreg	irregular	irregular
Iso	isofase	isophase
L	luz	light
La	lateral	lateral
	levante	East
M	millas	Nautical miles
Mte	monte	mountain
Mto	monumento	monument
N	norte	North
Naut	nautófono	foghorn
NE	nordeste	NE
No	número	number
NW	noroeste	NW
Obst	obstruction	obstruction
ocas	ocasional	occasional
oct	octagonal	octagonal
Pe A	peligro aislado	isolated danger
	poniente	West
Post	posterior	posterior, later
Ppal	principal	principal
	prohibido	prohibited
Obston	obstrucción	obstruction
Prov	provisional	provisional
prom	prominente	prominent, conspicuous
Pta	punta	point
Pto	puerto	port
PTO	puerto	port

Note 'puerto' covers any landing place from a beach to container port.

R	roja	red
Ra	estación radar	radar station
Ra+	radar + suffix	radar+suffix (Ra Ref, etc)
RC	radiofaro	circular (all-round) radiobeacon
RD	radiofaro dirigido	directional radiobeacon
rect	rectangular	rectangular
Ra	rocas	rocks
Rp	centeneallante rápida	very quick flashing (80–160/min)
RpI	cent. rápida interrumpida	interrupted very quick flashing
RW	radiofaro giratorio	rotating radiobeacon
S	segundos	seconds
S	sur	South
SE	sudeste	SE
sil	silencio	silence
Silb	silbato or silbido	whistle
Sincro	sincronizda con	synchronised with
Sir	sirena	siren
son	sonido	sound, noise, report
Sto/a	Santo, Santa	Saint
SW	sudoetse	SW
T	temporal	temporarily
Te	torre	tower
trans	transversal	transverse
triang	triangular	triangular
troncoc	troncocónico	truncated cone
troncop	troncopiramidal	truncated pyramid
TSH	antena de radio	radio mast
TV	antena de TV	TV mast
U	centellante ultra-rápida	ultra quick flashing (+160/min)
UI	cent. ultra-rápida interrumpido	interrupted ultra quick flashing
	Ventisquero	Glacier
V	verde	green
	vivero	shellfish raft or bed
	visible	visible
W	oeste	West

Ports and Harbours

a popa	stern-to
a proa	bows-to
abrigo	shelter
al costado	alongside
amarrar	to moor
amarradero	mooring
ancho	breadth (see manga)
cabo	warp, line (cape)
calado	draught
compuerta	lock, basin
dársena	harbour
dique	dock, jetty
esclusa	lock
escollera	jetty
eslora total	length overall
espigon	spur, spike
fondear	to anchor
fondeadero	anchorage
knudos	knots
fondo	depth (bottom, base
longitud	length (see eslora)
lonja	fish market (wholesale)
manga	beam
muelle	mole
nudo	knot
noray	bollard, mooring
pantalán	jetty
parar	to stop
pila	pile
práctico	pilot
profundidad	depth
rompeolas	breakwater
varadero	slipway
vertedero (verto)	spoil ground

Direction

babor	port
estribor	starboard
norte	N
este	E
sur	S
oeste	W

Administration

aduana	customs
astillero	shipyard
capitán de puerto	harbourmaster (an *armada* officer)
carabineros	police
combustible	fuel, in the general sense
derechos	dues, rights
dueño	owner
fabrica	factory
ferrocarril	railway
gasoleo	diesel
gasolina or bençina	petrol (UK) gasoline (US)
Investigaciones	CID and international police
kerosina	paraffin
manguera	hose-pipe or flexible tubing
parafina	paraffin
patrón	skipper (not owner)
prorroga	extension to a document, customs permit, for
instance	
petróleo	diesel
señalizacion	light dues
maritima títul	annual certificate

INDEX